THE CHILD AS POET: MYTH OR REALITY?

The Child as Poet: Myth or Reality?

by Myra Cohn Livingston

THE HORN BOOK, INC.
BOSTON 1984

Printed in the United States of America

Library of Congress Cataloging in Publication Data
Livingston, Myra Cohn.
  The child as poet – myth or reality?
  Bibliography: p.
  Includes index.
  1. Poetry and children. 2. Children as authors.
I. Title.
PN1085.L58 1984 809'.89282 84-10925
ISBN 0-87675-287-3

CONTENTS

ACKNOWLEDGMENTS

According to a Welsh proverb, there are three things for which thanks are due: an invitation, a gift, and a warning. The *invitation* from Ethel Heins and Lee Kingman to write this book is answered first, with warm thanks.

There are many people who have given the *gift* of time, information, and interest. The chapter on Langston Hughes could not have been written without the help of Alice Schlesinger, Alumni Director of the University of Chicago Laboratory Schools and Warren Seyfert, former director of the school. I am indebted to former faculty members Blanche Janecek, Ida DePencier and Eunice H. McGuire, and to former students Irene Pearlman Breckler, Dr. Carita Chapman, Alice Wirth Gray, Loise Grass Kuhr, Phoebe Liebig, Dartha Cloudman Reid, Judith Hayes Weir, Catharine DeCosta Wilder, David Zimmerman and others. For help in trying to locate materials I thank Margaret Burroughs, Ellen Hill, Dr. Donald Joyce, Effie Lee Morris, Basil Phillips, Dr. Annette L. Hoage Phinazee and Joseph Rollins.

Conversations and letters exchanged with educators, poet-teachers and teachers have been numerous. In addition to copyrighted material, acknowledged elsewhere, I appreciate the generosity of those who have given of their time and permission to use holograph letters, papers, and excerpts from publications. These include: Sandra Alcosser; Darwin Belfils; Lee Bernd; Dr. Jane Bingham; Dr. Robert O. Boord; Heidi Bowton; Richard Brown; Lee Bennett Hopkins; Jacquelin F. Howe; Dr. Leland Jacobs; June Jordan; Dr. Kenneth Kantor; Rolly Kent; Kenter Canyon Elementary School, Los Angeles; Robert King; Herbert Kohl; Arthur Lerner; Richard Lewis; Dr. Peter Neumeyer; Donna Northouse; Norine Odland; Bettie Day and the Office of the County Superintendent of Schools, Santa Barbara, California; John Oliver Simon; the Executive Board of the Southern Nevada Teachers of English; Karen Swenson; and Ruth Whitman.

To the Teachers and Writers Collaborative, my appreciation for permission to quote from the Collaborative's publication; particular gratitude to Phillip Lopate for sharing thoughts and classroom writing for many years.

I am grateful to Hilda Conkling for her letters and conversations, and for allowing me to use her work and that of her mother, Grace

Hazard Conkling. My thanks to Judd Marmor, M.D., for counsel concerning imagination and creativity and for suggesting source materials. Further gratitude to Geneviève Patte of La Joie par les Livres for obtaining materials pertinent to Minou Drouet.

To Lee Kingman, special thanks for her editorial acumen, patience, and abundance of understanding. For help with typing, returning overdue books, and finding misplaced notes, cheers to Rosemary Hulle. To Lloyd Alexander, who translated the French materials, offered friendship and suggestions at a crucial moment, and sounded the *warning*, my deepest gratitude.

And to my husband, Dick, our children Josh, Jonas, and Jennie, and my mother, the final thanks – for their understanding of the other world which consumes me. It is my family to whom this book is dedicated.

M.C.L.

PREFACE

Every age and culture imposes its own perspective on the persistent mythology of the child as a symbol of hope for its time. These myths are not new. They stem from peoples of all creeds who seek to renew themselves and to combat the chaos of their lives both as individuals and members of a society.

The tradition of the child as hope is inherent in the Romanticism that has pervaded English and European literature and philosophy for centuries. Yet the American view would seem to be unique: Not only is the child a symbol of that which takes us back to the beginning of experience and flouts convention, placing emphasis on immediate perception and primordial will, but the child is also the embodiment of all the qualities traditionally ascribed to poets, in particular the love of truth and the power to speak this truth through language.

The worship of the child-poet is not confined to a few. Parents, teachers, poet-teachers, educators, and purveyors of school materials, those who work within the establishment of schools and those who censure its outmoded, structured methods are in total agreement as to the brilliance of the child-poet. The adulation cuts across all educational and socioeconomic boundaries.

This book inquires into the nature of the phenomenon and examines many of the facets and implications of this curious mythology. Can children be called poets – even natural poets – or do we attribute to young people the powers they do not, in fact, possess? Are they capable of writing fine poetry, or is what is called natural, instinctive, intuitive writing merely a phase of their physiological and psychological development? What is the nature of children's imagination and of their symbolism, and how are these qualities repressed – or nourished?

Has creative writing for children been hobbled by the quarrels of adult poets among themselves and by teaching methodologies and dissension among educators? Have we enhanced the ability of children to write poetry – to use their sensitivities and imagination to create something which will add significantly to their growth and enrichment?

Is the child a natural poet? Is the mythology we have created one that will serve children well in years ahead, or is it but another Romantic attempt on the part of adults to impose order on chaos in a perplexing age?

CHAPTER I

The Child as Natural Poet

Oh, I know you have your own hymns, I have heard them –
and because I knew they invoked the great protector
I could not be angry with you, no matter
how much they outraged true music –

From "Gulls"
William Carlos Williams[1]

Walt Whitman's image of the "sacred faces of infants"[2] is ever with us. The literature of the Western world, from the Bible to contemporary poets, urges us to remember that it is the child who is nearest to God, that it is our duty to restore what the world has taken away from children. Poet Robert Duncan speaks of a parent's refusal to love a child as

> the crippling of the imagination or rather its starvation. The world of wonders is limited at last to the parent's will (for will prospers where imagination is thwarted); intellectual appetites become no more than ambitions; curious minds become consciences; love, hatred, affection and cruelty cease to be responses and become convictions.[3]

To deny children love, to repress their imaginations and thereby rob them of the ability to create, is to wrest from them their birthright – and that is a form of dehumanization. Such a denial is the false nurse of William Blake's *Songs of Experience*, who tells the children they may not stay up a little longer to play, whereas the true nurse in *Songs of Innocence* recognizes their need for play, dreams, and pleasure. It is Dickens's Oliver Twist at the mercy of Bumble, Fagin, and Monks; Nicholas Nickleby's Smike cowed by Squeers. It is Miles with his "fragrance of purity" and Flora with her "angelic beauty"[4] like one of "Raphael's holy infants"[5] subjected to the neurotic and the evil in Henry James's *The Turn of the Screw*; it is Dostoevsky's "blessed babes"[6] gone to heaven in infancy, and even the fated Smerdyakov, whose penetrating curiosity in childhood is rewarded with slaps.

These images from past centuries haunt us and generate new visions. It is the view of Christianity, Duncan writes, that the Lion is Christ. Duncan believes that the "Lion is the child, the unfettered intellect that knows in his nobility none of the convictions and dogmas which the human mind inflicts itself with – " "Sometimes," he says, "I dream of at last becoming a child."

> Can the ambitious artist who seeks success, perfection, mastery, ever get closer to the universe, can he ever know "more" or feel "more" than a child may?[7]

Such a view of childhood is often the province of the poet who glorifies the child's life, thoughts, and feelings, and defines the responsibility of adults toward children. To Ned O'Gorman, "All children are mystics. They embrace the world with breathless loving delight." It is therefore the "duty of a teacher of very young children to give a child back a world to love if the world has been plundered from him by men, governments and the city."[8] This conviction, echoed by many with similar views, is the direct legacy of Romanticism in literature, a movement engendered by the philosophy of Jean Jacques Rousseau. *Emile*, written in 1762, states Rousseau's beliefs in the innate goodness with which the child is born. It is the social environment and methods of education, he writes, which threaten that goodness. Under the tutelage of a compassionate and intelligent teacher, living with nature as his model, Emile is the symbol of the child whose full potential may be realized if he is properly raised and guided. It is the teacher who will protect him from the evils of the world – false authority, shallow society, and materialism. Thus, Emile's inherent goodness, in combination with the consummate lessons of nature and a caring adult will prepare him for manhood and serve him throughout his life.

This concept found its quintessence of poetic expression in the work of William Wordsworth. Here the perfection of nature and of childhood are synonymous. Children, like rustics, are the priests of nature, unsullied by the world. They exemplify Wordsworth's own assertions about poetry, its use of "natural language" portraying the "essential passions of the heart." In both may be found the superiority of imagination over intelligence and the "spontaneous overflow of powerful feelings."[9]

In his "Ode, Intimations of Immortality from Recollections of Early Childhood," and in other writing, Wordsworth seeks to assure us that indeed "The Child is Father of the Man."[10]

> Heaven lies above us in our infancy!
> Shades of the prison-house begin to close
>   Upon the growing Boy,
> But He beholds the light, and whence it
>   flows
>   He sees it in his joy;
> The Youth, who daily farther from the east
>   Must travel, still is Nature's Priest,
>   And by the vision splendid
>   Is on his way attended;
> At length the Man perceives it die away,
> And fade into the light of common day.[11]

Surely then, grown men often look to the child in themselves to retain the vision of a primordial will, a heaven lost by the symbolic "prison-house" that shackles them. Infancy and early childhood are close to this ideal state. Youth is "Nature's Priest," cognizant of the "light." Later circumstances of life and maturity cut off this energy and joy. Whether the fetters are Duncan's "convictions and dogma," O'Gorman's government and city, Rousseau's foppish society, or the constrictions on natural speech which Wordsworth opposed, they are images of a perniciousness that must be corrected. Rationalist and Romanticist, Idealist and Pragmatist, each try by means of imagination, intellect, or memory to recall "that dream-like vividness and splendour which invests objects of sight in childhood."[12]

Rainer Maria Rilke in *Letters to a Young Poet* advises a young man that anyone wishing to create poetry "must be a world for himself and find everything in himself and in Nature with whom he has allied himself."[13] Should Nature be cut off from sight, should the young man even find himself in prison, says Rilke, "would you not then still have your childhood, that precious, kingly possession, that treasurehouse of memories?"[14]

If we are not poets able to summon up our own recollections as Wordsworth does in "The Prelude" and as Rilke also advises, then somehow – in some manner – we wish to hear from the children themselves how it is to feel "more" and know "more." And so we turn to the child as "natural poet" to tell us.

"Children are natural poets, singing before they speak, metaphor-making before they prose their way to school,"[15] writes Margaret Meek. May Hill Arbuthnot goes even further:

> In truth, the child of one is a nearly complete poet. He has so mastered pitch, volume, phrasing, and cadence that through them, and without words, he can communicate his feelings and desires to others. And his ear is so tuned that he responds to similar messages from others. Such behavior may or may not be instinctive. But it is, we are told, strikingly similar to the way in which primeval man first employed his language—to tell us of his fears, joys, frustrations, and triumphs, and to listen to those of others.[16]

The doubts Arbuthnot has about instinct are allayed by many educators and teachers, for it is part of the Romantic tradition to pit instinct against reason. Primitive emotions, biological urges, "natural" feelings, and spontaneity come to the individual's aid as a basis for action in this regard. It is not through experience or intelligence, but through strong sentiments, imagination, and passions that man must move, developing feeling. What the heart says is truth; whatever seems natural is right; and therefore feeling is truth.

To Rousseau instinct is an innate part of the child's being but must be subject to strictures. Whereas instinct in the savage is praiseworthy and may operate without control – because living in and with nature, he has no need to deal with the pressures or rules of society – the child's instinct must be guided. Rousseau's observations may have much to tell us about an age where self-expression is often mistaken for creativity.

Richard Lewis, dedicated to the fostering of creativity in children through his writing and work at the Touchstone Center in New York City, ascribes much creativity to instinct. Children, he says, "create form and rhythm instinctively, and they don't understand the traditional sense of poetry as something perfected and stylized."[17] He praises the "human instinct to create – to make sense and give meaning to our experience of the world . . . found at all stages of our lives." In the tradition of Rousseau he recognizes that this "instinct is most vulnerable to dislocation and submersion—for children can easily discern what, in their immediate environment, is important for their future survival." Like Wordsworth, he believes that events of early childhood "have all but dissolved into the deeper recesses of memory, yet, as memories, they were the beginning of our innate ability to invent ways of 'expressing' and 'shaping' our experiences." The ability to create, he notes, becomes more complex and subtle, "but as children, we were basically unaware of the gift we were exploring, for such exploration was a natural part of the instinctive growth of our consciousness." Form, rhythm, creativity, and growth of consciousness are, therefore, in Lewis's terms, instinctive. Such instincts make possible, given the right circumstances, children's abilities to involve "themselves in the process of 'making' and 'doing' which will eventually be the fibers of their spontaneous playing and imagining."[18]

Phillip Lopate, whose book *Being With Children* is a landmark for those interested in children's creative writing today, asserts that "children should trust their own instincts."[19] Almost sixty years ago, Hughes Mearns, a pioneer in his work with creativity at the Lincoln School in New York, wrote in *Creative Youth*:

> We ask ourselves . . . how thoughts come to us; where we got this and that fine idea, this felicitous phrase, that stimulating picture or figure of speech; and while we never achieve completely satisfying answers, we learn to respect the instinctive self within us, that possible product of animal and spiritual race-accumulations which is, at its best, so right and so sure, so beautiful and wise.[20]

Mearns speaks of the "instinctive language" of children, their native ability and gift for using words and rhythms, a kind of "untutored speech." Whether this language is used in poetry or prose does not matter. It has a "rhythmic cadence, a sense for the right word, and an uncanny right placing of that right word for just the right emphasis intended. To me, and to many others, this language is too worthy to be neglected; we feel that it should be encouraged, brought out, allowed to grow to strength, beauty, and power."[21]

> Poetry, an outward expression of instinctive insight, must be summoned from the vasty deep of our mysterious selves. Therefore, it cannot be taught; indeed, it cannot even be summoned; it may only be permitted.[22]

Richard Lewis also makes reference to the "truly miraculous gift" of invention, "a language of feeling and ideas."[23] Terms such as *mysterious* and *miraculous* imply, of course, the Romantic view. It is indeed Wordsworth's heaven, joy, light, and vision. In an article, "A Love Letter to My Church," which tells of his work with the Teachers & Writers Collaborative in New York, Dan Cheifetz speaks of his fellow teachers as "monks on the path." To him the Collaborative is a "kind of personal 'church'," one of the "places set aside for spiritual expression" where he finds "spiritual energy." Here he can impart to students "the value of their own playfulness," show them how to "get in touch with one's personal powers" and the "supreme creative objective—the creation of oneself." The specter of children unable to play, at the mercy of "the still powerful puritanism that insists kids are in school to work"[24] and that puts them at the mercy of what Cheifetz believes is the elementary school educator's need to be "powerful," is tantamount to divesting children of their energy and spontaneity. "We must recognize," Richard Lewis says, "the enormous potential of children, no matter what their intelligence or background, to comprehend and create a use of language which they can easily claim as their own."[25]

And so we perpetually search for the uncorrupted meaning in the sounds of a new generation of children – the babble of infants, babies' first words, and early speech patterns. Later we delight in their ability to put words together in more sophisticated ways. Many adults note with wonder how children play with words, believing that whatever they write is a demonstration of this inherent gift of language. "Quite spontaneously," Kinerith Gensler and Nina Nyhart report in *The Poetry Connection*, "these children have incorporated onomatopoetic language (words that imitate the sound associated with a thing or action) into their poems."[26]

Claudia Lewis, a poet and educator closely associated with the Banks Street School for many years, writes in *A Big Bite of the World*:

> A four-year-old's definition of a cove is ingenious and convincing: "A cove is a cozy nest of rocks." Another four-year-old's description to her mother of a cake baked in school borrows a word which is singularly apt in this context: "It had eggs, flour, milk and affectionate sugar." A three-year-old's remarks to an adult who is singing off key: "That's not the right size is it?" Finally a five-year-old reveals her grasp of a common element in song and in painting; the teacher asks, after the children have been singing "Deck the Halls," "Do you know what this means – 'Fa la la la la, la la la la'?" "Why yes," replies our child. "It's just like when you paint a design."[27]

Adults admire such anecdotes of language. They are repeated continually and may even fall into the commercial niche of Art Linkletter's *Kids Say the Darndest Things*. Amusing and fresh in concept, they suggest to many adults that children are indeed natural poets because their speech is so often disarming. Rousseau's assessment of Emile's speech is pertinent. In him, he writes, will be heard no

> smart repartees or witty and agreeable discourses. You must not think he will retail to you a set of pretty phrases . . . All that you have to expect from him is simple and native truth, without ornaments, without preparation, and without vanity. He will as readily tell you his evil thoughts and actions, as his good ones, without giving himself any concern about the effect it may have on those to whom he is speaking. He will use the privilege of speech with all of the simplicity of its first institution.[28]

"Simple and native truth" is bound up with the recognition that "Childhood hath its manner of seeing, perceiving and thinking, peculiar to itself; nor is there any thing more absurd than our being anxious to substitute our own in its stead."[29] Certainly to read some of the writing of children is to be struck by their original perceptions written without vanity or pretext.

Many poets struggling to express themselves in imagery, to recall the suppressed dreams of long forgotten individual or collective knowledge, turn to their inward lives. What both poet and reader seek here is access to the hidden truths in varying degrees. Thus, by some sort of individual process, the poem may be born.

David Holbrook, who believes that "the creative processes by which we develop and sustain an identity are intuitive,"[30] describes part of the process:

> For reasons which don't yet seem clear, access to our deeper areas of inward life is too painful to be endured, possibly because we fear most our very inner weaknesses and need to defend our being against interference that we fear might destroy us. We can only work on inner reality by dreams, hidden meanings, symbolic displacement, and metaphor, and by this symbolic *work* construct something upon which to rejoice.[31]

While adults may have to struggle to gain this access, they tend to believe that the *work* is not necessary for children, who are already in touch with and close to the inner life. Whether joyful or painful, such dreams, meanings, images, and metaphors will spring forth spontaneously, truthfully, and naturally. If, as George Steiner says, mythologies "began with man's earliest attempts to rationalize their apprehension of the soul,"[32] mythologies engendered by children are, by virtue of their few years of life, yet unencumbered with apprehensions and what apprehensions they have are readily expressed. The child, as Rousseau says,

> pursues no formula, is influenced by no authority or example, but acts and speaks from his own judgment. Hence you must never expect from him studied discourse nor effected manners, but always the faithful expression of his ideas, and the conduct influenced only by his inclinations.[33]

This "faithful expression" is reminiscent of the overly-idealized "noble savage" concept which has found its model in primitivism, another area to which some poets respond. What they admire here is the seemingly superior virtue of the "natural man" and his surroundings in nature. Because the primitives are free of untoward influence, they can function more favorably, with easier passage to the subconscious – primitives, again, uncommonly reminiscent of Wordsworth's rustic and child.

To call children natural poets may, on the one hand, imply that the source of their ability lies in the realm of the mysterious, that it may be tinged with a touch of Romanticism. On the other hand, it is possible that the "simple and native truth" inherent in the language and speech of children, in their way of perceiving, thinking, and speaking has some basis in fact. Charles Olson, a poet of the Black Mountain School, asserts that "speech as a communicator is prior to the individual and is picked up as soon as and with ma's milk"[34] and that it is the breathing of an individual that determines his metrics. Both statements strongly suggest a Romantic viewpoint – and yet we live in an age when many branches of science, notably psychology, have made new discoveries about children. It is possible that these empirical observations may offer a further insight into the nature of creativity.

To create new combinations of language, perception, and rhythm, the adult poet draws from the conscious and unconscious, the known and the unknown, to produce his own expression and truth. To discover the difference between what the child does and what the adult does, we must look to the sources of this creation.

CHAPTER II

The Child and Imagination

Do you exist
my pretty bird
flying
above the snow?

Are you actually
flying
or do I imagine
it so?

Detail of wing
and breast
unquestionably
there –

Or do I merely
think you
perfect
in mid-air?

From "The Unknown"
William Carlos Williams[1]

"I no longer use the word 'Imagination' in my teaching," Phillip Lopate writes in *Being With Children*. "It has become a dirty word – an invitation for the child to ignore everything that is real and important to him." Lopate bases his beliefs on the fact that

> Many adults approach imagination as something extraneous to reality, as a holiday from reality. It seems to me, on the contrary, that imagination is *secreted* from reality through meditation on the concrete world. You look at something long enough and something starts to alter. The syrup in the spoon becomes a lake.

> But this in a way "delivers" you from your circumstances; it may be a way of connecting you even more to the material world that is right in front of your eyes.

Children, says Lopate, are "presumed to have wild imaginations. (Some do, and some do not.) The adult asks the children to take out their imaginations. The children oblige with ready-made images that corroborate the adult's fondness for the innocent, the picturesque and the happy."[2] Lopate is objecting here to what is certainly widely accepted, admired, and enthusiastically received by a multitude of teachers, educators, and parents as poetry.

> I live in the state of poetry
>
> It is in outer space
> The sky is pink and white and purple polka dots
> We have a main power plant shaped like a coil
> I live in wishes
> In Wishes wishes come true
> My friend lives in Colors
> There every body is red and green
> My house is a glass ball shaped one
>   it isn't green like most of them though[3]

This is the work of a sixth grade boy, Thomas Kennedy, writing under the guidance of Ron Padgett, a poet, translator, and teacher in the Teachers & Writers Collaborative in New York. The assignment to describe a state that "exists in our imagination only"[4] is one of the many "Utopian" or "imaginary world" assignments collected in Richard Murphy's *Imaginary Worlds: Notes on a New Curriculum*, published by the Collaborative. Its genre is similar to other assignments described in detail in the Teachers & Writers' *Whole Word Catalog* and *Whole Word Catalogue 2*, the most extreme of which is a suggestion to

> Imagine yourself dying: what does it feel like, what does it look like, what does it feel like to be dead – these questions may take the writers into the mythology of heaven and hell, devils, angels, and God. They could do a large mural of heaven and hell (like Bosch or Michelangelo.)[5]

Tommy Kennedy's poem brings into play the "wishes" and "colors" assignments that are part of the method advocated by Kenneth Koch, who pays homage to children who "can imagine what it feels like to be a dog, a fish, a teddy bear, a cloud or a piano. This is one of the fundamental poetic talents – and children have more of it than adults. . . They are likely to write more enthusiastically and more imaginatively from the inside than the outside."[6]

Koch, whose method is described in his books, *Wishes, Lies and Dreams: Teaching Children to Write Poetry* and *Rose, Where Did You Get That Red?: Teaching Great Poetry to Children*, has influenced countless teachers and poets working with children in the field of creative writing. Koch feels, as others do, that the imagination in the children with whom he has worked has been "repressed and depressed" and he sets about devising a method to bring it out by a series of prescriptives, among which are wishes, lies, and dreams. Wishes work well, Koch feels, because they are a "natural and customary part of poetry" and encourage the children "to be imaginative and free."[7] Thus a first grade child's wish poem reads:

> I wish me and my brother and my friend Paul were birds . . .
>
> David Jeanpierre[8]

Koch recommends lying as "a very quick way to the world of the imagination."[9] His students understand, he says, that he is not "recommending dishonesty in their everyday lives" but lies as a way to "very free imaginings. Often starting off saying untrue things as a joke, children become excited by the strangeness and beauty of what they are inventing."

> Calling the poem "Lies" is better than calling it "Imaginary Things" or "Make Believe," words that have a built-in childishness and fairytale quality. Using them, children are more likely to write about dragons and gingerbread houses than about things close to them. "Things That Aren't True" is probably the best way to put it. "Suppose" and "Pretend" are other possibilities. I don't like them much because they dictate a certain kind of wistful imagining. An exciting thing about invention is being caught up in it and starting to believe it; "Suppose" and "Pretend" keep saying it couldn't be true.[10]

A fourth grade student of Koch's writes this "lie" poem:

> I am in New York in a cow's head.
> I am still in New York in a cow's head.
> I am still in New York in a cow's head.
> Now I'm in New York in a flower.
> I'm now in New York in a cow's head.
> Now I'm in Spain taking a bath.
> Now I'm in Spain taking a bath tub.
> Now I'm in New England eating my friend in the bathroom.
> Now I'm still in the bathroom eating my friend but I'm on a cow.
> Now I'm in New York in a cow's head.
>
> Marion Mackles[11]

Dreams, for Koch, "are a frequent source of poetic inspiration," an "easy way" to make children "aware of their unconscious experience."[12] Another fourth grader writes:

> I had a dream that I was in a forest
> The trees grabbed me and tried to eat me
> I kicked them all and ran away
> Then I fell in a flower garden
> I fell in a flower the flower had closed
> I was trying to get out of the flower
> Then I woke up and found myself in bed
> instead of a flower
>
> Lenora Calanni[13]

Dream poems of this sort are printed in scores of pamphlets and books. *An Invitation to Poetry*, the third issue of an annual poetry magazine, publishes the winning entries in a contest sponsored for children by the Southern Nevada Teachers of English. Honorable mention was given to a third grade girl who wrote "The Funny Dream":

> I had a funny dream last night,
> I don't know what it meant.

Oh, boy it was a strange sight,
And this is how it went –

I dreamed I was a caveman,
The torches smoky light.
Upon the old bone table,
A pile of bones so white.

I dreamed I was a caveman,
I had a little bone.
And how I had to fight for it
To get it for my own.

I dreamed, but now I am awake,
We're going to the show.
I'm glad I'm not a caveman
A million years ago.

Christine DeLong[14]

Ardis Kimzey, who has worked as both poet and administrator in North Carolina schools, and whose book *To Defend a Form: The Romance of Administration and Teaching in a Poetry-in-the-Schools Program* has received much attention, includes a dream poem by a first grade pupil:

Last night I had a dream,
It was about a horse that I had got.
The color of it is black,
It feels very soft,
And it doesn't make a sound.

Sharon Walker[15]

Gensler and Nyhart, who are active in the Poets-in-the-Schools program in Massachusetts as well as the authors of *The Poetry Connection*, also explore reverie, daydreams, and nightmares.

> Poets rely heavily on the part of the mind that asks "what if?" – that speculates and fantasizes. Many poems are written in a state of reverie, when the imagination is given free rein.

> One of the most effective ways to help children tap this rich source within themselves is to show them poems in which all sorts of imagination are expressed. These include daydreams and nightmares, exaggerations and outright inventions. The kind of figurative language that compares dissimilar things, creating similes and metaphors, also springs from the imaginative activity of the mind. Looking at model poems, kids discover that they are in a time-honored tradition when they take odd leaps in their writing.

Models for reverie, for imagined "What if?" and invention, are used by Gensler and Nyhart to encourage "such dreamings-up." "Some poems," they continue, "are based on exaggerating, on seeing what it would be like *if* something outrageous occurred." To tell a lie, they believe, "stretches the imagination and allows an emotion, a dread, or a secret wish to be expressed in words. Dreams and transformations can also occur."[16]

Lewis MacAdams, who has been a director of the Poetry Center at San Francisco State University which administers the Poets-in-the-School Program in California, views imagination in broader terms:

> The imagination is like a muscle in a certain way . . . it atrophies in people because it isn't used. It goes back to the basic of the curriculum, of our culture. We're involved in the mind as rational, and we have these ideas of what the mind is. The imagination is not considered as important as the logical and rational mind. It's ignored, essentially, in schools . . . the emphasis is really changing, with all the books coming out on teaching poetry in the schools. It's not basically poetry that's being taught; it's the act of the imagination.[17]

"The act of imagination," in MacAdams's view, is based on the belief that it can be used by children to make "extraordinary images, to make *true* images." Encouraging children to "write things they know about" leads to his concept of poetry as "finding out your own personal truth." Imagination releases children from "reality boxes"; dreams give them "permission to be far out, to really use their imagination," and surrealistic exercises, such as automatic writing can be used to make up a language.[18]

This idea of language invention is also a component of Richard Murphy's "imaginary worlds" where imagination may be summoned to elicit new sounds and new words. An eighth grade boy writes about "The Nightmare World":

> I am a very queery, dreary eater
> Eating snake eyes, and ant skin froggy
> Legs, pickles and eggs slimy
> wormy chocolate gooey covered
> Pickle cream Echy Ecchy Ecchy
> Burp Glurp Chirp Bubble "Whew"!
>
> Fred Wolf[19]

Imagination and feelings are often linked. An article in *Scholastic Voice,* directed to the children themselves, tells them that

> Sometimes you have to remind yourself to let your feelings – and your imagination – rip, if you want your words to have impact . . . you don't have to be crude to liberate your imagination and feelings . . . Go back to your image lines. Can you make them stronger by using a wilder imagination?[20]

Imagination as an instigator of idea is also a common practice. Iris Tiedt in her book, *Individualizing Writing in the Elementary Classroom* published by the National Council of Teachers of English, speaks of children making books in which individual children can record their writing. Directions for an instruction poster are given:

> A Scary Night
>
> Choose a page in the Big Book
> Write the title of your story
> on the top line
> Write your name on the second
> line
> Then write your story.
> Use your imagination.[21]

Such directives, sprinkled liberally throughout hundreds of "creative activity" books, would seem to corroborate Lopate's observation that imagination implies a release from reality or some type of fancy injected into or apart from life. *Imagine and Write, Book 3,* part of the Creative Expression Series of *My Weekly Reader,* assures children they are authors if they will fill in lines provided for such instructions as "*Imagine* you often visit a zoo . . . *Imagine* that you have a new dog . . . *Imagine* a dog up in a tree . . . *Imagine* that you have been watching some giants . . . *Imagine* that an ugly witch has put you in a cage to fatten you up . . ."[22]

Imagination is constantly called into service for the language arts. Harvey S. Wiener in *Any Child Can Write* believes that "the child can write make-believe while practicing important language skills that you have been encouraging all along."

> What holds more promise than a child's imagination? In wonderful leaps the young mind wanders and connects, dreams and invents, projects and uncovers. Surrounded by a world of fiction – television, fairy tales, movies – the youngster absorbs models for imagined stories early into language experience. This delight in fancy is a sea of possibilities for developing writing skills.[23]

It would seem that imagination is expected to do everything.

Dr. Nancy Larrick, an educator and anthologist whose work with teachers and children is widely respected, describes in her collection of writing by children, *Green Is Like a Meadow of Grass,* the process by which the workshop in Poetry for Children at Lehigh University was held. Poetry was read, recited, and sung, and then created by the children both orally and on paper. "As a beginning," she explains, "we encouraged children to observe and then let their imaginations take over."[24] Rain, clouds, and seashells were observed, and new names invented for the shells. Among other activities children assumed the roles of animals petitioning God in the manner of Carmen Bernos de Gasztold's *Prayers from the Ark.* Fifteen weeks later thousands of "poetic images" had been recorded by the children, including "color" poems inspired by Mary O'Neill's *Hailstones and Halibut Bones.* The children realized, Larrick states, that it is not length or rhyme that makes a poem. But they did know that a poem does

> have to spring from imagination expressing some new idea, painting a unique picture, stirring the reader to think and feel as he has never done before.[25]

The writing that Larrick offers as evidence of this experience is often metaphoric. An eight-year-old boy wrote:

I wonder if my jack knife
Slipped out of my pocket
And cut holes in the clouds.

Joseph Ricci[26]

A ten-year-old girl describes rain:

What is that little pitter-patter
  on my window?
Could it be a little elf
  playing a trick on me?

Joan Fegley[27]

A nine-year-old girl describes a shell:

Lacy sea shell
So perfect and white,
Did a fairy leave behind
Her pink frill for your lining?

Debra Seip[28]

In this sense, imagination does paint a unique picture and gives a new idea. It is imagination that is called into activity by sensory observation, that same observation that Lopate describes "when the syrup in your spoon becomes a lake."

"Children's fantasies and imaginations are filled with magic, sometimes 'funny, cute' magic, but as often as not, magic of a very sinister variety,"[29] Marvin Hoffman writes in the *Whole Word Catalog.* Ideas for eliciting this sinister variety include categories such as Hypnotism, Invisibility, Superstitions, Charms and Witchcraft, Ghosts and Monsters, Cures and Home Remedies, and Tarot Cards. Here the child's imagination is not directed to the elf or fairy of Larrick's workshop. One child writes:

I am going to torture my
brother. I will put him in a

room with knives sticking
out. Right behind him is a
big cake. If he moves, he
gets scratched.[30]

Numerous variations on this theme are proposed by other poet-teachers. Tom Veitch believes in children's "natural sources of imagination" and advocates "The Trapdoor Method" by which children enter an "invisible and unknown world" or "the strange country that people call 'Imagination.' " For those unable to enter easily, he devises an "extended scenario" method whereby children end a story of his making by their own "further imaginings." These uses of imagination he recognizes as being in opposition to the "wish-fulfillment" imagination which is a "filling out of the self-image." "But both kinds of fantasy are very healthy and both kinds should be indulged in!"[31]

Still other teachers advocate the use of imagination focusing on a near-hallucinatory state. In his book, *The Power of Creative Writing*, Bernard Percy asserts that "the most rewarding part of any art form is hovering between . . . imagination and dreams and the reality of the world." He offers an example:

When on the earth, the sky
portrays a surreal mist of
unknown heights.
When in the sky, the earth
conveys a surreal mist of
unknown depths.
Perhaps what fills the space
between earth and sky holds
the visions which we seek.
Reality is where we are.
Visions lie just beyond that point
of direct focus.

Susan Cambigue

Percy follows this poem with instructions:

Take a moment and think of a dream that is important to you – something you wish to become reality.

Now visualize your dream and see it actually occurring. A nice feeling isn't it, bringing the dreams of imagination to the actuality of existence?

Teachers should help bring their students' dreams of imagination to the actuality of existence to nourish their students' artistic souls.[32]

Such claims for either dreams or imagination would seem to fall outside of any philosophy, romantic or rational, and contribute to an erroneous conclusion concerning the power of imagination itself.

The power of imagination is limited; it cannot of itself perform magic.

In his *Biographia Literaria,* Coleridge describes a poet as one who

> brings the whole soul of man into activity with subordination of its faculties to each other, according to their relative worth and dignity. He diffuses a tone and spirit of unity, that blends, and (as it were) *fuses,* each into each, by that synthetic and magical power, to which we have exclusively appropriated the name of imagination.[33]

Coleridge's claims are but one of a long line of theories about the imagination that have been proposed since Plato and Aristotle. St. Augustine states that the intellect is superior to the imagination, while Blake, in his denial of an external and intellectual reality, believes "Imagination is Eternity." Between these two extremes philosophers, critics, and poets offer a staggering number of interpretations regarding imagination. In his *Critique of Pure Reason,* Immanuel Kant sets the groundwork for the beliefs of the Romanticists with his assertion that the imagination is an active faculty for synthesis — that it is a mediator between sensibility and understanding. Without it, he believes, there can be no objective knowledge nor subjective judgment.

"We do not," writes Kant, "refer the representation . . . to the Object by means of understanding, with a view to cognition, but by means of the imagination (acting perhaps in judgment with understanding) we refer the representation to the Subject and its feeling of pleasure or displeasure."[34] In this view, imagination is free and not simply reproductive, but productive and capable of its own activity. In acquiring knowledge, therefore, understanding is more important than imagination, but in matters of art or aesthetics imagination clearly serves understanding.

In reading Tennyson's "The Eagle" the principles of this thinking can be applied:

> He clasps the crag with crooked hands;
> Close to the sun in lonely lands,
> Ringed with the azure world, he stands.
>
> The wrinkled sea beneath him crawls;
> He watches from his mountain walls,
> And like a thunderbolt, he falls.[35]

It is apparent to the intellect that an eagle does not have *hands*, nor can it get *close* to the sun; the sea does not *crawl* nor does a mountain have *walls*. But if the poem is read "by means of the imagination," the images (through Tennyson's use of personification and hyperbole) are striking, and may be subjectively accepted or rejected.

To Koch, Padgett, Murphy, Gensler and Nyhart and many adults, imagination is anything but the "synthetic" power that Coleridge described; nor does it fill Kant's role as a mediator between sensibility and understanding, as demonstrated in Tennyson's "The Eagle." It is rather a "world" or an area of the mind that is "extraneous to reality," reserved for fantasy, recall, and pretending, for invention and "free imaginings." As such it is strangely suggestive of the heightened self-emotion of the Romanticists as well as Wordsworth's "spontaneous overflow of powerful feelings."

Lopate's stance is characteristic of a number of contemporary poets who place faith in the image, as well as in the reality of experience and memory, to reveal meaning through observation and contemplation and thereby to spark the imagination. Here is a reminder of Rousseau's use of nature as a model, and of Wordsworth calling back the image of daffodils.

MacAdams acknowledges the potential of the dualities in the Romantic view; his "act of the imagination" comes closer to the view of Coleridge and Kant. It is the statement of creative unity, of the ability to synthesize both known and unknown. The imagination is active, not in a vacuum where it feeds upon itself, but as it operates upon externals and fuses both into the creative act.

The split can clearly be seen in the many statements made about imagination that appear in books and articles dealing with poetry and children's writing. Here the concept is used in such loose terms that it refers to imagination as *instigator of the idea*, as *fantasy*, as *metaphor*, as *a spur to feelings*, as *image*, as *language invention*, as *access to memory*, and even as *some fuzzy philosophical determinant*.

These disparate views of the imagination lend themselves to a logical arrangement built upon three classifications. If the imagination is conceived of as a functional mode of the mind, it may be said to be the means whereby mental pictures or images can be formed and expressed. This it does by three activities; the reproductive, the productive, and the creative.

The reproductive imagination calls to mind what has happened in the past. It is a recalling, a remembering and recognition of something seen, felt, heard, or experienced. Yet what is produced by reproductive imagination alone is usually dull and almost journalistic; certainly not the stuff of which fine poetry is made.

The productive imagination operates in a different manner. It is the daydream, the wish, and the lie that many teachers encourage. It is the release from reality that often negates the reproductive imagination or embellishes it, that reaches into the unconscious and builds "imaginary worlds," but as such it is egocentric in nature. It is autonomous to the degree that it eschews reality. It can even lead to hallucination because it does not recognize the limitations of externals. It is this productive imagination that is most generally thought to be creative.

The creative imagination, however, operates in a different way. It takes cognizance of the reproductive imagination because it acknowledges reality and accepts it; therefore, it cannot operate autonomously. It also uses the productive imagination to the extent that it speaks of subjective events not to be found in reality. In doing so, it transcends reality and puts together parts not to be found in the external world. The result is a creative product that does not destroy either reality or rationality but rather presents a new view of the world built upon symbols that are universally understood.

Vachel Lindsay's "The Moon's the North Wind's Cooky" serves as a simple example of how these three modes of the imaginative mind may work.

> The Moon's the North Wind's cooky.
> He bites it, day by day,

Until there's but a rim of scraps
That crumble all away.

The South Wind is a baker.
He kneads clouds in his den,
And bakes a crisp new moon *that . . . greedy*
North . . . Wind . . . eats . . . again![36]

Although not directly stated, it is the poet's reproductive imagination that recalls what has been observed about the moon's shape in its full, half, and waning phases. The rational mind, seeking to understand these changes, compares the moon to some other external object which undergoes the same change – in this case, a cooky. At this point a child might exclaim "the moon is like a cooky" or "the moon is a cooky" – and for many this suffices as a poetic statement, a simile or metaphor conjured up by the productive imagination that defies reality. But the creative imagination goes beyond this pseudo-statement: It enlists the rational mind again to ask the questions, *why, who, how?* and in so doing creates a new picture and complete synthesis. In this instance the North and South Winds, products of the creative imagination, are born. The poet has transcended reality, created something not in the external world but nonetheless credible because of the universal symbolism used. What is crucial here is that neither moon nor cooky has been destroyed but rather each takes on a new dimension and meaning.

The poet thus synthesizes in a manner where rationality is not destroyed but rather enhanced. All three modes of the imagination are used. Most writing by children, however, stops short of using this third phase. Imagination is confined to either the reproductive mode or the productive mode and nothing new is created. The result is a work based upon recollection and memory – the reproductive imagination as in the poem by Lenora Calanni, "I had a dream that I was in a forest," or some wish or dream that bypasses reality, as in the poem "I live in the state of poetry" by Thomas Kennedy which, although productive, is no more than a fancy of the autonomous imagination. While both poems may be thought to be creative by many adults, they do not represent the creative mind at its best because there is no synthesis in terms of what has traditionally always been understood to be art.

CHAPTER III

Symbolism and Inner Reality

There was a child went forth every day,
And the first object he look'd upon that object he became.
And that object became part of him for the day or a certain
  part of that day,
Or for many years or stretching cycles of years.

From "There Was a Child Went Forth"
Walt Whitman[1]

The forty-sixth annual report of the Bureau of American Ethnology, published in 1930, includes a lengthy section written by Edwin T. Denig containing his "plain statement of facts" about an Indian tribe, the Assiniboin. This tribe, descended from the Sioux and the Dacotah, is thought to have separated from the Sioux around 1760. Known among themselves as the Da-co-tah, they inhabit the region of the Upper Missouri River. Under the leadership of an intelligent ruling chief, Man-to-was-ko (Crazy Bear), the people, Denig reports, live by the land, content to hunt and sustain themselves on the prairie. They covet nothing belonging to anyone else.

> They do not think the Great Spirit created them on or for a particular portion of country but that he made the whole prairie for the sole use of the Indian, and the Indian to suit the prairie, giving among other reasons the fact that the buffalo is so well adapted to their wants as to meat and clothing, even for their lodges and bowstrings. To the Indian is alloted legs to run, eyes to see, bravery, instinct, watchfulness, and other capacities not developed in the same degree in the whites.[2]

The Assiniboin in many respects would seem to fulfill the Romantic idea of the noble savage, dependent on nothing but nature and making no claims on any other people nor territory. They are primitive and enjoy their beliefs in accord with primitive thought.

> They say the moon is a hot body and derives its light from its own nature, not as a reflection of the sun's rays; that it is eaten up monthly or during a given period by a great number of moles, which they call we-as-poo-gah (moon nibblers). These moles are numerous all over the prairies, have pointed noses, no teeth, and burrow in the ground. They (the Indians) believe that in eating up the moon their noses are burned off, their teeth worn out, and for their damage have been cast down from above, where they are doomed to burrow in the earth and get nothing to eat. The same operation is going on all the time by other moles, who in their turn will be thrown down. They think Wakoñda causes a new moon to grow when the old one has been destroyed . . .[3]

The Assiniboins' belief about the moon, unaffected by the scientific knowledge of the twentieth century, is as ingenuous as that of a young child:

Why the Moon Changes Shape

Someone bit off more and more of the moon
and didn't like it
and spat it all back together.

and someone else tried it
and he didn't like it
and he spat it all back together

Then someone else ate the moon,
didn't like it
and he spat it all back together.

The moon tastes like
asphalt eggs,
and the reason people want
to try it, it's like

something new,
and they think to themselves,
Can you eat it?
What can you do with it?

They think it's something
to eat, as they take
a bite out of it.

They also think that
the moon's made of green cheese
like everyone says,
and they wonder, "Can I reach it from here?"

And they try but they can't
so that's why people take space ships.
They go to it,
they say, "O, it's too hard.

I don't think I'll really like it."
They take it, and
instead of just a little
they take the whole planet.

James Lindbloom[4]

This work by a seven-year-old child in Poughkeepsie, New York, is another mythical invention to explain the changes of the moon. Published in *Stone Soup, a Journal of Children's Literature,* it is an example of what its editors believe to be "artistic," an expression of the child in "natural language,"[5] a work in which the child as author "will be called upon to explain the ambiguities"[6] but above all a work which draws out the creative spirit "with a very real and positive line to . . . experiences and perceptions."[7]

In *Spicy Meatball Number Five,* a publication of the Teachers & Writers Collaborative containing the work of children of P.S. 75 in Manhattan, another poem about the moon appears:

When the moon is getting lighter
The sky is getting darker
And the people is getting creepy
And all the people are going up in the moon
And the little girl stays down
And takes off her tongue and
Puts it up in the sky.

Grisel[8]

A ten-year-old from South Carolina places first in the October 1977 Poetry Contest of *Cricket, the Magazine for Children:*

The Night Sky

The stars are only letters
Of a line of strange language.
Every night the stars
Are arranged by a learned man
So that they will spell a line of poetry.
Beautiful poetry that makes me happy,
Beautiful poetry that makes me sad.
Each night another line appears,
As good and as lovely as before.
Every month a poem is finished,
And the moon, in its joy,
Is his whole self.
I wish I could read these wondrous lines,
But they belong to the stars that write them
And to the learned man in the moon.

Anne Elizabeth Murdy[9]

In Flora Arnstein's *Children Write Poetry* a California ten-year-old writes:

The moon is like a silver plate.
It is broken by strong fingers of sky and clouds,
Then put together by them again.

Edna[10]

"A Moon Child's Goodnight" by a Massachusetts high school student is published in *Reflections*, an Ohio publication:

Two astronauts are having a
tea party on the moon. One pours
moon drop tea into granite cups.
The second serves blue cheese
on a platter.
The sliver they eat

leaves the moon
suspended in space
breathlessly whispering
goodnight.

Amy Dockser[11]

An eight-year-old from Connecticut writes another:

The moon is a golden bracelet
that has been broken,
And an angel flew down from the
heavens,
took a piece up and hung it in the
sky . . .
Every night a light is left there
to make it shine.

Joya Moller[12]

There are numerous similarities in these myths and observations about the moon; children's minds and imaginations, eager to explain why the moon changes, display an interest in something eating the moon or a close association with food. They are works which may surprise us with their originality. They make assertions that bear close resemblance to the Assiniboin belief, and may even be thought to lend credence to Jungian archetypes. They seem natural, encompassing "native truth" and "faithful expression" in both thought and language. They are spontaneous, symbolic, and spring from an "inner reality." They show the ability of imagination to create and would seem, in Richard Lewis's terms, to encompass a "language of feeling and ideas."[13]

These works by children fulfill many requirements of what poet-teachers and educators believe to be the purpose of imagination: to elicit new ideas, fantasy, metaphor, and to serve as a springboard for image and feelings. They are, in terms of imagination, more creative than productive or reproductive. In addition, they give to adult readers, in varying degrees, a sense that their own imaginations are ignited and sparked by the child's vision.

"Entrenched in our poetics," George Steiner writes, "is the belief that art reveals to us, through allegory and metaphor, the 'real' world of which our own is but a corrupt or fragmentary image."[14] Here poetry serves as the "light" and the "real world" which we have lost. Here poetry offers that sense of mystery and mystique which adults seek to recapture through exploration of the child's imagination, the quintessence of which is given to them by the child as natural poet. The fact that a diversity of adults thought them worthy to be called poetry and published them as such is the final proof of this belief.

David Holbrook, whose "Creativity in the English Programme" was presented at an Anglo-American Seminar on the Teaching of English at Dartmouth College in 1966, recognizes that "while there is all the difference in the world between art poetry and the poetry of children, the *functions of symbolism in each are the same* because they are functions natural to man and their modes are archetypal."[15] Holbrook's paper lays stress on words as crucial to the teaching of effective English and to the act of creativity: Words cannot be separated from "the dynamics of personality, nor from the processes of symbolism by which human beings seek to deal with their inward life."[16] Words as symbols and the need for symbolization must be applied to both "outward communication" and to the "inner" or "psychic" or "subjective reality." To deny this inner world is to deny the "unknown self." Creative symbolism, he asserts, is not controlled by intellect alone. Furthermore, he stresses "the approach to inner dynamics, as a primary occupation of human beings in the preservation of identity."[17]

> It would be wrong, however, to elevate creativity into a mystique. Any teacher who has a sensitive understanding of poetry and imaginative fiction has the grounding for an understanding of creative work with children. The fundamental problem is that of responding to symbolic expression.

"How we can tell what the child or the poet means depends upon our acquaintance with all kinds of creative art and with criticism which illuminates its symbolism," he continues. The ideal teacher would need further to study growth of personality in children, "the symbolism of their play and expression" and "more attention to psychoanalytic studies of children."[18]

Holbrook's prescriptions for an ideal climate for teaching are indeed valuable and many of his insights cogent. What is curious, however, is that while he recognizes the difference between "art poetry" and the work of children, he does not make an adequate distinction between the use of the symbol by the child and by the adult, nor does he distinguish the difference in their "inner reality."

It is not the purpose of this book to become involved in arguments about linguistics and the origins of language; nor to debate whether there is some schema of universal grammar determined by deep or innate structures of presetting in the brain, as Noam Chomsky asserts; nor whether linguistics is one sign of development in thinking that, manifesting itself in oral and written words, is directed to some goal. Nor is the scope of this investigation to examine cognition either as thought directed to final purpose – as opposed to discovery and enrichment, whereby the modification results from learning to respond to new aspects of sensory stimuli – or as responding differently to the same sensory stimuli. Linguists, psychologists, and educators seem perpetually at odds over these matters, and little or no evidence can be found that anyone has studied, with any scientific purpose, the child as poet.

It is convenient, however, in attempting to separate the Romantic notion of the child-poet from the reality, to make use of some of the aspects of the findings of Jean Piaget, whose book *The Language and Thought of the Child* affords insights into certain thought and language patterns that turn up in the poetry children write. Piaget's concern is not with the origin and structure of language, but rather with its importance as a function of communication – spoken words as well as the unspoken thoughts which the child reserves for himself and keeps hidden. It is these that are of importance in any investigation of the child's writing.

The myth of the Assiniboin that the moon is eaten appears frequently enough in the work of children to assign the thought some importance. The Assiniboin believe that the moles, moon-nibblers, eat the moon and are punished by their god, Wakoñda, who "causes a new moon to grow." There is no doubt that they attribute to their god some special magical power, but it is this very lapse in explanation, in the failure to say "how," that a striking similarity occurs between primitive belief and that of the child. The primitive, like the child, Piaget says, "will substitute for things, as they are, a fragmentary world of his own in which everything has an aim, and in which everything can be justified."[19] This can be seen in the poem written by James where a succession of "someones" bit off the moon and "spat it all back together." Thus far, the reasoning is clear. He has explained how the moon is revitalized and made whole. But at the end of the work where the people "take it" – and indeed "take the whole planet" – the reader is left wondering *how* the moon ever gets back in the sky. There is no question that James, if asked, would invent an answer, just as the Assiniboins might. This same principle works in the free verse about the astronauts where the reader is told that "The sliver they eat/leaves the moon/suspended in space."

Similarly, the idea of the moon as a golden bracelet gives no clue as to how the moon will be made whole, although the child might explain that at some time the angels carry all the pieces up to the sky. The silver plate metaphor by Edna does carry through with the idea that the "strong fingers of sky and clouds" can both break apart and "put together" the moon, if the reader is willing to accept the idea that the sky and cloud have strong fingers. Again, if asked to explain, she would probably find a plausible reason!

Although Piaget's critics have been put off by his use of the term "egocentric" in describing the child, it is a characteristic of behavior and of thinking that is observable in children and exemplified in much of their writing. Young children believe that they are at the center of the universe, that the world was created not only for them but that everything in it shares their feelings and desires. Objects and animals, furniture and moons – all things are alive and function as they do. They are unconscious that they are any different from the things they know and observe and they confuse themselves with nature which, in turn, gives rise to a primitive animism whereby whatsoever comes into their experience takes on the qualities they feel. A fifth grader, whose work is published in *Poemmaking: Poets in Classrooms*, writes that:

> In space the moon is quiet
> And it is very slow.
> The moon feels very sad
> In space with nobody
> To talk to – the poor moon.[20]

To be lonesome means there is no one to talk to, and the child assigns his feelings about this loneliness to the moon. This thought is seen clearly in the work of Grisel when she attributes to all the people her own feelings of creepiness as the sky grows dark. "The little girl" is, of course, herself and the fact that she "takes off her tongue and/Puts it in the sky" is manifestation of another characteristic of children in believing that whatever they know must be known by everyone. The personal symbolism which children often hide, but sometimes reveal in their work, is part of their frame of reference, also uniquely personal. Is the tongue, in this case, a wish to taste or bite or nibble at the moon, or is it a metaphor of the moon as crescent resembling a tongue? It is what Piaget would describe as a "purely personal connection between ideas as they arise"[21] and can be observed in "Why the Moon Changes Shape" far more elaborately. Yet it exists in almost every example given.

It is in the nature of the child's personal, ego-directed view that very little attention is paid to logical detail. All gaps are filled in by invention, and children may even contradict themselves in order to fit everything into their schema. This is evident in "The Night Sky" when Anne speaks of the "learned man in the moon" who arranges "letters of a line of strange language" to make "beautiful poetry." Her first assertion is that she has read the "Beautiful poetry that makes me happy,/Beautiful poetry that makes me sad" but later she writes "I wish I could read these wondrous lines." In a like manner it is at first the man who arranges the letters, but later she states "they belong to the stars that write them/And to the learned man in the moon." Nor does she, incidentally, explain how the moon looks when he is not "his whole self." The reader knows only that the moon feels joy when the poem is completed and has become round. If a completed poem is equated with the joy of a full moon, it would be logical to ascribe to a quarter or half moon different emotions, but these are overlooked.

This negation of analysis, caused by subjective reasoning, is explained by Piaget; here "Syncretism is a 'subjective synthesis' "[22] while objective synthesis requires analysis. Richard Lewis marvels, for example, at a child's ability to write a story wherein she "traveled through the wildest spectrum of feelings – incorporating all the seemingly disparate elements of her experience, which included swimming pools, mice, bridges, muggers, monsters, kings of the world, bat girls, drunkards, snake birds, Shirley Temple, judges, spook houses, Dracula, kangaroos, and the Wizard of Oz."[23]

Whether by incorporating everything possible into their writing or by omission, children's inner realities vary from those of adults. It is as Piaget says, that

> Instead of looking for an explanation in spatial contact (visual realism) or in logical deduction of laws and concepts (intellectualism), the child reasons . . . according to a sort of "internal model" similar to nature, but reconstructed by his intelligence, and henceforth pictured in such a fashion that everything in it can be explained psychologically and that everything in it can be justified or accounted for (intellectual realism).[24]

The children's world is a world apart, a special kind of world, just as real for them as the adult's world, yet even more striking in its "pure realism,"

> an immediate taking possession of the object, but so immediate that the subject, who does not know himself, cannot manage to get outside himself in order to see himself in a universe of relations freed from subjective accretions.[25]

Here perceptions are more imaginative and intuitive, and therefore richer than those of adults whose imagination has been suppressed in favor of logic and reality. Here are symbols, private and personal to the child, analogies and comparisons couched in concrete symbols. Even order is often sidestepped in the exuberance of the schema.

A sixth grade boy, whose line serves as the title of a book published by the Los Angeles County Art Museum, *The Moon is as Full as a Suitcase*, writes:

> The rivers are like old people.
> with boney fingernails.
> The moon is as full as a suitcase.
>
> David Lorenzo[26]

This work shows not only the juxtaposition of lines without any relationship to each other, but points up how the child does not compare perceptions but perceives comparisons, using the word *full* rather than observing the actual shape of both objects.

Children often exhibit in their work a syncretism in both reasoning and language which is based on contiguity rather than logic. Whereas adults use logic and reasons to make a reconciliation between two different or opposing principles, children do not because they think in vague, personal, and unanalyzed terms. It is, to Piaget, a "confused perception which takes in objects as a whole and jumbles them together without order."[27]

> The desire for justification at any price is a universal law of verbal intelligence in the child . . . This law is itself derived from the syncretistic nature of childish reasoning.[28]

Such reasoning is a negation of analysis, and therefore displays a primitive quality. It leaves nothing to chance. It has no adaption to the point of view of anyone else, but subsists as a world unto itself.

> Syncretistic understanding consists precisely in this, that the whole is understood before the parts are analysed, and that understanding of the details takes place – rightly or wrongly – only as a function of the general schema.[29]

Piaget makes the point, however, that as they grow, children no longer use this syncretistic reasoning when it applies to their perceptive intelligence. Yet they are apt to retain syncretism in their verbal intelligence, when what they write is neither observed nor clearly understood.

The "natural" language that is found in all of the examples also gives a clue as to the nature of syncretistic thinking. Often it is an indefinite pronoun used without sufficient explanation. In James's last stanza, it is unclear, for example, to what "it" refers; is it the moon or the taste of "green cheese"? In "The Night Sky" the use of "its" would ordinarily be "his" as determined by the writer's analogy between the moon and the learned man. In addition, there is a surfeit, in many examples, of the conjunction "and," used instead of the more explanatory conjunctions "because" or "while," or the adverb "thus" which an adult would certainly choose to explain order or cause.

But what is most telling, perhaps, is the grammatical ellipsis in the writing wherein the reader can judge that all that is going on in the child's mind is not being verbalized. What prompted James to speak of "asphalt eggs" is known but to him; an educated guess might be that the moon may look like asphalt, or asphalt is thought to be a substance of which the moon is made. In *A Big Bite of the World* a child writes:

> A big day is here. The rocket hit the moon.
> A moon man came out. Watch out! John
> A moon man! Kill him I can't. Look
> at that thing! help![30]

In this instance, "thing" is presumed to be understood by the reader. A third, fourth, and fifth grade class in Long Island, working under the guidance of Alan Ziegler, asked to fill in "Poetry is like . . ." end a long collaborative effort with

> Poetry is like the moon because it floats all over the world. When I see the moon it looks like poetry is written all over his face.[31]

Although the idea is strangely similar to the myth created in "The Night Sky," there is no indication of anything at work to make this analogy. If the connecting link is "floats," the reader must presume that both the moon and poetry "float," an association which some child must surely have made. It is difficult to determine any connecting link with the other forty-odd descriptions of poetry in this example, ranging from "Poetry is like/eating a mayonnaise sandwich," to "a hamster running under a bed," to "a new born pain in the neck." The link may possibly occur because of an earlier statement that "Poetry is like/music in the air" or "Poetry is like/moonshine."[32] Here then is another instance of contiguity where vision, or lack of it, is distracted by idea, and shows up, as Piaget asserts, in verbal syncretism, as noted in "The moon is as full as a suitcase."

Children feel, in most cases, that it would be useless for them to use the correct conjunction, analyzation, or even a reasonable order, because there is no need to do so. When they are young, they use words "to bring about what the action of itself is powerless to do," thus romancing and inventing and creating their reality "by words and magical language, in working on things by words alone apart from any contact with them or with persons."[33] Their

> causal relations remain unexpressed and are thought about only by the individual, probably because, to the child mind, they are represented by images rather than words.[34]

They are, therefore, "hidden away by the child in the fastness of his intimate and unformulated thought." Such thoughts are subconscious, not adapted to reality and tend "not to establish truths," but to "satisfy desires." They are strictly individual and incommunicable by language and "have recourse to indirect methods, evoking by means of symbols and myths the feeling by which it is led."[35] Later children will learn from experience and logic, and while they will be able to distinguish between their dream worlds and reality, they will persist in verbal syncretism.

> The child alters reality at will, to see what would happen in such-and-such conditions. They are "experiments just to see," the work of imagination . . . whose function it is to loosen the spirit from the bonds of reality, leaving it free to build up its ideas into a world of their own.[36]

It is evident, therefore, that using Piaget's insights into the individual use of symbols and myth, Holbrook's dictum for teachers to study symbolism in literature would be somewhat futile. A parent or psychoanalyst would be in a far better position to explain this inner reality and relate it to the symbolism of an individual child. In the same way the reader is able to appreciate the obvious in the writing, but cannot go further into the subconscious mind of children to interpret what children have chosen to keep hidden for themselves. It is therefore naive for the editors of *Stone Soup* to suggest that children be "called upon to explain the ambiguities" in their writing. Neither the child nor adult is Wakoñda!

What adults praise in the work of a child does not seem to be so much a matter of its merits as a poem as it is an admiration of the intuitive and "natural" manner of the myth or metaphor. It is certainly regard for rich invention, for a use of language which is free of logical restriction, and praise for the spontaneity of what the adult believes children are giving through their thoughts and imagination:

Come with me to the other side of the moon.
I'll tell you where the moon comes from.
And where we come from
Where the sky came from
Come with me
This is not a side show, don't be mistaken
I can open the world with my brain, and yours can
do it too. COME WITH ME. . . .

Tracy Lahab[37]

This poem by a sixth grader, found in Koch's *Rose, Where Did You Get That Red?* is an example of what many adults call natural, unconscious, intuitive, and a key to the soul of the child. It is the very essence of Romanticism for it presupposes that children can unlock all the secrets of the universe through their poetry. It is self-expression, the celebration of individualism, the exaltation of nature, far beyond the clutches of materialism and rationalism. In addition, it flouts the tradition of poetry as a crafted work.

CHAPTER IV

The Outer Climate

How many will come after me
                singing as well as I sing, none better;
        Telling the heart of their truth
        as I have taught them to tell it;
Fruit of my seed,
        O my unnameable children.
Know then that I loved you from afore-time,
Clear speakers, naked in the sun, untrammelled.

"Dum Capitolium Scandet"
Ezra Pound[1]

"The secrets of individual imagination," the poet Allen Ginsberg writes, "which are transconceptual & non-verbal – I mean unconditioned spirit – are not for sale to this consciousness, are of no use to this world except perhaps to make it shut its trap & listen to the music of the spheres." Ginsberg speaks of his own poetry as "Angelic Ravings," and further advises his reader that "Who denies the music of the spheres denies poetry, denies man, & spits on Blake, Shelley, Christ & Buddha." In his *Notes for Howl and Other Poems* he describes how "I suddenly turned aside in San Francisco, unemployment compensation leisure, to follow my romantic inspiration – Hebraic-Melvillian bardic breath. I thought I wouldn't write a *poem*, but just write what I wanted to without fear, let my imagination go, open secrecy, and scribble magic lines from my real mind – sum up my life – something I wouldn't be able to show anybody, write for my own soul's ear and a few other golden ears."

Ginsberg's *Notes* relate how he wrote "a new poetry . . . continuing to prophesy what I really knew despite the drear consciousness of the world . . . "

> I went on to what my imagination believed true to Eternity (for I'd had a beatific illumination years before during which I'd heard Blake's ancient voice & saw the universe unfold in my brain), & what my memory could reconstitute of the data of celestial experience.[2]

This concept of the power of imagination is described by Ernst Kris in an essay, "On Inspiration: Preliminary Notes on Emotional Conditions in Creative States," as a state when "the unconscious is supreme." Ginsberg, indeed, would seem to be like Kris's "priests and prophets of old" who wove myths "similar to those which mold the fantasy life of early childhood."

> The story of this past is not entrusted to consciousness. In a state similar to that of intoxication, elated, in a trance, not conscious of what he does – thus Plato, to whom we owe this first description of the state of inspiration – the poet sings his song. The voice of God speaks through him to men.[3]

In primitive society, Kris continues, those who assume this "inspired leadership" communicate with their repressed fantasies and wishes by use of the mechanisms which are in the nature of projection and introjection. "What comes from inside is believed to come from without. The voice of the unconscious is externalized and becomes the voice of God, who speaks through the mouth of the chosen."[4]

> Through the idea of inspiration the communication gains in authority, and the person who communicates it is relieved of the burden of responsibility.

To further understand this authority, Kris cites the concept of revelation, in which the truth is not seemingly acquired through human effort, but through some other power, and therefore is "beyond criticism as well as beyond doubt."[5]

In a like manner other poets describe psychological and physiological states which Kris identifies in psychoanalytic terms that are not the concern of this book. Yet the "single breath unit" of Ginsberg and the "breathing" of Charles Olson's line are curiously linked to what Kris calls the "full metaphorical meaning of inspiration"[6] which is based upon the "immediate substitution of spiritual influence for breath."[7] Robert Bly's description of psychic energy and Robert Louis Stevenson's description of working with some unseen collaborator are also called to mind. The dream-like trance in which Coleridge wrote "Kubla Khan" is probably the best known of these states, which are described in varying degrees by other poets who, in one way or another, go beyond themselves in the act of creation.

Although Ginsberg's description may seem an extreme example, it should be noted how similar the process is to those very qualities which adults praise in children's poetry. Implicit in the "unconditioned speech" is the spontaneity and unrehearsed rhythms believed to be instinctual. The "unconscious as supreme" is set into motion by Romantic inspiration and the act of writing "without fear." "Magic lines" are scribbled because the imagination is allowed to flow without restriction. Furthermore, there is that same implied reference to the celestial experience and the angelic that has been observed in Transcendental philosophy. The voice of the child is the voice of the "chosen." Through the child adults may partake of the "music of the spheres."

The child himself, however, as Piaget asserts, listens to no other voice than his own. He is unaware that he is revealing the "secrets of individual imagination" or that he needs "romantic inspiration." He scribbles his magic lines unaware that he is writing with an "unconditioned spirit." To him there is no "real mind" because there is not yet a false one.

Ginsberg's beliefs about inspiration are not unlike those of other contemporary American poets who search for truth relayed by another power or person, or for voices from some bygone culture or race. Primitivism presupposes, like the noble savage concept, that there are qualities in earlier societies and modes of living superior to those of the present day; that escaping materialism or any of the variety of contemporary ills which are assumed to be evil leads to the discovery of poetic truths.

Primitivism and neo-primitivism argue that poetic vision, or truth, takes its roots in something deeper than personal experience. Yet the resultant creative offerings are so dependent upon cryptic and personal symbolism that the reader is left perplexed. Some argue that intelligibility is necessary to communication; others argue that the reader's response to the communication is not significant – that bringing forth the light or the truth is often considered an end unto itself.

Personal symbolism is used by many poets who weave these symbols into fantasy, who believe variously in the landscape of the mind, the psychic processes, the revelation of the dream, or a neo-surrealism that prides itself on obscurity and comic phantasmagoria. Again the reader often is asked to find coherence in incoherence. Personal experience is the raw material of other poets who offer it as a microcosm of the universal, a confessional or spiritual purge, and often merely a blatant egotism combining elements of rebellion with personal visions of truth.

Other poets, who believe that objects and things are more persuasive than subjectivity and personal symbols discard the idea of imagination and substitute the image for symbol. Here nature, everyday experience, immediate perceptions, even stark journalistic records and unedited factual detail are presented to the reader. Truth is thought to be found in the object or the word which weaves a magic of its own and persuades the reader of its importance by its mere existence.

It is customary to identify these poets by schools, yet a poet may embody the beliefs of a single group, of several groups, or may drift from one to another. Of these the Black Mountain School, the San Francisco Renaissance, the Beats, and the New York School are the most widely recognized. Or a poet may evolve his own poetic truths without allegiance to a school. What binds many of these poets together, however, is their dislike of academic poetry whose closed form, established metrics, complexity of thought, cosmic concerns, formal diction, and reverence for classical allusions are thought to represent restriction, insulation from experience, and, symbolically, an ivory tower. A new insistence on open form, natural language, and the abolition of restrictive rhyme and poetic tools is thought to be freer and more open to the natural mode of man's experience, a climate in which poets are better able to seek and find their own truth.

What also binds them together is a fierce allegiance to the groups of beliefs which they espouse. Richard Kostelanetz in *The Old Poetries and the New* speaks of a "complicated sociology of American poetry."

> The scene of American poetry is defined by the proliferation of parochial establishments which jell around various common ties

> – academic connection, geographical location, sexual persuasion, ethnic or religious or racial origins. Nearly, though not every, significant American poet belongs to one or another group, sometimes less by his loyalty to them than by the group's adherence to him; and what announces the existence of a clique is, first, a discernible network of writers who regularly and publicly praise each other's work, regardless of whether it is excellent or abominable, as well as, second, their blatant penchant for ritualistically either dismissing or ignoring poets outside their circle.[8]

As a corollary these poets have, in the words of Horace Gregory, the "American vice," a dispensation to "make all things new" without regard for the past. Thus most poets of the past are either assailed or ignored; old gods are toppled and new ones arise. The tradition of poetry as a mode of art which pays attention to form and uses poetic devices is summarily dismissed and not only ignored but *not even understood.* A new sort of Romanticism arises, a new sort of Transcendentalism whose roots are to be found in processes with which few contemporary poets are familiar. The ramification of this situation for children's writing will be dealt with in future chapters.

What these new views do not take into account, however, are the values which many adults put into the traditional idea of academic poetry – artistic unity and a synthesis which operates within some framework and goes beyond mere self-expression.

In an interview with the poet X. J. Kennedy in the May 20, 1972 issue of *Saturday Review* another poet, John Ciardi, suggests that Kennedy's stance on the poem as an artifact and his views on the subject of form, rhyme, and meter might be "well worth pondering at a time when so many poets are calling for a sort of untutored spillage of raw emotion." Kennedy asserts that:

> Many poets around the early sixties got turned off by the old forms. They saw rime and meter as parts of a whole traditional order that they found necessary to reject. They came to associate iambic pentameter with a dead aristocracy and to see open forms as more democratic, more fluid, more honest – more honest for them, that is.

Just possibly their sense of honesty was affected by the fact that

> they had not mastered stricter forms to the point of feeling free with them. Certainly, such a poet as [Richard] Wilbur feels honest within form and would probably feel dishonest if he broke out of formal containment.

"The tendency today is to adulate spontaneity," Kennedy asserts. Ciardi, therefore, introduces the question of spontaneity as poetry, versus poetry as artifact, and asks if believing in spontaneity and ignoring the artifact *"doesn't . . . imply a sort of dance of death"*? Kennedy answers:

> I see it as part of the whole attack on the notion of the responsible individual who labors with his poem until it is in the best possible shape and who then takes the blame or praise for it. The faith in an accidental arrangement that can be asserted as a work of art has helped many writers to justify to themselves a kind of poetry in which no particular human voice is to be heard. To me, poetry has to offer such a voice and to control its cadence, its inflections, and its emphases in some indesctructible order.
>
> The fact that so many are writing from other principles makes the real poetry harder to find, but it is there. Poetry always has room for every kind of excellence.

Ciardi asks Kennedy whether his views are not somewhat elitist. *"Aren't you insisting on a kind of preparation not immediately available to the socially underprivileged who yet have strong feelings and who might never get them expressed if they had first to learn the formalities?"* Kennedy's reply is important.

> The kind of preparation that makes a man a poet is not immediately available to anyone. A poet labors hard and long to prepare himself and finds joy in his labor. Form is his aid. It is important because it tells him, among other things, when his writing is going wrong. When the rime stumbles or the meter starts going ticktock, he is being told that he has shallowed out and that he must go back and make himself feel harder what he is reaching to say. Those untutored and underprivileged you mention will never really learn what they want to say until some sort of form leads them to it.[9]

The philosophies of those who shun tradition and those who cherish it are crucial to an examination of the child as poet. For many children *are* under the tutelage of poet-teachers, and to understand their beliefs is to learn more about what children emulate and believe poetry to be.

It is over fifteen years since poet-teachers have offered their manifestos to the young. Through the National Endowment for the Arts, the Teachers & Writers Collaborative in New York, and programs in states that send poets into schools, children are absorbing the viewpoints and methods of these teachers. In addition, these poet-teachers have published their beliefs and ideas in books that are offered to educators, classroom teachers, and parents. It is not difficult to spot, in a child's work, the influence of these methods.

The situation becomes compounded, however, when many who *call* themselves poets enter the scene. These "poets" number in the thousands. Their work may be published in small poetry magazines, local newspapers, or be self-published. Their knowledge of poetry is frequently based on their own inner truths which may incorporate some knowledge of current trends but is usually adamant in its denial of academic poetry, rhyme, and the necessity for any sort of form. They may know little of children beyond the fact that children enjoy playing. Poetry then becomes a sort of playing with words for the children, and has little purpose but to assure the poet-teacher local glory, poetry readings, and future teaching jobs. There is also an unfortunate tendency to make all things new by renaming traditional poetic devices or figures of speech to suit individual invention. Metaphor and simile, for example, become "clay words"[10] or "like poems."[11]

The classroom teacher is sometimes influenced by either the poet-teacher or the poet who proclaims himself teacher. Occasionally the brief visits of the poet-teachers will carry over into the work done after they have left, as the regular teacher makes an effort to incorporate some creative writing into the daily schedule. More often than not, however, this teacher's knowledge of poetry is vague. Some teachers, educated to a school of declamation wherein Beauty, Truth, and Wisdom abide, are apt to think that poetry no longer lives and are aghast at the poet-teacher's startling views. Younger teachers who may have little knowledge of children's literature or of the poetry to which children respond may accept the models given by the visiting poets or resort to a textbook poetry unit. In either case, children are at the mercy of conflicting views of poetry and, as their knowledge of poetry is limited, will model their own work on that of the visiting poet or on the teacher's idea of traditional and often poor, archaic, or irrelevant examples.

In a few cases there will be a teacher whose knowledge of poetry is sure and whose love of it is pervasive. Some evaluation can then be made of what is being offered to the children. But this is a rare situation.

There are teachers, moreover, so influenced by the poet-teacher that they will carry over writing assignments suggested by the poet. In this case the writing is apt to resemble that of visiting poets or, often, their lessons embellished by the teacher. Teachers' enthusiasms may further lead them to invent and try ideas that are then published in educational journals, suggesting tricks they have discovered to get children to write and, again, renaming traditional figures of speech. Now metaphor becomes a "Make-It"[12] poem, or a "mind-stretching exercise."[13]

Still other teachers rely on commercial methods, both in printed and audio/visual form. Here pre-selected recordings of poems are used – usually traditional poetry that may have no meaning for the contemporary child. Most often "fill-in books," in which children fill in the appropriate blanks, are used to assure teachers that their students are all "young authors" or "young poets." These are published by magazines or textbook houses employing writers who know little about poetry and certainly are not poets themselves. They masquerade as authorities. Now metaphor and simile are called a "makes-me-feel"[14] poem or "quickie sensory suggestions."[15] Occasionally someone who knows a little more about poetry will write a text, but the models of poetry used are those of the author himself, permission fees being too high for the publisher to afford good contemporary poetry. In this case, children may well be subjected to trite verse as a model that will show up in their work.

Yet another formidable influence is the use of children's writing as models for other children. There are a smattering of trade books and magazines which fall into this category and they are widely praised. But in many cases schools and classes will write their own material and "publish" their own books to be used in classrooms and on library shelves. Thus, children are led to believe that their own poetry is on a par with the finest poets, a misconception that even teachers, librarians, and parents espouse. Publication is often marked with a public event, a school celebration or even a school or regional fair devoted to the work of children as poets and authors.

If adults, including poet-teachers, teachers, and parents, conceive of children as natural poets – and there is every proof that they do – there is reason to presume that they interpret poetry as a spontaneous, instinctual product of which every child is capable. There is no need for work or labor, no need to view the process of creativity or writing as more than an act of the moment, as self-expression that is an end in itself. Every child then, if given the opportunity, is a poet and writing is an instinctive act.

If this is true, why then is it necessary to bother with poet-teachers or teachers? If form, rhythm, creativity, and growth of consciousness are instinctive, why should there be centers to develop the imaginations of children? If their untutored language is also instinctive, why do we teach them English? It is time to strip the romance from the idea of the child as natural poet and examine these claims.

"The concept of 'instinct'," writes a leading psychoanalyst, Judd Marmor, "has probably been more subject to misuse and confusion than any other in modern psychological thought." Instinct is not, says Marmor, "any seemingly automatic activity or habitual inclination"[16] as many believe. There has long been a failure to show the difference between biological need, aim, motor pattern, and its emotional concomitants. To some scientists, indeed, the word instinct has been discarded and in its place are "inherited biological structures" and "behavioral systems" with varying degrees of environmental influences.

> The fundamental error which the instinct theorists – including Freud – have made in this regard is to assume that the various characteristics which they correctly observed in all human beings *in a particular time* and *social milieu* were inherent in *all* human beings, in *all* times and in *all* social milieus.[17]

Marmor believes, based on the evidence of experiments with insects, birds, fish, primates, and even feral children (human beings raised among wild animals), that "the higher the ascent in the evolutionary scale the more variable is the behavior of the individual animals, and the wider its range of adaptability."[18] Thus behavior or instinct is dependent less on "phylogenetically predetermined patterns" and more dependent upon the influence of environment.

> The vast range and complexity of modern human behavior are dependent not only on the inheritance of a human brain and body, but equally importantly, upon that vast *social* inheritance called culture. This represents the transmitted learning and experience which one generation of men has handed down to its successors during thousands of years through the medium of language. It is this unique factor which qualitatively distinguishes man from all other animal forms.[19]

To speak of human nature, Marmor asserts, "*as some form of human behavior, thought, or emotion, which is determined by purely biological factors, and which exists even in a state of isolation, is clearly erroneous.* There can be no 'human' nature apart from some form of human society, and the character of that 'nature' will inevitably reflect the character of that society." This is in no way a denial of the biological needs or drives which are common to men and animals, "but the *aims* of these drives in humans, and the *objects* towards which they are expressed, can only be understood in terms of the specific social relationships to which the human being has been exposed."[20]

In man "each stage of development is determined by the cooperation of heredity and environmental forces." In humans the "cultural factors become indissolubly inter-related with organic process through the laying down of language patterns." Thus is born a "new unity, a 'socio-biological unity' called human nature" but it is not fixed, immutable, or universal. Rather does it depend on biological and social inheritance, and "significant changes in either sphere may alter it."[21]

To understand this view of instinct and human nature is to recognize that while certain children may be born with inherited capacities for the writing of poetry, it is the environmental factors which play an equally important role in this development.

Arbuthnot states that "the child of one is a nearly complete poet" who has so "mastered pitch, volume, phrasing, and cadence that through them and without words, he can communicate his feelings and desires to others." She has also asserted that "his ear is so tuned that he responds to similar messages from others." Such assertions do not make the necessary distinction between biological needs, the cries which an infant produces in order to satisfy his hunger, and the words he learns to demand attention. That these sounds and early words communicate thought is undoubtedly bound up with the primitive idea of word magic when, for example, animals accompany their actions with particular cries or sounds, or a warrior issues a cry to summon his troops to battle. To Piaget the patterns of sounds are an unconscious repetition of what the child has heard, known by the name of echolalia, which persists as a game up to the age of seven.

Certainly parents and teachers are aware that children who come from homes where few words are spoken, and few books read, reflect this lack of communication in their reading and writing skills. It may be said then, that given a particular environment at home and in school, children, because of their inherited capacity to learn and their ability to use words as communication, may seem to have a natural language; but this is so variable that no broad generalizations may be drawn as to the child's power as a poet.

Similarly, Richard Lewis's claims for the powers of instinct, form, rhythm, creativity, and growth of consciousness must be related to what is believed to be biological and physiological and what is acquired from the child's environmental background. Koch asserts that children "turn out poems as naturally as an apple tree turns out blossoms."[22] Treating children like poets is right, he insists, because it corresponds "with the truth." His encouragement to children "to get tuned in to their own strong feelings, to their spontaneity, their sensitivity and their carefree inventiveness"[23] is all to the good, but one questions whether all of his students possessed these qualities to the same degree and whether Koch's truth is upheld by all adults.

If, as Rousseau, Piaget, and others assert, children themselves do not possess, nor do they need logic and reason – *one of the factors in children's writing that charms adults* – it does not follow that adults themselves should relinquish their own reason in unabated enthusiasm for what is offered as poetry. Nor should they continue to operate on romantic premises about the nature of a magical power children possess.

An understanding of children, poetry, and the limitations and interactions of both is expressed by a number of critics, educators, teachers and poets, both in this country and in England. Rosemary Manning, reviewing the work of children in the *Times Literary Sup-*

plement, notes that poetry demands a "heightened intensity of thought and feeling."[24] Should not adults consider the possibility that the thought and feelings of children are not, in itself, poetry? Should they recall Rousseau who warns that

> A common error which you ought carefully to avoid, that of attributing to the warmth of genius the mere effect of opportunity, and to construe into an inclination for a particular art, that spirit of imitation which is as common to the ape as to the human species, and leads him mechanically to do what he sees done by others, without very well knowing to what purpose. The world is full of artisans, and particularly of artists, who have no natural talents for the arts they profess, to which they have been trained from their infancy, either from motives of convenience, or from some apparent zeal which has operated as well in favor of any other art.[25]

Ruth Whitman, a poet and co-editor of *Poemmaking: Poets in Classrooms*, is closely associated with the Massachusetts Poets-in-the-Schools program. She believes that

> children are still close to the primary sources of poetry with which every one is born: the ability to make images out of sense perceptions and emotions . . . and . . . still close to the myth-making and sense of play of childhood.[26]

In addition she states in her introduction to *Poemmaking* that not only "one of the best ways to learn is by imitating fine models" but that the "process is always more important than the product."[27]

Richard Lewis believes that children "aren't writing a poem as much as using the words as a means of discovery,"[28] and in his work at the Touchstone Center he places poetry among the other art forms by which children can learn to use their imaginations in pursuit of a richer, more meaningful life.

Claudia Lewis states that although "it is common to think of children – the younger ones especially – as natural artists, the process takes nurturing. More exactly, the individuality of the children takes nurturing."[29]

> It is evident that the ease with which pre-school children sing and chant and dictate what we call poetry is related to their full-bodied responsiveness, their emotional vitality. They have not closed themselves up against the appeal of rhythm and incantation; the sudden griefs and joys that rock them lead them to expressiveness that takes its color and movement from the mood. And because language is one of their playthings, they easily discover the magical edge of words.[30]

She understands children and views them as using words not as poets do but to discover themselves and grow. If she shows, occasionally, overenthusiasm in what the child calls a poem, it is because she is cognizant of the individual child whose private symbolism sends out a message about *how* that individual child is growing. Her ideal is shared by others who ask for an atmosphere in which the child is "at the center, able to make his own observations, honest and trusting enough to react in his own way to what he sees, and equipped with the knowledge and skills that must underlie any significant effort."

> After all, as teachers, we are primarily concerned with the growth of children. Writing is one of the tools. When the result is creative, it is a measure of the quality of growth.[31]

All that the child is doing, she says, "is learning in the way that is natural for him. He is organizing his concepts, the first step in a gradual process of learning how to generalize and think abstractly. If he delights us with the freshness of his images, it is because he is still anchored to the concrete, his senses are receptive and he will say what he thinks."[32]

It is children's "abilities to make analogies, to think in terms of vivid similes, that has led adults to call them natural poets,"[33] Claudia Lewis writes, and in these words lie a partial explanation of why children's work is praised. The other part of the explanation lies in the Romantic attitude of adults which catapults this ability – which is, after all, a simple psychological mechanism of growth – to the status of poetry, despite all other imperfections.

In reading the work of the child poet adults feel they are briefly humanized, rekindled, made aware of what children truly feel and think, of what brings them joy or nightmare. They admire the open subjectivity of the child because they have been conditioned to the idea that their own egotism must be suppressed. They extol the child's ability to escape from reality without censure or ridicule and the honesty of voice which they cannot summon in themselves. They respond enthusiastically because they want their dreams and wishes back again; they want a lessening of pain, an escape hatch from the everyday world. They marvel at the word play because they have forgotten how it is truly to play. They urge them to speak in their natural voices so that they may return again, through the child, to their own youth. They believe that by some magic children can restore to them their sensitivities and sensibilities, their spontaneity – a myriad of miracles. And so they accept everything and anything, never questioning whether it is poetry, a piece of poorly rhymed verse, a metrically mangled limerick, a flowery paean to nature, an inept haiku, an "untutored raw spillage of emotion,"[34] "a catalog of perspectiveless drek,"[35] or, as is often the case, a single sentence masquerading as artifact, an outpouring of what is called self-expression.

Leland Jacobs, a noted American educator who has influenced many generations of teachers, writes of this self-expression:

> I do not believe one should teach children that writing is self-expression. Rather, I believe one should teach them it is an ordering – the aesthetic order of selected components of experience, or of existence. I believe that self-expression is precompositional. There is a place for word play, for the playful use of what will possibly later be ordered aesthetically. But such self-expression is not the outcome of composition.[36]

Self-expression and spontaneity are viewed by the English critic, Aidan Chambers, in full light. "Frequently," he writes, "the problem lies in our misunderstanding of the nature of spontaneity."

> The elevation of self-expression into art happened as soon as we took a wrong turn about two things: first, that everybody is creative in whatever way he wants to be: and second, that all you have to do to realize your creativity is to be spontaneous. The first proposition is arguable. The second is nuts. Or to put a finer point on it, spontaneity becomes artistically useful only

> when it is backed by considerable hard work of a very particular kind.[37]

Phillip Lopate speaks just as plainly. "Not every child is a poet," he writes. "It is a nauseating sort of professional flattery to pretend that all children are poets until the spirit is crushed out of them. No matter what you do to keep the spark of imagination and language play alive, there will always be a very, very few who choose to write poetry as a lifelong devotion, and who are any good at it."[38]

But perhaps most interesting of all are the words of Herbert Kohl, who in 1967 launched a stunning attack against education in his book *36 Children* and whose *Teaching the Unteachable* set new trends in educational thinking. Kohl, who indeed became the guiding spirit of the Teachers & Writers Collaborative movement, wrote that although "it is no accident that children who have no preconceived notion of poetry can produce work that is interesting and moving,"[39] yet "it is a mistake to assume that all children have the energy and devotion to write novels or poems." His further injunction that "Writing must be taught qualitatively – how can one best express himself, in what way?"[40] serves to begin a further examination into the environments, both past and present, in which children are taught to write poetry. This environment is crucial indeed.

Whether arch-Romanticist or rationalist, adults have admiration for the ways in which children use imagery, metaphor, and imagination, and the senses themselves. What poet-teachers, classroom teachers, educators, and parents hope to create is an environment for children in which creativity and growth can flourish. Whatever side is taken depends a great deal on how creativity and poetry are perceived and what name may be given to the work that many call *natural* poetry.

CHAPTER V

Hilda Conkling: Child-Poet

Eyes of the eagle are yours, eyes of the dove are yours,
Heart of the robin is yours, heart of the woods is yours.
The long hair of Mab is yours. The long hair of Eve is yours.
And you are a cool clear river at play,
A river of light, that sweeps through the breast: —
Of healing and power,
That surely cures.
And I am young as Hilda today,
And all heavy years are hurried away,
And only the light and fire endures . . .

From "Being the Dedication of a Morning
To Hilda Conkling, Poet"
Vachel Lindsay[1]

Vachel Lindsay's admiration for Hilda Conkling, written over sixty years ago, the tribute of a poet in his forties for the work of a child, exemplifies the Romantic tendency to adulate children as poets. The concept of a child-poet who can heal, cure, "hurry away" the years, and restore to adults the "light and fire" is very much in the tradition of all those who find in the poetry of children a rebirth of themselves.

Hilda Conkling's first poems appeared in a number of magazines, *The Lyric, St. Nicholas, Contemporary Verse, The Delineator, Poetry: A Magazine of Verse,* and *Good Housekeeping.* Her first book, *Poems by a Little Girl,* published in 1920, is a collection of poems "spoken" between the ages of four and nine. *Shoes of the Wind,* writing done at age ten, was published in 1922. A selection from both books, *Silverhorn, the Hilda Conkling Book for Other Children* with illustrations by Dorothy Lathrop, appeared in 1924. The preface to her first book was written by Amy Lowell. Louis Untermeyer sang her praises as "the most gifted of all child poets." William Rose Benét wrote about her, Pathé made her the star of a newsreel. Hughes Mearns and Flora Arnstein used her work as models for students and her poems have remained a staple of anthologies both for children and adults to this day.

Other child-poets have come and gone; Scotland's Marjorie Fleming, France's Minou Drouet, America's Nathalia Crane, Katharine Carasso, and, in more recent memory, Aliki Barnstone. To read child-poets is to become aware of a precocity that spent itself at an early age. Others who started publishing in their teens, as did Edna St. Vincent Millay and Vanessa Howard, cannot be considered in this light for their work started beyond early childhood. Hilda is unique, for she began "speaking" poems at four that have stood the test of time because of their keen observation, appeal to the imagination, and metaphoric precision. Indeed, the poetry Hilda Conkling has written in her adult life is minimal and largely unknown.

To read Hilda's work and that of other child-poets is to raise a series of questions about the child's ability to create, the environment in which it may be fostered, and the influences by which it may be nourished, or eventually thwarted. Fortunately Hilda Conkling has retained strong memories of her childhood, memories tinged with perception, humor, honesty, and some pain. Her "gift," she recalls, is not a gift at all but a handicap from which it has taken her a lifetime to recover. Her story may serve as a guide to others about the nature of the child as poet, and the moot value of early publication and praise.

Hilda Conkling was born in 1910, one of two daughters of Grace Hazard Conkling, a divorcée, an Associate Professor of English at Smith College, a published poet, and a pianist. Her sister Elsa was twenty months older. "Mother loved Wagner," Hilda relates, "so hence Elsa's name and mine, from Brunhilde – (thank heavens she didn't give me the whole of it!)"[2] Both girls were raised in an environment in which music, plays, and lectures at Smith College, the woods and hills of Northampton, Massachusetts, and books played an unusually important part. "Evenings," she remembered, "were the best time, when mother read aloud, when she played the piano."

> Every time my mother played the piano I would sit dissolved in tears because all I could think of was that there would be a time

> when I wouldn't hear her play. I can still see myself to this day crying quietly in the dark while Mother played Chopin. I was seven or eight at the time.[3]

Hilda has vivid recollections of her mother reading. Grace Conkling "chose books regardless whether we could understand them, like Kingsley's *Water Babies* or de la Mare's *Three Mulla-Mulgars* . . . which was very mystical and over our heads but we were fascinated. I took off on my own in choosing books. I enjoyed such books as Sandburg's *Rootabaga Stories*."[4]

In 1928 the Hampshire Bookshop in Northampton published an essay, *Imagination and Children's Reading*, by Grace Hazard Conkling. The text focuses on the importance of the "concentrated and identifying and passionate vision"[5] of the child. "Children," she wrote, "see not only colors and contours invisible to us (adults) or long forgotten; they can see anything at all!" Her continuing theme focused on artists and writers who retained their childlike vision, Cellini, Blake, Keats, Dante, and Yeats. "I believe," she wrote, "that the artists of the world, whatever medium of expression they may use, are those who have kept the clear eyes of their early years."[6]

The importance of reading to children from only the "richest and the best" books, books that "appeal to the imagination," is emphasized throughout Grace Conkling's essay. Choosing glorious and beautiful books is a "tremendous responsibility, for it means the selection of a varied library, rich enough to satisfy the imaginative child eager and ready to live as Keats once said he lived 'in a thousand worlds'."[7] Grace Conkling believed that books should be strewn about for children to discover; that children should be exposed not only to the same books as their parents – the Bible, Shakespeare, Cervantes, Keats, Chaucer – but to a wide range of books written for them. "There are various and delightful approaches to the classics,"[8] she wrote. "With Hawthorne and Colum and de la Mare to turn to, there is no reason for children to miss all this joy."[9]

Among the books for children she cites are those which do not dwell on the "little hard pellet of an exact fact."[10] Facts abound, and children will find them as they wish. In *Moby Dick* there is factual material as well as description, but it is the "sheer power of imagination," its intensity and mystery that she feels draws boys to the book. Her love for the three Mulla-Mulgars appeals for its "sadness

. . . which the great stories of the world possess, and the light on it of a fancy pure and unearthly." The world of fairy, it is evident, is her own special realm, the world of de la Mare. "For although children like to read about other children exactly as they are, they are dreamers too, creators of a world of illusion in which they play important parts and themselves augment the fairy population."[11]

Becoming akin to "a fairy's child," Grace Conkling felt, is the next step and "not at all hard to take," for it means "certain escape from the cold world of parents" into those found in Kingsley's *Water Babies*, de la Mare's *Down a Down Derry*, Hans Christian Andersen's "The Wild Swans" or "The Snow Queen" – all of which "strengthens the imagination." The romances of the world "depend on impossible episodes and revelations from the invisible and supernatural," and "require faith." Grace Conkling also believed that "poetry belongs to children peculiarly: they have the capacity for wonder, they know the thin witchery of words. They need not have experienced things in order to respond to them. Give them genuine poems, not verse about children by grown-ups."[12] Conkling mentions de la Mare's *Come Hither* and *Peacock Pie*, as well as A. A. Milne's *When We Were Very Young* and Elizabeth MacKinstry's *Puck in Pasture.* Clearly in her mind was the belief that fine books would arouse and strengthen the imagination of each child. "There is no average child, they are all different. We need tact, humor, sympathy and imagination. The greatest of these is imagination. It will help us not to patronize them: it will keep us humble."[13]

To the list of books Grace Conkling appended at the end of her essay, Hilda has added her own notes. "She should have mentioned Hugh Lofting and the Dr. Dolittle tales, but maybe these came later. Also Carl Sandburg's *Rootabaga Tales* (The Potato family's adventures). Also *Jane Eyre* and Barrie's *Peter Pan* . . . I read that twenty-three times, then Kingsley's *The Water Babies.*"[14]

Hilda Conkling acknowledges that the emphasis on reading was a strong influence indeed, one of the sources of her gift. "Mother read to us . . . what she chose, not what we wanted," she remembers. "She would ask if we understood and I said, 'No, but I like the sound of your voice going on.' That is really how a child feels – keeping it simple."[15] Children need, she feels, the "stimulation of music and reading at home to offset the sterile atmosphere of school which can't help being so – with so many different types and needs." They need, she reflects, "time to themselves particularly if they have shown an interest in words."[16]

Hilda had time to herself in the hills and woods of Northampton, part of the environment which allowed her the gift of creation. Even now, she says, "I suppose my feeling is to be close to nature – the least change – season to season – has always been my interest (I don't say stimulation) but could be."[17] Hilda remembers that she would flee outside to watch the brooks, pick the flowers, and study the trees.

Grace Hazard Conkling was a strong woman. She set a strict routine for her daughters. "I had to be on time for meals," Hilda recalls, "even when I was busy with a poem."[18] "Mother," Hilda says, "was very dominating, and she was often high-handed and adamant in her decisions. It was always, Do this, that, and the other thing. To be fair, she was just as hard on herself as she was on my sister and me. But she was difficult to get along with. Being a Libra, I hated scenes, so I'd try to keep the peace, ever the obedient daughter. As long as I did as I was told, we got along very well."[19]

"Mother-daughter relationships," Hilda reflects, "are quite something. The more I talk about myself and Mother the clearer it comes in my mind. She was a very secretive, complex soul, more so than most. I admired her greatly and was her companion until her death (in 1958). If she had lived five more years we might have become even better friends."[20] Grace Conkling's standards of perfection for herself were severe. She was trained abroad as an organist and later transferred her talent to the piano. Hilda remembers that she would "practice eight hours a day trying to meet her highly critical standards. Nervous exhaustion eventually forced her to quit."[21]

Hilda thinks of herself, however, as someone who did not care for work, who was "born lazy" and given to daydreaming. "Mother couldn't believe she could have such a daughter. But as long as there were three meals on the table, I was perfectly content to stay at home and go on my own gentle way, not bothering anybody . . . Until I was 18 or 20, Mother made decisions for me. She had to push me out of the house to get some training. All the time I would wonder – why go into the world to work?"[22]

Hilda does not remember how she began "talking poetry" when she was four and can only surmise what led her to write about the things she did. "At four," she believes, "you are not yet influenced by adults. You go on your own self-centered way, a clean slate, a blackboard on which nobody has written."[23] She was told very few of the incidents that brought about the poems and that "it was mostly at bedtime that I did my 'talking' in free verse I suppose." She did not realize her mother was writing down what she said, aligning and punctuating them. "She wrote poems, too, and always had a pad in her hands, so it didn't seem unusual, me babbling, her scribbling. But later she'd read them back to me, and I always knew if she'd taken down a word wrong. I could always correct her."[24]

"I was never allowed to feel that what I said or how I said it was anything unusual, to the point that later as an adult I look at my poems of then in astonishment and as if they were done by someone else. I was lucky," she adds, "to have such a good mother who was always writing notes so I was never self-conscious about what I said." A poet, she believes, "really is – a voice of those who would like to 'sing' but can't."[25]

After Hilda's poems were first published in magazines, Grace Conkling was approached by Frederick A. Stokes who wished to publish a book of them. Hilda remembers being called in from outdoors to sign her name in the first five hundred copies. She also remembers being overfed with candy and ice-cream during an interview with the *Ladies Home Journal* and a day when she went to the movies with her friends and saw herself in a Pathé newsreel. Her reaction was one of horror. "There was my face on the screen. I could have died, especially when the other children started pointing and laughing. As you can imagine I took a dim view of the whole thing."[26] She remembers being approached by a fan who asked her how she wrote sonnets. "You'll have to ask my mother,"[27] she replied.

The purest language used by children – and the longest in duration, according to Jean Piaget – reveals itself in the monologues children use with adults, in which they can follow the threads of their imagination without interruption. On the other hand, conversation with peers is very different, because "being on the same level" the child "cannot enter into his most intimate desires or personal point of view as in the friendly adult world."[28] To their mothers or an adult who will listen carefully, children can speak without fear of being cut off. Nor do children realize that they are addressing themselves to another presence, for to speak of themselves or to speak to their mothers appears to them to be one and the same thing. Thus Hilda wrote:

For You Mother

I have a dream for you, Mother
Like a soft thick fringe to hide your eyes.
I have a surprise for you, Mother,
Shaped like a strange butterfly.
I have found a way of thinking
To make you happy;
I have made a song and a poem
All twisted into one.
If I sing, you listen;
If I think, you know.
I have a secret from everybody in the world
  full of people
But I cannot always remember how it goes;
It is a song
For you Mother,
With a curl of cloud and a feather of blue
Blowing along the sky.
If I sing it some day, under my voice,
Will it make you happy?[29]

"All that the child does," Piaget explains, "he shares with his mother and, from his point of view, there is no frontier separating his ego from her superior ego. In such a case the child's ego-centric speech is greater with the adult than with other children."[30] Furthermore, and most important, the "child's language does not depend upon only the child's development but . . . on the type of relationship which he maintains with the adult." A small child receives from the adult the "double impression of being dominated by a mind far superior to his own and at the same time of being completely understood by this mind with which he shares everything."[31]

> The child loves to know that he is near his mother. He feels that he is close to her in each of his acts and thoughts. What he says does not seem to him to be addressed to himself but is enveloped with the feeling of a presence, so that to speak of himself or to speak to his mother appear to him to be one and the same.
>
> His activity is thus bathed in an atmosphere of communion or syntonization, one might almost speak of "the life of union" to

use the terms of mysticism, and this atmosphere excludes all consciousness of ego-centrism.[32]

To Hilda Conkling, the word *listen* is almost a mystical word. Her feeling that children should be listened to appears to stem from the experience of her own childhood, when her mother not only listened but recorded what she was saying.

In 1929 Hughes Mearns, writing in *Creative Power*, touches on the subject of the interaction of mothers and children. "Mothers," he wrote, "have given us our best revelations of the creative spirit in the young. I pay my tribute here, as I have done elsewhere, to one mother who listened to the beautiful voice of the child artist and had the fine courage to give the result to all of us."[33] Mearns is speaking of the "voice of the inner spirit" and of Grace and Hilda Conkling, and of what must have been, following the appearance of Hilda Conkling in print, an "international interest in the unique contribution of childhood." Mothers pulled from "secret drawers" the "precious baby-books which record questions, fancies, soliloquies, indignations, and protests even."[34] Mearns praises the confidences that children may give to their mothers, the communication of the child's "most precious thinkings" just before sleep. But he also warns that at the age of eight for boys and perhaps the age of ten for girls this sharing of "inmost imaginings" will cease, and cautions mothers about the "greedy possessing"[35] of their offspring.

> Boys and girls must live their own independent lives. It is right and morally important that they should. She who interferes with that right unduly is wronging her own. Opportunity, of course, should be given for the confessional relationship, but it must never be forced; nor must one pry for the sake solely of one's own personal enjoyment. My fear is that in presenting this method of keeping a healthy relationship between mother and child I may be simply putting a weapon into the hands of those who would sacrifice their own for the orgy of selfish and unbridled mothering. I know too well the devastating effect of their work upon the whole existence of children. It gives me a kind of horror when I think of their creeping in at the bedtime hour and, possibly because of my revelations here, subtly coaxing confidences.[36]

Mearns expresses concerns about the "devitalization, physical, mental, and spiritual, that always follows when strong mothers give over their whole lives to the greedy possessing of their offspring."[37] This does not appear to have happened in the case of Hilda Conkling, for Grace Hazard Conkling was a woman who believed in discipline, in self-discipline and self-reliance, and wished to impart this to her children.

Grace Conkling's poetry reveals a keen and observant eye as well as a use of apostrophe – the formal term for addressing some inanimate object – and personification.

> The smooth road beckoned *Follow*!
> But the logs whispered . . . *Stay*![38]

Oak trees speak, thrushes "talk a bit in their own way/Or gossip with a star," a house is personified as something that could listen to a hymn or watch "the golden west go dim." She uses conversation and her apostrophe to the moon

> Moon, moon, what have you seen
> The other side of the sky?[39]

is clearly followed by Hilda's own interests in nature. When she was between five and six years old, Hilda wrote:

> Moon Song
>
> There is a star that runs very fast,
> That goes pulling the moon
> Through the tops of the poplars.
> It is all in silver,
> The tall star:
> The moon rolls goldenly along
> Out of breath.
> *Mr. Moon, does he make you hurry?*[40]

It would be natural to assume that Hilda's interest in animism and the world of the imagination would lessen as she grew older, a loss engendered by the encroachment of realism, common to most children. Yet as a poet she would certainly retain the keen metaphoric eye that distinguished her work from the age of four.

> There's dozens full of dandelions
> Down in the field:
> Little gold plates,
> Little gold dishes in the grass.
> I cannot count them,
> But the fairies know every one.[41]

One of her famous poems, "Dandelion," written between the ages of seven and nine, attests to this metaphoric vision:

> O little soldier with the golden helmet
> What are you guarding on my lawn?
> You with your green gun
> And your yellow beard,
> Why do you stand so stiff?
> There is only the grass to fight![42]

"I am told," Hilda Conkling writes, "that I still 'talk in pictures' and use unusual words in odd ways and sense and notice more than the usual person. I don't consider myself so," she relates, "and am not conscious of any of it. I guess I still startle people once in a while. I don't feel like a complex person but suppose I am as is most everyone. Since I was made to feel that my books were just a happening, that could have been achieved by anyone, I feel other children are probably saying, doing and acting even now much as I – but maybe no one is listening."[43]

Is it the *listening*? For Hilda relates how, after years of recording what she "spoke," Grace Conkling suddenly stopped. If Hilda asked her mother for help or information, she was "brushed off." Hilda understands that her mother meant to encourage self-discipline. But Hilda was bereft. Her high IQ of 186 and her photographic memory did not serve her well. School was drudgery to her. She had difficulty with abstract concepts. At home Grace Conkling would no longer help nor listen to what Hilda was writing. "My mother's attitude about not helping me in writing when I got stuck, later, was her own idea of discipline which is necessary too, for when I try my hand at prose I'm like a colt in pasture – I run away with myself and words become verbose."[44]

Is it possible that a child whose work was praised, who was the darling of literary figures and of the poetry reading public, felt that *no one* was listening? Is it possible that someone "born with a love of words" and a "vivid imagination," but who had no one to listen to her, could suddenly stop writing?

Hilda feels that any sensitive child might have the same imagination and the same perception as she. But she believes that her work was "squashed flat" by school or by her mother's lack of help. She also believes that she "grew up with a handicap in regard to reality. While I was just trying to be an everyday child, this poetry intervened. It's like talking about another person, another life."[45]

It was Amy Lowell, a friend of Grace Conkling, she relates, who visited the Conkling home and who often conversed about what would happen to Hilda. Amy Lowell's introduction to *Poems by a Little Girl* states emphatically that

> A book which needs to be written is one dealing with the childhood of authors. It would be not only interesting, but instructive; not merely profitable in a general way, but practical in a particular. We might hope, in reading it, to gain some sort of knowledge as to what environments and conditions are most conducive to the growth of the creative faculty. We might even learn how not to strangle this rare faculty in its early years.[46]

She is enthusiastic in her praise for Hilda's poetry and knows "of no other instance in which such really beautiful poetry has been written by a child." Yet she asks two questions:

> How far has the condition of childhood been impaired by, not only the possession, but the expression, of the gift of writing: how far has the condition of authorship (at least in its more mature state still to come) been hampered by this early leap into the light?[47]

The first, says Lowell, will have to be answered by Hilda herself "some twenty years hence." Yet even after sixty years, Hilda does not feel her childhood was impaired. Indeed, she is not the spoiled child-protégée who struts and boasts about her heaven-sent gift, but rather feels that her mother handled her success wisely. She was, Hilda recalls, "my source of information and my defense . . . Mother was determined that I think nothing remarkable had been done, so that I would not think of myself as special, or become conceited."[48]

"Even now," Hilda Conkling continues, "it is difficult to explain what I was doing. I was conscious of saying things without understanding. That's about as close as you can come to inspiration."[49]

Louis Untermeyer, reviewing *Poems by a Little Girl* in the August, 1920 issue of *Dial Magazine*, writes of the age of infant prodigies and *wunderkinder*: Erich Korngold, Pamela Bianco, Daisy Ashford, Opal Whiteley, Horace Atkisson Wade "and – most gifted of them all – Hilda Conkling." Her verses "many of which are astonishing in exactness of phrase and vision" may show, he suggests, "the natural impress and occasional preconscious echoes of the mother" yet "the quality which shines behind practically all of these facets of loveliness is a directness of perception, an almost mystical divination. It is its own stamp of unaffected originality, a genuine ingenuousness."[50]

Untermeyer speaks of the process by which Hilda tells her poem and her mother makes notes, or copies it down from memory, aligns the words and reads it to Hilda for corrections. "In this process," he suggests, "there is, of course, the possibility that certain modifications, certain subtle refinements may result; it is even more probable that a tentative and half-conscious shaping has already taken place."[51]

> Here we face the twisted problem of the child as artist. What force impels it? What supplies it with backgrounds that the child has never known? What directs its candour, sharpens its edges, illumines its clarity?[52]

Untermeyer believes that the answer "lies in its very immaturity. It is still the emotional primitive, still free of superimposed patterns, drawing its substance directly from the unconscious. The child knows beyond knowledge, tapping that vast source of intuitive wisdom." Yet he goes further and states that "every child is therefore an embryonic painter, poet and musician"; that "did the world so desire, it could have a race of artists in one generation; that it prefers to starve or 'sublimate' the creative hunger; to direct the expressive energy into channels of more efficient industry is one more cause of man's growing neuroticism, his wavering allegiance to the modern world, his failure to adjust. Civilization has broken down almost all his individualistic resources. When it first took away his art, it left him, as a substitute, his craft. But now, lost among his own machines, he turns in upon himself – a disillusioned and defeated child."

Only the artist escapes, Untermeyer continues, "the artist who is a child that has reached maturity without having its vision distorted or its contact with the subconscious made difficult by prejudice and pressure. But where the child pierces the subconscious from beneath, the artist sounds it from above. The great danger lies in reaching the dead level of reason and remaining there; getting stuck fast in tradition, education, and all that is derivative and conscious is what happens to ninety-nine per cent of us. Even in this extremely first book one sees it happening to Hilda. It is ridiculous to talk of 'stages' in the work of a ten-year-old child and yet the verses conceived between four and seven are more vivid, seem more spontaneous and less – absurd as it may seem – sophisticated than those written between seven and nine. Literature and an almost domesticated sapience rather than the child's naive wonder take hold of her 'later' poems."[53]

In the light of knowledge about Hilda Conkling's background and also in view of what Piaget has revealed about the thought and language of childhood, Untermeyer's comments are strikingly Romantic. To speak of "backgrounds that the child has never known" is again to suggest Wordsworth's "celestial abode" rather than the down-to-earth reading and music to which Hilda was exposed, and the surroundings of nature in which she played. To suggest that a "child knows beyond knowledge, tapping their vast source of intuitive wisdom" or making "contact with the subconscious" is clearly in the tradition of the Romantics. To suggest that Hilda's later poems (written between seven and nine!) are products of "domesticated sapience" and show less of "naive wonder" is to acknowledge only that the child *is* growing, casting off the syncretism that characterizes the writing of young children.

In her preface to *Poems by a Little Girl*, Amy Lowell notes the unusual relationship that exists between a mother and daughter, when the child can write:

> If I sing, you listen;
> If I think, you know.[54]

She places importance on the fact that Hilda's interest was not in playing games with other children, but rather that her devotion to books, to music, to nature, and to her mother superseded other interests. Hilda's book of poems she finds an "amazing thing" with its "perfectly original expression" of love. Lowell recognizes that Hilda is a "perennial child, thinking as children think; and we are glad of it. It makes the whole more healthy, more sure of development." Lowell indicates that she thinks "too highly of these poems to speak . . . as though it were the finished achievements of a grown-up person." Hilda's thoughts are those "proper to the imaginative child."[55]

Lowell also recognizes that Hilda "is evidently possessed of a rare and accurate power of observation. And when we add this to her gift of imagination, we see that it is the perfectly natural play of these two faculties which makes what to her is an obvious expression." Lowell notes, too, that the cadence of the poems, that Hilda's "instinct for rhythm is unerring," due to her "musical inheritance." She recognizes that Hilda

> has been guided by a wisdom which has not attempted to show her a better way. Her observation has been carefully, but unobtrusively, cultivated; her imagination has been stimulated by the reading of excellent books; but both these lines of instruction have been kept apparently apart from her own work. She has been let alone there: she has been taught by an analogy which she has never suspected. By this means, her poetical gift has functioned happily, without ever for a moment experiencing the tension of doubt.[56]

Yet here Lowell sounds a warning, for she wonders "how long the instructors of youth can be persuaded to keep 'hands off!' A period of imitation is, I fear, inevitable, but if consciousness is not induced by direct criticism, if instruction in the art of writing is abjured, the imitative period will probably be got through without undue loss. I think there is too much native sense of beauty and proportion here to be entirely killed even by the drying and freezing process which goes by the name of education." What Hilda's first book shows, to Lowell, is "high promise . . . pages of real achievement, and that of so high an order it may well set us pondering."[57]

Lowell does not fall into the trap of Romanticism, yet both she and Untermeyer sensed that education might play its part in tampering with Hilda's work. Although she relates incidents in which her teachers seemed supportive of her poetry writing, it may be that even Hilda feels she should have been spared the uncreative atmosphere of school. Algebra, for example, made no sense to her. "My teacher told me," she says, "that X didn't stand for anything. In that case I decided I wasn't going to waste my time looking for it." Hilda speaks of herself as "a great day dreamer outside the window of the English class," yet she knew she had to attend school "because it was a great discipline and I've been thankful for the discipline since."[58] A graduate of Northampton School for Girls, she later attended a school in Versailles and a nursery training school in Boston. Over the years she has held numerous jobs, including work with underprivileged girls in Boston, with the gifted in Virginia, with the Bureau of Standards in Washington, and as a bookstore manager and local bookstore buyer. Today she earns enough to "pay for the heating bill" by driving the elderly to grocery stores and doctor's appointments.

Hilda Conkling has not lived in an ivory tower; her life, in fact, has given her little time to pursue her poetry. She has had to come to grips with the world of reality, a mundane world which is at odds with Barrie's "Never-Never Land." Did this confrontation with reality diminish her ability to continue writing fine poetry? Is Hilda's own feeling that she had a handicap in regard to reality the answer? Is it possible that a child who read *Peter Pan* twenty-three times became lost in a dream world from which she could not emerge?

Is education that may recognize the gifted child but do little to encourage divergent thinking to blame? Is it possible that given a sparkling imagination, a sense of keen observation, a natural rhythm, a union with nature, and high IQ, a child can be quashed by the dull atmosphere of school — even if, at home, the freedom is given to create?

Or might it be the home itself? Is it the guess Hilda herself makes that once her mother refused to help, she was unable to write? Did Hilda Conkling awaken too late to the discovery that her "life of union" with her mother, her desire to please by her "singing" was submerging her own personality, gradually eroding her own inner voice? Was there, in psychological terms, some identity crisis? Was it necessary that her mother always be there to listen?

Erik Erikson views child development as a series of stages during which important crisis encounters occur. Successful resolution of these crises depends, he feels, upon the milieu. Piaget's work in cognitive development up to adolescence speaks of stages through which the child passes, from infancy to adolescence, where intelligent behavior depends upon a balance between intellectual functions of assimilation and accommodation. Did Hilda make these adjustments, pass through these crises?

Untermeyer states that if the individual is stuck in "tradition, education and all that is derivative and conscious," the artistic gift vanishes. It happens, he writes, to "ninety-nine per cent of us."[59] If he is right, there would be no poets, no artists at all beyond the early years; a poet, indeed, could only exist in contact with the unconscious and a wisdom that "knows beyond knowledge." It is a Romantic speculation, for it insists that children are, indeed, inhabitants of some celestial abode, the torchbearers of some light and truth not available beyond early years.

To understand what happened to Hilda, or to any other child-poet whose work ended with childhood, we need to examine all of these speculations. Is blame to be placed upon the harshness of the real world, the educational system, the parent-child relationship, or does the answer lie elsewhere?

CHAPTER VI

Hilda Conkling: Her Work

Your talk was soft in the wood.
You spoke small soft words like moss
Or green velvet mullein leaves.
You showed me mulleins holding the first snow:
You brought me wintergreen . . . squawberry . . .
A snail's coiled shell . . .

It was you who saw the wind
Perched like Puck
On a hillside boulder.
It was you who told me of his peacock feather
Made of air.

I remember hilltop birchtrees
Balancing marble clouds
On pale fingertips.
I remember your fingertips stained with earth,
With ground-pine . . . roots of fern . . .
Your hand was like a cold little stone
In a glove of lichen.

If there were to come a day without you,
If ever I look for you
And you are gone,
What shall I do with this memory
Soft-colored like your words,
Your wild small words of wind and mullein leaves
Furred with snow!

"Hilda in the Wood"
Grace Hazard Conkling[1]

In *Wilderness Songs* by Grace Hazard Conkling, published in 1920 by Henry Holt, there is but one poem, "Hilda in the Wood," written entirely in free verse. Another poem, "A Letter to Elsa," traditional in rhyme and meter, addresses Elsa as the child who feeds on the "magic fruit" of a "spiced garden" filled with Elsa's own "sweetness," tended by an elf-mother who ministers to her needs and "tired head."

> Russet-eyes, rose-mouth,
> When the wind's from the south,
> When he rustles and stirs
> In the plumed junipers,
> Does he bring coaxing words
> From the sly mocking-birds?
> Do they call you to come
> Where the wind is at home
> When he rests from his trips?
> Elf-locks, scarlet-lips,
> I am wiser than they.
> Hearken now what *I* say!

Grace Conkling, the mother, will build a house for Elsa, "Velvet-gray like a mouse" with peacocks and a talking fountain, a green cockatoo. She will spread a table with a "honey-comb" and "heaped mulberry-fruit," milk "white as the moon" and Elsa may sleep on a "smooth silken bed."[2]

The contrast between the form and mood of these two poems suggests that Grace Conkling knew the differences in her children well; Elsa seen within a framework of orderly structure, metrical exactness, and domestic security; Hilda seen in a freer pattern of abandonment to the wood and nature.

Hilda herself remembers that "Mother *tried to treat* us both alike" but the two temperaments were "like oil and water." She recalls that "when Elsa and two other girls we knew were making plans for their weddings, I was off teaching dogs to climb a ladder under our apple tree." Elsa, she believes, was hurt by the "furor" caused when Hilda's poems were published, and was left out of a lot of attention. Elsa later married a Swedish baron in the diplomatic service, had children and grandchildren. "I had my chances too, but though Mother tried not to interfere I didn't really care about anyone enough to fight" for marriage or for the young men. "I've not regretted it either."[3]

Grace Conkling's own poetry was published in many magazines of the day: *The Atlantic Monthly*, *Yale Review*, *Harper's Magazine*, *Good Housekeeping*, *Contemporary Verse*, and *Poetry: A Magazine of Verse*, among others. According to Ellen Williams, biographer of Harriet Monroe, the editor of *Poetry* magazine, Grace was one of the "polished, well-bred" poets who operated "between fairly fixed limits" and to whom Harriet Monroe was always kind; yet, according to Alice Henderson, Harriet Monroe's assistant, Grace was one of a group who "hasn't the *germ* of development, who will never *get* anywhere."[4] It is pure speculation that Hilda's own cadenced and free way of speaking might make Grace Conkling take stock of her own work; yet comments such as these might suggest that the daughter's success was all the more awesome to the mother. The expected, orderly pattern of life that the mother established was difficult for the daughter to fit into. Hilda remembers having to discipline herself to its structure.

A reading of the poetry of Grace Conkling demonstrates that the animism and the symbols – bird, moon, wind and tree, flower and fairy – were omnipresent. All speak and call. All represent some emotion, some association. Piaget has theorized about the imitation and echolalia which characterize the language of the young child: Can this be said of symbolism as well? Hilda was undoubtedly aware – because of the deep communion and love for nature she and her mother shared – that her mother considered that the "wind's a friend of mine" or that she had an "understanding with the hills."[5] A child who grows up hearing that there is "the other side of the sky" or that "I shall go dreaming till I die,"[6] that there are elves and "fairy seas"[7] might, the mother figure being omniscient, also believe in the animism of nature and adopt the symbols meaningful to that mother. Apple trees, blue hills, the sound of water, eagle and color, are important to both adult and child. Grace Conkling's "To a Tired Child" is part of that pattern.

This tall gray road that climbs the sky
   Is neighbor to a star,
But if you watch the trees go by,
   It will not seem so far:

And if you listen very still
  As though you were quite grown,
Maybe the thrushes on the hill
  Will think themselves alone,

And talk a bit in their own way
  Of gossip with the star.
Hush! for a star is shy they say,
  As any thrushes are.[8]

That Hilda listened to Grace Conkling and in turn asked to be heard is not accidental; the results may be followed in her own work. From her first poems spoken at four onward, there is a continual undercurrent of sounds; both animate and inanimate objects are constantly engaged in "listening"; whether it is by the use of apostrophe or the inanimate itself speaking. Indeed, one of the chief characteristics of Hilda's poetry is that of sound or implied listening.

The poems of her four-year-old period speak of the "moonsong," the sound of hills and of water, a "little winding song to dance to . . . " The last of a series of twelve "First Songs" is most revealing:

Will you love me to-morrow after next,
As if I had a bird's way of singing?[9]

Hilda, it would seem, discovered very early that the way to please her mother, to assure her of her love, was through "singing." Birds seem to be symbolic of this and appear throughout her work. But the singing, the listening is not confined to birds alone. It is remarkable that of the seventeen poems written between the ages of five and six, eleven employ this mode of music; there is a garden that sings, eagles calling, birds that tell and call, trees that laugh, a wind that sings, a chickadee that talks, and Hilda herself, asking to "Help me tell my dreams/To the other children." "Spring Song" reveals another interesting idea of the power of song. She addresses the listener, asking

Do you know anything about the spring
When it comes again?
God knows about it while winter is lasting.

Flowers bring him power in the spring,
And birds bring it, and children.
He is sometimes sad and alone
Up there in the sky trying to keep his world
  happy.
I bring him songs
When he is in his sadness, and weary.

She also "keeps reminding him (God) about his flowers he has forgotten," and asks in one line, "What can I say to make him listen?"[10]

Of the eleven published poems written from ages six to seven, six are strong in sound. A fairy queen walks to her throne "slowly, slowly to music." Hermit thrushes sing and answer, gulls swing and call, bees hum, birds sing songs of sun drops so that Hilda herself hears the music. She speaks to the rooster

Shouting all day long your crooked words,
Loud . . . sharp . . . not beautiful![11]

The tree-toad with his silver voice sings "patiently all night/Never thinking that people are asleep" while

Raindrops and mist, stariness over the trees,
The moon, the dew, the other little singers,
Cricket . . . toad . . . leaf rustling . . .
They would listen:
It would be music like weather
That gets into all the corners
Of out-of-doors.[12]

Hilda herself tells the tree-toad that

I hope to hear you singing on the Road of Dreams![13]

Of Hilda's poems written from seven to nine years of age, which number over seventy, half are concerned with sound. A lonesome wave whispers, a bridge moans and weeps, a pine tree sighs, birds and wind sing, and she speaks of the "sweet singing that the water sang." The Dew-man sings that "*The unknown world is beautiful!*"[14]

She invokes the Mother Sea, to *"send us up your song/Of hushaby"*[15] and birds with their various songs range from eagles to yellow summer-throats. Even a tower "made a new song/About himself."[16] Always the listener, she tells her reader at one point of the yellow summer-throat

> *I knew what he said, I knew,*
> *But how can I tell you?*[17]

The poems in *Shoes of the Wind,* written when she was ten and possibly later, show a marked difference. The pear is a singing tree and the iris sings a song, but in "Hill-Song" there is a warning that although

> . . . the gurgling of brook-water
> Makes me want to sing!
> This hill-song is over now . . .
> Ends suddenly
> Like a sapphire. . . .[18]

Yet the animism which pervades Hilda's work does not, as in the sound poems, show a similar tendency to fade as she grows. Animism, in Piaget's terms, purports that the world of nature is alive, conscious, and endowed with purpose: there are four stages of this type of thought. Up until they are four or five, children believe anything may be endowed with consciousness and activity. If experience teaches them that a thing is not alive, i.e. that a cloud will not move at their command, children may, in this second stage, contradict themselves, certain that either moral or physical necessity is responsible. In the third stage, only objects that have spontaneous movement are animated or alive while those which require human activity, such as riding a bicycle, are not. The last stage, in which only animals and plants are considered to be alive, does not occur until later.

In Hilda's case, however, as in her mother's – and in the work of many poets who, in personifying the world of nature or objects about them, use animism as a tool – the focus does not lessen. Observation and reason would certainly prove that the moon does not follow the movement of one individual, as the egocentric child wrapped up in syncretic thought might assert. But the power of imagination keeps alive this tendency which, indeed, is one of the bases of metaphor. That Hilda consciously chose not to relinquish animism and that she still thinks in "pictures" and speaks in a "different" fashion attest to this ability.

This may also account for Hilda's present belief that she has had a handicap in regard to reality. Yet a reading of her poems shows that both in the use of her imagination and in her concept of dreams, she progressed from the egocentric thinking of childhood to a sure knowledge of reality.

Dreams, to Hilda, were quite separate from her ordinary life: One of the unique qualities of her writing is her ability to tell these dreams. She did not ever seem to confuse what was in dream to what happened in everyday life, and her daydreaming was a conscious act to give life and animism to what she sensed was not real. Her dreams were not the zany convolutions of the fragmented psyche, not the forced efforts of a make-believe "candy land," but rooted in her background of reading and observation of nature.

Hilda's first poem about dreams, written between the ages of five and six, is filled with the mysticism that might well give credence to the idea of the "celestial abode." Dreams, she recognizes, come at night when she is sleeping and she finds her "pillow full of dreams." They are the "new dreams" which no one has told to her.

> They remember the sky, my little dreams,
> They have wings, they are quick, they are sweet.[19]

She wishes to tell her dreams to "the other children" so that "their bread may taste whiter,/So that the milk they drink/May make them think of meadows/In the sky of stars." Her dreams are so sweet, she insists, that she must tell them so that the other children "will remember what they knew/Before they came through the cloud."

Yet her next dream-poem, written at age six, is quite matter-of-fact and begins

> When I slept, I thought I was upon the
> mountain-tops,
> And this is my dream.
> I saw the little people come out into the night . . .[20]

Another poem, written at the same time, is equally realistic about dreaming, a record of "Evening" when the birds and fireflies engage her attention.

> I like this country,
> I like the way it has,
> But I cannot forget my dream I had of the sea.[21]

"The Land of Nod," written in the same period, describes wandering into a country "Where everyone is asleep," and where "I never think of home/For home is there." Clearly she was able to separate night-dreaming from her dreams of the day, her inventions and imaginary places peopled with fairies or deer, or a "Field of Wonder" where "Colors came to be." A scarlet bird who "went sailing through the wood" reminds her of "a mist of dream/That floated by." In "Hummingbird" she tells the bird that

> I dreamed you the way I dream fairies,
> Or the flower I lost yesterday![22]

In "Blue Grass" she writes

> Blue grass flowing in the field,
> You are my heart's content.
> It is not only through the day I see you,
> But in dreams at night
> When you trudge up the hill
> Along the forest
> As I do![23]

She relates dreams, after the age of ten, to going down "the highroad of the Milky Way" with the assurance that

> When I am asleep
> This is what I shall dream.
> Things can never really go,
> They come again and stay.
> When your thoughts are put on beautiful things
> They come alive and stay alive
> In your mind.[24]

Her dream to go to Bermuda or to remember the "Vermont Hills" because

I shall dream them again
When years have gone,
And I shall not have forgotten
You.[25]

shows that she was very much in touch with the nature of imagination and fantasy; there can be, in other words, no doubt that Hilda very well understood the nature of dreams. Even at five and six years of age, she is cognizant of the nature of daydreaming:

Shady Bronn

When the clouds come deep against the sky
I sit alone in my room to think,
To remember the fairy dreams I made,
Listening to the rustling out of the trees.
The stories in my fairy-tale book
Come new to me every day.
But at my farm on the hill-top
I have the wind for a fairy,
And the shapes of things:
Shady Bronn is the name of my little farm:
It is the name of a dream I have
Where leaves move,
And the wind rings them like little bells.[26]

Her own private world, a world of imagination, is always clear to her, but a place in which she often guards the secrets. "If I Could Tell You the Way" speaks of a place "Down the forest to the river" where there are swans, ducks, wild birds, and fairies who "know no sorrow," where "Birds, winds,/They are the only people."

If I could tell you the way to this place,
You would sell your house and your land
For silver or a little gold,
You would sail up the river,
Tie your boat to the Black Stone,

Build a leaf-hut, make a twig-fire,
Gather mushrooms, drink spring-water,
Live alone and sing to yourself
For a year and a year and a year![27]

That she "cannot tell" the way does not seem so much a desire not to communicate as to acknowledge that like any other human being she still holds some things in the "fastness of her thoughts."

One of her last child-poems recognizes that.

I felt the town asleep:
I felt people there in the great crisp dark.
When morning came in a waver of light
There was a breath of change . . . all the
  dreams going away from the dreamers
As dreams do go away in the morning.[28]

Thus she moves between the world of daydreaming as make-believe and night-dreaming.

Nor is there anything to suggest that she confused her keen observations, her extraordinary use of metaphor, and the synthesis she made between objective and subjective matter in her poems with an unreal world. Her early poems are less syncretic than those we find in other child-poets. She is not given to dull recitations of past experience, fragmented bits of simile, wild associations with color, the overuse of adjectives or the many ills which beset most child writers. Her use of animism brings life to a bird or a flower or tree; she turns a dandelion into a soldier, brambles into red candles, snowflakes into daisies, haycocks into beehives, or hills into a line of camels. By use of apostrophe, even before she is five, she is able to convince us of the sureness of her vision.

Sparkle up, little tired flower
Leaning in the grass!
Do you find the rain of night
Too heavy to hold?[29]

Between the ages of five and six she engages in conversation with rose-moss, speaks to a mouse, expresses sadness and notes how pansies resemble a clown, a girl, king, queen, and prince. Between six and seven she speaks to the red rooster with his "comb gay as a parade" and "pearl trinkets" on his feet.

As Rousseau would suggest, when using nature as a model the order grows from perception to memory to reasoning, and Hilda is in tune with this progression. Her happiness in the small world she has created about her moves from the sure knowledge that if sunflowers continue to grow, they will touch the sky, to a recognition that she cannot control either nature nor her own ways of looking. Hilda's blue mountains, which would seem to be symbolic throughout her years of unattainable climb, all come to a strange end when she writes of her joy at seeing a volcano, its "transparent colors, its long opal hair," but

> My thoughts are gone from me.
> Because of that splendid trembling iridescent
>   thing . . .
> I know it will fade
> I know it must go.
> Songs float over its crest . . .
> Dusk is coming on . . .
> *I will touch the mountain!*[30]

She senses the inadequacy of words that would, at an earlier age, have come easily.

> When the moonlight strikes the water
> I cannot get it into my poem:
> I can only hear the tinkle of ripplings of light,
> When I see the water's fingers and the moon's
>   rays
> Intertwined,
> I think of all the words I love to hear,
> And try to find words white enough
> For such shining . . .[31]

For the younger child who could see dandelions as gold plates, or a deer, Silverhorn, as "snowy deer" in the mountains, who dared believe that the brook's magic stones were its children, metaphor comes with more difficulty. In "Thunder Mist" she writes

Whirling vapor changing. . . .
Is it an opening flower?
Is it a fading prancing horse?[32]

She begins to wonder "Where all the beautiful things in the world/ Come from?" In "Big Dipper" she sees the "Pleiades like a bunch of grapes" but reveals that "It is harder to say what the roofs mean." Reality hits with full force after she is ten, when she writes of the "Eagle on the Mountain Crest."

His bronze shone like a haze:
From below you would think him
  an image
Of long ago.
But he is real . . . he is of now-a-days:
No one made him but God.[33]

She begins to think, looking into a gold-fish bowl "of things I'll see when I'm grown,/Thinking what is in the world beyond/Waiting for me . . ." She thinks of the horse she will have, the cozy cottage.

I cannot see the world behind the
  snow
But when I look into my mind
There with all its people and colors
The world sits smiling
Quite warm and cozy.[34]

Yet Hilda's brilliance enables her, in astonishing ways, to record what is happening to her. In "Mermaid" she writes

Do not grieve.
Do not be unhappy,
Do not look about
As though you saw nothing!

  Soon the black, the dark green ocean
  Will come back . . .
  Will clash against the rocks
  On the sliding sand . . .

Soon the sun will come from the eastern
  horizon
Up from the great blue hills,
To change the water to glittering heaps
Of pearls. . . .

Then you will remember![35]

In another poem, "I Shall Come Back," she speaks of herself directly.

I shall be coming back to you
From the seas, rivers, sunny meadows,
  glens that hold secrets:
I shall come back with my hands full
Of light and flowers.
Brooks braided in with sunbeams
Will hang from my fingers.
My heart will be awake . . .
All my thoughts and joys will go to you.
I shall bring back things I have picked up,
Traveling this road or the other,
Things found by the sea or in the pine-
  wood.
There will be a pine-cone in my pocket,
Grains of pink sand between my fingers.
I shall tell you of a golden pheasant's
  feather;
Moons will glitter in my hair . . .
Will you know me?
I shall come back when sunset has turned
  away and gone,
And you will untangle the moons
And make me drowsy
And put me to bed.[36]

All of Hilda's last poems, written as a child, reveal the changes that are happening. In "Jeanne D'Arc," she writes

If I were Jeanne D'Arc
It would be hard remembering the apple-
orchard in bloom,
With nothing about me but noise and armies,
All men, all women, unhappy,
No time for children (Let them be quiet!)
No time for anybody
But kings . . .
And the appletrees all the time wondering . . .[37]

This is perhaps the most poignant of all her work, for it suggests that Hilda did indeed react more violently to her mother's need for quiet, for being left alone, than even she can remember. *No time for children (Let them be quiet!)* is unlike any line she ever wrote. "The Deserted House" is another aspect of this feeling:

Do you remember the house
With many windows?
It looked through its cobwebs
At the blue mountain.
There were old rosebushes near the doorstep . . .
Queer bright single roses bloomed . . .
I used to think of people
Who had wanted them there.
Maybe there was a little girl
Going barefoot . . .
Maybe she thought summer began
With a rosebush.
Do you remember the maples
And the fence where we saw baby swallows
In a row?

I made a song about a princess.
She was a little girl . . .

In the cobweb house of stone she is hidden . . .
They have left her alone,
When she called no one answered . . .
They have left her alone.

She sang to keep her heart high . . .
They have left her alone.
But the silvery cold made her shiver and sleep
And her song went by.

After that I made a story about her
Out of the old house:
I put roseleaves on her eyes . . .
(You know how sunset . . . every afternoon . . .
Used to fill the windowpanes with colors
They had never known?)[38]

Hilda's repetitive line, used only twice in all her work, "*They had left her alone,*" is a song to a loss. The loss, in this case, may be interpreted in a number of ways, but in no manner so clearly as the cries that ring out when she is writing of her mother.

Hilda's first poems seem always addressed to the mother as listener, written in the belief that her mother knew her thoughts and shared them.

I know how poems come;
They have wings.
When you are not thinking of it
I suddenly say
"Mother, a poem!"
Somehow I hear it
Rustling.

Poems come like boats
With sails for wings.
Crossing the sky swiftly
They slip under tall bridges
Of cloud.[39]

This poem is firm in its belief that poem and mother are synonymous; she knows where the poems come from; she can explain the mythology. A little later in "August Afternoon" she will speak of the things that make up this afternoon: gentian, blackberries, goldenrod, tree fringes. "But more than fruit or flower or tree/Is my mother's love I hold/In my heart."[40] In a vase one peony will be Cinderella,

"But this is Queen Elizabeth/In my mother's vase."[41] In "Pigeons Just Awake" she thinks of "what it must be to fly," but "If I could fly/I should not have to leave my mother for long/Nor my dark-eyed sister."[42]

Hilda's communion with her mother (and possibly sister) is expressed in "Three Hyacinths." It shows, clearly, that the reality of the family circle, the loss of egocentrism and the beginning of self-identity has gradually taken hold.

> Three hyacinths grow gaily
> In the blue Chinese jar:
> My mother, my sister and I!
> We are curly-fingered,
> We wear pointed caps:
> We play ring-around– –rosy all day long:
> We look at winter through a silver
>   window
> Glad we are not made of frost,
> For hyacinths on window-panes
> Fade and vanish . . .
> They cannot look back at the sun
> Laughing softly;
> They cannot whisper together, I suppose,
> As garden hyacinths do,
> Or, as my mother, my sister and I whisper
>   and play
> Living in the blue jar.[43]

Hyacinths, Hilda tells us, once picked, no longer have their animate ability to laugh and whisper as flowers in the garden or as humans do. Yet the emphasis is not so much on the animism of nature as on people; the work reflects her concerns with reality. There are other aspects of change as well; poems written before she was nine are couched in apostrophe: she speaks directly to sunflower, petal, bluebird, poppy, a narcissus, a mountain. Later poems show more narrative; apostrophe lessens, as does her use of sound. She is viewing nature in terms of its reality. The period of sadness characterized most intensely by water, rivers, wave, almost ceases and she is thinking ahead to her life with real animals, real people, real places.

Whereas her earlier poems with personification and animism did not hesitate to put words into the mouths of flowers, moor or sea, she now waits for the words to happen!

While this in no way diminishes her abilities for animism, personification, metaphor, the use of simple language, or her love of nature, it does portend the intrusion of reality and usher in changes. To read the last poems of *Shoes of the Wind* is to see what is happening:

> Time is a harp
> That plays to you till you fall asleep;
> You are always spending it away
> Like a music . . .
> Suddenly you are left alone
> On a trail of wind.
>
> The mountains were asleep
> Long ago!
> Listen . . . the tune is changing . . .
> Do you hear it?
> You will sleep too
> Before too long . . .[44]

You are left alone . . . the tune is changing. No longer could Hilda write, as in the last poem in *Poems by a Little Girl*

> *If I am happy, and you*
> *And there are things to do,*
> *It seems to be the reason*
> *Of this world!*[45]

Imagination, dream, laughter, and even sadness must find a place in the real world. Like the penultimate poem in *Shoes of the Wind* Hilda has, because of her years, made the leap.

> Dragon Fly
>
> You jerk against the sun,
> You twist your diamond wires and green-gold scales
> You tilt your body . . . head down . . .

You quiver . . .
Are you angry or only excited?
I should think the ferns might be excited
Feeling you there:
And you never mention the reasons
For your coming.
Sure of your wings
You have time in the air for thinking:
You poise and are content.
But only lizards among old stones
Can find as you find the unexpected turning:
You say *It is time to go!*
And you have gone.[46]

It would not seem that Hilda Conkling has had any handicap in regard to reality. Indeed, her writings reveal that she made the distinction between dream and reality; that although she made use of her imagination, it did not infringe upon her ability to understand reality: Her writing shows that she did indeed come out of the "dreamworld" of her earliest years.

The difficulties Hilda has had in writing since her childhood would rather seem to stem more from her faint suspicion that at a point when she needed someone to listen, that person – her mother – was no longer available. She had to come to grips, as well, with the physical necessity of writing down her own words and "the act of writing things down hindered her."[47] "The concept of a mental image," she has said, "and what turns up on paper suffers some change in the transition. I don't know what happens, but it doesn't come out the way you think at all. Almost like a learning disability. It was a real handicap. Whenever I'd ask Mother for help or information, I was brushed off with 'Never ask my help with your poems unless you feel sure it is the best you can do and are really stuck.' She meant to encourage self-discipline. With that encouragement I struggled by myself to complete a novel. I was trained never to interrupt her although she was free to call me. Again and again I would reach out only to be thrown back on myself. Self-reliance became one of the first things I learned."

> If Mother had continued listening to me after the first two books, I would have produced more. She squashed it by her routine.[48]

The implications of Hilda Conkling's beliefs give pause for anyone interested in nourishing creativity. The help and encouragement needed by any young person, in whatever field, was certainly there, along with a home environment she enjoyed with a mother who believed in good books, and the model of nature. What is to be inferred from the inability of a child with an IQ of 186, with a gift for words and rhythms, observation, perception, and a photographic memory, who begins as a poet and whose mature work is never fully realized?

For given the talent, the nourishment, the right environment, is it possible to assume that the gift given to children of an ability to write can be lost so easily, that the products of later life can never measure up to the originality of the earlier work? Does the answer lie in the plunder of the mystical life, in exposure to school and reality, in some Romantic concept that the "celestial abode" has been lost and is irretrievable?

In his introduction to *Marjorie Fleming's Book*, published in 1920 by Modern Library, Clifford Smyth feels that the poetry written by Hilda Conkling is indeed beautiful, but asks "is it the poetry of childhood?"

> It has the maturity of thought, the spirituality, the deft phrasing that comes, if at all, with years of literary cultivation. How a little girl of seven could have hit upon such refinements of art is indeed a problem for the psychologist. But, for this very reason, without any wish to disparage Hilda's really incomparable achievement, one does not recognize a child's voice singing these limpid lines of hers.[49]

Rather Smyth believes that there is a "sort of biblical sincerity and downrightness about an intelligent, unspoiled child's utterance; a quaint gravity, a humor that knows not that it is humorous, a simplicity of expression that savors of some ancient saga. That rare being, a child-poet, is a wild rose in a garden whose fragrant many-tinted flowers are the last word in artistic loveliness and complexity. The wild rose has but a few petals in its coronal; its fragrance is as elusive as a summer zephyr. But we love it for its very uncultivation, its wayward habit of straggling off into unexpected nooks and corners, above all for its reminiscent flavor of the primitive things of nature."[50]

Smyth's statement about Hilda Conkling's work and his ideal of the child as poet is important, for it shows just what it is that he, and many others, would ask of the work of children. It shows as well how different the poems of Hilda Conkling are from other child-poets.

Certainly Hilda's simplicity of expression cannot be faulted. Her own admitted love for words does not depend upon the precocity of a large vocabulary to be found in other lauded child-poets. Her words are always simple, always understandable; they did not come out of dictionaries or a thesaurus.

Does Smyth intimate, when he speaks about the savor of an "ancient saga" and a "biblical sincerity," that the tone and language is simple; or does he suggest that it is in this sort of work the *truth* be found? The point is crucial. He may be referring to a moral and ethical tone, a belief in God, or the didactic moral lessons and messages that are part of a pseudo-sort of poetry. But his emphasis on the "flavor of the primitive things of nature" and its "uncultivation, its wayward habit of straggling off into unexpected nooks and corners" suggest that what he favors is the unpolished work; that he would expect a child to offer a syncretic view of life that would, in addition, offer "a humor that knows not that it is humorous."

In other words, he would ask of the child-poet that same sort of confusion of word and of incomplete thought, without polished metaphor or synthesis, that would allow adults to recall a time when reason did not invade the thinking. Here adults could give themselves up to the wild abandonment of fantasy one minute and realism the next, and they could chuckle over the confusion in language, the cuteness of childhood. It is the "unfettered intellect," the disarming vision, the "single and native truth," and the "untutored speech" – it is poetry as an "expression of instinctive thought" that he seeks. Smyth, like thousands – even millions – of others is seeking a myth, a Romantic view of life which he hopes to recapture through a child, and he cannot find this in the poetry of Hilda Conkling.

CHAPTER VII

Other Child-Poets

Three turkeys fair their last have breathed
And now this world for ever leaved
Their Father & their Mother too
Will sigh and weep as well as you
Mourning for their osprings fair
Whom they did nurse with tender care
Indeed the rats their bones have cranched
To eternity are they launched
There graceful form and pretty eyes
Their fellow fows did not despise
A direful death indeed they had
that would put any parent mad
But she was more than usual calm
She did not give a single dam
She is as gentel as a lamb
Here ends this melancholy lay
Farewell Poor Turkeys I must say

Dedicated to Mrs. H. Crawfurd
By the Author – M. F.[1]

Marjorie Fleming who was born on January 15, 1803 and died on December 19, 1811 is probably the first child-poet whose work has been chronicled. *Marjorie Fleming's Book, The Story of Pet Marjorie, together with Her Journals and Her Letters* by L. MacBean, with the aforementioned introduction by Clifford Smyth, is replete with the qualities most admired by those who view the child as poet, and with praise for this young Scots girl who died a month short of her ninth birthday.

To MacBean, Marjorie is "the immortal Child of all literature" whose "artless writings have been classed with the wonders of the world." Sensitive, thoughtful and spirited, warm-blooded, happy and humorous, she was a "real, natural child"[2] whose only faults were poor penmanship, poor spelling ability and a sharp temper, better described as "untamed passion."[3] Her writing, recorded in journals, showed her love for animals, nature, the outdoors, and books. Born into a family with a love for books, she enjoyed the work of Maria Edgeworth as well as the poetry of Pope, Wordsworth, Gray, and Shakespeare. Indeed, Sir Walter Scott is said to have remarked that "She's the most extraordinary creature I ever met with, and her repeating of Shakespeare overpowers me as nothing else does."[4]

Marjorie's gift for observation is shown in many journal entries written between the age of six and the time of her death.

> I love to see the morning sun that rise so long before the moon the moon that casts her silver light when the Horison sinks beneath the clouds and scateres its light on the surface of the earth[5]

As a child of her time, she was influenced by the religion and manners that were drilled into her. "God is kind and indulgent to us which we do not deserve," she wrote, "& do not deserve to be so kindly treated but god does not do so. Though we praay in publick that should not hinder us from private prayer."[6] Again and again she would bemoan her own bad behavior, "My temper is a bad one,"[7] and again, "Isa has given me advice which is that when I feal Satan begining to tempt me that I flea from him and he would flea from me."[8]

MacBean believes that "no one ever produced quainter effects with common English words"[9] than did Marjorie. Although he recognized that children often use a word before they know its proper meaning, he finds in her work "sheer inexperience" but always "mental alertness."[10] Thus he enjoins the reader to be amused at the fact that Marjorie found it a "melancholy consideration" when she portrays a wounded officer dying on a battlefield, and it is always to his "reader's enjoyment" that he directs his remarks – "hesitating penmanship, erratic spelling, moral sentiments . . . the personality of the 'Divil' " and other childlike writing.

> An annibabtist is a thing I am not a member of; I am a Pisplikan just now & a Prisbeteren at Kercaldy my native town which though dirty is clein in the country.[11]

Marjorie's verse, written in rhymed couplets, is praised by MacBean. In a rhymed history of Mary, Queen of Scots, he finds a "strange mingling of cleverness and childish limitations" but "food for serious reflection, as well as for enjoyment. Still more striking would it appear if we were able to show the little girl's own copy, with her careful corrections of spelling . . . Did ever epic poet attempt to ride the winged Pegasus under such trying conditions?"[12]

Poor Mary Queen of Scots was born
With all the graces which adorn
Her birthday is so very late
That I do now forget the date
Her education was in france
There she did learn to sing and dance
There she was married to the dauphin
But soon he was laid in a coffin[13]

Slightly over 200 lines in length, Marjorie parallels the life of Elizabeth and ends with the story of Mary's death.

But hark her soul to heaven did rise
And I do think she would not go
Into the awfull place below
There is a thing that I must tell
Elisabeth went to fire and hell
Him who will teach her to be cevel
It must be her great friend the divel[14]

Clifford Smyth's praise of Marjorie Fleming and L. MacBean's account of her life and writing are supplemented in *Marjorie Fleming's Book* by an essay by John Brown, M.D., who extols Marjorie, yet wonders if "we make too much of this little child, who has been in her grave in Abbotshall Kirkyard these fifty and more years?" Her affectionateness and her nature are not overrated, he concludes, but perhaps "her cleverness" may be. Brown also praises her "prattle," her "childish . . . strong and free" use of words, her "beautiful" remarks about God, her "confessions,"[15] her passions, her loves, and failings. Indeed, to read *Marjorie Fleming's Book* with its triple paeans from Smyth, MacBean, and Brown is to recognize that the admiration accorded Marjorie Fleming is not that she is a fine child-poet, but it is given because she is able to use words in a fresh manner, is able to rhyme, and, because of her training in literature and religion, is able to parrot what she has heard in regard to religion, ethics, and morals. Had she not written a journal and some rhyming verses, she would be no different from thousands of other children whose parents *neglected* to write down what *they* said! There is nothing unusual in a child misspelling or using words incorrectly, or even using words imperfectly understood. What is unique is that her work was rescued from oblivion and a cult developed around her. Her poem about the turkeys is extolled today. The myth of the child-poet goes back as far as the beginning of the 19th century, and Marjorie Fleming's untimely death from measles weaves its own romance to which adults respond!

The cult of the child-poet takes its twists and turns in a variety of ways. Katherine Carasso and Nathalia Crane are among those whose facility with rhyme and form astonished the public for a while and in whose work various critics or audiences found remarkable, instinctual, amusing, or beautiful verse. "Katharine Carasso is a born poet, with a muse that was not created to remain hid" wrote George Steele Seymour of this eight-year-old whose book was published in 1936. She is a "real little girl" who sews, helps make tea, plays the piano, and "gets bothered about school." But when she goes into her own room "then the poems come and her little soul expresses itself because it must express itself." It was, according to Seymour, "written in the Book of Fate" that Katharine would have a book of her own printed. Yet he also realized that whereas the "performance of childhood has always a spontaneity that no later age can attain . . . there is in it something precious that no later effort can score."[16] Katharine is a "straight-forward little girl who takes us into her mental sanctum sanctorum, lighting us now with a candle which we trust in future years will grow to the proportions of a flare,"[17] yet

> I will not make the usual remark expressing wonderment at the performance of a child poet. We all know that that remark is usually insincere. Early performances are incomplete performances; perfection comes from long dalliance with the subject and exercise with it.[18]

The work of Katharine Carasso written from age eight to age ten shows an unusual ease in the use of traditional form, a penchant for personification, and a love for sense of story. "Silence" is personified:

> Through the valley of Pale Light,
> Saunters Silence on tip-toes,
> Spreading magic where she goes.[19]

Rhythm is handled well in her work "Up in a Swing" which begins:

> Up in a swing, out of the door,
> As on a wing upward we soar;
> Clear is the trail, wide is the space,
> Free, without quail, upward we race![20]

Metaphor comes easily. She describes a friend as "a wave in motion" and her laughter like "a gurgling brook."[21]

Her work is chiefly in strict rhythms, precise rhymes, and shows the arch precocity of a child who has absorbed the lessons and mimicked the precepts of how she should feel; of lofty adjectives and high-flown thoughts. In "My Prayer" she writes

> Purge, oh Lord, from sordid sights
> This strange world of ours;
> Flood it with undying lights, –
> Shower it with flowers.[22]

Further injunctions to "save the helpless and the weak" and to "pour thy mercies forth, good Lord," indicate nothing more than a keen absorption of the diction peculiar to prayer and facility with form and rhyme.

> My Queen-Mother
>
> Mothers are the ripened fruit
> And children are the green, –
> My own mother I salute
> As all the mothers' queen!

Mother's crown – a chestnut braid,
The kingdom – a great heart;
Her rare beauty cannot face –
Jehovah's work of art!

Mother's court with love is filled,
And love beams from her face;
All her enemies are stilled
By her resistless grace.

Mother bears a regal mien,
Her look is frank and mild;
Mother is a rarest queen
And I – her princess-child.[23]

While this is the sort of verse that is the backbone of the greeting-card industry, it is so metaphorically trite that it becomes an embarrassment. It is such verse that sounds the death-knell for child-poets like Katharine Carasso and can only point up the extraordinary comparison between a Majorie Fleming who wrote

My mother is so very sweet
And checks my appetite to eat[24]

or Hilda Conkling who said

If I sing, you listen;
If I think, you know.[25]

Nathalia Crane's first book, *The Janitor's Boy*, published in 1924 when she was ten years old, also shows a use of form and rhythm that is mature. Fortunately, no such studied paeans to her mother appear. Mother is, in her terms, someone to whom she returns after "The First Snow Storm" with an account of how she got pushed into a ten-foot-high drift.

I feel that my shoes are wet, Mama,
  And I fear the same for my hose:
And I fancy I'm rather damp, Mama,
  Around my underclothes.[26]

Another verse about "Mother's Bonnet" is illustrative of what William Rose Benêt, in his introduction to the book, termed a "fancy that quickens into imagination."[27]

> This is her bonnet, with ribbons arrayed,
> Clearly a calico ambuscade;
> It dates from the days of the bricks of straw –
> This is the bonnet my mother wore.
>
> This is the bonnet my mother donned
> When she walked with a youth by Plymouth Pond;
> 'Twas the night she wore her beads of jade,
> And father fell into the ambuscade.
>
> This is the bonnet I found in a chest,
> Daisies and bows in a lavendar nest;
> It looks like the plumes the Persians wore,
> But it must have had wonderful power to draw.[28]

Here is a more reasonable attitude toward a parent, one that Nathalia Crane used again and again, weaving from an object or a person some imaginative picture. She sees a girl in Flatbush flirting with her "pa," and becomes a member of a group that protects fathers:

> Some day, of course I will mature and
> grow a little more.
> But now I am content to be my mother's
> Signal Corps.[29]

Listening to her father describe the battle he fought in the war, she recognizes that "Ma gets mad" when he makes a battlefield on the floor. Her love, it can be said, is a realistic sort of thing – no greater than for the Janitor's Boy ("Oh I'm in love with the janitor's boy") or her friend Marjory or for a statue or for all she sees and experiences in Brooklyn.

The "instinct for remarkable phrase and striking figurative expression is either inborn or it is not,"[30] Benêt says, and it shows itself in Nathalia's work. Her facility with rhyme is not remarkable in itself, but he senses that her work has possibilities.

On the one hand, with Nathalia, we have simply a rhyming gift turned to amusing descriptions of certain fairly ordinary episodes and characteristics of life that interest every healthy alert young lady. On the other hand we have the beginnings of a poet with a true ear for rhythm, an eye for the color of words, and a fancy that often rises into the realm of imagination.

Benêt hopes she will "perfect her technique. It needs perfecting."[31] But he marvels at her "spontaneous phrasing and the natural meditation of – a child of ten."[32]

In the darkness who would cavil at the
  question of a line,
Since the darkness holds all loveliness
  beyond the mere design.[33]

Four lines from "My Husbands" he finds "almost uncanny."[34]

I hear in soft recession
  The praise they give to me:
I hear them chant my titles
  From all antiquity.[35]

Nathalia uses the life about her as a spur to her imagination; occasionally she uses metaphor. Berkley Common is "Like a manuscript all yellow, and with many things deleted."[36] She often uses personification when "The Talmud stalks from right to left, a rabbi in a gown."[37] She personifies a shadow and a reflection as having a quarrel, flowers as gossips and chessmen as warriors. Yet this personification is but a form of animism, common to all children. She assumes persona as an old maid, a chess game, and "Regina Mendosena, queen of all of Shanty Town,"[38] but this would seem to be childish imagination at work. Nathalia displays in her verse the same use of poetic tools found in other child poets; yet of all, she has the greatest command of vocabulary. Benêt marvels at her likeness to Dickinson in "The Vestal."

Once a pallid vestal
  Doubted truth in blue;

Listed red as ruin,
  Harried every hue;

Barricaded vision,
  Garbed herself in sighs;
Ridiculed the birthmarks
  Of the butterflies.[39]

Nathalia's "gifts will simply develop according to the experience of literature and her experience of life," Benêt writes. "It is a very ticklish thing to endeavor in any way to direct so young a gift. It will find by instinct its own nourishment; that is my belief."[40]

Nathalia Crane is almost seventy years old; she has been teaching English and Irish Literature at San Diego State University and is recently retired. She does not wish to speak of the days when she was a child-poet. To read her work, therefore, is only to recognize, in the words of Nunnally Johnson, that she was "an extraordinarily articulate little girl, and if in some cases the conceits and fancies which she crystallizes are no rarer than those that, in all probability, throng the mysterious mind of every imaginative child, the explanation is simply that she is able to utter and clarify them, and these other children are for the most part normally unable to do that."[41]

The analyses by Benêt and Johnson escape the pitfalls of the "celestial abode" and the "unconscious," which trapped critics of earlier child-poets. They are realists who see in Crane's work a child whose vocabulary and expression is full of promise. But she did not fulfill that promise and neither, would it seem, do more recent child-poets whose work has been highly praised.

In 1968 *The Real Tin Flower*, poems written by nine-year-old Aliki Barnstone, was published with a foreword by Anne Sexton. "Here is a marvel," Sexton writes. "Here are poems that startle the senses . . . fresh merchandise in a world of style supermarkets." Aliki Barnstone, Sexton continues, is a child with "big words in her mouth. Was she born wise?"[42] Her "child-eye view is everywhere, even in the bland innocence of the endings of poems . . . She is not the self-conscious surrealist nor is she controlled by a didactic adult world . . . Aliki Barnstone is the child imagist in each of us."[43]

Aliki Barnstone was born in Connecticut, daughter of a mother who is a painter and a father who is a poet and translator. In 1961 and 1962 she attended school in Spain and Greece. Her first poems were published in magazines. Her book was published in 1968 and no other book by her has appeared since. The forty-three poems reveal a preoccupation with color reminiscent of Mary O'Neill's *Hailstones and Halibut Bones* (which appeared in 1961, seven years before the publication of Barnstone's book) and a number of brief metaphors sprinkled throughout.

Here one can find that "Blue is Greece"[44] or mention of a "blue kiss," or "Vick Vapo-Rub bluey world."[45] "Purple is a funny color," she says, adding in the same poem that the "sun is yellow."[46] White is "warmth and kindness"[47] or "a snake, tadpole, valley."[48] Red "is the fire/of sparks blazing in your face."[49] Metaphors state that

> The moon is the match of the candle
> the sun is the flame.[50]

or

> The sky's teeth are clouds
> in a blue mouth.
> The poet's teeth
> are swans.[51]

Thunder, she writes is "a big black sound/coming out of a cloud,"[52] and lilies of the valley are "the bell/of day."[53] Spring is "barefoot children/and blooming daffodils."[54] Of the Big Dipper she writes that it "twinkles like a roll/of Scotch Tape in its holder."[55] Her most famous poem, used as the title for an anthology, *Zero Makes Me Hungry*, is "Numbers."

> I hate and like math.
> The letter O
> and the number zero sound like
> poems about O snowflake. Zero
> makes me hungry. It is the emptiest
> number in the universe
> which is – and is not – round.
> The wonder of zero, O snowflake
> and the universe
> will never be solved.
> I want my lunch.[56]

In a poem titled "Time" Barnstone writes:

> The calendars pile up in a neat stack.
> I knew they would.
>
> I tried to forget about them
> yet the days . . .
>
> I am older now and still a child
> but time is a thirsty germ.
>
> I have one year left to play in this lot
> and am afraid.
>
> Some people think about
> what they do
>
> or the school they are to lose.
> Others just let a river go by.
>
> I never see what I am looking at.
> I see what I think.
>
> At night life is blue waves,
> piers with stairs going down,
>
> people who jump off and frighten
> fish who swim away,
>
> boys who dive from the top of the rail.
> This is my real life.[57]

This is a far cry from the simple observations of Hilda Conkling, the rhymed observations and retold histories of Marjorie Fleming, the metaphoric and traditional modes of Katharine Carasso, and the academic vocabulary that often characterizes the work of Nathalia Crane. Barnstone's poetry wanders and meanders, moreover, with fragments of thoughts ranging from images of a group of calendars to piers with stairs; people jumping off and boys jumping from the rail. "Time is a thirsty germ" or "life is blue waves" are so metaphorically obtuse as to seem meaningless in context. Her leaps from one thought to another, in a pseudo-sophisticated manner, are interlaced with subjects thought proper to children – toothpaste or bubble gum – or unlikely subjects, war and death – and go beyond even the syncretic nature of childhood expression. Although she may not be in Sexton's eyes surrealistic, there is no real synthesis in her work. What does the line "yet the days . . ." (with ellipsis) mean? Perhaps the clue lies in her stanza

> I never see what I am looking at
> I see what I think.

These lines are most telling for they put into focus the realm of the intimist. Observation and objective data are only appendages to the subjective self, the precious ego, coddled and praised, throwing out a series of flashed images that dazzles the reader into believing that these images, strange juxtapositions, and sparklings of synaesthesia are poetry.

Yet Barnstone's book received praise at the time of its publication. Diane Farrell in the February, 1969 *Horn Book* agrees with Sexton that the poems are a "marvel."

> One part of the marvel is that the author of these poems is twelve years old; most of the poems were written when she was nine. The other part of the marvel is the precision of language, the richness of the imagery, and the depth of perception evidenced in the poems: the subjects are within the experience of childhood . . .

Farrell believes that "More adults than young people may find the poems appealing. But for those who savor sharp images and sensuous words, here is treasure."[58]

In the *Bulletin of the Center for Children's Books* of March, 1969 Zena Sutherland states that although "an occasional poem seems flat or self-conscious, most of the selections have sharp imagery and fresh concepts; a few are wholly conceived and even in their excellence . . ."[59]

Booklist, January 1, 1969 calls *The Real Tin Flower* "a rare achievement of excellence and originality in children's poetry." Barnstone's "language and imagery are unjaded, and whether serious or funny the tone of her work never becomes cute, patronizing, or sentimental. That the poems . . . express so honest a vision with such skill is all the more amazing since the author, now twelve, was nine years old when she wrote most of them . . ."[60]

Della Thomas of the Curriculum Materials Laboratory, Oklahoma State University Library, writing in *School Library Journal*, calls Barnstone's poems "a remarkable production for that age." She finds "striking imagery" in many of the lines but notes that "As might be expected, thought and expression are of uneven quality throughout the collection." Barnstone's observation about the Big Dipper as a roll of Scotch tape is "certainly not the equal of 'Every painting in the world/has a little tadpole/of white, for the artist/drops snowflakes on the canvas.' "[61]

Here, with a few reservations on the part of Sutherland and Thomas, is adulation for the child-poet in our time, a praise that is repeated for countless "young poets" and "young authors" who have become the subject and the *raison d'etre* for so many programs throughout the country today.

In 1970 the work of Kali Grosvenor was published by Doubleday. *Poems by Kali* is a collection of thirty-three pieces written by Kali at the ages of six and seven. In prose aligned to resemble poetry, the majority of the work speaks of the Black experience. In "We Black People Should" she writes

> Why did the Pilgrems
> discouver this country?
> We Black People Whould
> have this world.
> It's ours[62]

Kali's use of "natural" language, replete with misspellings, is characteristic of work that has come to be accepted by many as fresh and sensitive. Yet it typifies the voice of the child espousing adult sentiments with a candor that in children is often equated with truth. There is no evidence that Kali has published any work since 1970. Will she be heard from again?

A spectacular event that rocked France in 1955, the publication of *Arbre, mon ami (Tree, My Friend)* by Minou Drouet, born in 1947 is – because of its ramifications – of intense importance for a further look into the phenomenon of the child-poet. The literary furor that accompanied this publication brought cries of delight from many, outrage from others.

The title poem of Minou's first book, *Tree, My Friend*, published when she was twelve, begins in translation:

Tree, my friend
  you are like me,
    so heavy with music
under the fingers of the wind
  that leaf through you
    like the pages of a fairy tale
tree
  who like me
knows the voice of silence
  who swings
the deepness of your green locks
  the trembling of your living hands
tree
  my friend
    mine alone
      lost like me
        lost in the sky
          lost in the mud
lacquered with dancing light
by the rain
tree
  echo of the wind's rain
  of the bird's joy
tree stripped by winter
I watch you for the first time . . .[63]

René Julliard, the publisher of *Tree, My Friend*, in his preface to the book finds in Minou's work a "rich blossoming . . . every sign of freshness, vivacity of feeling, a gift of imagery, an exceptional strength of expression." Although he admits to being "disconcerted by an astonishing mixture of ingenuousness and skill, of naive spontaneity and advanced knowledge of language" and recognizes that certain phrases are imitative of Maeterlinck, there is still, to him, "an exquisite freshness, an abundance of rare pearls, a real enchantment."

Julliard relates Minou's background. Adopted by a foster mother, Mme. Drouet, who would seem to have been a frustrated poet and writer herself, she was given piano and solfeggio lessons at a young age and read to constantly. Julliard describes the relationship between the two:

> Mme. Drouet has raised her daughter with as much tenderness as discipline, she has constantly encouraged her to work: piano, solfeggio, general instruction, and certainly correspondence – though Minou, as I can testify, loves to write. Spending all day close to her mother, Minou, curious like all intelligent children – "I'm a living question mark," she told me once – asks question after question. Mme. Drouet is a dictionary consulted endlessly. The conversation between her and her child does not stop from morning to night; and it is this conversation, this sort of oral collaboration which is, without doubt, the source of Minou's writings.

"For the rest, that is to say the essential," Julliard continues, "for the *gift*, we are faced with the mystery of artistic creation and, confronted with that mystery, we are silent."[64]

Silence, however, was not the reaction to the publication of *Arbre, mon ami*. André Rousseaux, writing in *Le Figaro Littéraire*, speaks of Minou's "mastery of words and their music," her "innate awareness of the resonances of verbal music" and the "privilege of genius." Jean Rousselot, a well-known Marxist poet, expressed strong doubt about the authenticity of the poems, charging that a strong press campaign had been well-arranged by Julliard. André Breton and Jean Cocteau said that Minou's work was but a pastiche of the work of Max Jacob and Jacques Prévert.

Pierre de Boisdeffre, a literary critic, wrote with great irony of "a delirious press" who asked the public "to applaud the poems of an eight-year-old child, not as a collection of graceful images but as the authentic expression of genius." He believed Minou to have been "force fed" reading and music by the most authoritarian of adoptive mothers, yet notes that even then her sensitivity and natural spontaneity were not destroyed. Her letters he found "falsely poetic, with badly disguised little tracks, marks of commonness, and naturally, a great many mistakes in spelling." His quibble was not with her talent or gift "so fresh and so true" but with those who forced her into a "shameless publicity campaign . . . habituated her to generals and studios, exhibited her like a movie star in casinos and department stores." He wonders what will happen to Minou's talent in the future. "Will an idolized woman of letters still be able to sing, like the drunkard son of Bach, with the winged hands of a piano teacher?"

Hands richer than a summer garden
Hands so heavy with music
Even when you lie quietly on a table
Like two birds
Still singing
. . . Hands
Last of the fairies
Forgotten on earth
Hands sliding like a cloud
Deep as the sea
Attracting like the sea . . .[65]

In Minou's poetry simile and metaphor, *tools of poetry*, are used *as a substitute for poetry itself*. Her facile use of these figures of speech becomes a gimmick, a trademark, a trick that is substituted for a synthesis, for a finished product: This was recognized during *l'affaire Drouet* by writers such as Jean Cocteau who chided those who wanted to call "an empty drawer a treasure."[66] To read the title poem is to be aware of the constant succession of such metaphor, couched in the same animism and apostrophe characteristic of all children, but strung together so cleverly – in what may be thought to be a poetic diction – that a public believes it to be poetry.

Roland Barthes, a linguist, who attacked the problem in his article "La Littérature selon Minou Drouet" ("Literature according to Minou Drouet") published in *Mythologies*, states the problem squarely. Whether or not Drouet's work is authentic, he writes, is not the central issue. What is crucial is that Drouet's work is "precious mythological material." The writing "lets us read precisely what society believes to be childhood and poetry." Those who should be responsible, who should seek to examine the true nature and the reality of childhood and poetry, fall back on preconceptions of what they wish or imagine poetry on the one hand, childhood on the other, to be. This results in an image "both astonishing and necessary to society" – that of the child-poet. It is an image born of irresponsibility that makes the child "a purely magical object" who is both prodigy and victim.

Society's myth of childhood, Barthes states, "postulates a child as an asocial being," as a being who lives outside the mainstream, as an ideal being, "as if use of vocabulary were strictly regulated by nature, as if the child did not live in a state of constant osmosis with the adult world . . ." In this view, literature and poetry are conceived as a "gift of the gods," as if culture were absent. Thus, whatever the child says seems spontaneous. Addressing himself to the commentaries of one of the modernists, M. Henriot, Barthes states that in Henriot's view "Childhood receives its dignity by its very irrationality . . . whence the comical confusion with surrealism." In this myth, the "child can be neither trivial nor vulgar, which is still to imagine a sort of ideal childish nature come down from heaven, outside of any societal determinism . . ."

Barthes deplores the idea that insofar as the child is able to accomplish such work, he is thought a genius; that he can do at age eight what is usually done at age twenty-five. Whereas the classicists believe that it takes work and patience to write poetry, the Romantic myth enables him, as if by magic, to incorporate all of the insights and experience of the adult. Childhood, in this view, thus becomes the "privileged place of genius."

Barthes also writes of the myth that governs poetry, of those "venerable neophytes who were amazed to discover (in 1955) the poetic power of childhood, and called a 'miracle' what was a literary commonplace known for a long time." In this view, "Poetry is an uninterrupted succession of findings, which is an ingenuous name for metaphor. The more a poem is stuffed with 'formulations,' the more it passes for success." Such a view presupposes that poetry, "being a vehicle of unreality," has only to "*translate* the object, to pass from the *Larousse Dictionary* into metaphor, as if naming things badly were enough to poeticize them."

These "findings" and "formulations," Barthes points out, are "the antiphrasis of all Poetry, to the extent that they shun the solitary weapon of writers: literalness; yet it is that alone which can remove artificiality from poetic metaphor, reveal it as a lightning bolt of truth, a victory over the continuous nausea of language." The poetry of Drouet "babbles endlessly, like those people who are afraid of silence; it visibly dreads the literal and lives on an accumulation of expedients: it confuses life with nervousness." But it is a "stock of 'findings,' this calculated order of bargain-rate profusion, all of that provides the basis for a Poetry that is gaudy, tinseled, and cheap . . ."

Minou Drouet, while regarded as a prodigy, says Barthes, is but a victim of society. She is "the child martyr for the adult badly needing poetic luxury; she is the one sequestered or kidnapped by a conformist order that reduces liberty to prodigy. She is the girl that the beggar woman pushes ahead while, behind, the mattress is full of coins. A little tear then, for Minou Drouet, a little shiver for poetry . . ."

If there are to be tears and shivers, they must be also felt for Hilda Conkling, and to a lesser degree other child-poets adulated and praised for early performance, catapulted, because of one gift or another, into the limelight. Society, "should not lament hypocritically" because it is society who has made these children into conciliatory victims, "sacrificed so that the world can be clear, so that poetry, genius and childhood – in a word, disorder – can be tamed and put to good account . . ."[67]

Society's need for what Barthes calls the "bourgeois elegaic feeling," for "successful verbal acrobatics," and for "predictable formula" persists to this day in even more startling ways. Children in classrooms with far less talent than child-poets such as Crane, Barnstone, or Grosvenor are hailed and honored throughout our country by those who in Cocteau's words "want to call an empty drawer a treasure."

If there is lament for Hilda Conkling, it must be because she has found her solace in incomplete answers. It was not, it would seem, her inability to come to grips with reality, not the fact that her mother would no longer help her. It was not due to the schools. It was society who made of her another victim; the more lamentable because she – of all the child-poets – did not rely on the "findings" or "gimmicks," the "acrobatics" or "formulas" that characterized the others.

Yet society in the United States today persists in repeating its myths of childhood and poetry, since adulation is irresponsibly afforded hundreds of thousands of children who are praised for "findings" which are neither gifts nor treasure. And it is, unfortunately, these children who will awaken one day and discover that they have been exploited.

CHAPTER VIII

Langston Hughes: Poet-in-Residence, 1949

Hold fast to dreams
For if dreams die
Life is a broken-winged bird
That cannot fly.

Hold fast to dreams
For when dreams go
Life is a barren field
Frozen with snow.

"Dreams"
Langston Hughes[1]

"Shortly after the end of World War II," Warren Seyfert, former Director of the University of Chicago Laboratory School, recalls, "a number of us on the Lab School faculty became involved with an effort to revive the Progressive Education Association, which had fallen on hard times in the war years. The outcome was a national conference held in Chicago at which Langston was a speaker and where several of us began our friendship with him. Those were the years when having a writer-in-residence was developing as a frequent collegiate pattern, and we wondered why the same arrangement wouldn't be productive with younger students of the kind the Lab School enrolled and with a faculty committed to exploring new ideas."

"I can't remember," Seyfert continues, "where we got the money to support the residence, though I do remember that even then it was hardly a persuasive sum. I learned that Langston was planning to take a kind of sabbatical to work on his autobiography, and we dreamed up the notion that he come to Chicago for a few months . . . and we could provide a modest subsidy if he'd spend a little time during the week at the school. Doing what, we said we didn't know, since there were no precedents for that sort of an arrangement."[2]

The youngsters at the University of Chicago Laboratory School, according to Eunice H. McGuire, an eighth grade teacher at the school, were middle and upper class white, with a few black students. The faculty were middle class white. It was, she recalls, "an odd experience for our poet. We didn't know quite what to do with him or he with us . . ." Yet Langston Hughes arrived on March 1, 1949 and left in May. In his book *The Dreamkeeper*, an inscription to Mrs. McGuire reads, "with my thanks for listening so patiently (and so often) to my amateur teaching."[3]

In his report to Seyfert following the end of the writer-in-residence stint, Hughes explains that his contacts with young people had, heretofore, "been limited to a winter of the teaching of English to business academy students and preparatory school girls in Toluca, Mexico, and to a semester at Atlanta University where I gave seminars in poetry and conducted a group in Creative Writing on the college level." He had, however, spent the previous twenty years reading poems to groups of people from kindergarten children to adults and "often, especially in the rural South, before audiences combining the entire age range from pre-school youngsters through high school." He had talked to "hundreds of grammar, high school, and college assemblies throughout the country. But never, before coming to the Lab School, had . . . worked with Creative Writing students below the college level."[4]

The students Hughes attracted to his creative writing classes came on a volunteer basis, from grades six through ten. About eighty came at first but a change in schedule reduced the number to sixty. Although most came regularly, the high school students attended sporadically. Some came just to listen, others to write. Weekly, during study periods, ten groups came. There was a group that met after school. Individual consultations were offered; about a dozen students came for these.

Seyfert relates how Hughes was housed at the International House. "One day he appeared at the School to get acquainted with the faculty. It had been decided previously that, to get the residency moving, teachers who would like to have our poet join in a classroom discussion would arrange a time that was convenient for him. Meanwhile, he proposed to offer one or two seminars on writing and related matters. Not surprising, the operation took off slowly, for not many people had had firsthand experience with a poet, not to mention a Negro in those years – the Lab School had become an integrated school about five years earlier, but misgivings lingered. Very quickly, of course, everyone found Langston to be a gentle, wise, and an altogether special person."[5]

Hughes's report to the Lab School indicates that he spent ten periods weekly at creative writing with the students, six periods weekly speaking of the Negro in poetry, one period weekly reading poetry aloud and one period weekly in a class titled Basis of Jazz. "During the free periods I visited classes, the Senior Kindergarten, or consulted with individual creative writers." This, Hughes and Seyfert agreed, did not leave any time for Hughes's own creative work. This was, Hughes commented, "not serious for a short period. But I suggest that if a Writer in Residence is invited to the Laboratory School for a longer period, the schedule be a lighter one in order to allow the writer time for his own writing which is, after all, the thing that makes the writer of unique value to the students – the fact that he is a *practicing writer living and working* in their midst."[6]

An examination of the philosophy and methods of Hughes in his work with the students illustrates the many differences that characterize the work done by poet-teachers today, while the follow-up on Hughes's students may give clues as to the influence of a poet and how he is remembered. Will students of today look back upon their experience thirty-five years from now in the same way as a number of Hughes's students do now?

The University of Chicago Lab School is remembered by a former student, Irene Pearlman Breckler, as being attended by children from both the upper middle class and lower upper class. Their parents were largely professionals, successful executives, business men, and professors at the University of Chicago. The students' intellectual level ranged from high to gifted. Most of the students were Caucasian, although around 1945 some blacks were admitted. They had been selected for entrance by examination and interview and tended to regard themselves as superior to their public school peer group.[7]

Langston Hughes was "intrigued by the maturity of the questions asked by many of the pupils, even little youngsters." He viewed the student body as "delightful, attentive and courteous in every way." His "impressions of the Laboratory School are good ones . . . I would say its students have more initiative, freedom of expression, and independence of thought than any I have known before. There is about the school a sense of fun in learning."

In his report to the Director, Hughes described his "Methods of Guidance."

> My first talks and discussions with each group were designed to indicate to the young people the pleasures that lie in individual creation – not in imitating anyone else but in making one's own world in words on paper; in pointing out the difference between objective, factual, journalistic writing and individual, personal, creative writing; indicating the differences between fact and fiction, verse and poetry; and how in the wonder of creation each sea shell, each animal, each tree, and each person is different; so if each person writes as he is, his writing is bound to be different, individual, and therefore interesting.
>
> Picking at random from the daily paper any factual account of an accident, a murder, or some such news item, we examined its possibilities as a basis for fiction or poetry if used imaginatively, creatively. We considered our reactions had we known any of the people involved in the news story. Group discussion brought out that each person saw different possibilities, felt differently about the happening, and each if on the scene would have had a reaction different in some way from the rest of us.
>
> Then at the end of our first talks I gave my first and only writing assignment explaining to the groups its two purposes: (1) to use facts creatively and (2) to enable me to see, since we were strange to each other, how each would use words. The assignment was to take as a subject one's home, one's neighborhood, one's street, or one's city and write about it in any form desired, poetry, verse, narrative, or fiction; in other words, to begin with something one knows well, since even fantasy must spring from known facts.
>
> A portion of each group meeting was devoted to the reading, discussion, and group criticism of the week's manuscripts. No student was required to read his work to the group, and those

who did not wish to do so received personal comment and criticism privately from the teacher. But most of the young people liked group reading sessions and felt that each other's comments were helpful.[8]

These group critiques are well remembered by a number of the students who participated. Alice Wirth Gray, whose poetry has subsequently been published in *Chelsea*, the *Christian Science Monitor*, *Helicon 9*, the *Atlantic Monthly* and *American Scholar*, recalls the sessions "where six or seven students sat at a collapsible table in a very cold room . . . the great warmth engendered by the radiant presence of Langston Hughes, the exhilaration of working with this man. There was good literary talk, and we had a vague understanding that we were lucky to be able to work with him. Yet I remember thinking – it is so pitiful that there are so few of us. I know other people thought this too . . . When he left I felt a sense of loss at not seeing him again. None of us knew much about him, how good he was. It was a 'lost opportunity'."

Yet Gray, in the ninth grade at the time, took from that classroom the knowledge that poetry was involved with discovering that urban life was part of poetry, that metaphor was necessary. She remembers that Hughes read poetry to them, "his own very simple, lyrical poems" and that he wanted to "unlimber us,"[9] to move towards unconventional forms. She also remembers that what Hughes gave of himself was friendly and kind.

Dartha Cloudman Reid, who was in the sixth grade in 1949, reveals that discussions were encouraged and Langston Hughes "showed us how to improve our poetry and how to better express ourselves . . . The only specific session that I can recall clearly was a poem written by my classmate . . . about an organ grinder's monkey. Mr. Hughes read it aloud to us and read slight changes that made it better and we could see how to work with the ideas to improve the poem. He had an easy way with us – encouraging not criticizing." The main thing he offered, she recalls, was "encouragement. He was very positive and definitely affected the goals and quality of my life style . . . We respected him because he was a 'real poet' and we were excited with the opportunity to work with someone of his ability . . . his comments and instruction had a greater impact on me than the help from just a teacher of many subjects."[10]

Judith Hayes Weir, now Director of the Center for Urban and Regional Affairs at the University of Minnesota and mother of four children who have gone through the Minnesota Poets-in-the-Schools program, was in seventh grade then. She remembers Langston Hughes reading his own poetry and was impressed with him as a "magnificent, humane and warm"[11] person. Indeed she feels he may well have had something to do with the idea that she always wanted to "grow up" and become a writer. His encouragement still lingers as a possibility for her, although her current interest is in photography and community affairs.

One student remembers that "he did help us and offer suggestions but mostly he worked hard to get us to criticize our own work – did *we* like it? did it say what we wanted it to say?" Hughes was "so encouraging and eager that each of us write . . . that was the most important thing to write – to try – not to worry about rhyme/ meter/verse but to write . . ."[12]

Phoebe Liebig remembers Langston Hughes as a "different kind of teacher." While others taught skills, Hughes allowed a chance for self-exploration, for having fun, for a kind of learning that did not demand the follow-up of information. She welcomed the lack of competition in creative writing that permeated other classes. To her, Hughes represented a kind of "thinking and feeling" that was entirely different. Hughes was encouraging; he accepted and praised what was good but would always ask, "Is this what you mean?" He would "question as to why a certain metaphor had been used. If he felt he could be helpful, he offered suggestions." Yet she always felt that "a piece of work was mine, not something he had overlaid," and remembers that he encouraged feelings in terms of images, that he was "strong of imagination." He worked in metaphor, in a "single concept such as love and tried to dimensionalize it."[13] He suggested that his students go beyond the adolescent experience and write in the persona of an older person.

David Zimmerman, a journalist and free-lance magazine and book writer who was then in the ninth grade, retains a "quite vivid memory of Langston Hughes and of the classes with him." Zimmerman is the author of three books and numerous articles appearing in *Smithsonian*, *Natural History*, and *Audubon*, and is the winner of many prestigious prizes for his writing in medicine and the natural sciences. "It seems possible that work with Hughes might have contributed to my choice of profession. I frankly do not know whether this is so or not."[14]

In Langston Hughes's report there is a paragraph that outlines the material he presented.

> Each student was also asked to indicate the fields of writing in which he wished to work most intensively during the Spring. These were quite varied, ranging from factual and editorial writing to poetry, short stories and scientific fantasy. Since it was not possible to further sub-divide the ten groups of young writers, succeeding sessions were devoted to topics which might be helpful in various broad fields of writing, such as Humor in Writing, Methods of Working, Getting Started, Use of Dialogue, Single Plot Construction, Writing as Communication, As Personal Expression, Advantages of Poetic Prose, Use of Visual Words, Moral Obligations in Writing, Various Ways in Which Writers Collect Ideas, Helpful Books to Read, etc.[15]

This presentation ties in with Zimmerman's statement that he was "particularly impressed by Hughes's methods: we wrote stories, poems, etc., and they were typed and reproduced for class reading, discussion and criticism and editing in story meeting with Hughes. In a sense, this demystified writing, and made it into a manageable and real process – and I am reasonably sure that this comforting understanding remained with me at the time I made my decisions to work as a journalist (and later as an author)."

Zimmerman says that his "interest has always been prose. I neither read nor write poetry." Yet it would seem that the climate created by Hughes, the model as writer, could have influenced Zimmerman; he was "most certainly, one of the first persons whom I knew as a teacher who was clearly identified in my mind as a writer."[16]

Lois Grass Kuhr recalls that "I have no memory of ever writing – poetry or prose – during these years . . . but I was then . . . not a creative writer. I may have attended that one session because of the enthusiasm of my more creative friends . . . I never wrote poetry. I managed to get a college degree in journalism without ever studying poetry. I rarely read poetry. I don't understand or enjoy it. (Those two thoughts are related, I realize.)"[17] Memory plays strange tricks, for records of the Lab School show that two of the works of Lois

Grass, "Love and My Roommate" and "Poem," did appear in a school magazine.

"I do have clear memories of that year," Catherine DeCosta Wilder, another former sixth grader, wrote, "but Langston Hughes or any teacher other than my classroom instructors does not figure among them. I do remember writing a poem that year (I think it was that year) on the theme of snow. I think it was published in the school magazine. My (then) little brother repeated it so often – and made such a fuss that I never wrote another one." The list of contributors to the magazine shows, indeed, that "Morning Snows" was the work of Catherine DeCosta, written for the class.

It is Wilder's feeling, however, that because of the nature of a laboratory school, the students were accustomed to "part-time teachers, substitute teachers and classroom observers in *abundance*. They became part of the 'background noise,' so to speak." This may also account for the fact that a number of the students interviewed by telephone or responding to a letter do not remember Hughes. "Was he the principal?" one man asked. Yet he made a deep impression upon others. The Lab School, Wilder notes, was "ahead of its time in many ways, among these, desegregation. It is appropriate and natural that Langston Hughes was invited to be on the staff."[18]

Another student, preferring to remain anonymous, recalls that having Langston Hughes was the "first and last time" that a "school situation was so filled with excitement, openness and creativity . . . I remember that suddenly, words became so important."[19]

Lois Grass Kuhr felt that something different came from Hughes, an opportunity to be exposed, for the first time "to the realities of being Black and surviving ghetto life. Consciousness-raising didn't become popular for 20 years,"[20] she notes, but the day that she heard from Langston Hughes about the experience of the Negro was a day she will always remember. Phoebe Liebig speculates that Hughes remains not only the first "Negro teacher I ever had" but that "he is one I do remember (at school) always at the top. Maybe because he was racially different" but it was "probably more than that . . . "[21]

To one student, Hughes represented someone who gave confidence to enter "into the 'scary' world of poetry," to teach that not only could poetry be appreciated "but I even dared to write some of my own."[22]

During April, 1949, Hughes relates how he gave four seminars "on the Negro theme in our poetry as expressed by both Negro and White poets from Colonial times to the present, linking this theme to the general stream of American poetry and its changes in poetic patterns and content." It was his intention to show how almost all the great American poets from Longfellow, Lowell, Whittier, and Walt Whitman to Lindsay, Carl Sandburg, and Karl Shapiro have written about the Negro and the racial problems in our democracy."

> I tried to show how poetry does not grow out of a vacuum but out of life, and is related to its times. To that end, a brief historical background prefaced each period – the birth of a new nation two hundred years ago with its paradox of human slavery; the Reconstruction period with the Negro's struggle for education and democratic rights; the Prohibition and Depression periods between World War I and World War II with the problem of Negro life shown as segments of much more general problems affecting everyone; and finally our contemporary post-war, post-Roosevelt period. Indicated were the folk influences on poetry – folk verses and folk songs merging into the minstrel music and that of Bland and Stephen Foster, up to the blues and jazz of today.
>
> The poems chosen to read aloud for the students were selected not only on the basis of representing adequately their authors, the subject matter and the period, but also on their attraction for the ear. Many poems, particularly of contemporary poets, do not project well when read aloud. This factor, it seems to me should be considered when reading poetry to young people who must be kept awake in order to absorb information. An attempt was made to relate almost every poem used to incidents in the poet's own life and to relate his life to the historical period in which he lived so that life, history, and poetry would emerge as one in the student's mind. Just as Walt Whitman wrote about the problems and potentialities of our democracy because he felt so deeply about them, so did Negro poets write about the problems and *limitations* of our democracy as it affected their lives . . . The tie-up between poetry and social studies, art and sociology was indicated from 1746 to the present.[23]

Hughes used as his basic references three anthologies, *The Poetry of the Negro*, co-edited by Arna Bontemps and Hughes himself; *The Negro Caravan*, edited by Brown, David and Lee; and Arna Bontemps's *Golden Slippers*. He scouted out as much poetry of Chicago poets and poems about Chicago as he could, "the desire again being to relate poetry to life within the student's local understanding." He invited Gwendolyn Brooks to attend the tenth grade seminar to explain the background of her *A Street in Bronzeville*. In addition, Hughes played recordings of Vachel Lindsay's "The Congo" and James Weldon Johnson's Negro sermons in verse from *God's Trombones*.

David Zimmerman remembers that Hughes read his own poetry and especially recollects hearing the work of Paul Laurence Dunbar. Lois Grass Kuhr remembers being "entranced, awed and entertained." She remembers vaguely hearing "The Congo," but whether it was Hughes reading the poem or a recording she cannot recall. Phoebe Liebig recalls that he "read a lot of Black literature and Johnson's 'The Creation,' and Lindsay." Alice Gray remembers that he read his own poetry and E. E. Cummings.

"Each Friday morning," Hughes reports, "with one of Miss Rusk's eighth grade classes, we had a half hour of Poetry Aloud. Selected around a single theme every week, the young people brought poems to read. I also made a brief selection." Some of the subjects around which selections were grouped were nature, animals, people, historical events, humor, religious subjects, and love and death.

> Reading clearly and simply was an aim – poetry as communication and enjoyment. Discussions brought out the various forms of poetry, the differences between verse and poetry, rhymed and free verse, and narrative, dramatic, philosophical and mood poems. The young people were intrigued by Gertrude Stein. Records were played of Miss Stein and Robert Frost reading their own poems.
>
> From the reading aloud of the poems of others each week, the young people went on to the writing and reading of their own original compositions in class.[24]

Although none of the students seemed to remember hearing the work of Gertrude Stein or Robert Frost, it is Langston Hughes's own poetry and that of Lindsay and Johnson that are most often remembered. Langston Hughes's Reading Guide shows that he divided the reading that was probably done by him into four distinct periods; the Colonial Period through the Civil War included work by Lucy Terry, Phyllis Wheatley, Francis E. W. Harper, James Edwin Campbell, Whittier, Lowell, Longfellow, and Whitman. The Civil War included readings from Paul Laurence Dunbar, William Stanley Braithwaite, James Weldon Johnson, and Georgia Douglass Johnson as well as the Minstrel Songs, Stephen Foster, Vachel Lindsay, and William Ellery Leonard. The World War I through World War II period included Claude McKay, Fenton Johnson, Jean Toomer, Countee Cullen, Carl Sandburg, Du Bose Heyward, Witter Bynner, and Kenneth Porter. World War II to the contemporary period included Margaret Walker, Gwendolyn Brooks, Robert Hayden, Langston Hughes, Karl Shapiro, Kenneth Patchen, Selden Rodman, and St. Claire McKelway. To the recommended anthologies, he added books by individual poets Dunbar, Hughes, Cullen, Brooks, Walker, and Owen Dodson.

In addition to giving seminars and classes, Hughes also visited classrooms, talking on subjects requested by the students. These were usually related to his own literary activities both in publishing and in the theater. He would speak about "how poems are written, how books are published, or else my travels to various lands, Africa, China, Russia, the Caribbean . . . With each group," he states, "I attempted to relate poetry to every day living, to show how the things one does become materials for creative writing, and to indicate how pleasant an adventure writing can be. In the classes there was always time for questions and discussions by the pupils."[25]

One other seminar was given with Robert Erickson on The Basis of Jazz. Selecting both from the *Library of Congress Alan Lomax Folk Song Recordings* and those modern recordings collected by Mr. Erickson, "we conducted once a week a record seminar on the basis of jazz, from the folk music of the deep South and the jug and tramp bands with their improvised instruments to the best of the modern commercial arrangements such as Benny Goodman and Artie Shaw."

> Discussion and comment by the class, Mr. Erickson and myself, brought out the value of freedom and originality in folk expression and how it might be used in more disciplined and formal

> patterns, and of what value this folk expression – originally largely Negro – has been to American popular music, dancing and general enjoyment.[26]

There was also a project on rhythm as expressed in human life, nature and art, and its various forms of communication through athletics, the dance, the motion picture, photography, the graphic arts, music, and the spoken and written word. "The students chose their own working groups and a week was devoted to exploring the various forms of rhythm. My group of four students devoted their time to Rhythm in the Spoken and Written Word, mostly as related to humor, producing limericks and nonsense verse to be read aloud. During the following week two demonstration programs were presented showing the results of the various studies and activities."[27]

It is likely that Phoebe Liebig may have been part of one or both of these groups, for she recalls that although Hughes, to her knowledge, never spoke of metrics and rhythm, he indicated the presence of these through sound. "I latched onto being a sound person," she recalls, "I would listen to what was going on in a piece – I believe that music was played."[28] She remembers too that he talked about concepts, gave examples from literature. The concept of creative expression to her, as well as to Dartha Cloudman Reid, and probably to Alice Wirth Gray and David Zimmerman, has remained as a way of life, whether in writing or in other fields. "I feel very strongly," Dartha Reid says, "that each person must have an escape valve for his feelings and emotions."[29]

Langston Hughes's emphasis on poetry and creativity as part of life and for its pleasure also stresses in his report that

> Aside from the pleasure of personal achievement and the fun of creating, writing may have, I believe, for some adolescents a psycho-therapeutic value in that, unconsciously and by indirection, they may get down on paper some of the things that trouble them – and thus relieved, live better, freer, less confused lives. It would seem to me that words being so direct, might have a greater value in helping young people see themselves clearly than do paints or music.[30]

In his report Hughes echoes his joy at the cooperative group of people who made possible his three months at the Laboratory School. They were, he stated, "full of interest, revelation, and a re-affirmation of my faith in American youth . . . A few in the Creative Writing group, less than a dozen, seemed to be there more for appreciation than for writing – but perhaps . . .

> Eight weeks is much too short a time to be of any real help to young people seeking to express themselves in writing. It is hardly enough time for teacher and students to become accustomed to and at ease with each other, or to develop an understanding in which so intimate a thing as a poem may be discussed sincerely and frankly. Eight weeks is just about time to begin to understand a student's trends in writing and his possibilities for development. So I suggest that the next writer in residence remain for at least a full quarter, or better still, an entire year. It would also seem desirable perhaps after eight or ten weeks to be able to work more intensively with students who show *definite* talent, and, if possible, to permit them to have a bit more time for individual consultation and creation. A school literary publication (or a page in the school newspaper devoted entirely to creative work) might be desirable, also, as an outlet for student work. Creative writing as a part of the regular English classes undoubtedly has its value. But a freedom beyond that possible in a class – freedom for ungraded and entirely individual expression would certainly be rewarding to some young writers. Therefore, just as there are special people in art on the staff, it might be desirable for the Lab School to have a permanent writer in residence.[31]

Hughes's recognition that too short a time was allotted to meet with students agrees with how many poet-teachers feel today. Yet Hughes stressed an aspect of writing that is not mentioned by a majority of poet-teachers now: He was intensely concerned with the need for revision. Present day insistence on the spontaneity of the act of writing, on the immediate product as being complete, would not have satisfied Hughes. "Those manuscripts which seemed to need revision (and most of them did) were returned to be polished up and brought back the following week. A number of them did not come back to me. One of the problems of guidance in creative writing is, I believe, to instill in the young the discipline of revision and the desire to stick with a good piece of work until it is *as good* as the writer can make it."[32]

Hughes also recognized the difficulties of giving children free rein as to subject matter. "The younger children," he reported, "seemed to me more spontaneously creative than the older children, and had to think less hard in order to get ideas for writing."

> Broad suggestions on the part of the teacher as to possible subjects for writing, I discovered as the weeks went along, seemed to help many children get started who had complained that "they couldn't think of anything to write about." However, those who showed most talent in writing seldom needed suggestions as to subject matter. Almost all the children brought in their "home-neighborhood, street-city" assignment. But, left on their own for voluntary choice of subject matter, many who came regularly to the groups brought no other finished piece of work during the remaining weeks.[33]

Present day methods also recognize the need for suggesting assignments, although the recognition that the talented do not need such assignments is germane to an understanding of the mythology of all children as poets.

Hughes also believed in rhyme and rhythm. At the kindergarten level his "half hours and moments of practice rhyming with the five-year-olds were most rewarding."[34] The sixth graders, Hughes reports, "wanted to work only on rhymes and poetry. We did practice rhymes in the group meetings, reading them aloud for criticism to detect and correct false rhymes and bad rhythms. At our last two sessions the whole group worked out a practice-verse play, 'Two Elves and a Pie'."[35] Dartha Cloudman Reid does not remember the emphasis on rhyme or rhythm, but she does remember the play to which Hughes refers. But this did not please her. "The individual help with expressing my own thoughts meant more to me." This play was the only collaborative effort of students fostered by Hughes, and it seems pertinent and important that he addressed the point of classroom environment.

> It was pointed out that seldom is serious writing done in groups or in a room full of people, and that, if the spirit moved them, poems should be put down quietly at home. Some did write at

home, and a few lovely little poems were brought to class as a result.[36]

In our present age when so many poet-teachers welcome and extol pandemonium and noise in the classroom and the practice of writing collaborative poems, it is important to contrast Hughes's feelings about these two matters.

However, Hughes did believe in allowing the children to see their work typed out. In May, sixty-seven manuscripts were given to him and were rexographed. "Seeing their work typed gives the writers a more objective eye for its defects. And if it could be printed, that finality would show how much better each might do next time."[37]

It might be added that in our age when children's work is not only typed up and reproduced, with publication viewed as an end rather than a means, Langston Hughes's feeling about work in print as a spur to seeing the defects stands as one of his most important contributions. Hughes called his students "young writers" but he knew the value of teaching them about rhythm, metrics, the use of repetition, the necessity of revision, and of using good models.

It was Henry Adams, while he was at Harvard, who said that if he could reach one student in a classroom of four hundred, he would be satisfied. The response to the presence of Langston Hughes at the University of Chicago, thirty-four years ago, as recalled by his students, attests to the dynamism of his personality. Whether or not his students remember everything with accuracy, they do remember the vibrancy and warmth of his personality.

"When he left to be about other business," Warren Seyfert recalls, "it didn't occur to any of us that what had been created under his stimulation and guidance was in the class of 'collectibles,' and he would have been the last one to make the claim, I'm sure. And in those years the Lab School staff wasn't much given to preaching about the efforts it was continuing to make to improve educational opportunities for youngsters, so nothing was made of this experiment with a writer-in-residence in the professional press. Alas!"

Seyfert recalls "that indeed we did have a great time, kids and faculty, working and living with an honest-to-goodness writer and learning from him, all of this thirty-five years ago."[38]

In addition to his work at the Lab School, through their courtesy and as time permitted, Hughes made himself available for other appearances in the University community and Chicago. In a letter written to Charlemae Rollins in 1967, Helen Rand Mills recalls the three memorable times she saw Langston Hughes.

> He came to visit my class at the Abraham Lincoln School. The students could hardly write at all but they had visions of themselves as writers. He made them feel that they were writers. One said, "But I can't spell." Langston Hughes said, "Neither can I" and he went on to say spelling wasn't the important thing about writing.

In addition to remembering an afternoon when she heard him reading his poetry, Mills tells of a correspondence he had with one of her students. "He wrote to her charming and encouraging letters that thrilled her and inspired her." Once I said to her, 'Do you know he doesn't know whether you are white or black.' For a moment she was surprised; she was white. Then she said, 'That's all right.' I said, 'I love you for saying that.' "[39]

It is unfortunate that even after a three year search, the rexographed work of the students is not available. But a list of the titles indicates that Hughes's directive, "to begin with something one knows well since even fantasy must spring from known facts," established the importance of observation, of attention to reality. Poems by students in sixth and seventh grade classes – "Tree," "Summer," "Watching the Clouds," "Morning Snows," "The Steeple," "The Old Piano," "Books," "My Sister," "Pal," "The Clock," "Macaw," "Morning Rush," and "My Neighbors" – far outweigh those that suggest preoccupation with the self – "Sadness" and "Something Should Be Done." Eighth grade students wrote of "Home," "Description of My Neighborhood," "A Window at Night," "Spring and the New Community House," and "Broadway"; "My Day" and "But It's Mine" suggest a more subjective approach. The writing of ninth and tenth graders shows a broader range of titles, but there is still the focus on observed life – "Youth Fights," "The Tale of a Barber Shop," and "Prayer for a New Car." While it is impossible to state what these writings contained, Hughes's belief that *facts should be used creatively* is in sharp contrast to the present-day tendency to elicit the intimist approach, to dig into the unconscious, to honor fantasy, dream, wishes, and feelings as a sole basis of poetry.

Alice Wirth Gray remembers, however, that Langston Hughes may have saved one poem of hers that "came floating back in part."

> It was about the courtyard of the apartment building I could see from my bedroom and I remember it had some lines about a woman with hennaed hair and it ended up with what I thought was the most cosmic metaphor ever about the moon resembling a street lamp. I seem to remember that Hughes took it seriously which was the way I was desperate to be taken, and that looking back on it what remains important to me is that it was my first recognition that city life and everyday dull existence was a subject for poetry not just by men but by me. It felt wonderful to be so worn and world-weary.

"We were all VERY SERIOUS about writing,"[40] she says.

The University of Chicago Laboratory School still has a set of pictures Hughes gave to the library, pictures of Arna Bontemps, Gwendolyn Brooks, Countee Cullen, James Weldon Johnson, Claude McKay, Richard Wright and himself. The class he taught in The Basis of Jazz eventually became a book he wrote for children, *The First Book of Rhythms*, published in 1954 by Franklin Watts. In it he speaks of the power of rhythms, the restful and the rapid, the effect of one rhythm on another. He writes of the source of rhythm, the beauty of upward rhythms and their models in nature, in architecture; the rhythms in nature from the planets to the seasons, the musical rhythms for work and play. To show rhythm in words he quotes nursery rhymes, William Blake, the Bible, Whitman, Lincoln's Gettysburg Address and two of his own couplets. He speaks of the mysteries of rhythm in nature, the rhythm of athletics, of machines, of motor and transportation vehicles as well as the rhythms of furniture or handcrafted stitching; rhythms in fashion. The book is a paean to rhythm and life about him as it shows its individual rhythms, and it is evident that the very rhythms of his life touched children many years ago in a way that will remain with them and their children for years to come.

What emerges from reading Langston Hughes's report of his activities in this early Poet-in-Residence experience and the reactions of his former students is, in the broadest sense, the knowledge that such an experience can enrich the lives of young people in both tangible and unknown ways. Those students who fell under his spell were changed; by other students, he has been long forgotten. Children studying under the direction of poet-teachers today may follow the same pattern.

But it would seem that, in the broad overview of methods and expectations, Hughes placed values on a literary history; a respect for tradition in addition to his own sociological emphasis; a love for a craft that is, nowadays, largely neglected; and an emphasis on the importance of good models. In his teaching there were no easy ways, no prescriptives, no immediate satisfaction with what is first written and blindly accepted as perfect. He did not praise the child as poet because he knew that poetry is the result of craft, of revision, and of respect for the tools of poetry; that its roots are in individual experience and *observation*. It would never have occurred to Hughes to laud himself, or to praise and view the products of his students as "collectibles." He knew that he was not creating a "new literary tradition" but fostering and nourishing an old one. He would never have said that every child is an instant or natural poet.

CHAPTER IX

The Poet as Teacher

What an abyss hath fruitless knowledge dug round the hapless youth! Tremble, presumptuous man! Thou who are about to conduct him through its dangerous paths, and to draw from before his eyes the sacred curtain of nature. Be first well assured of his capacity and your own, lest the intellects of one or the other, and perhaps both, be perverted in the attempt. Beware of the specious allurements of falsehood, and the intoxicating fumes of pride.

From *Emile*
Jean Jacques Rousseau[1]

Poetry written by children in the United States, published during this century, reflects not only the trends in education but the nature of creativity as well. The Romantic view of children as natural poets lends credence to the reality of the imagination and self-expression: This subjective viewpoint is countered by those who view creativity as the interaction of the self with that which lies outside the imagination – the external forces and the reality that discipline imagination and go beyond raw self-expression to produce a creative product that communicates, through universal symbolism, to others.

An objective view of poetry was present in the early decades of the century, at a time when the writing of children reflected the utilitarian mode of the times, with an emphasis on mental discipline and preparation for life. "Learn to live, and live to learn," the motto of the St. Nicholas League for Young Contributors, which began in 1899 as a regular feature of *St. Nicholas Magazine*, stressed poetry as a craft. In founding the League, Mary Mapes Dodge and Albert Bigelow Paine hoped to give to children from five to eighteen years of age a "creative adventure" which would "stimulate them to strive toward higher ideals both in thought and in living, to protect the oppressed, to grow in understanding of all forms of nature."[2] Contributors to the League, if their efforts merited approval, might receive honorable mention, a gold or silver badge, and if work was outstanding, a five-dollar cash prize. They also received membership and a button with the name of the League and the stars and stripes of the American flag.

But there were rules. All contributions had to be neatly written on one side of the paper, with originality endorsed by a teacher, parent, or guardian. And while each issue of *St. Nicholas* expressed "earnest gratitude"[3] or commended children for their "undiminished allegiance to democratic precepts,"[4] or praised the contributors for "an array of fine things,"[5] no child was ever called a poet or author. Boys and girls were constantly reminded that the "results they achieve afford ample proof that these League competitions form an excellent drill, for young folk, in the art of writing, which cannot fail to be of service to them in after life."[6]

Unbridled self-expression, however, was not to be tolerated. The poetry accepted for publication had to adhere to the standards of the time. As late as 1924 the editors repeated warnings they had often given before

> . . . there is one point which we wish to whisper a hint to a few of our poets of the high-school age, – a word of counsel or guidance which for some time we have had it in mind to offer, – namely: If your intention is to write a set of verses containing lines that rhyme, make sure that the final words of these lines really do rhyme. Be careful to avoid, for instance, such rhymes as "bloom" and "soon;" or "known" and "home;" or "stream" and "green;" or "nine" and "time." Even though these, or rhymes closely resembling them, may be found occasionally in the writings of famous poets, they are blemishes, and the poems in which they occur are held in honor not because of them, you may be sure, but in spite of them. Still worse are such false rhymes as "clothes" and "hose," "fields" and "wheels" and "leaves" and "waves." All these have appeared at intervals, in stray contributions to the LEAGUE; hence this caution.
>
> As this is the month heralded by "Good Resolutions Day," will not our young verse-writers make a note of the foregoing admonition and resolve that correct rhyming shall be one of their

standards, holding out the "Stop, look, and listen!" warning during 1924?[7]

However strange this guidance may seem today when most poet-teachers inveigh against rhyme itself, the message is clear. Romanticism must be tempered with self-discipline, that quality which Rousseau stressed as necessary to life: Unmitigated freedom in art would not serve those, the editors believed, who would go on to make contributions in later life. And the St. Nicholas League had an impressive list of contributors – Edna St. Vincent Millay, Corey Ford, Margaret Widdemer, Ring Lardner, Edmund Wilson, Elinor Wylie, Alan Seeger, Bennett Cerf, Sigmund Spaeth, and Morris Bishop among others. The editors did not hesitate to reject work which did not come up to standard or to offer criticism that might help to guide the young. The "excellent drill," they believed, would pay off.

Nowhere is there a better look at the verse-writing of children in the first few decades of this century than in the pages of St. Nicholas. It would be out of place today with its exact rhymes, strict meters, and special diction: Such writing as "a low mud hut 'neath the setting sun," or "The gold of sunset fading o'er the hills" falls strangely on contemporary ears. The League's insistence on standards of form as well as higher ideals made their mark; *to grow in understanding of all forms of nature* and to protect the oppressed carry a ring, not of self submerged in self, but of a sense of community and audience.

Discipline, then was seen as a form of personal development, a way in which the child should have to come to terms with the reality of his world. But the seeds were sown; a child could indeed, given the fine models with which Dodge insisted the pages of *St. Nicholas* be filled, proceed to imitate, and possibly, to succeed. The excellence of the St. Nicholas League has been acknowledged, by, among many others, E. B. White who wrote in *The New Yorker* of what it meant. *St. Nicholas* always stood for high standards in children's reading as well as in performance by the League contributors.

Yet a movement for greater spontaneity and freedom, with its emphasis on use of the creative imagination, was gaining strength among educators. In an excellent article, "Creative Expression in the English Curriculum: An Historical Perspective,"[8] Kenneth J. Kantor traces the influences of educators who sought to give children greater access to self-expression. The "progressive" movement is nowhere more evident than in the writings of Hughes Mearns, a writer and teacher at Lincoln School, associated with the Lincoln School of Teachers, Columbia University, and later as Chairman of the Department of Creative Education, New York University. His books, *Creative Youth* and *Creative Power* published in 1925 and 1929, set forth precepts that recognize the value of both subjectivism and objectivism as it is reflected in children's writing.

Mearns believes keenly in the potential of the child as poet; his Romanticism is evident when he writes that "children speak naturally in a form that we adults are accustomed to call poetry, and without any searching for appropriate use of the medium."

> This is because their minds are wholly intent upon something real within them; the language is instinctive and really of secondary consideration; they fashion it to the significant form exactly as other artists handle their medium, swiftly and without disturbing thoughts of standards outside themselves.[9]

Children, Mearns believes, trust their instinct and in this they are like the artist. "In their best moments they seem to know exactly what to do without fear." To Mearns the child "is a genuine primitive" and "It is fitting that our educational leaders should be rediscovering with joy and understanding the work of our own young 'natives'."[10] He enjoins the child to write, to pay no attention to spelling, punctuation. "Get that stuff out and down on paper while it is still hot!" he writes. "Scribble! Say everything, whether it belongs or not. Don't stop to think even . . . away with you and scribble!"[11]

Yet Mearns also recognizes that the scribbling must be further refined. He does not accept whatever the child puts down as poetry, although the very act of getting inner thoughts down is to be commended, and more importantly, he respects the privacy of the child's inner life and provides a "Poetry Drawer" into which students can put that writing which is not to be read aloud, shared with peers, or published. The drawer is itself a symbol of the respect of the child for a trusted adult, and the teacher's respect for the inner life of the child; and this can only occur in an atmosphere which has been carefully cultivated.

To Mearns, the environment for developing this mutual trust is crucial. The adults in a child's life, the parents, librarian, and classroom teacher, play an important role. It is the home which must strike a balance, and be willing to accept children's confidences without prying into or exploiting their inner lives. The teacher must carry on this delicate matter, but go even further by rejecting the imitative, by drawing out the natural voice and helping to give it form. Mearns believes that it is the teacher who must encourage the child.

> You have something to say. Perhaps you don't believe that. But, nevertheless, you do have something to say. Everybody has. It may be so deep inside of you that it is below consciousness. Waiting to be brought up. Perhaps you have had glimpses of it at times but have thought it worthless. On the contrary, it is one of your most valuable possessions. The world always pays a high price for it, because it is rare; so few persons are able to discover it within themselves, or, having discovered it, so few are able, or have the courage, to bring it boldly forth.[12]

Once the raw stuff is down, the teacher must guide the child beyond: He must not nag or scold, but show the right way, beyond imitation and copying, beyond the stale and pedestrian to the fresh. Mearns feels that because children are not product-oriented and tend to believe that what they write is never good enough, the teacher should not hold up standards of perfect work. Children do not consider themselves "poets" not should they.

> Children seem to be driven by an inner necessity of putting forth something; that it shall turn out to be beautiful is not their concern. Their impulse at its best is to place something in the outside world that is already (or almost ready) in their inside world of perceiving, thinking, feeling; they measure their success or failure by the final resemblance of the thing done to the thing imagined.[13]

To Mearns there are no magic pills, no formulas for creativity. What is imperative is an environment that not only allows freedom of expression but guides children away from an imitation of trite adult language, adult standards of "beauty." Mearns enjoins adults to remember that while praise is needed at times, children instantly recognize false adulation and welcome criticism as a way to learn.

Teachers must listen for what children have to say more than how they say it; they must make children believe they have something to say and not ask for a finished product but rather some evidence that the child is thinking and growing. "While scholarship may be the proper goal for some," he writes, "for others the way to wisdom and enlarged living may come through a broad cultivation of spiritual and creative powers."[14] The attention is never on the word but the "force that creates the word."[15]

Mearns notes how few teachers are able to distinguish between what is truly creative and what is merely imitation and copied. Yet it is "the pattern copiers," he asserts, who win approval in most educational systems, while "crude attempts at individual expression are passed by."[16] Creative education is as important as creative expression and is in the hands of the teacher and the school. Thus Mearns makes a plea for better school environments, for support of good models, for recognition of what is originality and what is mere imitation. He is both idealist and realist.

> To secure teachers who know the good from the bad will take time. We cannot adopt a national creative program and have success overnight. One should be aware of the slow nature of our undertaking and be cheerful about it, nor demand too much at the start. The first outcomes, in enlarged freedom are most worthy. Here and there we shall have a superior result. At first we shall credit it to gifted children or to social advantages or even to the I.Q., but eventually we shall find as a constant factor a teacher who understands some of the mysterious ways of the creative spirit, one, too, who appreciates and approves its crude and original manifestations.[17]

It is children, Mearns stresses, who can bring to light their creativity because they "have not been too much molded by the prevailing taste for the copied article," and in addition "they have a more ready access to the source of all creative activity, that inward world of unreality."[18] Mearns thus appreciates how children are able to deal with metaphor, yet he does not stress the fantastic or implausible. Writing is not raw self-expression but "guided self-expression," and the writings of the children that he teaches reflect a deep concern for meaningful symbolism as well as traditional form and rhyme.

Mearns, like Flora Arnstein who patterned her work after Mearns in the 1940's, believes in the natural abilities of children. Both emphasize that a "real knowledge of the good will always drive out a taste for the inferior"[19] and that there is in the "guarded secrecy of child thinking and child feeling, an amazing potential power which could some day remake a troubled and distracted world."[20] Both stress the need for an environment in which children can grow and in which a teacher is there to guide. But Arnstein, who worked in a progressive private school in San Francisco and who has written her own books, *Adventure Into Poetry* in 1951 (later reissued as *Children Write Poetry*) and *Poetry in the Elementary Classroom* (also reissued as *Poetry and the Child*), is inclined to be Romantic, a supporter of the mythology of the child as poet. Children, she believes, "take us for a moment into their world, a world we adults have lost, mostly beyond recall."[21] She believes that everything a child says or does has validity, and that the teacher must not impose standards. Children must be freed from criticism. The guidance she provides, therefore, is not so much to help the child write better but to give an "indirect moral guidance." All that the teacher can do directly is "to help the child gain access to his real self, to overcome the insecurity which makes him repudiate what he does, often before he has had a chance to try."[22] For this the teacher must provide a "relaxed, informal atmosphere."[23]

Children, she believes, are naturally creative but many forces conspire to restrict this creativity. Creativity can only function in an environment which eventually, through a familiarity with reading and sharing good poetry, results in learning that sensitivity of self comes from "security in relation to the group and the teacher."[24] A child's access to his creative soul is built upon this security.

> The importance to a child of parental backing cannot be overestimated. We teachers can do little where home conditions are adverse. Children's loyalties are so rooted, antedate our influence by so long, that even if we would want to, we could not pit ourselves against the home. Nor would we risk this. The child cannot build on a substratum of conflict. We must strive to bring him security, and more security, so that he may be free from distrust of self, from the need to effect reconciliations – free to create from his own center, from the core of his own being.[25]

Detriments to creativity occur when the child has an inadequate self-concept due to lack of opportunity or early discouragement, shyness, self-consciousness, ridicule, overpraise, ill-advised criticism, or standards set at too high a level. It is up to the teacher to be patient, understanding, sympathetic, and to wait "in an atmosphere of faith and trust in the powers of every child, no matter how meager the evidence of the presence of such powers."[26] The most favorable circumstances for good writing, she believes, grow out of discussion about some poem read – and "strangely, the weather."[27]

Whereas Arnstein's stance on the use of good models is admirable and her discussion of children's response to literature shows thought and insight, her conclusions as to the natural abilities of children remain somewhat simplistic and naive. She does not seem to realize that the background she gives her children in poetry through reading it aloud has anything to do with the children's writing. She asserts that children possess creative language, picturesque expression, poetic cadence, lyric tone, an innate sense of form; that they learn that rhyme can be superfluous or crippling; they recognize stilted diction and seem to know when a poem has gone wrong. Her effusion over the quite unremarkable writing of her children indicates that she views this work apart from a discussion of the guidelines which she herself has instigated and fostered.

Her insistence that she does not present poems as models sounds a discordant note when she asserts that children "naturally" show an affinity with simile, metaphor, repetition, refrain, onomatopoeia, and personification. In this writing, which she calls "Child Ways," she notes the recurrent patterns of needs for classification, use of rhyme, and other stereotyped forms which say more about her lack of knowledge in child psychology and child growth than anything else. She is adamant that "uncritical acceptance" and disregard of the spurious should be accorded any poem, regardless of its quality, yet she maintains that the teacher must always "try to entice the child back to his creative sources, commending especially the poems revealing true experience expressed in the language of genuine feeling."[28]

While Mearns would inveigh against imitation and actively guide the child beyond it, Arnstein's stance is that a child must find his own way out of the "muddied stream."[29] While Mearns would recognize the "inward world of unreality," Arnstein measures by "true experience." Yet both place equal importance on the idea that poetry writing is not easy for children, that "access to the inner self is not easily attained and difficult to sustain."[30] Almost everything in our environment, Arnstein asserts, "seems designed to remove us from the source of the creative power. The child is hard put to find a direct relation to himself and his own values."[31]

Current beliefs about children as poets would coincide with the latter view; indeed, the entire Poets-in-the-Schools program sprang up, another twenty years later, predicated on the belief that the educational institution robs children of their right to express themselves honestly in poetry. It is this belief as much as any one thing, which lies at the basis of the entire mythology of the child as poet. Yet this mythology has dramatically swept away the belief of Mearns and Arnstein that access to the inner self is difficult. Many adults today believe it is simple for a child to reveal his feelings, his wishes and dreams; and that given the right "method" and the correct "fill-ins" a child will become an instant poet.

The history of the Teachers & Writers Collaborative in New York has been so carefully documented by Phillip Lopate in *Journal of a Living Experiment* that to be aware of its beginnings, it triumphs, conflicts, and policies up to 1979, the book itself should be read. To understand the influence of the Teachers & Writers Collaborative during its first ten years is to note the degree to which its philosophy, methods, and ideas have been copied, emulated, and adopted by educators, teachers, and poet teachers nationwide. Its publications, cited throughout this book, as well as the beliefs and methods of its teachers, have proliferated widely. It is an organization which, Lopate notes, will probably never be rivaled because of its unique make-up and its federal, state, and corporate support.

The Collaborative's strengths, Lopate writes, "have been the freedom it accords artists to define their tasks as they see fit; its support of deep, long-term work; the fostering of a pedagogy built on close personal ties between children and adults; and the generous sharing of its experiences, both good and bad." It has, he states, "carved out a small niche for itself as an experimental 'laboratory'."[32]

This "laboratory" came into being as a result of four seminars and conferences held during 1965-66 at Tufts, Sarah Lawrence, Columbia, and the Huntting Writers and Teachers Conference. From the last emerged principles that centered around how writing and reading could be best freed from the fetters of standardized English curriculum, tests, and methods that had little relevance to the child's background, interest, or inner life. What emerged was a belief that it was the writers themselves – those who understand the power of language and fight against the trite – who could make language live for children and could ultimately effect changes in the educational system. According to Lopate:

> The forces which converged to create Teachers & Writers Collaborative (among many other similar groups) in the late sixties were various and sometimes so contradictory in outlook that perhaps we should wonder more that they meshed at all. It so happened that certain educational and aesthetic and political ideas that were in the air managed to coalesce into organizational form at a particularly ripe moment, when anger at the power structure, heightened social consciousness on the part of artists or writers and some extra government money floating around fortuitously came together.[33]

Among those who hoped to effect changes was Herbert Kohl whose experience in the classroom armed him with knowledge that the writers, untutored in the ways of children, did not possess. Author of *36 Children* and *Teaching the Unteachable*, his beliefs reflect those of Rousseau. "In the usual method of education," Rousseau wrote, "the master commands and thence imagines that he governs his pupil; whereas it is in fact the latter who governs him."[34] Kohl recognized that children struggle against the system, seek to preserve their liberty and devise their own ways of dealing with such an education. "Oppressed and galled by the yoke imposed on them, children try all means to shake it off," Rousseau writes, asserting that there are meaningful ways to engage the child in "making the best use of everything about him."[35]

> Let him observe in you the same struggles he experiences in himself; let him learn to overcome himself by your example . . .[36]

Kohl, like Rousseau, believes that the instincts of children are good and their sensibilities innate; that there is potential in children ignored by most educators and teachers; that this potential is at odds with an educational system that presents a "vision of life which does not correspond with what is real to the child, and does not help him make sense of his experience." A successful classroom, Kohl asserts, "has to be based upon a dialogue between students and teachers"[37] in freeflowing discussions, both planned and unplanned. Kohl also perceived that "one of the most valuable qualities a teacher can have is the ability to perceive and build upon the needs his pupils struggle to articulate through their every reaction."[38]

What also distinguishes Kohl is his recognition that for the writer to enter the classroom and work with children without an understanding of children, and to work without the partnership of the teacher, perpetuates an indictment of the teacher as responsible for the "false representations of life" which irrelevant materials and meaningless studies represent. This only tightens the yoke. Kohl's experience had taught him that not every child was capable of producing poetry, and that writing well can only occur if there is a firm basis on which to build – a *need* to communicate after communication is established between student and adult.

Kohl's hope for a Collaborative that would engage student, teacher, and writer in a three-way dialogue is reflected in his suggestion that writers keep diaries of both successes and failures and that these be circulated for a meaningful inquiry as to how both students and adults could best be served. It is fortunate that this plan was followed for it gives a picture of what actually happened in classrooms and how various poet-teachers worked.

Previous experience as a classroom teacher also enabled poet-writer Phillip Lopate to contribute to the Collaborative in important and meaningful ways. Lopate, who, according to Kohl, brought to a Romantic movement an "unromantic sensibility,"[39] recognized that children were capable of more than an instant product and he engaged them in learning the value of process. Through his guidance children developed a sense of discipline about their work. While Lopate viewed imagination as a valuable mode of the mind, he did not see it as autonomous. As a writer he understood the necessity for the struggle that results in a meaningful experience with the arts – and this he gave to children through writing, drama, and film. His concern was that the arts should be a vital part of the curriculum, touching every aspect of school and community life and affecting the individual even beyond formal schooling.

Since its inception, there has been a curious dichotomy within the

Collaborative of those who accepted the challenge to work on deeper levels and those who have subsisted by the quick prescriptive approach. Some poet-teachers have developed methods which have grown in scope; Richard Murphy's *Imaginary Worlds* is an example. Some poet-teachers have established a place in a particular school; Ron Padgett worked for over eight years in one school, thereby making a commitment to a particular group of children and parents. *The Voice of the Children*, compiled by June Jordan and Terri Bush, is a record of work done in a Saturday workshop, and Jordan's diaries attest to the commitment made. But there have also been those whose prescriptives and instant gimmicks nurtured the myth that whatever a child put down in a few minutes was poetry.

Yet the successes of the Teachers & Writers Collaborative are many; keeping poetry alive by bringing poets into the classroom introduces children to the joy of writing, to the importance of their own feelings and thoughts, and reaches children who otherwise might not be exposed in the public school atmosphere to the same advantages as those in the private schools where Mearns and Arnstein worked. Team teaching, as practiced by the Collaborative, has made it possible for children to be involved in an exchange of ideas with enthusiastic artists who convey the excitement of what they are doing. The Collaborative's publications have enabled all interested adults to keep abreast of a variety of ideas which have meaning beyond the New York City scene. A publication such as *Journal of a Living Experiment* is, in itself, a valuable history which records the contributions made to both poetry and education, as well as a document on which future ideas may be built. Many other publications offered by the Collaborative vary in quality, but the shift from the early *Whole Word Catalog* with its instant gimmicks may be contrasted to the more thoughtful consideration of writing as process which characterizes Alan Ziegler's *The Writing Workshop, How to Teach Creative Writing*.

As for the flaws in the Collaborative's program, many are past history. It is moot whether the original goal to let teachers become true partners in the poetry experience has actually happened. Lopate speaks of this in his *Journal:*

> From the teachers' standpoints, the writer seemed to come in, "do his thing," get the kids all excited if he did it well, bored

and sullen if he bungled it, and leave; there was little opportunity for communication about ways to improve the program or work it better into the classroom framework. One teacher accused a writer of merely collecting material for an article – of "ripping off" her students, in effect, to help his career. (Interestingly, there was some truth to this charge: an article did appear in a national magazine based on three visits to the class.)[40]

There has been little evidence in the Collaborative's newsletters of input from the teachers themselves; if they have been treated with less than a nod, it may well be because, as Lopate suggests, poet-teachers and classroom teachers "had professionally very different habits, career goals and modes of thinking. In addition, writers got paid to do the Collaborative's work, and the teachers did not."[41]

But it may also be that the constant criticism by poet-teachers of teachers and the educational system has been partly responsible. It is unfortunate that a number of poets who worked in the Collaborative chose not only to ignore Kohl's idea of working *with* the teacher but instead to revile the entire educational system. In many instances the poets were justifiably horrified at the meaningless gimmicks previously employed, and the inability of educators to understand the nature of true creativity. But the desire of some writers to overthrow the old order led them to enlist the support of students in criticizing the teachers and their methods, and even to usurping the teacher's place. An exercise in the *Whole Word Catalog* is envisioned by the editors as "a grand opportunity for students to satirize the kind of textbooks they often feel victimized by."[42] One poet-teacher writes derisively of a high school class "where the teacher was intoning Tennyson to a group universally sunk in torpor, virtual catatonia,"[43] an often-repeated condemnation by others wherein both traditional poetry and the teacher who adheres to tradition is ridiculed. Another writer records in his diary of how the school system is "completely in the hands of the know-nothings and the Yahoos."[44]

This attitude showed in many postures as the poet-teacher adopted the image of the "outrageous" or the "weird" artist who specialized in stage showmanship. Often poetic energy became equated with overly physical response that merited a "riot of desk thumping, foot stomping, laughing, squealing, saying hello, hand waving, and talking"[45] to herald the poet's arrival, and a subsequent high level of noise and physical activity among students as proof of the poet-teacher's success.

To others the Romanticism of the revolutionary approach signified total freedom of expression for both poet-teacher and child in their language and actions. Lopate speaks of the "phobic alienation" recorded in poet-teachers' diaries. "Consider," he writes, "the imagery behind popular educational titles of the day: *Teaching as a Subversive Activity* made creative pedagogy into a giddy adventure of infiltrating enemy lines, and altering the curriculum became a delicious sort of sabotage." The "horror and anger" with which writers first entered the schools is indeed, to Lopate, "a little false-naive" for certainly "to respond with such culture shock to what they must have known, on another level, was a norm – most probably, one they had experienced themselves as children . . ."[46] Nevertheless many writers like David Henderson express the view of others. He asserts that "I tried to be the exact opposite of what a teacher is to them."[47] Such an attitude in conjunction with the poet-teachers' constant disregard for poetic tradition – for the disdain with which they treat any trappings of the "old" poetries – is bound to work to the detriment of a goal which Kohl envisioned as paramount to revitalization in the classroom.

The same disdain for literary tradition coupled with lack of knowledge of children suggests other flaws. Lewis MacAdams's statement that

> Kids seem to have better imaginations when they are in the first grade than when they're in the tenth grade. That seems to be almost always true, at least in my experience with kids.[48]

is surprising in its naivete, lack of understanding about the nature of childhood, and the further revelation of how many poet-teachers have lost contact with their own childhood. The handling of such a subject as death, for example, can be done well as Ohio poet-teacher Robert McGovern believes. Using Richard Snyder's "A Small Elegy" with lower grade students, McGovern notes how eager children are to speak of those "they have known who have died."[49] But suggestions to have children imagine themselves dying or write suicide notes as assignments in the *Whole Word Catalog* seem an inappropriate way for children to come to terms with the experience of death.

Another possible area in which goals have gone astray relates to the presumption that "underprivileged," "bi-lingual," or "special group" children will, through contact with poet-teachers, be given a pride and self-confidence that they might not otherwise have known. Poet-teacher Julia Alvarez has answered this well:

> Too often in these bi-lingual programs or programs for "special groups," we tend to focus on what is underprivileged in the kids, what has been left out, what they do not have that they must get: we must bring them up to grade level; we must make them confident and dominant in one language; or, Ay Dios, we must make them proud of who they are. Such a philosophy assumes that they aren't already proud, or if they aren't, confirms that they need to be made proud. I am not minimizing the very real difficulties, gaps, insecurities these children have endured. But why always approach them at the sorest, bleakest place in their experience?[50]

Another area in which the Collaborative has been weak is a lack of understanding by some that all of the United States is not New York City; that there are children who do not respond to the bizarre, the crazy, the surrealistic; that the "autonomous imagination" is not everyone's view of poetry. Nor should it be. It might also be suggested along this line that those in the Collaborative who believe their prescriptives are "new ways to help children utilize their natural talents" and that this "hadn't happened yet in poetry" are speaking of *poetry* in their own terms, oblivious to the work of Mearns, Arnstein and others who preceded them.

Yet the Collaborative has survived in its sixteen years amid many growing pains and seems to be moving toward a re-definition of the poem, not as an instantaneous product, but rather as the expression of a process. The one-class visit has been extended so that both teachers and teams can form long-term relationships which benefit both student and classroom teacher. It is to be hoped that the Collaborative will continue to introduce "new curriculum ideas and new approaches to teaching writing and to arts education"[51] that will, like its original aims, involve poet-teachers *and teachers* as well as children, so that some of the original dreams, as proposed by Kohl, may find fruition.

The history of the Poets-in-the-Schools component of the National Endowment for the Arts runs roughly parallel, in time, to that of the Collaborative. Funded in 1965, two years before the Collaborative started, its first grant was made to the American Academy of Poets who made possible in the 1966-67 school year the work of Kenneth Koch in New York City. The success of a pilot program for visual artists in 1969 led to a further grant which began in the 1971-72 school year at which time four hundred poets were sent into over a thousand schools in forty-nine states. Figures for 1979-80 indicate that the number of poets by 1979 had reached 875. Among its many goals the Endowment's Literature Program

> sees it as a way of stimulating creative self-expression in children; of arousing interest in reading, grammar, and writing through the recognition by the students of their own creativity; of assisting teachers in their effort to find new ways to stimulate student interests in poetry and literature in general; of making contemporary writing a part of the regular curriculum in English; of assisting contemporary American poets through providing them with employment directly related to their craft; of demonstrating to educators that the creative artist can play a constructive role in the daily educational process; and, of helping children learn by creating within them the desire to learn.[52]

Whether or not these goals have been met is debatable. Lopate, who writes of the Endowment's work, notes that a lack of guidelines and "educational vision," its resistance to evaluation and analysis, and "its lack of professional seriousness in regards to a discipline in arts education and a lack of educational direction"[53] is evident, because while it asks for government funds for children's creative expression, it has never defined what it believes that expression to be; and while it points to the jobs it creates for poets, its policy of a constant turnover does not allow for any in-depth teaching nor adequate compensation. Elliot Eisner, an aesthetician at Stanford University, believes that this program "represents a tendency to seek image over reality, public relations over significant improvement, approbation over critical appraisal."[54]

What can be learned of those who work within it can only be gleaned by the various publications of state arts councils. Repeated requests for information, both by telephone and mail, over a period of six years to the office of the National Endowment for the Arts and to numerous Poets-in-the-Schools programs in many states, have been ignored. There is no accurate record kept of the number of poets employed nor the number of children served. There are few statistics available, and few publications which, like those of the Collaborative, give insight as to what has been accomplished. Occasionally articles in newspapers or magazines by a poet working in the program are headlined "The School Board Sucks" or "Diarrhea is a Dirty Word: An Account of Censorship in the Public Schools," establishing quite clearly the tenor of the poet toward the educational system. A poet in the Minneapolis Public Schools gleefully describes a teacher as "a pale, driven-looking young lady who looked like she'd last only for a few more weeks and then she'd give in to a delicious breakdown."[55] Another poet contrives to introduce herself and behave towards students as though she is "totally weird."[56]

Yet, as in all groups, there are those who take their work seriously. Poet-teacher Karen Swenson's statement concerning the committed poet who works in the Poets-in-the-Schools Program shows both idealism and pragmatism.

> When one walks into a classroom of grade school or high school students one would have to be mad to think that in a week one is going to turn them into poets. What I have to achieve in that time is to break down some of the barriers that our culture has built up around the idea of poetry as an awesome, incomprehensible, eggheaded art, to get them to play with words and ideas in an original way, to get them to want to write *their* words, not clichés, and to get them to write something totally different from their usual school assignments, something that is them, that belongs to them, not to the teacher or their parents.

None of this, she notes, is easy to accomplish because "most young people have a very large file of clichés stored in their heads by fourth grade. Most of them have learned that what anyone walking into a classroom wants from them, no matter what they say to the contrary, is something that sounds like what everyone else says, that no one wants them, their ideas, their emotions, their experiences."

> The average teacher, and I do not mean that one does not run into wonderful exceptions, reinforces very thoroughly all these

> ideas. They take the poems away from the children and never return them, thus proving that what you do in school does not belong to you but to adults. They incessantly praise the most turgid clichés and are always amazed that the silent, shy student who has done poorly all year is the one who, given a chance to speak in his or her own voice for once, outshines all the more studious others.

It is unfortunate, Swenson believes, that the Poets-in-the-Schools Program has a "tendency to talk as though every child's poem is a miraculous manifestation of genius, a tiger's egg . . ." because through its programs children can be led to interest in reading poetry and be capable of enjoying it, as well as show intelligence in their appreciation "rather than being quite so dependent on critics or not reading it at all." To Swenson this "seems to be the *honest* aim of these programs."[57]

Within the framework of the American educational system, the poetry writing of children reflects the changing trends in belief about creativity itself. Shifting from a concern for art as a form of social communication with utilitarian overtones in the first two decades of this century to a view which places greater value on the exploration of the inner life of the individual and undisciplined self-expression, the pendulum swings back and forth. Such is a view of poetry itself, for those who regard it as the unique vision of the individual are opposed to those who believe that poetry must communicate the vision to others. It is but another argument that exists concerning rationality, order, and discipline on the one hand, and on the other, imagination, instinct, intuition, and emotion.

Those who gave meaning to the Collaborative in its early days have gone on to other pursuits; those who have remained with state arts councils have done so because of a deep commitment to children and poetry. In some instances there has been growth, none so striking as that of John Oliver Simon in California who has moved from a belief in the quick assignment, the instant product, to establish instead a program with concern for process. In an era of waning funds and support for the arts, the work of all Poets-in-the-Schools must be reassessed, goals reevaluated, and some measure of rationality applied to the Romanticism which has contributed to the mythology of the child as poet.

CHAPTER X

A Basis for Models

The white man drew a small circle in the sand
and told the red man, "This is what the Indian
knows," and drawing a big circle around the
small one, "This is what the white man knows."
The Indian took the stick and swept an immense
ring around both circles: "This is where the
white man and the red man know nothing."

From *The People, Yes*
Carl Sandburg[1]

"Time of the Indian" is a magazine published under the auspices of COMPAS, the community arts program of the St. Paul-Ramsey Arts and Sciences Council which also supports the Minnesota Poets-in-the-Schools. In 1976, a retrospective issue of the magazine appeared. As an introduction, Thomas D. Peacock, Director of Indian Education in the Duluth Public Schools, points out how Indian children "are grasping for a spiritual and cultural rebirth . . . " To Indian children, he writes, "life is earth and there is little distinction between man and all those natural elements that make up earth: to children who have grown up without ready-made everything and had to invent their own they have acquired an imagination to capture the spirit of their culture. They must be inquisitive and air those feelings. This, you see, is what the magazine has offered to them, a very necessary outlet of human feeling. The children have the spirit of the old ones and for that I am most grateful."[2]

One of the contributions to "Time of the Indian" is by a Heart of the Earth School student:

A white man drew a small circle in the sand and said that's what the Indian knows, and drew a bigger circle around the small circle and said this is what the white man knows. The Indian swept an immense circle around the two circles and this is where the white man knows nothing.[3]

The striking similarity between Sandburg's lines from *The People, Yes* and the child's writing might well suggest that however the piece correctly ends, it was, at one time, told by the "old ones." Perhaps Sandburg heard it told by the Indians. Perhaps James L. White, the Poet-in-the-Schools teacher who has worked with children, shared a similar story with his students or introduced the Sandburg poem; perhaps the student read Sandburg and adapted it. So alike are the beginnings, and the use of the verb "swept," and the phrase "know nothing" that there would seem to be more here than the individual creativity of a child writing in the 1970's and an American poet publishing his work in 1936. The reader can only guess what happened.

In the *New York Times Magazine* of August 31, 1975 is an article by Phillip Lopate, "Getting at the Feelings." One of the featured poems by a girl is:

They Are Calling

They are calling Nan come at once
But I do not answer. It is not that I
don't hear I am very sharp of ear
But I am not Nan Go and wash. But I
don't go yet their voices are quite clear
I am humming but I hear But I am not
Nan I am poet They are calling Nan come
to dinner! And stop I stop humming I
seem to hear clearer now that dinner's
nearer Well just for now I am now and I say
Comming[4]

In 1970 Felice Holman, whose poetry for children has been published in several volumes, included among other work in *At the Top of My Voice*, published by Charles Scribner's Sons, the following:

They're Calling

They're calling, "Nan,
Come at once."
But I don't answer.

It's not that I don't hear,
I'm very sharp of ear,

But I'm not Nan,
I'm a dancer.

They're calling, "Nan,
Go and wash."
But I don't go yet.

Their voices are quite clear.
I'm humming but I hear,

But I'm not Nan,
I'm a poet.

They're calling, "Nan,
Come to dinner!"
And I stop humming.

I seem to hear them clearer,
Now that dinner's nearer.

Well, just for now I'm Nan,
And I say, "Coming."[5]

The student's version of the Holman poem was also published in *Spicy Meatball Number Five*, written and collated by the students of P.S. 75, Manhattan, with the help of the Teachers & Writers Collaborative Team: Teri Mack, Karen Hubert, Sue Willis, and Phillip Lopate. This publication of the school year 1973-74 was supported by a grant from the New York State Council on the Arts and the book itself received funds from a grant given by the National Endowment for the Arts.

Within the same issue another poem by the same girl appears:

When I stamp the ground thunders When
I shout the world rings When I sing
The air wonders oh how do I do such thing[6]

Here, again, the poet imitated is Holman whose poem is included in *At the Top of My Voice*:

When I stamp
The ground thunders,
When I shout
The world rings,
When I sing
The air wonders
How I do such things.[7]

In the May/June 1980 issue of *Stone Soup, the Magazine by Children*, a poem written by two nine-year-old boys is published:

White Season

In the winter the rabbits
Match their pelts to the earth
With ears laid back they go
Blown through the silver hollow
Through the silver thicket,
Like puffs of snow.[8]

Different only by virtue of alignment and punctuation, this is clearly "White Season" by another children's poet, Frances M. Frost.

Reflections, a National Student Poetry Magazine by Seventh and Eighth Graders, published in Duncan Falls, Ohio, included among the contributions to its second issue in 1982 a verse by an eight-year-old from Fremont, California.

First Snow

Snow makes a whiteness where it falls;
The bushes look like popcorn balls,
And places where I always play
Look like somewhere else today[9]

Bearing the same title, this is in fact a much-anthologized verse by Marie Louise Allen, differing only in the addition of the article "a" in the first line and in its punctuation.

Language Arts, a journal of the National Council of Teachers of English, published in its February, 1983 issue a work by a seventh grader:

Witch's Child

Tell me a story
Said the witch's child
About a beast
So fierce and wild,
About a ghost
That moans and groans,
About a skeleton
That rattles its bones.
About a monster
So crawly and creepy,
Something nice to make me sleepy.[10]

This is clearly with several word, article, and punctuation changes the work of Lilian Moore, a noted children's poet:

"Tell me a story,"
Says Witch's Child.

"About the Beast
So fierce and wild.

About a Ghost
That shrieks and groans.

A Skeleton
That rattles bones.

About a Monster
Crawly-creepy.

Something nice
To make me sleepy.[11]

Wombat, a Journal of Young People's Writing and Art, published in Athens, Georgia, included in its first issue in September/October, 1979, a poem by a child in an Athens, Georgia school:

Safety Pin

Closed, it sleeps
On its side
Quietly,
The silver
Image
Of some
Small fish!

Opened, it snaps
It's tail out
Like a thin
Shrimp, and looks
At the sharp
Point with a
Surprised eye.[12]

Again, with but two changes in punctuation, this is the work of another fine children's poet, Valerie Worth, found in her *More Small Poems*.

In *A Magic Place Is . . .* , an anthology of poetry by children of Santa Barbara County, California, one seventh grade girl writes:

There was a young lady named Bright,
Who traveled much faster than light.
She took off one day,
In a relative way,
And returned on the previous night.[13]

This is the anonymous limerick that properly reads:

There was a young lady named Bright
Who traveled much faster than light.
  She started one day
  In the usual way
And returned on the previous night.[14]

In the same publication another seventh grade girl writes:

My Rock

This is my rock
  And here I run,
To steal the secret
  Of the sun,
This is my rock
  This is the place
I meet the evening
  Face to face.[15]

This is certainly an imperfectly remembered version of David McCord's "This is My Rock" with a stanza missing.

This is my rock,
And here I run
To steal the secret of the sun;

This is my rock
And here come I
Before the night has swept the sky;

This is my rock
This is the place
I meet the evening face to face.[16]

In *Easy Thing for You to Say*, a statewide anthology of work by California Poets-in-the-Schools in 1980, a poet-teacher, Nan Hunt, broaches the subject of "Plagiarism and Appreciation"

> Early into our thirty sessions of poetry writing, I had delivered a caution about plagiarism. "Do not copy someone's writing and then pass it off as your own. This is called plagiarism. It is against the law – not honest." After some questions and discussion I assumed the message was clear.

Hunt relates how an assignment to a seventh and eighth grade class based on the theme, "If I Could Be Anything . . . " produced a rhymed poem from one boy which struck her, when she read it aloud to the group, as "too perfect." Confronting the child and asking if he wrote it himself, she received an affirmative answer.

> I hadn't been with the class long enough to know them well. A snake of ego-gratification slithered into my rationalization. Perhaps, just perhaps, I had facilitated such a burst of inspiration from this young talent. Still – that suspicion. I stopped at his desk later and quietly asked again. "Did you really . . . ? His dark eyes looked steadily into mine; he nodded.

Yet subsequent writing from the boy did not measure up to his first effort. The time came for the children to display their work in the school's creative arts fair. "When I saw the final product, I realized that . . . three students had substituted poems I had not seen and obviously not their own work." To add to her discomfort she had also, at the same time, learned from some teachers that the boy's work she suspected of being copied was a work widely used as a choral reading, written by a children's poet.

> Now, there had to be a reckoning. Passing off these pretties as their own had to stop. Luckily I had a few days to get over my anger. It was rather humiliating to know that parents, faculty, and most of the school as well as the County Board of Education saw the poems. No one noticed the falseness of those four except me. Mentally I hashed over several ways to confront the culprits. Further thought convinced me that this kind of stealing by youngsters involved more than duplicity and laziness. There were genuine elements of aesthetic appreciation. It could be the act of absorbing into themselves and claiming something they admired. At least they had recognized quality – except for Jad who leaned toward greeting card verse. If I were harsh in reprimanding them, I might quash a sincere budding interest in poetry . . .
>
> Instead of accusation, I decided on a positive approach. I met with the four plagiarists outside the classroom "This is very serious. It is all right to copy other people's writing if you admire it. I can understand how you could think that someone else said it for you just the way you would like to say it. But you *must* always sign the real author's names. I've been tempted myself to borrow a great line from another poet . . . "

While acknowledging that the poem the first boy had chosen to copy showed his "good taste" in the selection, Hunt explained to the group the necessity of giving credit when copying or receiving help from anyone.

> I went on to explain that if they could find a way to tell of their own true feelings it would be much more valuable to them and to me.
>
> This approach was fairly effective. All four students went on to write awkward but authentic expressions of their own . . . [17]

Nan Hunt's experience has probably been repeated hundreds of times. Her comment regarding duplicity and laziness is cogent, for there are children who wish to impress both teacher and fellow students with their ability and, by copying, make their mark. Her point about aesthetic appreciation is probably best of all, for it takes into account that absorption of phrases, words, or ideas that can become part of any human who reads poetry, and who seems to make it his or her own.

In the August 1978 issue of the magazine *Human Nature* Edward Hall, a teacher working in a classroom in Africa, makes a plea for the writing of good English. His own teaching methods are described, as well as examples of the work of his students. Among these is a poem which is a copy of "White" from *Hailstones and Halibut Bones* by Mary O'Neill. The editors of the magazine received a letter, after publication, from a woman who pointed out that Edward Hall "had best look to the honesty and integrity of student outputs in his own African classroom" and cited that the poem was a "direct steal." Perhaps Edward Hall feels, the reader wrote, "that it is useful and legitimate to plagiarize . . . in learning to write direct clear English . . . "[18]

Stealing and plagiarism are stern words! It is doubtful that Edward Hall realized that the poem was copied. Nor did poet-teachers, James L. White, Teri Mack, Karen Hubert, Sue Willis, or Phillip Lopate know the work of their students was derivative. Certainly the editors of *Stone Soup*, *Reflections*, *Language Arts*, *Wombat*, and *Human Nature* would not knowingly publish work that they knew to be copied or imitated. To do so serves no purpose for students, audience, or the publications. Nor need the children always be blamed. Occasionally there is a child who will knowingly plagiarize a piece of work and must be called to account. The examples given show that Nan Hunt's students did indeed copy, as did probably those children who submitted "White Season," "First Snow," "Witch's Child," and "Safety Pin." The imperfect ways in which one girl imitated the poems of Felice Holman suggest that the poems meant more to her than an act of plagiarism.

June Jordan, whose poetry for children and adults is most respected, compiled with Terri Bush an anthology of children's writing, *The Voice of the Children*. During the time she taught at the Church of the Open Door in Brooklyn she kept a diary. An entry on February 3, 1968 expresses her joy over two poems which she sent to the Collaborative. "I must insist," she writes, "that the first two pages, the first two poems of the attached writings by eleven and twelve year old children are, unequivocally, two of the most beautiful poems I have read, ever. I trust that the Collaborative will concur. Regardless, I count my reading of the first two poems among the happiest, most sobering events of my last year."[19] The second of these poems reads:

> Travel
>
> I would like to go
> Where the golden apples grow
>
> Where the sunshine reaches out
> Touching children miles about
>
> Where the rainbow is clear in the sky
> And passbyers stop as they pass by
>
> Where the red flamingos fly
> Diving for fish before their eyes
>
> And when all these places I shall see
> I will return back home to thee
> The end
> by Deborah Burkett[20]

Those who know Robert Louis Stevenson's *A Child's Garden of Verses* will recognize the similarities in the poem "Travel" which begins:

> I should like to rise and go
> Where the golden apples grow; –

Where below another sky
Parrot islands anchored lie,
And, watched by cockatoos and goats,
Lonely Crusoes building boats; –
Where in sunshine reaching out
Eastern cities, miles about, . . . [21]

Six of the lines in Deborah Burkett's poem are clearly derivative of the Stevenson poem. The title remains the same as well as three of the couplet rhymes. Jordan had brought a large number of children's books to her class – picture books, the poems of William Blake, Robert Louis Stevenson, and others. Her report to the head of the Teachers & Writers Collaborative met with resistance; the child, Jordan was told, was not being *true to herself, to her black world.* She was imitating a white man. This was clearly to be discouraged as it was a "route away from the true." To Jordan the child had internalized the poem to make her own statement.

Jordan answered the letter to the head of the Teachers & Writers Collaborative.

> Deborah's poem, as you acknowledge, differs from Stevenson's. You say hers is superior. I say hers is her own poem. I submit that Deborah's not only equals the arresting force of loveliness of Stevenson's, it makes a very different statement – as any proper reading and comparison of both poems would reveal.
>
> Contrary to your suggestion, Stevenson was not "foisted" on Deborah. In my opinion, Deborah is clearly a writer. And she has presumed, she has dared to do what other clearly gifted children do: they learn a kind of creative mimicry. They consume and they incorporate, they experiment and they master.

"No great poet," Jordan writes later in her letter, "has emerged without knowledge and mimicry of precedent."[22]

Whether or not Burkett's poem is thought to be "superior" or "different," it is important to recognize that models may be used to spur further thoughts and feelings – to internalize, in Jordan's words, personal responses.

What Jordan calls Deborah's "creative mimicry" is the apprehension, rather than comprehension, of Stevenson's idea – a practice of poets who often pay tribute to the original poet by the use of the word "After" in the title. This can be seen even more clearly in the writing of a fifth grade girl whose work appears in an issue of *Wombat*:

> Summer Day
> (As influenced by
> Edna St. Vincent Millay's
> "Afternoon on a Hill")
>
> I will be glad
> Under the sun
> I will touch flowers
> And not pick one
>
> I will watch the wind
> Blow the grass
> On the town. And
> Then start home.[23]

The superlatives in the original poem, "the gladdest thing," "a hundred flowers," the "quiet eyes" that look at cliffs and clouds, the wind that bows down the grass and grass rising, the marking of the lights, are not within the interest of a fifth grade girl. She has, in short, simply marked as important the idea that she can be glad in the summer, make a short journey and then return "home," which says more than starting "down." Again, the apprehension of what the poem means is important to a child; the comprehension of detail is not.

This can also be seen in a poem by a seventh grade boy which appeared in the March/April/May issue of *Wombat*.

> Some days my thoughts
> are like cocoons – all
> grey and dull and dry.
>
> And other days they
> are such Free and Flying
> things.[24]

This version differs greatly from the original and much anthologized work of Karle Wilson Baker:

Days

Some days my thoughts are just cocoons – all
  cold, and dull and blind.
They hang from dripping branches in the grey
  woods of my mind;
And other days they drift and shine – such free
  and flying things!
I find the gold-dust in my hair, left by their
  brushing wings.[25]

It is impossible to know if the boy's version is imperfectly remembered, or whether it has been adapted in what Jordan would call "creative mimicry." To the child, in either case, cocoons are not cold and dull and blind, but grey, dull, and dry – as *he* knows them to be! He has eliminated the elaborate (and indeed far-fetched) metaphoric stance of the mind's "grey woods" and chosen the appealing idea of thoughts as "free and flying." Again, he has wisely discarded Baker's fuzzy statement that thoughts, within the mind, could leave gold-dust in the hair!

The work of Deborah Burkett and the other two children offers important clues to what children find in their models when they are, in Jordan's words, internalizing or involved in "creative mimicry." Ideas may be employed that relate to them as individuals; the wish to travel, to see flowers on a summer day and return home, to describe thoughts. The details they seize are those which hold appeal – golden apples, sunshine, red flamingos, flowers, grass, and cocoon, but which are presented as they relate to their own understanding. Thus, abstract concepts and imagery which are not within their interest or comprehension are discarded. Stevenson's travel is not that of Deborah Burkett, yet his poem has fired her with longing. The girl does not look at "cliffs and clouds/with quiet eyes" nor is she interested in the number of flowers; she does not see the town as her point of return, but rather her own "home." The boy similarly discards the idea of a cold and "blind" cocoon, the "dripping branches," and the gold-dust.

Children's imitations, copyings, and borrowings are found at all levels of the writing process; from a line to an entire piece of writing. They may appear on a scribbled piece of paper, a class bulletin board, a school or district collection of work by students, submissions to contests, or in magazines. Whether such work is plagiarism, the *conscious* act of copying, or borrowing *unconsciously*, the motive for such use gives concern. Alan Ziegler, in his book *The Writing Workshop*, believes that plagiarism occurs among those who "are unable to support their creative selves." Copying may be due to a need to please the teacher, to measure up to what is expected, by a student who may not be able to write something new. Ziegler believes that students "should not feel pressured to produce new work constantly" and suggests that they be given "an awareness that writing ideas often don't come right away during any given session . . ." It is often "desperation that breeds plagiarism."[26]

Yet while adult writers know that writing cannot be hurried, most children do not have this option. Time allotted for creative writing suggests productivity based on several circumstances. Poet-teachers, whose living may depend on an accounting of work engendered from their students, must answer to the program that supports them. A teacher, who must justify time away from language arts and basics, must give evidence to the principal, school board, and parents that children are not wasting time with frills. The pressure is therefore placed on the children as well: If they wish to be part of a classroom display, to be represented in whatever publications are produced, to earn the respect of teachers and peers, to be the lauded young authors or poets, they must produce a poem. Often they are driven to copying or imitating.

Going beyond plagiarism, however, are the children whose "creative mimicry" is the beginning of a process which leads to real creativity. But this creativity can seldom exist if the models are not present; those models which speak to children in terms of their emotions and interests, which engage and lead them on to test, as Holbrook would put it, "their natural exploring energy."

There is a general agreement among educators, poet-teachers, and classroom teachers that children should have models for their work, although most would agree with Richard Lewis that children are apt to lose interest when a teacher "gets up in front of a class and tries to ignite her pupils with her idea of what the poem means, or is trying to say, or how it is made, or why the poet created it."[27] Yet those who work with the writing of poetry know that this approach is often a prerequisite for good writing and while it may run the risk of turning the average student away from poetry appreciation, it is a meaningful and necessary adjunct to firing up children who are writing. Poet-teachers and classroom teachers spend much time discussing model poems by which they hope to impart some idea of inner reality, of image, or to emphasize a poetic tool.

Explication by poets differs, however, from that of teachers in a variety of ways, most important of which is their enthusiasm for and familiarity with poetry. While this would seem to be meaningful, it introduces other problems in regard to what has been, prior to the advent of poets-in-the-schools, a traditional point of view about models.

The belief that only the best is good enough for children when it comes to literature is a long-held opinion of many educators and teachers. Claudia Lewis, both poet and educator, stresses the "strategic importance"[28] of books and exposure "to a wide variety of poems read aloud."[29] This is "crucial if children are to have a broad knowledge of the ways in which words can be put to work and made to act powerfully on the mind and emotions."[30] Such poetry for children must be "old and new, free and structured, read aloud by their teachers, by themselves, and by poets on records . . . e. e. cummings, Yeats, Robert Frost and others."[31] The use of all kinds of poetry, "opening lines from the beginnings of 'The Dry Salvages,' T. S. Eliot's third poem in *Four Quartets*, the image of the river as a 'strong brown god' is certainly one that many nine year olds can appreciate."[32] In the poetry of Dylan Thomas, the exposure to a new voice, to the knowledge that an artist can make language spring up into new sounds and forms, "as well as the teacher's enthusiasm" is, in Lewis's terms, more important than the "writing attempts that followed."[33]

> Teachers know that for better or for worse, it is the exposure in childhood to styles, textures, and qualities in language that will leave its mark, as the writer – young or old – tries to discover in what ways he himself can make words work. And it is partly for this reason that teachers read aloud to children all through the elementary grades, knowing that in this way they can open up a great deal that might otherwise remain unavailable. In fact, this is one of the great challenges of teaching – to locate those varied stories, styles, ideas, and voices that are appropriate to bring to a given group of children.[34]

Helen Hill, a children's literature specialist and anthologist, in an article in *The Horn Book*, "How to Tell a Sheep from a Goat – and Why It Matters," points out that in poetry for children both subject and technique must be excellent. To choose work only because a child can relate to it is a false premise. Too many anthologists, she feels, "seem to assume that the child, with an uneducated ear and mind, won't notice inadequacies in concept or language; that it is all right to force rhymes, to pad lines, to use images that are merely cute, and to let the poem run down at the end like an old Victrola record." To offer children poems because they are easy to read, because they engender laughter, because children will sit still while listening is to emphasize the wrong thing. Such criteria exclude the serious poems which many believe "must be too difficult and uninteresting."

> I would like to argue, along with Frost and de la Mare, that even an uneducated child deserves the best and that no poem is good enough for children that is not good enough for adults. Nor should any poem be acceptable to adults if it does not have integrity. By integrity I mean wholeness or soundness of thought, perfection of technique, and sincerity of tone.[35]

While Hill is speaking of choices for sharing, her sentiments are echoed by others who apply these same criteria to models. "Young poets certainly need masters, and mistresses, to whom they can become apprentices," Margaret Meek asserts. "They need models and the grasp of conscious striving after the thing to be made . . ."[36]

Hughes Mearns's view of the need for models is both ideal and pragmatic. Books should be at hand, he writes, "at the moment they are needed. Without a large library and a gifted librarian" his work with children and creative writing "would have brought no worthy results." Yet many teachers today, and certainly poet-teachers, tend to become their own "gifted librarians" both by necessity and choice. Mearns, who believes that children's taste grows through the stages of "saturation and surfeit" and moves from a liking for inferior material to a high literary standard, proposes that teachers

> Never be dogmatic and never be superior. To sneer at taste is caddish at its best; and certainly it is futile. Taste is taste and should be respected at whatever level found.[37]

Whereas most teachers who must be pragmatic are apt to adopt this viewpoint, poet-teachers today are, for the most part, inclined toward an opposite stance, venting their beliefs about *correct* and *incorrect* models. In an age when the home no longer provides, for many children, an opportunity to hear poetry, that which is chosen by teachers and poet-teachers in the schools becomes more important.

There is heated debate concerning taste and models. There are those who decry the use of poetry written *by* children as models; those who believe in the use of traditional poetry and those who sneer at it; there are individuals who use only their own poetry as models, or the work of a particular school to which they belong. There are those who shun, in Holbrook's words, "false modernity" and those who espouse it wholly. These groups represent the various camps into which poetry itself has been divided. At the center are the children as well as many classroom teachers and educators who struggle to sort out what creativity and the writing of poetry means.

Because of the gulf that separates those who believe in the use of children's work as models and those who don't, all of these attitudes and beliefs bear investigation. Given the syncretism of the child's writing, its purely subjective synthesis, its personal imagery as opposed to the synthesis and symbolism common to great works of literature, a crucial question is raised: can there be standards applicable both to the mature poet and to the child?

"It is important," asserts John Warren Stewig, author of *Read to Write*, "that children read what other children – not just adult authors – have written." Stewig, who has served as president of the National Council of Teachers of English, adopts this belief because it "establishes the understanding that writing is a legitimate activity for children and that reading what other children have written can be interesting and informative." Teachers, in addition to using published collections, "should make concerted efforts to get samples of children's writing from other teachers." The purpose is "to help children see that reading and writing are closely linked."[38]

Stewig's stance is that of the educator whose goal is to keep children writing; who suggests discreetly that peer pressure may play an important part in the process. Using children's writing as models is clearly a way in which children may be led to believe that writing is not an isolated activity; the model is the *means* and *process*. To many poet-teachers and adults, however, the children's work becomes the *end* and the *product*.

In *Wishes, Lies and Dreams* Kenneth Koch writes that a part of his presentation was "reading other children's poems aloud"[39] because of the "good effects." Koch comes to this view because of his feeling that

> . . . the obviously difficult modern poets I read to them – Dylan Thomas, Theodore Roethke, John Ashbery. But adult poetry – even that of Whitman and other apparently easy writers – was too distant from the way they thought, felt, and spoke to touch them in so immediate a way that they wanted to write similar poems of their own. A hasty look at and a long memory of poetry for children by adults showed me that it was not what I wanted either. It was too often condescending and cute and almost always lacked that clear note of contemporaniety and relevance both in subject matter and in tone, which makes the work of a writer's contemporaries so inspiring to him.[40]

"The best poems I found to read, finally, were those that the children at P.S. 61 were writing,"[41] Koch says, and many who espouse his methods echo his sentiments. Children, say Gensler and Nyhart, should be their own models "because the concerns and feelings of peers tend to be highly contagious. Reading poems by other children moves children to write their own."[42]

"Often," writes a poet-teacher, Andrea Nold, "I read aloud from other poets. I consciously steered away from many of the conventional children's poems that rely heavily on rhyme. I wanted to help them think in different directions. They enjoyed Frost and Sandburg and the music of Dylan Thomas but the poetry of other children always made the biggest hit. 'Gee, that's really good!' And we would pause and look at what made it good. Slowly the children developed a sense of critical judgment, dependent not merely upon my word but upon their own emerging sense of what constituted effective writing."[43]

Bill Zavatsky, one of the compilers of *Whole Word Catalogue 2*, also feels that among his most cherished notions is that the "poetry best suited for children is poetry written by children."

> "Children's verse" of adult manufacture is usually the worst junk, cutsey-wootsy beyond any decent poet's sitting still. I include the

> famous Dr. Seuss in this category. I have observed a neighbor's daughter learning, from the pages of *The Cat in the Hat*, that poetry is *always* rhymed, is *always* goofy, and never has anything at all to do with real life. Why should she believe me when, in five years, I walk into her classroom, the visiting Poet, and tell her just the opposite? Parents want to be entertained too. Why bother to summon the strength and seriousness necessary to read poems from *There Are Two Lives* to a child, when Dr. Seuss is so much fun? "Children's verse" exists for the edification and entertainment of parents. But the whacky situations and the rhymes and pounding meters reverberate in the growing child long after they have served their purpose. They leave the impression that Poetry is a Never-Never Land where real thinking and human feeling are banished.[44]

To Zavatsky *There Are Two Lives: Poems by Children of Japan*, edited by Richard Lewis and translated by Haruna Kimura, is "one of the finest collections of poetry produced by anyone, anytime, ever. Most importantly, it is completely written by children, and sensitively translated."[45]

Alan Ziegler, the other compiler of the *Whole Word Catalogue 2* and an active poet-teacher, shares Zavatsky's thoughts. Under the auspices of Teachers & Writers Collaborative, his student, Gerry Pearlberg, had her own book published.

> Teachers & Writers published a book of her poems *Night Quiver*, at the end of the school year; Gerry participated in all stages of the book including a visit to the typesetter. I sent the book to a well-known poet, who responded: "My goodness, a book at 14; . . . I hope she's a strong girl as well as being talented. At 14 she's got a long way to go, and most of the journey she's got to be able to make herself." I thought about this – what had I gotten her into? Whatever it was, Gerry seemed to be the better for it, and so were the increasing number of people who were enjoying her poems. It is true that part of the "journey" she will have to make herself, but there will always be teachers, friends, other poets, and – perhaps someday – students, who will travel with her. And in moments of solitude there will be language.[46]

Ziegler used Gerry's poems with many other students. She wrote, he says, "magical poems, each a unique world inhabited with such characters as porcelain monkeys; satin sheets; a hugh, hollow black egg that when killed gives birth to millions of tiny vengeful eggs; a dust speck that contains an engraved picture of the poet as an embryo. Gerry created unnatural environments, yet the actions within them reflected internal logic; her poems were comprehensively strange. They were bright with imagery ("false teeth rest/on a chair/grinning like a/piece of death") and most of the poems had metaphorical implications."[47]

Ziegler does not state which of Gerry's poems he used as models but a few he does quote in his article about her include:

Breaking the Law

I love to break the law,
it shatters in slow motion
and bounces,
then lies still.

Stapling My Face

India ink babies crawling on my linen.
roaches disfiguring apples, smoke making my
    eyes sweat, lashes fall out.
not noticing beggars clad in chinese silks, nor
    the windmill drowning in the tide.
passing the buck, paper dolls running the
    casinos of vegas.
dogs barking. city. city. valentine dates and
    purple hearts. tell that to the G.I.'s.[48]

Susan Mernit, another poet-teacher with Teachers & Writers Collaborative, offers as a model for a sixth grade class a poem written by a tenth grade student:

Poem

I ask her if I can go away
She says no.

I ask her why.
She never answers me.
My brother asks if he can go.
She says yes.
I get mad.
She hollers at me.
I tell her it's just not fair.
She tells me to shut up.
I tell her I'm leaving.
She says go ahead.
It's just not fair.
He gets to do everything he wants,
She never lets me do it.
He smokes pot,
He drinks beer.
She never says a word.
It makes me so mad.
One of these days
She will be sorry.
I will go away
and never come home.[49]

Student writing is used as models in many publications distributed and sold in schools. *Imagine and Write*, issued by My Weekly Reader Books, is one of many that offer inept, jejune haiku as examples for children to emulate. In *Helping Children Become Writers*, Jacque Wuertenberg uses the work of "Young Authors" to illustrate language patterns, as well as suggesting that children can write "best-sellers" and blurbs for themselves as authors. In his book, *Teaching Poetry to Children*, David Greenberg advises teachers to "Always stress that the examples you're presenting were written by students of the same age (perhaps it's an expedient prevarication)."[50]

Do these models offer anything to other children? There may be value in demonstrating to students that the process of writing is being attempted by other young people – but to equate prose arranged as free verse, fragmented, surrealistic images, banal phrases, erratic rhyme patterns, and stilted diction with poetry is but another bow to mediocrity in literature.

In *The Whole Word Catalog* the editors offer a section on "Literary Models," which advises:

> Children especially like their own literature. They like to read the work of their classmates; they like to hear and read stories and poems by other children. They enjoy discussing their own literature and writing for an appreciative audience of their peers.[51]

In its appended bibliography, the books cited are *only* those anthologies made up of children's writing. One of the editors, Marvin Hoffman, a former director of Teachers & Writers Collaborative who with several others organized a resource center for teachers at Fairley Elementary School in Vermont, explains in the *Catalog:*

> For some time, we have been trying to convince publishers that students enjoy reading the work of other students. They often find it more engaging than the machine-turned prose and poetry of adult writers who "specialize" in writing for children. Now the number of anthologies of children's (and young people's) writing has skyrocketed in the past few years, to the point where it's virtually impossible to keep track of all of them. So please forgive the omissions.
>
> Yet, many of the books are not what we bargained for. Rather than serving as vehicles through which young people can talk to each other, they are coffee-table books for adults who are interested in finding out what kids are thinking about these days and whether they're as cute as they used to be on Art Linkletter's show.[52]

Hoffman's list includes eight anthologies, all collections of writing by children.

This intended emphasis on using children's work as models, in conjunction with castigating adult writers for their "machine-turned" specialized writing for children, is sobering, for it almost insists that *children can have no better models* than the work of other children. It is also the opinion of the editors of *Stone Soup*, who laud the making of books by children. Once they are made, the editors declare, "they can be used as the reading books for reading units. They can also be placed in the classroom library and treated as equals to the adults' books." Such use "will help 'blurr' some of the distinctions between children's books and adults' books. This blurring is important because it provides children with the feeling that they are real writers and artists . . ."[53]

Kenneth Koch's statements in *Rose, Where Did You Get That Red? Teaching Great Poetry to Children* are even stronger. His hope to introduce children to the great poetry of present and past, to give them new ideas for their own poems and present them with adult poetry to enjoy for life, "seemed unlikely to be produced by the poetry children were being taught in school. The poems my students wrote were better than most of those in elementary school textbooks. Their poems were serious, deep, honest, lyrical, and formally inventive. Those in textbooks seemed comparatively empty and safe."[54]

Koch maintains that the textbook poems were not connected to "any serious emotion or to any complex way of looking at things. Everything was reassuring and simplified, and also rather limited and dull. And there was frequently a lot of rhyme, as much as possible, as though the children had to be entertained by its chiming at every moment."[55] as well as "condescension towards children's minds and activities in regard to poetry in almost every elementary text I've seen."[56]

The particular text series which Koch cites does indeed, upon examination, reveal a use of *some* poor verse. But the series also uses the work of Carl Sandburg, Langston Hughes, Gwendolyn Brooks, James Stephens, Vachel Lindsay, and other fine poets. To say that children's poets such as David McCord, John Ciardi, Harry Behn, and others are "reassuring and simplified" and do not deal in serious emotion, show condescension, use rhyme, and that his children wrote better poems than these poets is indeed astonishing!

"One aspect of childlikeness which is particularly likely to work against children's loving poetry and taking it seriously," Koch writes, "is a cloyingly sweet and trouble-free view of life. Even Blake's "The Lamb" alone or in context with other sweet poems, could be taken that way. It is constant sweetness that is probably the main thing that makes boys, by the time they are in fifth and sixth grade, dislike poetry as something sissified and silly."[57]

While some selections within the text Koch cited are typical of poor versifiers, most are no more cloying that examples Koch gives of his own students' writing. Koch's children see daises, rose petals, the woods, the bottom of the sea, the edge of a river, "pink bananas," color TV. What could be sweeter, more of a cliché, and devoid of serious emotion than a fifth grader, writing in imitation of Shakespeare:

Will you come with me in the woods and hear the
birds chirp, the bees, buzz, buzz, and the rabbit
going hopity, hop, hop.[58]

Indeed, the poem from which Koch took his title hardly seems to be "serious, deep, honest, lyrical, and formally inventive."

Dog, where did you get that bark?
Dragon, where did you get that flame?
Kitten, where did you get that meow?
Rose, where did you get that red?
Bird, where did you get those wings?[59]

To say that it is the "constant sweetness" that turns boys away from poetry may indicate that Koch does not fully understand a number of things about teaching poetry in elementary schools. The imitating, copying, and creative mimicry, as well as the outright borrowing by children, attests to the fact that children do indeed enjoy poetry written *for* them, because it is not condescending; it does take into account their emotional needs, and children – contrary to statements and dictums of many poet-teachers – *do* enjoy rhyme.

Zavatsky, Hoffman, Ziegler, Koch, and many others seem in agreement that not only is poetry written for children poor, but it is of no value. "Try to stay away from poetry collections 'for children' AND READ ADULT POEMS TO YOUR STUDENTS" is part of a directive issued in 1978 to teachers in an elementary classroom by Natalie Robins, a visiting poet in the New York State Poets-in-the-Schools Program. While Robins does not recommend using children's writing as models, the choice of her poets, from W. S. Merwin to Anne Sexton to her own poetry, is moot. She asks teachers "to browse in libraries and bookstores for little (and literary) magazines and individual poetry collections . . . to use younger less established poets"[60] in the classroom. It is particularly interesting that the majority of those who believe that children write as well if not better than adults, that poetry written by adults for children is without merit, have *little or no background* in poetry written for children. It is the rare poet-teacher – June Jordan and a handful of others – who recognizes the wealth of poetry that speaks to children from Robert Louis Stevenson to the present. It is one thing to castigate poor verse, but quite another *to be ignorant* of the broad spectrum of poetry to which children respond, and to state that the best models are the work of the children themselves.

This belief raises some deep questions as to the value of art itself, the traditions of the past, the gulf between what children write and what adult models they are given, if any. It would suggest that many adults take very seriously their conviction that children *are* poets, that what they create and write, in a matter of minutes, is true art, instead of words and ideas that serve to *begin* the process of creativity. This belief also suggests, in Nold's terms, that children's writing *can be explicated to the same degree* as that of the established poet, and in the view of the editors of *The Whole Word Catalog*, that children's writing is, indeed, *literature.*

The clearest answers to these questions of the value of art, tradition, and adult models, however, come from the children who, in their imitations and borrowings, demonstrate that they are seeking *more* than the writing of peers. They take from excellent models what they need, whether it is a conscious style imitation of Shakespeare (directed by a poet-teacher) or the emotional or conceptual ideas written by an adult who remembers what it is like to look, see, and feel as a child – a Stevenson, a Worth, a Holman; their internalization of a piece of poetry *apprehended* rather than *comprehended* attests to this creative mimicry.

Fortunately not all teachers or poet-teachers or editors subscribe to the belief that children's work is the best model, nor that poetry written for children is anathema. There are other beliefs about the need for models that go beyond the limited syncretic instant writing of children themselves; models that are offered by those who speak with more knowledge, assurance, and understanding of children.

CHAPTER XI

Further Models and Related Matters

They sought it with thimbles, they sought it with care;
  They pursued it with forks and hope;
They threatened its life with a railway-share;
  They charmed it with smiles and soap.

From *The Hunting of the Snark*
Lewis Carroll[1]

While many teachers and poet-teachers regard models as a spur to the writing of poetry, David Holbrook is concerned with models in a dual role. Creativity, in his view, is the only basis of an approach to the teaching of English as an art; it is a "natural function" in children and must therefore "develop naturally whenever possible."[2] Believing that literacy in its "deepest and widest sense" is "the capacity to use words to deal with inner and outer experience," he places emphasis on fostering the child's "adequate capacity to be on good terms with oneself, and to find inward order, by means which *include* words."[3]

It is imperative, he believes, that teachers be aware of the symbolism of the child's writing. The creative arts are "one major source of insight into our inward problems" and nowhere do individuals express their inward thoughts more than in poetry. "Poetic exploration," he states, therefore "should be at the center of English teaching."[4] It is in literature that the child can find a confirmation of the struggles of the inner life. Holbrook begins with the writing of children as evidence of these inner struggles. "Examples to prompt creative work should, I am sure," he says, "preferably be creatively symbolic in themselves – that is, pieces of music, poems, paintings, stories, rather than real objects or accounts of real events." To Holbrook, photographs, newspaper accounts, or actual objects do not contain the "unconscious content and symbolic quality" that are necessary for "involved creativity."[5] He would, therefore, prefer "good examples of children's own writing which often prompts the best kind of imitation, because of its unconscious or involved content" and "imaginary family situations," a subject with potential for elaboration. Children, he observes, have a "natural desire to thrill, entertain, and share feelings," and to this end duplication, oral reading, drama, taping, publishing, and displaying are all worthy outlets. All of the children's effort, he says, is praiseworthy "for in creativity we all identify with our 'inner contents' and to be cribbed (as by reviewers) gives us a good deal of pain."[6]

Creativity, Holbrook believes, is to be found in all children, yet the easy transition from fantasy to reality characterized in younger students becomes more difficult as the "movement between the inward and outward life becomes more difficult, because more complex."[7] It is here that the teacher has a vital role to play, for beyond the stage of facile expression links must be established between what the children write and what may be found in literature to correspond to their struggles. Here models fill their second function.

> From his experience of language-art the child can be led to discover how other greater and finer minds have tackled the same inner problems as torment him and he has tried to solve.[8]

A fine model for Holbrook will "cherish naivety." He deplores the "fashion for false modernity," and leans toward "the more direct and simple poets"[9] — Clare, Crabbe, Blake, Edward Thomas, Frost, Po Chu-I as well as folksongs, nursery rhymes, and games.

This approach places emphasis on the child's writing as a bellwether for growth and connection with the outer world. And while Holbrook does believe that "there is all the difference in the world between art poetry and the poetry of children, the *functions of symbolism in each are the same* because they are functions natural to man and their modes are archetypal." All humans, he believes, express themselves symbolically.

> How we can tell what the child or the poet means depends upon our acquaintance with all kinds of creative art and with criticism which illumines its symbolism. So the first need of a teacher of creativity is a wide acquaintance with arts of all kinds.[10]

To read Holbrook is again to be struck with some fascinating questions. Are all children, as he believes, creative? Do the *same* problems and struggles beset both children and adults? Is it possible for teachers to be so highly educated in and conversant with literature, art, childhood education, and psychology that they are able to fulfill the role Holbrook assigns? His ideals are admirable, but another generation has been born since Holbrook's paper was delivered at the Anglo-American Seminar on the Teaching of English held at Dartmouth in 1966, and there is little evidence that teachers are being trained to view or foster creativity in these ways.

Herbert Kohl began his teaching career in the early 1960's by making a unique contribution in terms of relating his models – myths, history, philosophy, and literature – to the interest and language of a group of children in Harlem. Kohl's view goes beyond the development of the inner self to a communion with others.

> Spiritual richness consists primarily of a knowledge of self and an ability to listen to other men's voices. Only secondarily does it involve openness to poetry, literature, music and other expressions of the spirit. Being rich spiritually is what some people call "being together." It makes it possible for one to act for motives that are not personal but rooted in the quest for a sane and just society of men.[11]

This willingness to listen to others is often expressed in theory by poet-teachers who write of their dialogues with children and purported success in the classroom. It is also a trademark of teachers who become tuned into the need for children to vent self-expression through feelings. But the chasm between theory and practice is deep. While poet-teachers may be more attuned to symbolism and "expressions of the spirit," they are often woefully ignorant of the minds and hearts of children; similarly, educators and teachers may be trained in childhood education or child psychology but lack understanding of what poetry, or any art, may mean or the ways in which it may be nurtured. This is often a no-fault situation, recognized by a few who search for solutions through the Teachers & Writers Collaborative and the Poets-in-the-Schools programs.

June Jordan, in her answer to the head of Teachers & Writers Collaborative concerning the work of Deborah Burkett and relevant models, displays an ability and sensitivity to listen far beyond the ability of most.

Yet some poet-teachers who have known success in urban classrooms with fast-paced techniques, models in contemporary poetry, and pop culture, surrealistic imagery, prescriptives that pander to the autonomous imagination, demonstrate in their diaries and articles an inability to relate to the rural child. They do not listen to these children, but are quick to equate tradition with backwardness, politeness with lack of "creative intelligence," serenity with "weak self-image." Although they seemingly admire these children's "appreciation of Beauty" and their "directness and literalness," the poet-teachers' underlying scorn for tradition – both in poetry and in society – blinds them to the possibilities of the metaphoric and symbolic values in nature and appropriate models.

Nowhere is this attitude more evident than in an article, "Teaching Poetry Writing to Rural Kids," a conversation between poet-teachers Ron Padgett and Dick Gallup. Decrying the children's ability to respond to surrealistic imagery, irony, and wit, Padgett proposes that "simple poetry events or happenings, nothing complicated by a lot of machinery or anything" might work.

> For instance, have each kid get a pencil and paper and go outside and run in different directions counting to a hundred. When they get to one hundred, stop, write down the first thing they see, turn around and run back to the classroom. Obviously what they wrote down would be of little importance here, but it would be fun to do that kind of thing. You could even have the teachers running the hundred yard dash![12]

Gallup agrees that this is a "terrific idea." Yet neither recognize that what the child might actually see and write down is the *very* thing that could be the foundation for reaching that child, to be developed in later writing sessions. To these children nature *is* meaningful, perhaps more so than the surrealistic imagery and wit. Yet, not only does Gallup apparently agree with Padgett's statement that "what they wrote down would be of little importance," but he has failed to search out meaningful models of nature poetry that would be of value to these children. Such poet-teachers have not yet learned to listen.

Most teachers and poet-teachers strive to find meaningful models for what they wish to impart, but many have a limited knowledge of poetry. It is not an easy matter, moreover, to know what will succeed with a given group of children. The importance of a well-rounded background is obvious. Holbrook's standards for *literature* are not those of the editors of the *Whole Word Catalog*, not necessarily those of Helen Hill in "How to Tell a Sheep from a Goat and Why It Matters" or Claudia Lewis in *A Big Bite of the World*. The emergence of the schools of poetry, as well as reaction to traditional forms and styles, have set in motion a confusion about models. But does not Kohl's "spiritual richness" imply that models chosen reside in more than the work of a single poet-teacher, the poems of a preferred school of poets, the choice of contemporary poetry without regard for the past, the body of poetry written only *for* children, or poetry written only *by* children? Poet Theodore Roethke in his essay, "Five American Poets," asks for curious readers who will not be afraid of emotion, who will not be afraid to step into a world different from their own.[13] This plea is relevant for any adult who chooses models.

In a report written in 1982 concerning the work of the Poetry Writing Workshops sponsored by the Commonwealth of Massachusetts Committee on the Arts and the National Endowment for the Arts, Ruth Whitman addresses the subject:

> What poetry should the poet use as models for the students? No writing can be taught without reading. It is the imitation of excellent models that made the writers of every generation. During the course of our experience in the States, we began by agreeing to use contemporary models – poems by contemporary poets at the beginning of every class. We often used the models subliminally – by writing a poem on the board, passing out copies of a poem, playing the poem on a tape recorder or record. The model poem was always relevant to the exercise we had in mind. We never used more than one or two poems in a single class so that the student would not be overwhelmed and would have time to respond. We began to compile our own anthology of the poems that worked best in class. Our criteria for including a poem were (1) that the poem should be excellent, (2) that the language should be simple, and (3) that the experience or perception described should be comprehensible and that the student should be able to identify with it.[14]

A *Small Teaching Anthology*, compiled by Whitman and Sam Cornish, however, includes more than contemporary poetry. It ranges widely in scope, from a nursery rhyme to the work of Robert Bly, from Emily Dickinson to the poem of a fifth grader. William Carlos Williams, Carl Sandburg, Theodore Roethke, and David Ignatow are represented in fifteen of the forty-four poems, with a single contribution from Cornish and Whitman. This is an eclectic anthology, one that employs both traditional form, rhyme and meter as well as free verse, a collection of the familiar and the unfamiliar, poems of levity as well as serious import. All poems included fulfill the criteria established by the Massachusetts poets, and the choice of poems appeals to all aspects of the poetic sensibilities. Rhyme and metrics are honored as free verse, a rare happenstance today!

Robert McGovern, a poet-teacher working in the Ohio schools, believes that the choice of quality poetry is important. While his book, *A Poetry Ritual for Grammar Schools*, "advocates the use of mature poetry . . ."

> I would not like to preclude the use of children's verse since I, personally, find much of it absolutely delightful. However, it behooves the teacher to be very careful about that transition point at which students seem to want to put away childish things. In the early grades, a mixture of children's verse and more sophisticated poems would probably make the most sense; in this way teachers should be able to track the growing sophistication of their charges. After the fourth or fifth grade, there will be many years before the students will have reached again the maturity necessary to enjoy *A Child's Garden of Verses*.

McGovern, like Whitman and Cornish, further enjoins teachers to mix poems of nonsense and humor with those that express the emotions of joy or pain. Not only should they choose "poetry by adults for adults in language that children can come close to understanding" but select "poetry that is relevant to what the children are thinking about." He encourages teachers to be fearless when approaching serious themes, but also "to beware of didactic poems – e.g. poems that teach children to be good boys and girls or good citizens and the like."[15]

Directives to choose humor are rare. The seriousness with which poetry is approached by most poet-teachers precludes attempts at humor in almost all cases; poetry, to most, is no laughing matter, but rather a concerted attempt to elicit revelation of the secrets of the unconscious.

In *To Defend a Form* Ardis Kimzey, a poet-teacher in North Carolina, would seem to sound the death-knell for humor when she writes:

> A special word about humor. I've given up trying to find good humor poems that don't rhyme, so I simply tell the kids that obviously funny poems drop right out of the category of no rhyme and I can't explain it. Funny poems are still those in which part of their appeal lies in being able to fit them together like a puzzle.[16]

There are many poet-teachers like Kimzey who move between wild enthusiasm for student writing and that of adult contemporary poets, who find their models in the small literary magazines, and who cling to the several dozen poets and poems mentioned over and over again by members of the New York School. To them, *The Whole Word Catalog* and the *Teachers & Writers Newsletters* are, in Kimzey's words, "the promised land."

Their criteria are of interest; even as they espouse the principles of listening and spiritual richness, they seem to close their minds to whatever does not come under *their* definition of creativity or poetry. Kimzey does not want her students to "write poems like the ones they see covering the poetry sections in most bookstores and whose author shall go nameless here because we all know who it is." Her goal – to show students "what an image is" and then see "if they can put it into practice" – is limiting. She deplores those students who "already have poetry books they have written ready for you when you arrive. Mostly the poems are metered and rhymed, but usually the student can be reformed in a few sessions."[17]

Kimzey, for example, wants to "provide good poems and many of them and in many different styles for the students to read and ponder over," so she keeps her eyes on the "little" magazines, using what she can because:

> I will have to admit that I'm not that fair in most of the classes about what I read, because I'm trying in most cases to read poems

> which show something about poetry that I'm trying to get across that particular day. It is only natural to use poems in that instance which I admire and know well.

She is also quick to zero in on the idea that "most teachers are not competent" in matters of poetry to give their attention to creativity, to open imagination, and "they are the first to admit it."

> They went to school in a time, which could be a few years ago, or now, when contemporary poetry was not taught. And . . . most of them are educators and not poets. The final thrust of the Poets-in-the-Schools Program as I see it is that you can give the students all the above, but from the viewpoint and sensibility of a practicing poet. The poet, by virtue of his profession, is going to bring things into the classroom that a teacher, no matter how fine, is not going to be able to give to the students.[18]

While the goals expressed by Kimzey – "attention to ability, example, and expansion of awareness" – sound admirable, the prejudices of those who agree with her are clear. They will reform those who have a penchant for rhyme and meter; eschew traditional poetry in favor of their chosen contemporary writers; and give to children what teachers cannot give, a sensibility that they believe peculiar to the poet. While the quest purports to be one of expansion for students, it is, in fact, a limitation. Students may become acquainted with James Wright, Wallace Stevens, Gary Snyder, Sylvia Plath, Charles Simic, James Dickey, Ted Hughes, Richard Brautigan, William Stafford, and Diane Wakowski among others; yet they will never learn in the classroom of Homer and Shakespeare, Frost and Sandburg. Poetry, in the terms of these poet-teachers, belongs to the present-day and to the sober. It is as though an entire body of work does not exist; no W. S. Gilbert nor Edward Lear nor the ability to enter into the escape hatch of nonsense – to laugh with Falstaff or hunt for the Snark. Surely anyone who purports to teach children must be aware of not only the serious poets of earlier centuries but the value of humor as well. Yet all of this is cast aside in favor of an intensity and concentration on something called the "image" and "imagination." Often poet-teachers' accounts of the pleasure their showmanship engenders seem to substitute for the pleasure of poetry itself. The focus is no longer on the poem but on the poet; the motives are no longer rooted in the quest, but in the self-approbation of poet-teachers who consider their own sensibilities superior to those of the teachers.

Yet there are poet-teachers who search honestly for a way to listen and to learn from students, who do not march in intent on reform, who do not turn every lesson into a panegyric in praise of their discoveries and masterpieces. There are poet-teachers who work quietly, although unheralded, to test out their own ideas and who do reach children. It is unfortunate, for example, that the many excellent essays in *Poemmaking* have not been expanded into books which would be significant to those teachers and educators, as well as parents, who wish to learn. *Beyond Words, Writing Poems with Children* by Elizabeth McKim and Judith W. Steinbergh is a good start.

Gensler and Nyhart have expanded their two essays in *Poemmaking* into *The Poetry Connection* but it is a slick series of quick lesson plans that lose the intimate flavor of the essays, in which there is a more caring and human flavor; in *Poemmaking* both poet-teachers and classroom come alive with a step-by-step discussion of how the lessons worked; in *The Poetry Connection* a short introduction to one chapter on "Fantasies and Dreams" seems only a hasty, impersonal rundown and clinical analysis of all sorts of imaginings – dreams, nightmares, exaggerations, and outright inventions. Model poems as well as posters and recordings are suggested "to create a climate conducive to the expression of fantasies."[19] Model poems by Kenneth Patchen, Randall Jarrell, Kinereth Gensler, Alan Tate, Siv Cedering Fox, Ruth Whitman, Denise Levertov, Linda Pastan, Donald Hall, David Ignatow, Mark Strand, Charles Simic, W. S. Merwin, and Jacques Prévert, as well as seventeen poems by children, are included. One "excellent way to turn kids on to writing," the authors believe, "is to show them a variety of evocative poems."

> In the process of collecting model poems for this purpose, we realized that the poems in anthologies for children are selected for pleasure and entertainment, rarely for the particular quality we were looking for – the capacity to start an original poem moving within a child.

They list three criteria for choosing models:

1. Is there something immediately appealing about the poem: its shape, title, a particular word or phrase?
2. Does it contain specific elements that can get children started on their own poems: a strong feeling that reverberates, a particular poetic technique, a way to play with words, subject matter that the child can explore?
3. Is the poem good enough to stand up under repeated readings? Does it remain evocative?[20]

Nyhart and Gensler explain that they also use model poems by children in *The Poetry Connection* "because the concerns and feelings of peers tend to be highly contagious. Reading poems by other children moves children to write their own." Does this suggest that model poems by adults do *not* elicit the same response?

In introducing their adult models, the authors explain:

> There is no one "correct way" for a child to make use of a model poem. Different elements of the poem will appeal to different children: one student will pick up an aspect of the form, another will be turned on by the subject, a third will be entranced by a particular line. Some children will write a close imitation of the whole. The sudden recognition of a poem's emotional wallop makes some children want to become poets, too. Sometimes the response is hidden. Ideas and possibilities are being stored up, to be incorporated into poems written at a later date.
>
> A wide variety of spin-off poems can be anticipated, for example, from May Swenson's "Bleeding." A child might respond to this poem by writing a conversation or a poem about a knife, or a poem employing the persona device . . . or a shaped poem. The title alone might be borrowed to begin the child's own poem.
>
> Some children's responses to model poems are: "I want to write a poem like that" or "I could write a poem like that" or "I want to write my own" or "I can't do that." We have made every effort to exclude from this collection poems that are likely to elicit the "I can't" feeling. Poems that are technically or intellectually too

sophisticated make children feel inadequate, stymied when it comes to their own writing. Many of the poems in anthologies for children, ones which children enjoy listening to, fall into this category.[21]

There are a number of points here that bear investigation. First, the assertion that models are not selected because they are pleasing or entertaining, but rather because they have a capacity to evoke a response toward writing, intimates that no one poem can do both; it must either be pure entertainment *or* evocative. Second, the belief that certain poems must be discarded because children cannot imitate them places an emphasis on the poem as a source of total comprehension rather than a work of art which may be only apprehended and enjoyed for the sake of its mystery, rhythm, or sensual pleasure in words. Third, the idea that poems are discarded because they will make children feel inadequate suggests that the children must be coddled as well as led to believe that they are capable of achieving what an established adult poet can. This is closely allied to the assertion that given the models of other children's writing, they will be able to function and feel comfortable. Thus, listening to a model poem, they are not necessarily expected to feel pleasure, but rather to respond instantaneously with their own words and writing – and this response is called a poem.

This view of poetry is quite in opposition to the idea of the poet as craftsman, of someone who works to make a synthesis that will either elicit pleasure or, in Tolstoy's terms, a communion with others. Rather it asserts that every child, indeed even every adult, *is* a poet by the simple act of spontaneously committing to paper a reaction to a prescribed model or poem. Writing poetry thus becomes a comfortable, peer-oriented activity within the grasp of every human being; a chance to turn into a few words some personal reaction to the word or idea of another. While on the one hand it is not the prescriptive fill-in, it requires little more than the ability to read or listen to carefully chosen models. The belief: *every* child is a poet; *any* child is a poet by virtue of being able to be exposed to the right teachers, to the right models!

There is also a curious twist in the introduction written by Nyhart and Gensler as they state that "We view the children's poems as stages in a developing process rather than as polished artifacts. Most of these poems were written quickly in class; few were revised."[22] Yet almost eighty children's "poems" are included to serve as *models*, the same criteria applied to the work of children as to that of the adult poets.

Meredith Sue Willis, a poet-teacher, speaks of models used with third and fourth grade students for a lesson on mood and style: "an advertisement for a furniture sale from *The Daily News*, a strongly conversational piece from Hemingway's *The Sun Also Rises*, something from Virginia Woolf, part of a sports article."[23] Another class with the same group centered around writing from "raw material" after the reading of Eliot's "The Wasteland." While these selections seem unusual for children of this age, they are, in turn, preferable to the models of Rod McKuen and James Whitcomb Riley chosen for students in a Lompoc, California, junior high school, or the imitation of greeting cards by others.

"It is not advisable to use bad examples from children's work," Sandy Brownjohn, author of *Does It Have to Rhyme?*, writes, "to illustrate what should be done. Teaching by positive example is better and will help to build up confidence."[24] Such a remark seems self-evident and yet it is astounding to find poor examples in dozens of articles by teachers and educators. Those who proffer them must believe they are adequate, representative, even good. Certainly educators and teachers are well meaning, yet they often lack the background that Holbrook asks for, the sensibility Kimzey notes, and the search for the quest urged by Kohl. Under a heavy workload and timid about approaching poetry at all, most teachers find themselves bewildered. Kohl states this position.

> One of the problems teachers face is that they don't know all the forms of poetry. When someone says try modern forms and nonwestern forms, many of us don't have a clear idea of what poets are talking about. And it's not our fault. Poetry has been divorced from our everyday experience and we lose a lot because of it.[25]

Teachers, caught between the injunctions to choose the best, but uncertain of how and where to find such models, and convinced that writing poetry is a good thing, but wary of proceeding, have a number of choices. They can seize upon the old warhorses which have been dubbed great poetry but which bear no relevance to children today – in which case children are tuned out. They can turn to the self-appointed experts who offer methods in commercial guises; who assure them that anyone can teach poetry writing and any child can write it; and who offer models ranging from these same warhorses to original jingles and a convoluted and inaccurate version of modern and non-western forms. The more adventurous teachers tend to become their own experts, seizing on pop culture as a way to relate to students, and choosing models from the most mediocre of songs and media hype. Some even write articles about the tricks they use to get children to write. Some invent new forms based on acrostics, shapes, or syllable counting which are but exercises in the language arts, and as such, writing which masquerades as poetry. Still others call upon local poets to come to their classrooms and work, or they attend conferences to gain some insight into the poets' methods – and models.

Parents, too, believing that poetry contains some mysterious quality of beauty, truth, or wisdom may buy an occasional anthology for children to read, one that they feel may contain poems to which children will respond. Or they will pull from a shelf a volume in which they find some familiar poem once learned or heard about because it bears the name of a recognized poet. A few may buy a book by a contemporary poet for children because of its appeal to either parent or child. And they will cherish, however inept – or beautiful – the original "poetry" which their child brings home from school.

Those of us who seek to define poetry do so in vain, as do those who seek for the "perfect" models. Poetry has as many facets as those readers and listeners who listen to the voice within, who seek to find a richness of spirit and an inner voice which brings not only pleasure, but communion with an individual, a poet from the past or present. Like Holbrook we may find a symbolic rendering of the inner life; like Kimzey we may search for the image; like Lewis we may choose models to foster enrichment and growth. But the poetry that speaks to us must also reflect something of our own emotional and physical selves; echo with a rhythm or a sound that somehow strikes a tune and changes our way of looking, thinking, or listening forever. What we seek from poetry is not the beauty, truth, and wisdom as *abstract* concepts, but as a *concrete* statement that can be translated into some image or emotion that may arrest or surprise, delight, or lead to further contemplation.

But before this can happen, there must be, in Kohl's terms, a spiritual richness, "a knowledge of self and an ability to listen to other men's voices." There must be, in Holbrook's terms, a respect for the inner self of every human and every child. Without this beginning there can be no openness to poetry – nor, indeed, to any art.

What needs to concern all adults, parent, educators, classroom teachers, and poet-teachers is a choice of models that will not only serve the children's immediate inner needs, but lead them to a broader appreciation and understanding of what the writing or reading of poetry may mean in terms of their own lives and their communion with others. To introduce them to only one kind of poetry or to poems that can only be appreciated in terms of a particular lesson and only to that which can be imitated easily, rings a death-knell for appreciation itself. Cannot models be apprehended even if they are not yet comprehended? Those children who indulge in creative mimicry or even broad imitation prove that they can.

Each model, therefore, takes its place, but only if it is an *honest* expression of what a writer feels, sees, or experiences. Poor verse and jingles will not do; they have no true voice. Children's writing *may* serve if used by an adult aware of the limitations of this genre. Prescriptives may be immediately appealing to children and adults because they are easily filled in, but this is no more creative or poetry than coloring in a painting-by-numbers. Good writing takes time. If the idea of a poem is that it is spontaneously conceived, written down quickly and therefore natural, why, indeed, bother with models of adult poets who labor to balance idea with form, subjectivity with reality, to produce an artifact that speaks beyond the personal image to the universal symbol?

Children's writing reflects, for the most part, the fact that children are just beginning to learn something about themselves. Their syncretic view is a personal view, one that is rooted in prelogical response and thinking. While their use of metaphor, for example, may be charming because it is fresh, it is rarely broadening. It is still an attempt to make comparisons, to sort out the world, to shed the self of its personal schema.

No one questions that children like to read original work to each other and listen to what other children have done. But to applaud this as art seems, in the long run, to give children the idea that they can, without a knowledge of craft or revision, produce work that is worthy of emulation when – in years to come – they will find otherwise.

No one questions that the writing of children, enjoyed by peers and adults, helps to give a child a sense of self-worth and marks a personal growth. No one questions that the writing of children as model may be an expression of child art, but the idea that this is *literature*, in the sense that it is a broadening, enriching body of work that has survived because it humanizes mankind and because it extends self and social consciousness for others, is debatable.

What some children's writing and the work of established poets *do* have in common is an ability to see something freshly, an honesty of perspective, a new way of looking. The beauty in children's work is seldom in the form, the ability to use the tools of the craft well. This cannot be expected of children. The beauty, therefore, is not in some lofty concept or use of adjectives, a nature scene, or a feeling that adults believe children harbor in their secret lives, but rather a beauty that is found in honesty, untainted by the clichés of language. Such work is beautiful because it is fresh and artless; because it reveals, without false words or use of gimmickry, what Koch calls "the strangeness and silence of their deep and private feelings"[26] *without false injunctions to do so.* It is beauty because it is still child-like. It is not expressed clearly; it is in no way concerned with logistics, the "how" of the happenings, the cause and effect; it is not factual. It is syncretic, and that is *true* to childhood, and childhood alone. It is, in Piaget's words, "not genuine understanding, but a convergence of acquired schemas of thought." It is a realism *true to childhood. This* is its beauty, its truth, even its wisdom.

Those who believe that this kind of beauty is sufficient for models will continue to use children's writing as further models. Those who believe that there must be more, an attention to the world that recognizes another reality into which children must grow, and into which they *will* grow, chose from other models. The richer the spiritual awareness of teachers, poet-teachers, or parents, the more they believe in the necessity to listen and to be part of the "quest for a sane and just society of men." Such teachers and poet-teachers will embrace more than their own individual voice; they will not spurn the great poetry of the past, nor the work of those who understand

and write for children in a meaningful way. They will not deny the importance of levity, of the power of metrics or rhyme when well-used. They will rejoice in *all* poets who open up the child to creative mimicry in the knowledge that this is a first step to the writing of poetry.

CHAPTER XII

Poetry and Language Arts

What I'm saying is that, in the long run, to break the rules you must know *about* the rules. Now all this is very obvious, but in spite of its being obvious, it doesn't seem to be understood by most young people, let alone elderly ones . . .

From *Borges on Writing*
Juan Luis Borges[1]

In her introduction to *Singing Youth, An Anthology of Poems by Children*, published in 1927, Mabel Mountsier sums up the feelings of many adults when she writes:

> In this century of the child, children are encouraged to develop their powers in a natural manner; and since rhythm of thought and emotion is as much a part of their nature as rhythm of motion, the child trying to express his feelings often answers in verse Swinburne's question, "O Child, what news from heaven?"[2]

A young child, she adds, "sometimes creates a poem so fresh and unaffected that it reveals the soul that has not yet felt 'her earthly freight'." Such beliefs, of course, not only support the myth of the child as poet but reinforce Wordsworth's image of the child in his "celestial abode" not yet shadowed by the "prison-house."

In an article in the *American Poetry Review* almost fifty years later, the poet William Jay Smith takes to task those who worship the child as poet. "Poetry in the Schools – at the Mercy of Genius" is stinging in its attack:

> Now in the fifth grade when students are just about to be turned off poetry by exposure to some dreadful traditional doggerel . . . into the classroom strides a modern young poet, whose message

> is freedom. Don't be frightened of poetry, he tells the kids. We're all poets together, and what you write is just as good as what I write (in many cases this is absolutely true) so start screaming, release all your inhibitions, and follow me. Soon there is complete pandemonium in the classroom, the kids are all scribbling down repetitive displays of verbal fireworks suggested by the poet, and when calm returns, the poetic efforts are scooped up and ready for publication. The logic behind this is that the students will be encouraged to produce poems when they see those that others their ages have written, no matter how little merit they may possess. Anthologies of student work are published far and wide . . . and praised by teachers and librarians. Much of what they contain is as bad as anything that we were handed in my day. The only difference is that it is written by children, most of whom have never written anything before, and, since it follows current poetic fashion, it sounds as zany and freakish as possible, and, of course, does not rhyme. What good it does in the end, and what it has to do with poetry is certainly questionable.[3]

While Smith's description of the poet-in-the-schools leans toward hyperbole and seems ultimately unfair to a number of poet-teachers who work honestly and carefully, his assessment of poetry written by children often hits home. "As soon as anything by a child genius appears anywhere, all critical judgment seems to go out the window," he states. Everything and anything is accepted in an age when there is

> a need to see everything cock-eyed and presented in a show-biz, Madison Avenue, television-tempered, baby-surrealistic imagery that is mistaken for the language of genius. Most of the exercises conducted in the classrooms are designed to this end. Children are told to be a flower, a hibernating bear, or a horseshoe. They are asked to compose riddle poems about the contents of paper-bags; they are led blindfolded through a maze touching a series of differing textures and then asked to write poems about what they experience. They listen to tapes of noises of traffic, airports, subways, and trains . . . They are required to respond poetically to all sorts of music and to dreamlike art prints of Magritte, Chagall, and Rousseau, and more particularly to modern photographs. They are told to cut up newspapers, which, as one offi-

cial report of the exercise describes it, "enabled them to make sentences, poems, whatever without the self-consciousness of having to drag up the words so obviously from inside, though in a sense the words were 'inside' for the selection process itself dictates a communication with the words chosen."

"The truth is," Smith asserts, "that there is little real communication of any sort with the *inside.* Almost all these exercises are like the barker's noises outside a carnival tent . . . There is a great deal going on *outside*, but what does it all add up to? Most of it is all fun and games, 'creative play,' and children react to it with a tremendous release of pent-up energy. But there is little of the intense inner energy that can lead to any true exploration of the psyche."

Smith believes that the noisy climate, the horseplay, is not conducive to the sensitive child's ability to "listen to his or her own heartbeat," that many teachers are "walling in the imagination rather than making it . . . a readily accessible and ever-continuing source of psychic energy." His censure of both the methods and attitudes of many poet-teachers is strong:

> Many of the young poets visiting our classrooms today are poor in everything but self-assurance. They have nothing but their genius to declare, and they declare it in no uncertain terms – in wild and wacky computerized metaphors and zip-zappy lines of free-wheeling verse. And the kids eat it up. Here is true democracy at work: everybody is a poet and everybody's poetry is of equal merit. Leading the young on to great poetry demands an attitude of humility to begin with, but most of these poet-teachers have all-encompassing egos. They do not bother to read what their students write; they read only themselves. And their students, following their example, read only themselves – so in the end we are spawning yet another generation of self-regarding geniuses.

Yet Smith asserts that there is much children *can* do in writing poetry if they are given an appreciation of fine poetry and better models. He believes in learning the rules and in an exposure to "the many poetic devices that the English language possesses." His attack is not against children writing poetry, but upon the notion that whatever children write, by whatever methods, is, *per se*, poetry. What Smith wants is "the best from the Poetry in the Schools program, which has accomplished much and which offers unusual possibilities."[4]

But just as Smith sees the imperfections in this program, so poet-teachers find in the average classroom the sort of poetry writing, albeit admired by teachers and educators, that is trite, sterile, and devoid of imagination. Alexander McIntosh, a poet-teacher writing in *Teachers & Writers Magazine*, states that "The people in these groups are often literary enthusiasts only, who do not (and why should they?) have the personal background in writing from which to tell what is good and what is not in kids' poetry. Their jobs often depend on a basically static, formula-oriented educational system, which attempts to contain the kids, much as a corral contains horses walking back and forth through the gates." A child who does "go outside the formulas," McIntosh continues, is "marked absent, that is, invisible. I have found that when a poem is written by a kid who does make it outside the gates, I usually have to point out its virtues to the teacher . . . "[5]

This problem is a real one, discussed constantly by poets who despair over the ability of educators and teachers to plumb the poem for originality and real creativity. Kohl points to the work that children do to please teachers and which takes a "particular form because the author wanted an A in poetry."[6] John Holt writes:

> It would be easy to compile a bookful of horror stories about schools and classrooms where neatness, mechanical accuracy and orthodoxy of opinion – i.e. agreeing with the teacher's spoken or even unspoken notions of what is right and proper for children to believe and say – count for far more than honest, independent, original expression.[7]

Tom Arrington, a teacher, speaks of how "Too often teachers impose a personal criteria of evaluation which silences many children's unique, individual voices. Too often a teacher's sole concern is proper usage, form or punctuation, rather than really listening to every student communicate in his own way."[8]

But this idea of a child "communicating in his own way" often leads back to the heart of the myth itself, the idea that a child brings "news from heaven." If this myth is to be believed holus-bolus, no further investigation need be attempted for all arguments would be futile. To red pencil, to grade, to insist upon correct grammar, to revise, only destroys self-expression. Criticism is a taboo. Lee Bennett Hopkins asserts that:

> Children will only create and reveal their inner thoughts to a teacher who will accept them for what they are. When children write like this – when they create from their hearts – it is useless to take a red pencil from the desk drawer and correct spelling errors or misuse of grammar and punctuation. If teachers attempt this, they will not obtain creative responses, the next time round; inner thoughts will be kept inside, and deep feelings will be turned into superficial sentences.[9]

The threat of children withholding their inner thoughts looms as a spectre for others. Arnstein believes that "the foremost enemy of creative functioning is criticism."[10] Revision in any form "only serves to erect an obstacle between the child and the poem."[11]"All effort," Holbrook believes, "should be praised."[12] The intrusion of adult standards, therefore, suggests that any teacher's criticism or interference will destroy not only children's natural expression but their ability to create in the future. Spontaneity, in fact, will be crushed.

Such thinking, when put into action, seems responsible for the countless pedestrian listings that many consider poetry. Aidan Chambers describes the process:

> A teacher stands up in front of a class and says, "We're all going to write a poem for this competition. Here's the subject: pollution. Now tell me what you think of when I say that word." After five minutes a list has been written on the board: Atom bombs. Fallout. Horror, Waste. Etc. Ten minutes later every kid in the room has copied the list down on a piece of paper, putting the stuff into lines "like poetry." Spontaneous, certainly. Self-expression, perhaps. Poetry, never.[13]

Chambers's example is apt:

> Atom bombs
> Fallout

Horror
And waste
Who's to blame?
You? Me?
Governments
All of us are to blame.[14]

In a "Dialogue on Creative English," Geoffrey Summerfield has much to say about the role of the teacher and creativity. The danger of "running hothouses for articulate introverts" can only be countered by developing a "proper sense of what can be expected" of children "who will be diminished if our expectations are mean, and harried or hurried if our expectations are premature."[15]

> It's important, of course, to escape from the current myth that "creative English" is simply a matter of getting the pupils to write little poems; such a notion is obviously limiting and, indeed silly: at worst, it degenerates into a game in which the kids write the sort of half-baked, facile free (licentious?) verse that they know the teacher wants or will tolerate.[16]

Summerfield notes a falseness in the notion that creative English exists as "a nursery for the cultivation of literary talent; one is not cultivating poets: one is trying to foster the growth of more articulate, more effectively human people."[17]

> Unfortunately, our current notions of creative achievement seem to rest on the post-Renaissance and more especially on the Romantic notion of the artist as solitary or isolate.[18]

Rather than succumbing to the Romantic notion of creativity, to "intense and often overwritten spasms of response to sensory experience," the "absurdity of a situation in which forty pupils are all expected to make a poem, simultaneously, and before the bell for the end of the lesson rings,"[19] Summerfield views creativity as something more. It is not a matter

> of simply eliciting verse or worse, but rather of establishing a relationship and an ethos which will promote experiment, talk, enquiry, amusement, vivacity, bouts of intense concentration,

seriousness, collaboration, and a clearer and more adequate self-knowledge. This will involve us in talk about ourselves, our language, our behaviour, our attitudes and beliefs, and when appropriate, in recording such things in writing. And the teacher's sense of his role is crucial. If he is prescriptive – knowing what *he* wants, knowing all the answers beforehand – he will be less effective than if he is prepared to allow the pupils' awareness of criteria to grow for itself in the business of making, modifying, and so on.[20]

Like Kohl, Summerfield believes that the product is only secondary to the process. What is creative, therefore, for both student and teacher is part of a much larger process which occurs in the classroom and in which the teacher's role is central to the functioning of the child. Here, the teacher is more than someone who instigates word lists to be spontaneously whipped into instant poems. The teacher is not afraid of destroying the "natural" product but rather of involving the child in the act of "making."

This "making" as well as revising, improving, and correcting is essential to the adult poet. Even those who claim, like Koch, that fifth grade children "turn out poems as naturally as an apple tree turns out blossoms"[21] must recognize the need for a teacher's role in the process. A "Lies" poem by a fifth grader is published in *Wishes, Lies and Dreams*:

I fly to school at 12:00 midnight
I run to lunch at 9:00
I go underground to go home at 11:00
My name is Clownaround James Jumpingbean Diego
  Spinaround Jimmy and Flipflop Tom
My head was born in Saturn my arms were born in
  the moon my legs in Pluto and the rest of me
  was born on the earth
My friend the bee zoomed me home
    Eduardo Diaz[22]

The poem was not written in this form originally. A photocopy of the original reads:

I go to school at 12 midnight
I go to lunch at :900
I go home at :1100
My name is James Diego Jimmy Tom and Bill
I was born in saturn part in the Moon
a part in plouto and a part on earth
I walk home my friend the bee

The beginning of a second draft shows further changes:

I fly to school at :1200 midnight
I go to lunch at :900
I go underground to go home at :1100
My name clownaround James Jumpingbean
Diego pinnaround Jimmy and flipflop
Tom
My head was born in saturn my arms was
born in the moon my leg in ploto and the rest
of me was born on the earth.[23]

Although the spontaneous thought of the child is retained, there has been rewriting, beginning with the change from the trite "I go" to "I fly . . . I run," an elaboration on the names he is called, and further changes from I was born" to the particulars of "head," "arms," "legs," and "the rest of me."

Mearns speaks of the difference between product education and creative education. Creative systems, he asserts, "turn out a comparatively ragged product," as opposed to the "good patterns in large quantities, seemingly every hour on the hour" of product education which allows the child "gratification."

> If a child punches clay, splashes paint, or writes a rhyme, that seems to conclude the educational obligation of the school. School officials show me the primitive work of children, announce with pride that there has been no instruction, and end with a satisfied, "Yes, we have creative work."

But is it not, asks Mearns, "the business of education to improve ability, to add to strength, to secure superior results?"[24] Should the child be allowed to believe that whatever he writes is perfect? There is a cop-out on the part of many teachers who subscribe to the myth today, just as they did over fifty years ago, and who cling to the idea that whatever a child produces is an artifact. "It's not too hard to get people to freak out, to just write anything they want to," poet-teacher Lewis MacAdams writes. "It's harder to get them to see the sense of discipline that it takes to be a poet."

> Somehow everybody has this idea that it's easier to be a poet than to be a violinist. And it ain't true. Somehow, because people know how to write their names, or descriptions of apple trees and stuff, they think they're more quickly qualified to be a poet. That's a hard thing to get people to see, to be clear about, without trying to quash them. To get free, but also to realize where that freedom lies. That's hard; that's really hard.[25]

This sense of discipline is often at war with what Summerfield describes as the credo of the "progressive angels," those who "stand or fall for all that is ill-formulated, permissive and antiacademic, learning-made-easy, and the abandonment of standards." While he agrees "that the word – '*creative*' – has too often been reduced to a mere political gesture, to a slogan, whose purpose is to show the world . . . that we 'care'," he notes that "discipline is too often equated with 'decent' standards in matters of spelling, syntax, legibility, speech – the accomplishments and skills that society, in the guise of employers and the professions, expects of us."[26] There is a difference between submission to discipline in this sense and the discipline that an artist or craftsman uses, because the artists identify what "they *want* to do with what they *need* to do."[27]

Summerfield points out how this control, discipline, and reliability often take place on a moral bias:

> To spell correctly is a sign of grace: it signifies that you are not only able but also willing, even anxious to toe the line that your elders and betters have laid down, and to "work hard" in order to refine and extend your skills is a token of moral virtue.[28]

Hard work as a way to the kingdom of heaven is thus often equated with discipline, and its opponents worry lest it signify difficulty for the child, a blockage to his inner self.

In a fascinating chapter in *Journal of a Living Experiment* Lopate tackles the question of language as basic to the beginnings of the Teachers & Writers Collaborative:

> The founders of Teachers & Writers Collaborative, the Huntting Conference members, perceived the educational crisis as first and foremost a crisis in language. They diagnosed an alienating separation between standard English as it was taught and the language people actually spoke and used for communication; they saw a rusting of the tools of language, partly as a result of the influence of public speech, which was "a language for evasion, for cheating and lying . . . "

The idea that children needed exposure to the visual arts and to music was not sufficient reason to fund a program, Lopate asserts, but the federal government's interest in language programs *was*, and the argument that "student-generated texts would have a positive effect on reading comprehension" was appealing to artists, educators, and to the government.

> Thus, language arts were central, both for those who wanted to maintain the educational system and those who wanted to undermine and transform it. For, if language is the door through which all else that the school teaches has to enter, it is also the gate that excludes. The writers attracted to T & W in its infancy were, as a rule, anti-Establishment in their politics: either radicals or reformists sympathetic to the anti-war movement, and the struggle for social and racial justice. It is no accident that they formed the Collaborative around the question of language.[29]

Kohl's beliefs, espoused in *Teaching the Unteachable*, are at the core of the movement to change the schools:

> . . . the values which had been traditionally rewarded in classrooms were orderly exposition, logical progression, correct grammar and spelling, neatness, length and wholesome attitudes. By contrast, the first writers going into the schools (and this is still to some extent true today) favored the jagged, the harsh, the surrealistic, the poetically disjunctive, the visceral, talky, vivid, possibly anti-social point of view. The new standard called for

> was "authenticity of voice" – honesty, immediacy and freshness, however ungrammatical – and this was counterposed to safer, grammatically smooth "middle class" compositions, which sounded deader or more socially conditioned to the writers' ears.[30]

Lopate tells of the "pioneer writers in Teachers & Writers who "*were* united by an awareness of the need to defend voices that had been repressed, for whatever reasons."

> They came on as champions of the repressed. Sometimes this repression was spoken of in psychoanalytic terms – the wasted or untapped potential in the individual child's unconscious: sometimes it was connected to larger forces.[31]

It is not difficult to see how a writing program which stressed the child's need to speak of his experience in plain everyday language dovetailed with that of poets and writers who were expounding their distaste of the academic poets, their diction, sense of tradition, and classical forms. Their worship of Williams's sweeping changes in poetic structure, their put-down of meter, rhyme, and form, took root as they molded children in their own likenesses. Their declarations that children were natural poets because they spoke in their own authentic voices burgeoned into tapping the child's unconscious and imaginative powers. It did not take long to equate the truthful and honest utterances of children with those of poets which, as Lopate points out, "has helped to get programs started and writers-in-the-schools accepted, if, at the same time, raising false hopes."[32] Lopate's belief that the poets and writers "formed an alliance with the lower orders, the students, over the heads of the teachers" may help explain the dilemma in which classroom teachers find themselves. If writers pay no attention to correct English or grammar, if the fashion is to accept anything, why should the children and their teachers do more? This snowballing movement has resulted in a most tenuous position for teachers who respect the poet-teacher's ability to elicit creativity in the child, but yet must produce to a school board's satisfaction some adherence to standards of correct English.

The problem is made even more difficult because *no one* – poet-teacher, educator, child, parent, or classroom teacher – wishes to explode the myth, for it provides the poet-teacher with employment;

the school board with a proof of children's linguistic abilities in the respectable guise of poetry; the child with a bursting ego; the parent and the PTAs with pride; and the teacher with an opportunity to display the product of his language arts *enrichment*. Everyone is able to enjoy the "news from heaven"!

Yet a few nagging doubts surface when the product and process do not satisfy. When publications display not the work of genius but a surfeit of mediocrity; when test scores plummet; when the economy is overburdened with high school graduates whose self-expression and individuality override their ability to use their own language efficiently; when support of liberal arts dwindles at the college level and state universities cry that students are unprepared; when state and federal governments as well as foundations withdraw support for the arts, something has gone amiss.

Today, however, the myth still holds: Poet-teachers have established their territory. Many of them, who are supported by the school community, are convinced, as Whitman and Feinberg state, that words must come "in an uninhibited way and spelling, punctuation, and awkward or inappropriate language is of far less moment than the releasing of creative energy and the opening of new pathways to insight and self-discovery." While there is merit in this view during the process – when a child is actually writing – the situation changes when school administration, parents, and patrons find misspellings and poor grammar.

McGovern is aware of the "pedagogical difficulties" inherent in the situation, yet asserts that when he sees "many expensively printed books of the poetic emanations of children from all over the country" he is

> appalled by the eagerness of editors and teachers to suggest the cuteness (out of the mouths of babes?) of bad grammar and spelling. This cannot by any sense of the poetic tradition be called creative. Many incorrect poems found in these books have some striking childish insights and turns of language, but they could have been revised with the help of the teacher (many times a poet in the school) to be even better; after all, art is reflective as well as spontaneous . . . "[33]

Brownjohn "makes no apology for mentioning the teaching of

grammar in connection with some of the poetry games. I feel it is important; and good writing, in the end, should be correct in grammar and spelling. Teaching it this way is not only more enjoyable but also more relevant."[34] Yet those in agreement often sacrifice process for the product.

The editors of *Stone Soup* believe that the more precisely children "spell, the more complex rules of grammar they have assimilated, the more easily and unambiguously they will be able to express themselves;" yet children should write in their "own natural language . . . If children fear extensive corrections, they will become self-conscious and too frightened of making errors to feel free to write comfortably and at length on topics which might become too complicated for them . . . "[35] Such a view supports wholeheartedly the myth that what children write cannot be tampered with, and raises perplexing questions concerning the point at which they, the editors, feel changes may be made.

Donna Northouse, a teacher in the Arts Magnet High School in Dallas, Texas, puts the blame on educators who are unwilling to teach the "rules of grammar, to reinforce those rules with *frequent* and *guided* writing exercises, to encourage more reading, all on both the elementary and secondary levels."

> It is all too easy to have students write their feelings freely on whatever moves them at the moment, without anyone paying attention to grammar or spelling. In fact, the current fashion is to do so under the guise of "creative writing."

The rules of writing should be taught, she believes, before students are encouraged to write creatively. If educators "choose to ignore the teaching of grammar, they are only doing their students a great disservice." Far too often do "students suffer from a false sense of security about skills they only *think* they have."[36]

Kohl believes that teaching spelling and grammar is not the same as teaching writing. Children "easily accept the discipline of learning to write correctly. Vocabulary, spelling, and grammar become the means to achieving more precise and sophisticated forms of expression and not merely empty ends in themselves." In an atmosphere where teachers care what children want to know, what they think and care about, where a "romance with words and language"[37] is at the core of their education and not an adjunct, language arts are no longer a drudgery. But it does involve an attitude on the part of the teacher to effect this approach. Teachers, Kohl states, "must be taught to look for sensibility and feeling in their pupils, as well as the abilities to perform intellectual tasks."[38] Taking children seriously, recognizing that children's thoughts and honesty cannot be inhibited or concealed if the atmosphere is right, begins with the teacher's willingness and ability to discuss with children their ideas, problems, even anxieties. This in turn leads them beyond the spoken word into the arts. The problem, Kohl seems to say, does not occur because creativity and grammar are opposed; the problem arises as a result of inadequate attention to the children themselves and their needs for experiment and play. Teachers err when they

> try too hard to interpret their pupil's work. If a child writes about violence, he is looked upon as expressing violent impulses that are "really" within him. If he writes about loneliness his teacher tries to provide him with companionship. This usual view of writing condescendingly implies that the child is incapable of literary exploration. Worse, it implies he is as humorless as the adults who assume responsibility for his education. I have laughed, cried, been duped, outraged, and sometimes bored by what my pupils have written – and I have told them this. Their effort to understand themselves and the things around them demands no less.[39]

Yet many teachers interpret play and experiment as a way to combine poetry and language arts. They offer word games, acrostics, syllabic patterns that mask as poetry; they seize Iris Tiedt's recently invented diamante because it makes a nice diamond pattern and enables children to practice their use of nouns, adjectives, participles, and antonyms. They bastardize the cinquain by turning it into a language arts display of noun, adjective, and verb. They invent dozens of other syllabic patterns. None of this is poetry but only a quick and easy way to facilitate language arts in the name of play. There is little regard here for the child's ideas or thoughts. This is not the play and experiment of which Kohl speaks.

Mearns recognizes that teachers who are unaware of what creative writing entails are often the ones who insist upon finished, trite products. They pour many students' energies into punctuation, spelling, and grammar. Many have "too clear an idea, learned solely from textbooks, as to how imaginative writing should be done, producing patterns that all must follow." Perhaps, Mearns adds slyly, "it is for these reasons that successful writers speak so seldom of their courses in English!" The satisfied teacher, to Mearns, operates on the thesis that "The world needs the obedient, the unthinking, the uncreative, the workers." Mearns would "summon the individual spirit; I try to give it its chance to grow in strength, although the process is worrisome and fraught with peril."[40]

The restrictions placed upon teachers in most classrooms, however, are tremendous. At the mercy of school boards, state testing standards, administration, and accountability studies, and with the taboos placed upon certain means of expression by society, their ability to create the environment – which is considerably freer for poet-teachers – is hampered. The schools, Ned O'Gorman observes, "know one rule: order, order, order. Joy, wonder, freedom, abandonment to the world are revolutionary ideas."[41] Richard Lewis cites the "demands of institutionalization" that turn learning, which should be one of our "most personalized, integrated human experiences," into a matter of "increasing fragmentation and expediency."[42] The *individual*, the *personal* becomes one of the lowest priorities in the schools. Those who advocate creativity, as Lopate suggests, do push to overthrow an establishment which, in many cases, relies on testing and grading, even when applied to creativity.

Some educators have spoken against these practices. Alvina Treut Burrows maintains that creative efforts "are not exercises to be corrected, scored, rewritten or graded. (NEVER graded! Who can grade imagination, especially that of a young child with a lifetime of growing to do?)"[43] Yet grading is a common practice. Carol Staudacher, author of *Creative Writing in the Classroom*, believes that children's work must be evaluated by giving it "some sort of grade." First the child is graded for "original ideas, interest, and completeness of his creative work" and second he is given "a mechanical grade because it evaluates his spelling, punctuation, neatness, and the actual construction of his project."[44] Both grades, she writes, have equal value!

An alternative to red pencils, fill-in blanks, and naming parts of speech is described in one method called a process approach conducted in the East Brunswick, New Jersey schools, where children "write about their own experiences . . . tap their memories," question, listen, respond, "exchange, revise and proof-read drafts after comments by their classmates and instructors." Board members, PTA members, pupils and teachers all applaud this method. The excitement engendered caused one student to make notes even as she was playing soccer, others to ask for a thesaurus for Christmas. Teachers are required to keep folders for each student, respond to writing and drafts, display work (because writers need readers), and stress through writing the correct forms of language. The enthusiasm for the project runs high, although teachers have had to learn to "curb their desires for immediate results." Louis J. Hebert is quoted as saying that "Of course my basic concern is the end product. Yet there are many ways of getting there. Grammar and punctuation are taught as they come up in a real situation, not one that's fabricated."

The results of this writing, however, do not seem to bear out much originality in the way of poetry. One example by a sixth grade girl should suffice:

> I see the sun
> Shining through a rainbow
> Emerging from the sky
> Flowing into the green grass.
> Fluorescent, frosted colors of
> Red, yellow, orange, pink
> Striped into a rainbow
> Full of life.
>
> Julie Berish[45]

It is moot how this sort of writing can be considered creative beyond a familiarity with a thesaurus, a tool many would hesitate to put in the hands of a child! Jacqueline Jackson, poet and author of *Turn Not Pale, Beloved Snail*, comments on an approach of this sort when she writes:

> There are, of course, exceptions, but too many teachers don't want rewrites for getting even better, deeper writing. Their sneaky purpose is usually to perfect the form, to use this way to teach you paragraphing, etc. etc. etc.[46]

Rather, she feels, revision should be attempted "because you love what you've written, and you want to work on it some more. The first writing has brought up additional thoughts, has stirred the still waters of the well" or "Because you love it so much you want to share it with others, and therefore all the etcs. need attention – your spelling, your crummy handwriting, etc."[47]

Langston Hughes's desire to "instill in the young the discipline of revision and the desire to stick with a good piece of work until it is *as good* as the writer can make it"[48] may come with difficulty to both poet-teachers and school administrators who are looking for a product. Poet-teacher Anne Cherner speaks of beginning revision "by asking for comments from the class to distinguish the poem's strengths and weaknesses. From this follows how to criticize constructively and how to revise."[49] Alan Ziegler writes of how "I try to run around the room as much as possible, helping them 'revise' as they write . . . revision can do wonders for a poem." He also speaks of helping to "make the imagery of the poem stronger."

> If a child writes, "It was a nice house," ask why it was nice. If he/she answers "because it had smooth carpets," then we're getting somewhere that helps the reader experience the house. One more step: "Maybe you could tell me what it feels like to walk on the carpet." So then the child might respond, "The carpets were like whipped cream that feed your feet."[50]

Brownjohn notes that a writer's "notebook is often messy"[51] but when a poem is in its final version it should be written with correct spellings and neat handwriting. To ask for this when children are first writing will interfere with their spontaneity. "Encourage children to re-work poems as a 'real' poet does."[52] Arnstein believes that revision can happen only after a long period of time, that a teacher should not interfere, but allow children to grow in critical judgment.

But this is not the difficult revision which most poets know. Writing is not an easy matter, nor is rewriting and revising. Ciardi enjoins students to

> Write! Write hot and revise cold . . . Set it down and then change it. You fill wastebaskets. What slips away, provides. It's hard. It's joyously difficult. It's what Robert Frost called "the pleasure of taking pains."

To Ciardi "the rate at which someone recognizes he has done badly or less than well is the rate at which he improves." Writing requires a "soul-consuming effort."[53] Education, to Ciardi, is not possible without failure. Mearns is most eloquent on the labor that writing takes:

> Long after the script has been done the thing winds and unwinds through all the waking acts and thoughts; constant mental revision goes on; rereadings must be made; addenda, elisions, expandings, interpolations, all these trouble and torture. Interest dies and revulsion takes its place, but the driving force of patching and remodeling goes on. Oh, those who fashion creative stuff out of the welter of consciousness, they know what an interest is, and, according as they know, they both love it and fear it.[54]

Peter Bower, writing in the *Connecticut English Journal*, points out that "The most difficult concept for a student – and many teachers – to understand is that time is needed if writing is to be carefully crafted."[55] But for the very young or even the middle-school child endless revisions of their work are generally not possible since poet-teacher's time is limited. With a strange pride, the Artists-in-the-Schools Program of the National Endowment for the Arts prints a poem in its brochure with the note that it was written thirty minutes after two poet-teachers had come into the classroom:

Rain in the night makes me
feel dark
cold and wet. Makes me feel
hungry.
Spring storm makes me feel
sad.
Rainbows make me feel
happy.
Green, red, orange, makes me
feel colorful,
the smell makes me –
fresh.
Rickina Moss[56]

Continual testaments to the power of poet-teachers to get children talking and writing appear in the newspapers and media. Teachers, encouraged by books and reports of such successes, can therefore adopt these methods themselves, sometimes using their own verse, setting up creativity centers, producing and publishing poetry, and advising colleagues how to obtain easy results. A typical example of a teacher who believes poetry writing to be easy is found in Virginia M. Dunlap's "Flights of Fancy" article in *Teacher* magazine. "For example," Dunlap writes, "the following poem was written as strings of words and loose sentences. By following breath pauses, this series of ideas can be broken into lines, and a natural, or organic, verse structure emerges."

> I like candy.
> It's hard.
> It smells good.
>
> It's pink,
> red, blue, yellow,
> green, white, purple.
>
> It's gray, black and orange.
> It tasted good.
> I love candy.[57]

While Dunlap is "more than pleased" by the outcome of her method, her ignorance of what poetry is all about or how it is made and crafted is self-evident. As a believer in the myth, her enthusiasm overrides her knowledge and ability. Nor is she alone. Dozens of such articles flood educational and professional journals. The results, even as demonstrated by the one example, speak for themselves.

There are those, too, who believe that children cannot be harmed by such methods, because they have the power to develop their own criteria. Andrea Nold reports how "Slowly the children developed a sense of critical judgment, dependent not merely upon my word but upon their own emerging sense of what constituted effective writing"[58] in model poems offered to them. Eleven- and twelve-year-olds, Claudia Lewis asserts, begin to understand something about "the relationship between form and feeling in a poem."[59] Children, writes Harold Bond, respond to the idea of using forms "once they realize the forms are the means and the end is the creative process itself."

> It is not adequate simply to turn children loose, enjoining them to write a poem on subject X. They want to know the rules of the game, what they can and cannot do; the number of syllables they may use or the number of lines or the shape of the poem or whatever. And they take these rules most seriously. When the rules come together, they make a net, and it is through that net that the child can catch his poem.[60]

Children know how to resist intrusions into their inner lives and how to reject subjects and suggestions, as Arnstein notes when she asks children to write about sorrow:

> Children are not occupied with sorrow in the abstract, nor has the emotion anything of the universality, the immediacy of fear – not, at least, in the lives of these children. Of course, it may not have been the subject matter that the children rejected, it may have been the imposition of *any* subject matter after the freedom they had enjoyed to write whatever they chose. In any case, that freedom was their right; and their tacit protest of any infringement on it was a healthy sign of having established the habit of looking to themselves for the source of inspiration. Moreover, my motivation was not legitimate. However desirable it might be for me to seek to understand the children, the prime reason for their writing was not to supply me with laboratory material.[61]

Margaret Meek also understands that children do not easily disclose their feelings. The idea that writing poetry is therapy for children is too facile, too appealing to many poet-teachers and teachers who often indulge in instant analysis. Children's symbolism is a matter for the trained professional, and lay analysis is dangerous. "After several years of schooling," Lopate writes, "most children will have internalized the voices of censorship to a degree that they protect themselves in advance through *self-censorship*."[62]

Many children are far more capable than most teachers give them credit for – they know when they have shallowed out. The drawing of a trashcan on the cover of a booklet of writing done in an after-school library class has something to say about what children think of their easily written, pedestrian verse. The children who begged a teacher to go outdoors, when presented with slides for inspiration, knew better than the poet-teacher where their real subject matter resided. As Kohl suggests, children know how to groan when one of their peers writes to impress a teacher, to get an A. Children also know when their teachers or poet-teachers are prodding. In the *Whole Word Catalog* a sixth grade pupil writes:

> My mind is wiped clean by this idiot
> who comes here once a week and sucks
> my head clean of ideas by putting my
> ideas on paper and printing them and
> handing them to other students for
> their knowledge enlargement.[63]

Children also know what will please certain kinds of teachers when they write:

> I am thankful for my mom, dad, and brother Randy.
> I am also thankful for my grandma,
> great aunt and their candy, too.
>
> I'm thankful that we see the moon and stars,
> I'm glad that I can eat candy bars.
>
> I'm thankful for my home and trees,
> And even for the little bees.
>
> I'm thankful that I can read a book,
> I'm very thankful that I'm not a crook . . . [64]

But there *are* things children do not yet know about the real *making* of poetry. The idea that they use onomatopoeia or assonance unconsciously is moot; the idea that they use metaphor and animism is not. The idea that they resist criticism, do not wish to use form or learn style, but are satisfied with the first thing they write with all of its grammatical and spelling errors may be more wishful thinking on the part of some teachers than truth. Children, says John Oliver Simon, "want to get the stuff right."

> What if they do something that you find interesting, charming, or poetic because of its unconventional grammar, or even the sequence is missing many of the logical steps that ordinarily con-

nect, and you like that; but they're really trying to get it correct, and what do you do? How do you point out the value that you find?[65]

Poet-teacher Roberto Bedoya characterizes himself as "almost lax about the atmosphere I was trying to create . . . I would encourage them to associate freely and just be free that they could be off the wall. But I realize now that I didn't give them enough formal structure, cause some kids really wanted it."[66]

Jack Grapes, another poet-teacher, believes that in a poem it's a special world, anything's possible and anything's allowed, but the more control they have over, quote, correct usage, the better they'll be able to express the way they talk when it's disjointed, or they can write it correctly.[67]

"If our emphasis that writing's the thing is sound, why should the quality matter?" Arnstein asks. As long as the content is not poor, as long as it is not "facile, superficial, 'cute,' or 'smarty'," as long as it shows "the mark of honest thought," why bother with quality? All that matters, Arnstein says, is that the children be pleased because they have shared their thoughts and feelings, have had their work accepted by others, and have achieved an "enhanced sense of personal status arising out of such acceptance" and a "release accompanying the *losing of self*" and a liberation of the spirit. It is not that the aim is to make poets of children but to "help them gain access to what creative powers they possess, so that they may grow *as people*, with the enjoyment of poetry (reading or writing it) ministering to that growth."[68]

Arnstein's stance would be admirable were it not for the fact that a great deal has happened since she taught and wrote her books. The simple pleasure of children writing poetry within a self-contained school is one thing, but today poetry writing among children has changed dramatically. Neither adults nor children view themselves as living within a classroom, enjoying the limited plaudits of friends and a classroom teacher. They are now "young authors" and "young poets" whose work is offered throughout the community — and often the country. Everyone is now, indeed, in Borges's words "at the mercy of genius."

Ruth Whitman in 1973 wrote in the *American Poetry Review* that

> recognition of the natural poetic capacity of children has recently, as all too frequently occurs in our exploitive culture, been turned into a fad, which like all fads, will inevitably crest and fade out.[69]

Quite to the contrary, the myth persists and with an increasing profusion of publications and conference activities centering around the poetry of children, seems far from a fade-out.

Today the acceptance of poor writing and spelling, incorrect grammar and impoverished language abounds in newspapers, over television, and in books. It is not likely that anyone will quibble over children's errors in their poetry writing. But what will happen when a present generation of children grows up *is* of concern. For children who are praised and flattered may find that life outside the classroom and the confines of home and of childhood does not take so kindly to their self-expression, their facile ability to toss off whatever idea or thought may enter their heads.

In 1927 Mearns wrote that the function of the school is "to remove the traditional bars of unfruitful suppression in order to get the mental set that will permit the hidden powers their freest exercise, but equally essential is the compelling duty to present the inviting materials upon which these powers may work to the best advantage. Mere freedom is not enough."[70]

The myth of the child as natural poet, however, rests partially in the belief that freedom *is* enough. It enables children and poet-teachers to flout tradition and authority, to revel in their passions. This is a new sort of Romanticism. There is no longer room for Whitman's Transcendentalism, for Wordsworth's Pantheism, or even Rousseau's self-discipline. The natural powers of the individual prevail.

The poet, I. A. Richards writes, has an "amazing capacity for ordering his experiences";[71] his style, furthermore, is a "direct outcome of the way in which his interests are organized."[72] The poet's work is, therefore, "the ordering of what in most minds is disordered."[73] This would suggest that what is called *natural* is an *inability to order*. Furthermore, order requires responsible educators, teachers, parents, and poet-teachers who will lead the child to a more meaningful sort of "making."

CHAPTER XIII

Process and Product: Children as Young Authors

What, are they children? who maintains 'em? How are they escoted? Will they pursue the quality no longer than they can sing? Will they not say afterwards, if they should grow themselves to common players, – as it is most like, if their means be no better, – their writers do them wrong, to make them exclaim against their own succession?

From *Hamlet*, Act II, Scene ii
William Shakespeare[1]

There are probably few ages and few countries that do not have a group of children applauded for performance in the arts. Hamlet's questions concerning those who "berattle the common stages" gave rise, in his time, to "much throwing about of brains" even as the issue of child poets is of interest today. Rousseau, in eighteenth century France, marveled at the ability of child acrobats and pantomimists, noting how children's bodies could be trained to perform with agility. But the premature cultivation of the minds of children, of their verbal discourse and language was, to Rousseau, another matter. For this required abilities children did not yet possess; a "degree of understanding they appear to have"[2] but, in fact, do not, as well as the "language of passions" which "animates speech." Children "cry out, it is true, but they lay no accent on their words; and, as there is little energy in what they say, there is nothing emphatic in their voice and language."[3] It is this necessity for the "language of passions," energy, and emphasis that distinguishes the poet.

Child prodigies in chess, in music, in higher mathematics, and in certain other areas of science have not been uncommon throughout history. Unlike child poets, their abilities do not depend so greatly on experience, observations, and emotional responses. The gifted child may exhibit a facility for language and observation, but it requires life-experience for this child to grow. Kornei Chukovsky, author of *From Two to Five* published in 1963, speaks about writing by gifted children:

> No one can question the value of our careful and devoted attention to gifted children. However, we must admit that at times it is too unrestrained. Instead of training young people to take their literary efforts more seriously, and instead of teaching them to set high standards for themselves, we give them so much encouragement and praise that some of them, with their noses in the air, begin to regard themselves as divinely inspired geniuses who do not need to observe any rules.[4]

"By praising in advance of achievement this or that child who shows artistic promise," Chukovsky comments, "these teachers develop in the child conceit and presumption, isolate him from his peers and prepare him for a life of failure."[5]

The opinions expressed by Chukovsky should concern more adults who are attempting to foster creativity among children. No matter what the methods or emphasis, at heart there is a desire toward a two-fold goal. The first focuses on the need to give children self-confidence, a belief in themselves, their ideas and feelings, and a continuing pattern of growth. The second attempts to link this self-concept with better expression, with a way to approach literature so that it may be applicable to everyday living, as well as understanding, and – particularly among educators – with a facility for language arts. These goals are stated by the National Endowment for the Arts as well as in the credo of Teachers & Writers Collaborative, and they are elaborated upon in the texts written by educators and read by teachers. They are the rationale upon which countless examples of children's work are gathered, published, and distributed, whether under the aegis of a classroom or a school district; by a national publication – book or magazine; or through contests intended to excite and inspire children to do their best work.

Undoubtedly most informed adults would agree with Rousseau that in children's work there can be no "perfect union."[6] Yet there remains an element of extravagance in the newspaper accounts, in the publicity afforded all of these published efforts that bears examination. For on the one hand the rationale is put forward that writing is a *process* – that the value lies in children's ability to grow through their creativity; while on the other there is an overwhelming amount of evidence that many view the writing as a *product* – to be awarded prizes, published, and publicized.

Process, in this instance, is that aspect of children's growth that involves them in writing, rewriting, and revising; a process that follows the germs of their ideas for a poem from its inception to its completion, and often into publication. It is a measure of what they are learning as they share their writing, accept criticism, and as they learn to listen to their own voices. It is a means of developing both as a writer and a human being.

Ruth Whitman and Harriet Feinberg in *Poemmaking* state emphatically that "the process is always more important than the product." Misspellings, uninhibited use of language, "awkward or inappropriate language" are all unimportant and secondary to "the releasing of creative energy and the opening of new pathways to insight and self-discovery."[7] Claudia Lewis spells out what is meant by this process most clearly:

> Though it is common to think of children – the younger ones especially – as natural artists, the process takes nurturing. More exactly, the individuality of the children takes nurturing. What we have been implying every time we have used the word *process* is that a child is there at the center, able to make his own observations, honest and trusting enough to react in his own way to what he sees, and equipped with the knowledge and skills that must underlie any significant effort. After all, as teachers we are primarily concerned with the growth of children. Writing is one of the tools. When the result is creative, it is then a measure of the quality of growth.[8]

Process, in this view, assumes therefore that whatever is written by a child be accepted in light of the background of each individual child; that there can be no real standard for judging creativity unless one knows the circumstances of that child's home life and performance at school, as well as that student's emotional life and growth. This standard is an ideal that can be easily understood and appreciated. But it presents a myriad of problems for the reader who obviously cannot know any of these factors when presented with the product. The student of literature may wish to know what elements in a poet's life led him to focus on particular symbols, but exegesis is not the point of art for the average readers of a child's work. Presented with a "poem" written by an eighth grade boy, Randy Wittstruck,

> I do not want to be a city slicker[9]

in poet-teacher Daniel Lusk's *Homemade Poems,* a reader may accept or reject this as *poetry.* It could be that for this boy this single line represents some sense of self-discovery or growth that was important enough for Lusk to include it as an example of an artifact; but most readers expect more of poetry. There is no question that process is very important, but there is a point when the *product* needs to offer more, if the reader is to believe that children can write poetry.

The publishing of children's writing has become an accepted vehicle and those who advocate it cite many reasons for doing so. Langston Hughes's belief that reproducing the work of his students gave them a chance to criticize and improve their work would seem strange to many adults today who believe that the child's work – as first written – should be respected. Zelda Dana Wirtschafter, Director of the Teachers & Writers Collaborative in 1968, cites two reasons for publishing:

> Seeing their work in print affirmed for the children the validity and importance of their own thoughts, feelings, and words, and inspired them to write more and more and more. They also, when confronted with the printed page, became more aware of spelling mistakes and more interested in spelling correctly.[10]

It is the second point that engages educators and teachers interested in language arts. Although obeisance is paid to feelings and the importance of children's thoughts, the writing of poetry has been literally sold to thousands of teachers as a way by which children can play while learning, whether the goal is to correct spelling or to further interest in the use of the language. Brownjohn's lessons and games all stress this point, for if children "use a word in the wrong part of speech it is very easy to show them gently the correct form (commenting meanwhile on the choice of such a good word!)" Children can also, she writes, be taught to "grow more familiar with, and find their way around in a dictionary – making it more like a game than a daunting task."[11] Tiedt speaks of the positive reinforcement that a teacher should give by "spoken words of encouragement directly to each individual young writer."

> Positive attitudes can be conveyed also through displaying student writing as something highly valued, by allocating time for sharing writing in small groups, or by publishing student work in a class booklet.[12]

As "one of the natural activities" that evolve, Tiedt's "Writing Center" would have "the construction of *books*," an idea which has been seized upon by many for "classroom authors,"[13] who even form school publishing companies. Such an idea, practiced by one second grade class in New Hampshire, moves from brainstorming for topics, to first drafts, to peer conference, to second drafts, to teacher conference, to third drafts, to a group conference, to a fifth draft, to final revision and typing, to illustration, to binding, to placement in a class library, to an entry, as it would be, on a publishing company's list of its books.[14]

Arnold J. Pakula describes in *Teacher* "A Fifth-Grade Publishing Company" whose purpose "was to help the children conjure, imagine, role play and express fantasies through prose and poetry, while learning and practicing basic writing skills."

> The incentive to write carefully is high, because the focus is on writing manuscripts for possible "sale" to the editor and qualifying for an editorial position.

Pakula's idea is that "while students are usually taught sentence structure, grammar, punctuation and spelling, they often have no idea how to apply these skills. Our publishing company enables us to develop these skills and go several steps further . . . We study poetry, arrange visits with professional writers and enter a writing competition to thoroughly immerse ourselves in a writing atmosphere." Pakula wants children "to gain some insight into the world of commercial writing"[15] and brings in copies of *Writer's Digest* and *The Writer* for them to read. He stresses the necessity for correct grammar, for rejection of inferior work emphasizing to students that "a rejection of their work is not a rejection of *them*, nor does it reflect how I feel about them."[16] Yet he continually emphasizes "that writing is hard work and that results are often disappointing."[17] His own enthusiasm leads him to reflect that "Learning to communicate thoughts, opinions and feelings in a well-written form is one result of our project. But equally important is seeing the children develop an enthusiasm and a love for writing."[18] To Pakula process and product would seem to be equally important.

The popularity of such endeavors is ever burgeoning: There are few who question the importance of such an enterprise. Yet Jacqueline Jackson, in discussing "How (Maybe) to Write a Book," states:

> My own children have gotten this approach, too, and specifically in "creative" writing. They had a teacher who has her classes write books, and illustrate and bind them. But she had the kids work out their stories by plotting and outlines, so that they wouldn't end up with all sorts of unfocused material that didn't go anywhere. All right. You avoid that problem, but often you get into others that are more serious, I think. She also said that her purpose in having them do the book was for what they'd learn about composition, grammar, spelling, and so forth, and that goes along with the outlining. I think it's putting the cart before the horse, using the writing as a means to an end, rather than the writing itself being the higher goal.[19]

Classroom publishing has become a thriving activity beginning with "Author Centers" or "Writing Centers" where, according to a LaVerne, California teacher, Dolores G. Gonzales, the "development of word skills, sentence structure, paragraphing, book designing and illustration takes place . . . but each child's product reflects individual thinking and effort."[20]

In each step of the venture children are encouraged to believe they have something of worth to contribute. "Like individuals of all ages, children need the experience of success, which breeds confidence and the ability to move ahead to new endeavors. And since early experiences are particularly critical in building a positive self-image, teachers of young children must maximize the opportunities for children's successful expression."[21] The highlight of book publication is the Author Party where the student is honored, autographs his book, and reads it aloud. "Grandparents fly in from Chicago. Parents take days off work. And the young writer is puffed up with the knowledge that 'Now I am an author'."[22]

Many teachers and poet-teachers enlist volunteers to type children's classroom work, explaining that the "confidence building experience of seeing their words in print" is important. Yet there are problems in copying a child's work, as Lopate points out.

> For instance, in typing a child's piece of writing as it was written and scrupulously following the line-breaks, there was the danger of reproducing as a delicate, artfully laid-out poem what had actually been a hastily written prose paragraph (children are not great respecters of even right-hand margins). Or a mistake might have been patently made out of sloppiness, rather than personal expression, such as when a child left out a key verb: should one respect the "purity of the text," as though one were copying out a Dead Sea Scroll, or slip in the one word that would make the whole passage intelligible?

"The desire to preserve the exact flavor of the student's language, understandable as it was, sometimes had the effect of making into a precious 'found poem' what had not been written with that intention,"[23] as Lopate points out.

This is certainly the point at which *process* and *product* must part company, for the process is scarcely ever the artifact as spontaneously and naturally conceived. Those at school and at home who encourage children to write take pride in what children have accomplished. The allurement of print beyond the classroom is as enticing to adults as to the children themselves. In an article "Share Your Students: Where and How to Publish Children's Work" in *Language Arts*, Kathleen Copeland sounds the invitation:

> How many times, paging through magazines for children, have you lamented the missed opportunities to have your own students' work shared in print? While we don't want our students to consider publishing the primary goal for writing, submitting

> their work for publication can be suggested to children as one worthwhile way to share their ideas. Through publishing, not only do young writers share their ideas with a large audience, they gain pride and satisfaction in a job well done.

Copeland gives a list of ten magazines that accept poetry, half of which have contests. She cautions teachers, however, "whether or not a submission is accepted, writing remains an exciting and worthwhile adventure," a panacea that is as loaded as her remark that "Often work is returned not for lack of quality, but for lack of space." She also suggests that additional outlets for work "include school district publications, school newspapers, classroom publications, and professional journals."[24]

McKim and Steinbergh note that poems written by children "can be submitted to a school paper if there is one, and the children's magazines if the teachers and children are so inclined. Sometimes the values of these national magazines do not coincide with the values I am trying to instill in my younger writers, and I do not want them to lose confidence if their poems are not accepted for publication."[25] Thus to these poet-teachers the process is infinitely more important than the product; the knowledge, in short, that what is published is often a piece of writing which had been better put in a classroom booklet or on a display board. This viewpoint, however, is not the most popular, as evidenced by the amount of publication of children's work, for teachers often value publication in terms of reflected glory, or parents spur their children to become "young authors." More and more educators, teachers, and poet-teachers are redefining the role of writers as those who write *for* an audience, who *must have* an audience if they are to grow; audience is thus invoked as a symbol for bolstering self-confidence in the child, but the implications are far broader.

Within a class the sharing of writing *is* a positive force, for the child who has approbation from his peers is certainly the richer for an ability to communicate. Children who may not be at the top of their class scholastically often have the greatest need to express their thoughts; the writing of poetry enables them to compete on a different level. The ability to listen and to respond to inner needs of self-expression is undoubtedly served in this way. Mearns notes the value of such an experience.

> "These pieces of writing," they seem to say to themselves, "were done by boys and girls just like me; written because they wanted to write; done the way they wanted to do them. I have things of my own I want to write about. In my own way, too. They must have had fun doing it. Why shouldn't I?"[26]

But sharing often leads to the idea of an audience beyond the classroom. Lusk believes that writing songs, collaborations, nursery rhymes, and "Playing God" (picking out something in a person that needs changing and writing about it) may help children "prepare to write for an audience."[27] Marvin Zimmerman suggests that students who do not know what to write about or what they are going to say can be helped by a sense of audience; students should, when writing, think of all phases of the educational environment which provide "direction, topic, and audience"[28] awareness.

The goal of publication, however, goes *beyond* classroom sharing or working. What most adults have in mind is the talent that may be showcased in district and statewide publications, in magazines that are published as an outlet for children's work, as well as in trade books such as *Miracles*, *The Voice of the Children* and *Here I Am*.

A young pupil in the Teachers & Writers program who had her work published in a book speaks of being "really proud. I felt like a literary figure at age eleven."[29] Koch tells how children, even when writing what "was not a great poem," still "made them feel like poets."[30] "It is inspirational," says a blurb from the *Chicago Tribune* about *Stone Soup*, "for children to read the contributions of their peers in a published magazine."[31] "Get the Mark Twains and Pablo Picassos in your class to contribute to *Stone Soup*, a top-notch literary magazine written and illustrated by kids," *Instructor Magazine* states.[32]

The concept that children can be Mark Twains, stars, literary figures, and even inspirational is supported by countless school districts who listen to those who tell them that poetry writing is easy. Nold believes that "There is nothing magical in writing poetry; nor does poetry belong to a special few."[33] Such beliefs filter down quickly. Milan Kralik in *English Journal* tells how each student writes a word on a piece of paper and dumps them on a desk.

> I announce (somewhat over-dramatically), "I am now going to write a poem," and I usually manage to throw one together in thirty to sixty seconds.[34]

The Southwest Regional English Teachers' Conference, sponsored by the National Council of Teachers of English, features among its events a workshop given by Jesse Hise on Anyone Can Teach Poetry Writing.[35]

Similar workshop sessions are part of numerous conferences throughout the country where teachers learn how poetry can be easily taught and quickly written. Publishers' booths often offer gimmicks from "classroom author kits" to flash cards to "books" which can be disassembled and used as 3x5 card files. Some of these include activity cards for sensory development, cassettes to recreate response to sound, scent samples, "thought activities" to feign blindness, as well as anthologies for reading. Some are cottage industry products, booklets that rely on a teacher's own poor verse to serve as models, or are filled with spotty or incorrect information about poetry itself. But all are aimed at instilling the idea that because children are poets and authors, it takes but a brief time to bring these "natural" gifts to fruition.

Since many adults believe that it is easy to write poetry, the belief often spills over to the children. A nine-year-old prize winner in a "Jive to My Sneakers" contest sponsored by the New York City Department of Recreation and the Police Athletic League told a *New York Times* reporter that "Poems are easy to do . . . Next year I may want to do another one."[36]

Such contests are becoming a part of city, regional, and statewide planning, with all the attendant hoopla and publicity that accompanies state fairs. A recent International Reading Association conference featured as a two-day preconvention workshop a "Young Authors Extravaganza" with almost forty separate workshops, focusing on all aspects of conducting Young Author conferences. Bookbinding techniques, publishing, planning conferences, "Fun Day Awards for Young Authors," "Recognizing Young Authors' Successes," student testimonials, "Making Writing Fun" were but a few of the group sessions offered with participants from twenty-one states. Intended for "teachers, curriculum specialists, reading council officers, and school administrators, grades K-12,"[37] there were but five sessions involved with actual writing, and no mention of any poet-teachers as part of the program.

A National Council of Teachers of English preconvention program in 1978 offered a three-day "Young Authors Conference" featuring fifty Kansas City school children "who have previously written and developed their own books" speaking about "the writing process and expansion of their written language."[38] Young Author Conference procedures as well as bookbinding techniques and writing activities comprised the second day, whereas the third was devoted to learning about how a Hallmark book is made.

This is only the tip of the iceberg when the amount of time and energy devoted to such enterprises, carried on in all states, is considered. Typical of such events is an annual Authors' Fair sponsored by the Department of Education of San Diego County, California, in cooperation with the greater San Diego Reading Association. Here some two thousand "budding young authors and professional authors" are brought together so that authors may acquaint children with "rough drafts, galley proofs and rejected manuscripts, so that the children become aware of what is required in authoring a book." Children, the department believes, "can only fully understand the reading process when they have experienced authorship themselves."[39]

Other activities focus on children's work as a product worthy of a place in school libraries. A directive from the North Area Publications Committee of the Minneapolis Public Schools states among its guidelines for selection that not only should material contribute to the students' self-esteem, be in good taste, and "represent the largest number of children feasible," but "be suitable for use as library material for a wide range of ages, kindergarten to adult."[40] The growing tendency to use student books as part of a library, to call children authors and artists, is ever spreading.

While many adults, teachers, administrators, curriculum specialists, and parents involve themselves in these activities, an examination of the material published serves to point up the moot value of this *product* as opposed to *process*. A first grade winner in the fourth Annual Young Authors Conference sponsored by Administrative Area H of the Los Angeles School District has her work cited in the *Los Angeles Times*.

> Blue is the sky – some days;
> Blue is a hat I wear;
> Blue is a desert flower;
> And water in a rumbling sea.[41]

Nor does the quality of writing in the majority of school and district publications fare any better. A sixth grader in a Carpenteria, California school writes about "Summer Fun":

It's fun, in Summer, at the beach
To see how far the waves can reach;
To picnic underneath a tree
Where nosy ants all come to see.
To row a boat across the lake
Until my arms begin to ache.
All the seasons are very fun
But Summer – that's the funnest one.[42]

A poem by an eleven-year-old published in *Highlights for Children* is pedestrian:

I like summer–
It's very nice.
There is no snow:
There is no ice.

The days are warm:
The nights are cool.
And we don't have
To go to school![43]

A nine-year-old has a verse published in *Wombat*:

Summer is hot,
Summer is cool.
You can go fishing,
And jump in the pool.[44]

In an article published in *Language Arts*, "Thinking and Writing: Creativity in the Modes of Discourse," Ken Kantor and Jack Perron speak of creativity as "a staple rather than a luxury in the elementary classroom – and that is encouraging." Yet they also note that "What many regard as 'creative' is sliced a bit thin. To many teachers, creative writing means writing that is 'cute' or 'clever' – or simply 'nice'." There is also a tendency on the part of many to "connect 'invention' with imagination and creativity (the use of inner resources) rather than the discovery of established knowledge."[45]

But the writing that usually wins contests and is chosen for publication focuses on established knowledge rather than any imaginative thrust. Educators and classroom teachers are caught up with the process of teaching fact and, indeed, encourage it. Imagination serves only as a reproductive function; the writing has a surfeit of pedestrian and trite remarks about summer having no ice or snow, or beautiful flowers blooming in spring. The most commonplace imagery seems enough for most teachers and most readers, as well as a touch of the occasional "I" to prove that somewhere is a voice that has "feelings."

Lee Bernd, an elementary teacher in Stevens Point, Wisconsin, sees the problem:

> Poems, composed by classes, those brain-stormed word lists on specific topics – a color, a dream, a wish, a lie – help children express themselves, build students' self-confidence, and encourage some to write independently. Sometimes the children may come up with something good.
>
> David McCord once said, "The child is not only a potential poet but every now and then is likely to write a line that any older person would be glad to have written." That is a good and fair remark, *if* we remember the words "potential" and "every now and then." Too often today we make children think they *are* poets *now* and that nearly everything they write is worth keeping.
>
> Let's consider McCord's word "potential." Webster defines it as "existing in possibility; capable of development into actuality." That's the key. The teacher's responsibility does not end with the listing of dreams or lies, although it may be written in the form of a "poem." The teacher's responsibility *begins* there. Will it be easy? Of course not. It is not easy to write a poem. It takes a lot of learning and a lot of thinking . . .[46]

Bernd expresses a philosophy rare among teachers, for in countless publications that purport to honor the work of children, the quality of this work falls so short of creativity that a reader must gasp in disbelief at the inability of educators to understand what poetry really is.

The judges of *An Invitation to Poetry* have chosen as the winner for first grade entries a poem titled "Abraham Lincoln."

Abraham Lincoln read books,
  Most he had to borrow
to read by
  the light of the fireplace.

When he grew up,
  Our President he became.
To be shot
  in a theater called
Ford.

Brian Leavitt[47]

Honorable Mention goes to another boy with a poem about a "Pussy Willow."

I wonder why
  the pussy willows
are soft, fuzzy and white.

I wonder why
  the pussy willows
stick like cotton candy on me.
  I guess I'll have to find out.

Matt Davies[48]

What is the rationale behind such a choice? The winning poem indicates that a *process of learning* has certainly taken place. The child is stating facts about Lincoln which indicate a measure of his intellectual growth. But the meaningless alignment, stilted diction, and lack of voice are not the stuff of poetry.

The boy who wrote about a pussy willow, however, has employed all the elements of the *creative process*; he has not only observed, but in an effort to understand, has compared the pussy willow to cotton candy in a fresh and surprising simile. He has used his imagination, a sensory response, curiosity, and his own honest voice which indicates, at the end, that he is growing. He speaks in the cadence and language true to childhood.

Yet the judges' choice bespeaks how, far too often, the pedestrian product that states fact, that attempts to be falsely poetic, is chosen, while the more creative artifact is not recognized. This is a nagging problem that is not easily solved, for it indicates a confusion about the creative process which many educators and teachers have not been trained to understand. Yet the reverse is true for poet-teachers who often revere the creative process at the expense of what are commonly called the language arts.

There must inevitably rise in examining the work of children in fairs, in contests, and in publications the ugly thought of the exploitation of children. Arnstein discusses this when she speaks in an interview with Lopate of a group of children taken around the country "to answer questions about their writing."

> One little boy was asked what happens when he writes a bad poem; he says he never writes any bad poems! Imagine! . . . It's just an exploitation. It's the wrong emphasis. You can't *plaster* culture on people. You can only develop it . . . under certain circumstances.[49]

Although it is fashionable for poet-teachers to confess failure in their diaries, articles, and books, they never publish the work of children which they believe to be flawed or inept. It is as if each work, written quickly, arose spontaneously because of excellent teaching. Too often the examples prove otherwise.

In an interview with Wayne Dodd, Robert Bly speaks about the "genial corruption" of publication at too early an age. "It seems to me," Bly states, "that workshops are extremely destructive in the way they prepare students for publishing ten years too early."[50] Bly, of course, is talking not about children but about young people in their *twenties*. How then are classroom publishing "companies," contests, and "Young Author Fairs" to be viewed with their emphasis on early adulation, when teachers and poet-teachers use the work of children to reinforce their own self-concepts, to espouse their own methods?

There is no question that *process* and *product* are important. It is also important that the efforts of children not be thrown away. Displays of children's writing can be a spur to children proud of their work. Display, without teachers' markings or corrections, as Burrows points out, "is a powerful builder of further energies for writing."[51] Display, in its broadest sense, can be folders on a desk, an original booklet, poems mounted on a bulletin board, a class project, and even, as Langston Hughes conceived of it, a program or a play. But a problem enters when this display becomes so product-oriented that the value of the process is disregarded. And this must inevitably happen in publication because of the myth that has been perpetuated about children as natural poets.

In an article in *Elementary English*, "Is the Display of Creative Writing Wrong?" Wayne L. Herman Jr. takes to task those educators, teachers, parents, and "patrons" of schools who insist that creative writing be displayed as product. Process, he believes, with all of its grammatical errors, misspellings, and inadequacies is more valuable to children who are only inhibited by a need to correct everything they write in order to prove to school boards and adults the worth of their educational climate.

> If children are required to put their creative work in near perfect form, we have prostituted our purposes of creativity to the objectives of the Establishment or to our personal motives. And children, of course, are cognizant of our changing gears. Subsequently creative writing activities will be characterized by inhibitions, the very thing we were trying to free children from.[52]

If children's work as process cannot be displayed, Herman asks, without fear that teachers, school boards, principals, and children will be put into a bad light, how is it that they do accept "poor products displayed in the visual arts" or inept ideas expressed in social studies or poor performance on the baseball field? Why is it that adults will not criticize a "skinny elephant" or an "improperly proportioned giraffe," a wrong answer, or a missed ball? Herman suggests that patrons of schools be informed that "errors in creative writing are used as a base for the instructional program in practical writing" and that creative writing "should be clearly labeled as creative writing"[53] in order to avoid such censure.

But such a solution does not begin to answer the central and crucial issue. For what Herman – and many others – fail to see is that the myth of the child as "natural" poet, the aura of "divinely inspired" genius that is thought to be the poet, is being challenged at its very roots, when imperfections exist. Errors are something that cannot be tolerated in the hero. The concept of children as poets implies that their natural gift is without flaw.

Most adults will accept failure in visual arts, in performing arts, in the classroom, and in sports because they are able to see the inept representation, the grotesque proportion; they understand that a growing child makes errors, cannot always hit the ball. But the average adult is not conversant enough with poetry to know what it is and what it is not. Educators and teachers themselves often stand in awe of the very word poetry. They subscribe to the idea that seventeen syllables, properly counted, constitute a haiku; that a given number of words that rhyme or are spaced in random fashion on a page are poetry; that if children express some feeling, observe some object, write down an idea, or use their senses, they are poets!

The myth has, indeed, triumphed! No amount of explanation that Herman or anyone else can offer will suffice because even the children themselves come to believe in their own powers as poets; in their natural gifts. Such gifts need no explanation, no improvement, nothing but raw self-expression. These gifts win contests, are published, and the children are stars.

Few adults have ever claimed that a child is a natural artist, a natural athlete, or a natural scientist. Imperfection in any of these areas is accepted because a child is growing and learning. No myth has been proffered in behalf of any other endeavor of a child's life.

But the myth of the child as poet has taken such firm root that whoever dares to explode it, to suggest that its product is not perfect, must answer not only to its perpetrators but to its heroes, the children themselves, who have come to tolerate the process in order to glory in the product.

CHAPTER XIV

Exploding the Dream

I prefer myself to everything which exists; it is with this self alone that I have passed the choicest moments of my life; this "I" in isolation, surrounded with graves and invoking the Great Being, would suffice to content me amid the ruins of the universe.

From *Cataractes de l'imagination*
J. M. Chassaignon[1]

"Mythologies," George Steiner asserts, "are the shapes which we seek to impose, through will or desire or in the shadow of our fears, on the otherwise uncontrollable chaos of experience. They are not, as I. A. Richards reminds us . . . mere fancies but 'the utterance of the whole soul of man, and as such, inexhaustible to meditation . . . Without his mythologies man is only a cruel animal without a soul . . . a congeries of possibilities without order and without aim.' "[2]

Mythologies root themselves in religion, in philosophy, in psychology, in politics, in economics, in history, and in literature. They occur in all forms, from the most primitive beliefs to the mythologies imposed by great works of art, which, as Steiner contends

> pass through us like storm-winds, flinging open the doors of perception, pressing upon the architecture of our beliefs with their transforming powers. We seek to record their impact, to put our shaken house in its new order.[3]

Steiner's insights on mythologies "of justice and of the ideal state" are curiously pertinent to the myths of the child as poet. "Throughout history," he writes, these mythologies "have tended towards one of two directions."

> Either they postulate the inherent fallibility of man, the permanence of a measure of injustice and absurdity in human affairs, the necessary imperfection of all mechanisms of power, and the consequent perils of attempting to establish a mortal utopia. Or they will affirm that man is perfectible, that reason and will can conquer the inequities of the social order, that the *civitas Dei* must be built now and upon earth, and that transcendental justifications of the ways of God to men are cunning myths intended to stifle the revolutionary instincts of the oppressed.[4]

Central to the conflict, Steiner believes, is the "mystery of the Kingdom of God."

> If this Kingdom exists beyond mortality, if we believe that there is a redemptive judgment, then we may accept the persistence of evil in this world. Then we may find it bearable that our present lives do not exemplify perfection, total justice, or the triumph of moral values. In this light, evil itself becomes a necessary adjunct of human freedom. But if there is no "other life," if the Kingdom of God is merely a fantasy born of man's suffering, then we must do everything in our power to purge the world of its failings and build Jerusalem of earthly bricks. To accomplish this, we may have to overthrow existing society. Cruelty, intolerance, fanatical rigour become temporary virtues in the service of the revolutionary ideal. History may have to pass through Armageddon or decades of political terror. But in the end the state shall wither away and man shall awake once again in the first garden.[5]

The two courses open to man, therefore, are to "either create the good life here on earth or resign himself to suffering his term in a chaotic, unjust and frequently incomprehensible journey between the two poles of darkness."[6]

But the myth of the child as poet *negates* the need for making a choice. It is a stunning myth, a myth that would supersede all others: for it places at its core the belief that children are the ones in the "first garden," the "celestial abode," the "heaven." They speak the truth that the "prison-house" shades cannot reach. It is this perceived truth with its innate rhythms, its pure language, its instincts and intuitions that permits adults to forget all the social injustice, the evils and absurdities, and it is possible *because they* – the teachers, educators, poet-teachers, and parents – are building the "Jerusalem on earth" that allows this expression. The two poles of darkness no longer matter. Children reveal the images of the unconscious with their poems; they give back to adults all that has been lost – their dreams, their memories, their pure and naive beliefs which the world has taken away. Adults play their role by devising methods that bring to light the images, the experiences, the revelations.

It is no accident that Blake invoked the child as his symbol. It is the dreams of children, their play, their innocence that must be defended against the encroachments of false priests and nurses, prejudice, and the horrors of the world. Myths conceived by poets vary. Some, Steiner asserts, are built on the "dislocated immediacies" of the subconscious mind. Others evolve from tortured minds. These are not new; "they began with men's earliest attempts to rationalize their apprehensions of the soul." But there are also

> mythologies whose conceptual content and symbolic forms are primitive and unique. Blake and Yeats developed highly complex and idiosyncratic bodies of myths. In contrast there are the great mythologies that have been assembled and codified over long periods of history and that are part of the poet's formative inheritance.[7]

The poetry which children write is not rooted in a sense of tradition, but rather comes in the nature of the "primitive and unique." Their own personal view of the world is, as Piaget writes, a single intuitive act; a series of "purely personal connections between ideas as they arise," an essentially unanalytic vision, distorted by contradictions. Children's schemes of analogy are often incommunicable. They attach their ideas to images which are no more than their own inner qualities and thoughts. They reason to an internal model which has little basis in fact and which follows no traditional logic. Children are inventive, spontaneous, and egocentric, and what their writing shows is a syncretism that is something apart from the real world, yet it is just as real for them as the world is for adults. Children's absolutes are of a purely subjective origin.

This syncretism as evidenced in the poetry of children is one of the intermediate links between logical thought as adults conceive it and the symbolism of dreams. Piaget writes:

> Like the dream, it "condenses" objective disparate elements into a whole. Like the dream, it "transfers" in obedience to the association of ideas, to purely external resemblance or to punning assonance, qualities which seem rightly to apply to one definite object. But this condensation and transference are not so absurd nor so deeply affective in character as in dreams or imagination. It may therefore be assumed that they form a transition between the pre-logical and the logical mechanisms of thought.[8]

Syncretic schemes, as Piaget asserts, are not unintelligent. "They are simply too ingenuous and too facile for purposes of accuracy." They lead the child to make progressive adaptions to life and eventually they "will be submitted to a rigorous selection and to a mutual reduction, which will sharpen them into first-rate instruments of invention in spheres of thought where hypotheses are of use."[9]

The myth of the child as poet – the child as the bearer of truth – must therefore undergo one more rigorous examination. For this idea of truth has come, of late, to be equated with the unconscious mind, the realm of dreams and wishes – as if in plumbing its depths poetry is instantly and spontaneously conceived, startling adults with its revelations. Zavatsky writes in the *Whole Word Catalogue 2* of a "Dream Workshop."

> Learning to take dreams seriously by writing them down can be an important method confronting the irrational. Our daily lives, like our dreams, sometimes defy our attempts at interpretation. Rather than flee from the strange or unknowable, it is to our advantage to find strategies that will allow us to co-exist with it . . . Dreams are often unpleasant experiences because they show us things about ourselves that we would rather not see – our anger, our terror, our vanity. Once we can stare unflinchingly into the mirror of self the dream holds up, growth and change are possible.[10]

Poets, say Nyhart and Gensler, "rely heavily on the part of the mind that asks 'What if?' – that speculates and fantasizes. Many poems are written in a state of reverie, when the imagination is given free rein." Daydreams and nightmares, exaggerations, and outright inventions are all to be drawn out. Telling "a 'lie' stretches the imagination and allows an ambition, a dread, or a secret wish to be expressed in words."[11]

Richard Lewis's workshop on dreams bases its actions on recognition that dreams are a "manifestation of human thought" that has "significant ties to the poetic and imaginative process." Dreaming, like playing, is "related to a fluid inner consciousness" which is a "necessary means towards understanding and expressing the meaning of experience."[12] Holbrook writes:

> access to our deeper areas of inward life is too painful to be endured, possibly because we fear most our very inner weaknesses and need to defend our being against interference that we fear might destroy us. We can only work on inner reality by dreams, hidden meanings, symbolic displacement, and metaphor, and by this symbolic *work* "construct something upon which to rejoice."[13]

In 1948 William Carlos Williams, in a talk given at the University of Washington, spoke about the poem as a "field of action": "The poem is a dream, a daydream of wish fulfillment but not by any means because of that a field of action and purposive action of a higher order because of that." The poet, he says, "is a wisher; a word man."[14] Williams wants all the help he can get from Freud's "theory of the dream – as a fulfillment of the wish" but he reminds his audience

> to keep in your minds the term reality as contrasted with phantasy and to tell you that the *subject matter* of the poem is always phantasy – what is wished for, realized in the "dream" of the poem – but that the structure confronts something else.[15]

What Williams is saying is that the poem as a whole must always spring from and convey the dream, the hope, the wish that the poet carries within him: It is not calling up a dream or wish that makes the poem. Nor is the dream or daydream in itself a "field of action." The poem is of "a higher order" – its structure "confronts something else." The something else in this instance is Williams's call for a new structure that will answer to contemporary needs, a new language commensurate with the speech of the times, an end to traditional meters. Williams also makes clear that he is not opposed to tradition, that "There is no such thing as 'free verse'," [16] that imagism disappeared because it was not structural, and that a structure is necessary.

Williams has been misunderstood in the present-day effort to make everything new. But nowhere has this misinterpretation been so blatant as in an erroneous emphasis on the calling forth of dreams and wishes as the complete poem, as the "field of action." Dream and wish are to Williams the totality of the poem, the synthesis, that which is to be *made through structure*. Poets of the past had varying wishes – for beauty, for aristocratic attainment – and expressed them in their terms, just as the modern poet has "admitted the whole armamentarium of the industrial age to his poems." [17]

The gravity of this misunderstanding among those who believe that filling in prescriptives makes the poem is far-reaching, for it has produced an outpouring of lines which bear little relationship to real creativity. Koch is correct when he writes that wishes are "a natural and customary part of poetry;" [18] that "children are great makers of wishes," and that the making of wishes "engages children's imaginations quickly." [19] Richard Lewis is right when he recognizes that giving children the "license to express their dreams" [20] gives them a freedom they might not enjoy otherwise. But Holbrook's comments on the "work" needed to "construct something upon which to rejoice" [21] are crucial to the idea of creativity itself.

Having children write about dreams, Koch states, "is an easy way to make them aware of their unconscious experience and to encourage them to bring it into their poems. Children can write about dreams directly, as if it really happened, and they enjoy doing it – even the scary parts." But what should be made of Koch's assertions? What is the response to his statement that "The more thematic and sensuous material they have experience in using, the more they will be able to put into the description of their dreams"? [22] What is to be made of his remark, "I emphasized that dreams didn't usually make sense, so their poems needn't either"? [23]

The implications of these assertions must concern everyone interested in the writing of poetry by children. The first suggests that the dream is easily recalled; that the child has ready access to his unconscious and is willing to share with an adult "even the scary parts" of dreams and enjoy doing so; and that none of this presents difficulty for either teacher or child.

The second implication presumes that a child, given a certain training in use of senses and writing, can use images and descriptions of dreams not only easily recalled but described. The third remark places emphasis on the unusual nature of dreams, their seeming incoherence, their lack of reality or adaption to everyday life, and their often surrealistic quality – a quality which Koch seems to condone in the poetry he encourages children to write.

For those who believe that poetry written by children should display the incoherent and the senseless, Koch's last remark is apt; but the first two statements are at odds with all that is known about dreaming and about creativity as it is usually understood.

It *is* true, as Silvano Arieti states in his book, *Creativity, the Magic Synthesis*, that "in dreams, thoughts are transformed into visual images."[24] It is true that the dreamer has a capacity for imagery and for "orgies of identification."[25] But it is also true that the dream is limited; it is a restriction and not an enlargement, and as such it is original, but *not* creative. Arieti writes:

> The difference between originality and creativity becomes particularly evident when we consider dreams. When we dream, the vigilance of the environment is removed; we are alone with our inner self. What is even more important is that we can place few or no restraints on the floating content of the dream. Dreams occur spontaneously and are always original. When we dream, we lose control of our actions, and as characters of our own dreams, we do many original things. Even when dreams repeat certain themes, they present something new in each instance. Unexpected connections occur. Some combinations of scenes and events do not seem to have taken place ever before in nature or in the dreams of other people. On rare occasions dreams have been reported as conducive to the direct acquisition of insights, or even the formulation of inventive procedures that generally occur in waking life. . . .[26]

In spite of this, Arieti asserts, "dreams cannot be considered products of creativity. They are of value only to the dreamer, private experiences that cannot be fully or correctly produced. They consist mostly of primitive mechanisms that are not sufficiently integrated with conceptual processes, so that they cannot be shared or communicated in the original form. When they are told to others, and even more, when they are interpreted, they are expressed with the usual words and with the ways of thinking of the waking mind. But then they are no longer dreams; they are translations of dreams."[27]

In dreams, Arieti points out, there are different levels of meaning and different levels of cognition. The dreamer "is only aware of what he sees in the dream, or of what he says at a manifest level . . . If there is a unity, it is in the atmospheric quality or in a sort of primitive, affective gestalt."[28]

The dreamer needs an interpreter, for it is not the "truthful image" which he reports, but one that has been changed and often subjected to symbolic displacement. Even those poet-teachers who believe in using dreams as a source of imagery note this change. Ruth Whitman observes that in asking children to keep records of their dreams and to recall what they remember, "what they want to write about is not necessarily the dream they really want to write about at all."[29] Zavatsky in his "Dream Workshop" wants "kids to take the dream seriously . . . to write down everything, but *everything* they could remember."

> I tried to convince them that no detail in a dream was unimportant, even if it seemed silly. What people wore, exactly what they said, what their faces looked like, the colors (if they dreamed in color) and how the things in the dream and what happened in the dream made them feel. I insisted that their written dreams be as detailed as they could make them.[30]

To Zavatsky not only are "dreams an inexhaustible source of writing material"[31] but a way to "make children recognize that good writing consists of concrete details that have sensual appeal, not in generalizations or abstractions . . ."[32] While this is a commendable goal, it is also true that his insistence on the students elaborating their notes with further description is not a purely unconscious, but rather a conscious act. Zavatsky believes that "much of the history of poetry is composed of images drawn from the unconscious mind and fashioned consciously to link objects, events, and emotional states, that seem at variance;"[33] yet he seems to ascribe to children an ability to detail from the dream more than they really remember. His interpretation of the children's dreams is also at variance with his statement

> Dreams are important indications of the emotional state of the dreamer. A child who has nothing but terrifying nightmares, or a child whose writing is filled with negative self-images, can perhaps gain a simple therapeutic value from recording his dreams. Some of the terror drains away in the saying of it, and the child who feels his work is worthless may be nudged to a reconsideration when faced with the existence of the piece of writing he has done. The temptation to play psychologist can become overpowering when working with dreams, however, and I successfully resisted it.[34]

Poetry is often viewed as therapy: a baring of emotions, fears, or angers that allow the child to vent feelings; of nightmares that the teacher accepts and even welcomes as a sign of personal rapport. In this way the myth gains further power for the adult, who sees himself as a receptacle, even a pseudo-psychologist or analyst who can interpret for the child and be there to help. Having urged the child to express feelings or wishes, dreams or nightmares, adults thus fulfill their part in the myth and become an indispensable part of the process.

While classroom teachers are inclined to use the dream and wish as a pleasant, uncomplicated exercise, many poet-teachers believe that dreams should be elicited to effect the image, or to bring out the unconscious, the true inner feelings of the child. This is, according to Arieti and many others, a psychological fallacy. Furthermore, in the hands of poets or teachers it might be considered irresponsible; for, having coaxed out of a child a symbolism which cannot really be understood – the "description" of a dream which is impossible for any human to remember accurately, a memory of something that "doesn't make sense" – adults then content themselves with the idea that, since dreams make no sense, *poetry does not have to make sense.*

The value of these methods then is open to many questions. Should children be told that it is easy and enjoyable to state and share their dreams? Should they be led to believe that in so doing they are describing things in any real way? Should they be told that poetry, like the dream, need make no sense; that anything crazy that comes into their heads is the stuff of creativity and of poetry? It is one thing to teach children that what they have to say is important – that their ideas and concepts are important. But the dream is, as

Williams points out, the totality of the poem and it is *not* something that comes to mind completely from the unconscious: It is only part of a higher order, a structure, a making that is not always easy.

The use of the unconscious in poetry is valid but, as Arieti points out, there is no trick to doing this. It is a natural function for everyone. The images the unconscious brings forth represent a human way of freeing the self from the bounds of reality. These images are a way of dealing with the absent; or even to create something which the individual wishes and to give it a form. The image is a powerful tool for the poet who does not wish to adapt passively to reality. This is what Williams means by the poet as a "wisher," someone who can transcend his usual state by his dream. But it is not the nocturnal dream, the unconscious dream; it is the dream that is rooted beyond the self; it is a dream that is achieved through a conscious making by transforming the image into the symbol, a new concept beyond the immediate and easily called forth dreams of the individual child – or poet.

It is not just a matter of naming the image, then, but a matter of transforming it, externalizing it in a creative product. Josephine Miles, a poet-teacher, is direct when she "disagrees with Kenneth Koch and others who try to tell students a poem is like a dream or a lie or something like that. Students may be able to work with these ideas and do beautiful stuff, but it's not where they're at – it's not coming from inside them. That's dangerous."[35]

Poet-teacher Anne Martin also recognizes that there is some danger that such methods are becoming "a new orthodoxy, that the excitement of the process and the easy excellence of the products are overshadowing some very important purposes of writing: to learn to know what we need to say and how to say it." What Martin feels is needed is "for teachers to try to help young children write honestly out of their own needs and obsessions, even when this may result in writing that is often quirky, unpredictable, and not necessarily a source of pride on bulletin boards."[36]

It may be, Martin says, that adults enjoy "Koch type exercises" because the "products are often so charming."[37]

> But most of the time I think they are just complying with a writing assignment, giving the teacher what he is looking for, coming up with the kind of writing that is sure to please other adults and children.

To Martin, however, such writing has a sameness "beyond the similarity caused by a common form." Children were writing what sounded "like Koch's own ideas" and it sounded hollow. Perhaps, she speculates, such "joyful writing experiences are useful and maybe necessary, but they should be only a preliminary to more individualized writing."[38]

Like Martin, McIntosh sees strengths and weaknesses in Koch – as one whose "pure idealism and naivete carried him along" – and applauds his use of dream material, but suggests that Koch did not stay with Teachers & Writers "long enough to bite the apple of knowledge himself, to fall from grace."[39] Dick Lourie in an article, "Kenneth Koch's Wishes, Lies and Dreams: The Scriptural Fallacy" written in 1974, points out that while Koch is aware of some of the dangers of his methods, "some of his readers are not." It is not difficult, he says, for any teacher to create, like Koch, "a literary tradition," given a certain classroom situation and a particular group of children. Lourie is more outspoken than most on the methods:

> What I'm suggesting . . . is that *Wishes, Lies and Dreams* has sometimes been influential in harmful ways – it has been taken as How To Do It, not How I Do It; it has been treated as the work of a master rather than that of a colleague; it has been enshrined as gospel rather than incorporated into a body of useful knowledge.[40]

What Lourie worries about is that teachers will adopt the ideas extolled in Koch's book. The first, that poetry written by children "should almost always (not just sometimes) be concerned with fantasy – which our theoretical teacher might have taken to mean poetic imagination"; second, that the "children's poetry should hardly ever concern itself directly with their lives, their feelings, their experience, directly stated, unfiltered by fantasy"; third, that "precise observation (and precise rendering of it) is not appropriate to the poetry children write"; fourth, "Perhaps that the proper stance for almost all (not just some) children's poetry is playfulness."[41]

Lourie is both courageous and, unfortunately, prophetic, for all of this has indeed happened. Teachers have come to believe that poetry writing is easy; that children must be in a state of excitement; that rhyme must be discarded. Poet-teacher Norman Weinstein believes

Koch is wrong in letting children "believe only in the imaginative fun. Let the struggle be declared for them also. Don't make writing any easier or any harder than it is."[42] Kathleen M. Sewalk in *Poemmaking* writes about the results of an "exercise in 'no realidad' – wishing." This she said could not be translated for many of the children she worked with because they were not brought up in the fantasy world "which sustains many American children past Santa Claus and the Easter Bunny. The Armenian children 'wish' for Jesus to have a happy birthday at Christmas, Santos wishes his mother would come home . . ." Their reality, Sewalk writes, "is 'here and now.' I must not play 'no realidad' with them."[43] There are others who recognize that children are wary of exposing themselves; that there are some who cannot remember dreams, who wish to keep their secrets, their wishes and fantasies within.

While some teachers and poet-teachers disagree with the ideas expressed by Koch, a great majority praise both his book and his methods. Writes Kimzey in 1977:

> Do people realize what chaos would have reigned about the country four years ago without Kenneth Koch? Do they realize what points of departure he has given the ones of us who teach poetry and stay in the classroom all of the time?[44]

That one poet-teacher could make such an impression upon so many and that so many have no knowledge of the pioneer work done by others is unfortunate – work done by Mearns in New York, by Siddie Joe Johnson in Galveston and Dallas, by Arnstein in San Francisco. They do not realize that Hilda Conkling wrote in the 1920's

> If I were Jeanne D'Arc
> It would be hard remembering the apple-
>   orchard in bloom
> with nothing about me but noise and armies
> All men, all women, unhappy . . .[45]

They have not read in Arnstein's work

> I have a boy. Yesterday he was small,
> But today he is large.
> "Big, big, big," I thought to myself,
> "My boy is an elephant." . . .[46]

Nor have they looked through the pages of Mabel Mountsier's anthology of poetry by children, *Singing Youth,* published in 1927, and read

> When pigs begin to whistle, and cows
>   sing operettas,
> When birds begin to giggle, and mother scolds
>   and frets . . .[47]

or

> The moon is a hunchback
> Who carries a load of silver
> On his crooked back, . . .[48]

nor found in the July, 1905 *St. Nicholas League*

> (Extract from the "New York Courier.")
>
> "A dragon was found sleeping on the third rail of the subway, just above Forty-second Street. He stopped traffic for four hours, until he was blown up with dynamite. That cleared the track."
>
> Morris Bishop[49]

Here are wishes, lies, daydreams and dreams, comparisons, noises, metaphors, If I Were, and more! But with these notable exceptions: The first, and least important, is that prescriptives were *not* and are *not* needed to elicit ideas, moods, lies, or any other sort of writing with children, for these things come to them without prodding. The second is that these children with their capacity for imagery were not consumed by the precious and everlasting self that announces with every line what it dreams, wishes, feels, sees, or hears; these children used the self as a springboard to something bigger, more universal, less boring than self – something that escapes from the world of private images (of interest only to the individual) to create an effective experience for others.

Poetry is not a series of self-engendered images; it is not pure subjectivity. The poem must discard the *image* and present a *symbol* that is understood; it must shed its *subjectivity* and give *objectivity.* A reader grows tired of the preciousness that purportedly offers news of the memory, experiences, dreams, or wishes of the child. This may be of interest to the parent, to the teacher in observing the child's growth, or even to the psychologist, but poetry must give more. A poem must go beyond a statement about what *a child feels:* What is wanted is the evocation of *a new feeling in the reader.*

Children may respond to prescriptives spontaneously; but spontaneity and originality are not always as they seem. The originality with which children make their early metaphors is lost as they enter society.

> Many of the private, unusual, very subjective experiences that the baby undergoes do not have names, or the child does not know these names and therefore he forgets them. . . . Later the child accepts the verbal clichés offered by his social environment and learns to use these clichés profusely. They may occur to him spontaneously, but of course not originally, unless he recombines them in unusual ways.

A use of verbal clichés, Arieti states, implies the adoption of usual ways of thinking. Thus, as children become more social, they lose their "primordial nonderivative originality" which cannot be recaptured "because it consisted of nameless experiences which he cannot remember. To become original again, he must use different ways, and the new forms of originality will be at least partially derivative."[50]

It is this process of socialization that alters a child's ideas and thinking; that must – if he is to grow – involve him with reality, force him, beyond the "I" of the self, to recognize the "it" of the mind. A child who has been in a classroom such as that described by Kohl or Summerfield where ideas are discussed, where writing is an outgrowth of larger issues, will have his horizons expanded and will no longer be consumed with himself. But a child who is only offered an opportunity to write of his own sensory perceptions, his own dreams as well as wishes, is left to feed only upon himself.

It is this escape from reality, mentioned by Lourie, that characterizes a great deal of the poetry done by children under the influence of the New York School. It is a poetry that does not deal with reality or daily life but with irrelevance. David Ignatow describes it as a "conscious contrivance as a metaphor for disengagement from social commitment."

> I can understand why the school of irrelevance exists; because of the despair of man. I can sympathize with it because where do we go from total despair? We go back into ourselves. And when you go into yourself actually you lose touch with yourself. That's a paradox. Once you go too far into yourself you lose touch because your self is only found through interaction with others.[51]

If Ignatow's observations hold any validity, they would certainly explain the stance of many poet-teachers who, in order to recapture their power – the role of the "shaman," the prophet and magician – seek to manipulate, to rearrange life. Is it possible to suggest that the antics Smith describes, the poet-teachers' alliance with children over the heads of teachers as described by Lopate and the statements they make themselves about school boards or classroom teachers, are an indication of this power? Certainly they feed the myth that not only are children natural poets but that their role as poet-teachers is central. They have founded a new literary tradition, named everything anew, and have led many to believe that their methods produce a poetry that, like theirs, not only breaks with tradition but is often contemptuous of tradition. Central to this stance is the use of "unconscious imagery," which is so vague a term to the lay public that it becomes a license for "writing crazy": which is, in turn the kind of writing interpreted as a truth which comes from the mouths of children.

Even those who do not regard themselves as shamans or as poetic revolutionists may fall under the spell, seeking to find in children's writing the secret meanings behind "clusters of sounds" or images. In her essay in *Poemmaking,* "Fingerpainting with Words," poet-teacher Ruth Lepson cites, among others, two works with the notation that the reader may find the images "too arbitrary because they are not tied to one another in a logical or familiar manner."[52]

Making Cookies

shoot, pool, corner, oil
crunch a bunch
fritos, doritos
crunch a bunch
run for your gun
never on a Wednesday.

Anon.[53]

retina of the I
speaker of an eagle
something to be pondered
cocks comb
and
swans can twist from
anywhere rotating, spinning.

Jenny Nason[54]

But, she continues, "they are no more arbitrary than the images of the surrealists, who were searching for the deeper connections that were found only in the unconscious; words that seem to be strung together because they sound right together to the author may have deeper connections, too. And, of course, if you object to fooling around with language because the results seem arbitrary, you might also object to the equally arbitrary yet often the most exciting aspect of a child's work – the series of fantastic images that he or she is able to create."[55]

Unusual juxtapositions of words and images, as well as "crazy" writing are often explained in terms of Surrealism, a French movement that favored "experiments with states of mind in which logic was suspended," automatic writing, word games, and a belief in the significance of dreams. It was a revolutionary movement that broke completely with classical European tradition, questioning "the validity of the premises upon which Western culture was developed."[56] Like another movement, Dada, it chose literature and art to express its precepts. But as one critic wrote

> Dada and Surrealism are not art movements: they are not even literary movements with attendant artists. They are religions with a view of the world, a code of behavior, a hatred of materialism, an ideal of man's future state, a proselytizing spirit, a joy in a membership of a community of the like-minded, a demand that the faithful must sacrifice other attachments, a hostility to art for art's sake, a hope for transforming existence.[57]

To one of its leading exponents, André Breton, Surrealism was

> the total recuperation of our psychic forces by a means which is no other than vertiginous descent within ourselves, the systematic illumination of hidden places and the progressive darkening of all other places, the perpetual rambling in the depth of the forbidden zone . . .[58]

To the Surrealist, words are images with an independent life of their own, and these images are brought together to reveal a world free of rationality and control, a world in which there is no censorship, no accession to social convention or education. Its exponents used for their themes revolt, love, freedom, the exaltation of desire, black humor, and the world of subconscious thought.

An affinity for juxtaposition of certain words or certain images is often expressed in Surrealistic terms, a theme that runs through Lepson's essays as well as the work of many poet-teachers. Thus the mode of Surrealist poetry is invoked, although a true Surrealist would ascribe neither form nor meaning to what is written. "Honest-to-goodness surrealistist poetry will have nothing to do with meaning clearly stated and accessible,"[59] Ignatow points out. "Systematic surrealism," writes poet Louis Simpson, "does not permit moments of true unselfconsciousness to occur . . . Instead of emphasizing the irrational, it seems to emphasize the calculating mind. Systematic surrealism makes us think of store window decorating – calculated shocks."[60]

To Simpson, Surrealism grows monotonous because the construction is predictable. It is only "a series of forced juxtapositions. Two things forced together by conscious effort do not make an image."[61] Surrealism, he believes, did add to literature the idea of invented images and it is these images, represented by the unconscious rather than by what has actually been observed, that have resulted in "deep images," as in the works of Sylvia Plath. But the constant insistence on writing irrational poems eventually leaves the reader bereft. There is no connecting link. "Total poetry, like the total human being, must include so-called rational as well as irrational states – the poem must be logical as well as unpredictable. Images that move us do so because they are connected, to logical thought processes which we all share.

> Poetry in which there are no dream states is trivial, but dream images may be trivial also, when they are produced by automatic writing, without a necessary direction by the psyche of the poet. The answer, therefore, seems to be that the poet dreams and produces the images of his dream, but that only by meditation and selection can he discover poetic images – those which move other people. Poetic images are not picked up in the street or from a common stock of clichés such as can be obtained from a textbook of psychoanalysis. The poet must discover the logic of his dream.[62]

Children can hardly be presumed to be able to find such logic, in which case the poet-teacher or adult must supply an explanation. The futility of such an endeavor is of course self-evident. Yet the myth persists that poetic images emanate from a mysterious abode and that the adult, in uncovering the key to the child's unconscious, has performed a miracle.

Within the past decade many of the tenets of Surrealism have appeared in new disguises in the poet-teacher's classroom. The word games invented by Surrealists, the experiments with language, the emphasis on the dream as a way to the unconscious, the use of imagination as a defense against reality, and the disdain for education as it has been practiced exhibit themselves in a variety of ways. It is implicit in invectives against poetry written for children; poetry that is not contemporary; in the renaming of poetic terms; and the substitution of their own new rules for the old, their own literary tradition. An underlying proselytizing and revolutionary spirit is apparent, for example, in Zavatsky's statement that

> I think it is important for teachers to recognize that in the search

> for illuminating details, poetry parts company with the tendency toward generalization and abstraction that forms the warp and woof of American education.[63]

Today the art and poetry of the Surrealists are used as models by many poet-teachers, their names – Rimbaud, Breton, Magritte, Eluard, Artaud, Tzara – invoked to elicit the dream, the incoherent, and the fantasy.

To those who seek from poetry some measure of understanding there must be, and can be, more. Karl Shapiro speaks of this when he writes in 1970 of "The New Poetry – a Literary Breakdown." Students in college, he asserts

> do not want to read; they want to "experience." They do not want to learn; they want to "feel." They have become almost impossible to teach.

"We are," says Shapiro, "experiencing a literary breakdown which is unlike anything I know of in the history of letters. It is something new and something to be reckoned with. We have reached the level of mindlessness at which students and the literate public can no longer distinguish between poetry and gibberish."

> When critics and university students can no longer tell the difference between rock lyrics and the songs of Shakespeare, teaching is no longer possible; standards of good and inferior disappear; discrimination dies; and the true artist goes into hiding.
>
> We are in the time that Yeats predicted, and when everyone is quoting his famous lines: "The best lack all conviction, while the worst/Are full of passionate intensity."[64]

Shapiro's comments reflect a situation which has not been helped by the myth of children who focus on themselves, their experiences, and their feelings as poets. It is not possible to rewrite history because of the shift in thinking that has resulted from man's inability to believe in some unifying power or principle. But those who *do* believe that educators, teachers, parents, and even poet-teachers can have some impact on students, must take a hard look at the influences that have given rise to the myth of the child as poet and at those who most loudly support it. Today, as ten years ago, those who speak loudest still, in Ignatow's words, have "no intention of dealing with life as life, but dealing instead with the imagination as an autonomous experience." This leads poetry to strange byways and none stranger than the belief in the image over the symbol and of subjectivity over objectivity.

If the ideas of Kohl, Holt, and Summerfield hold any validity, then the child as poet must be put into a new perspective. The private voice of the child must coexist with a sense of community, with meaningful communication and symbolism. There must be attention to more than the unconscious; and an attempt must be made to relate writing to the process with less attention to the product. For too long, poets – with their ideas of the unconscious – have foisted on children what is really beyond them. The child's mind is not the adult mind and to use on children techniques that only an adult is capable of using is not only a disservice, but irresponsible.

It is one thing for O'Gorman to make a plea that children be allowed to "FEEL the juices and the nerve endings of their 'selves'."[65] No one wants less and those who deny the importance of doing so also deny the child a chance for creativity. But it is also time to recognize, as Bernd points out, that

> Self-expression focuses everyone's attention on *yourself*: art focuses everyone's attention on the thing made. We recall art: the lilt and lines of the poem, the exquisite watercolor; the haunting melody, not in terms of the person who produced it, but we remember, and see and hear in our minds, the object itself.[66]

In *The Identity of Man* Jacob Bronowski speaks about the poem –

> A poem tells us how to be human by identifying ourselves with others, and finding again their dilemmas in ourselves. What we learn from it is self-knowledge.

Bronowski elaborates. "I do not mean by this a narrow knowledge of our foibles only. On the contrary, the self that we discover in this mode of knowledge is every self and is universal – the human self. Or better, each of us discovers the outline of his self within the human totality. We learn to recognize ourselves in others, and the character of others in ourselves. We compare ourselves with others, and the comparison shows us what we are and at the same time what man is, in general and in particular."[67]

This concept of poetry goes beyond the autonomous imagination. It goes beyond children listening to the work of other children with nothing but an exchange of syncretic schemes. It goes beyond residing in the self alone and suggests that there are models, real models, which are far more important than those within the fancies of dreams.

If the recognition is made that the new literary tradition has not enabled children to write poetry but merely to spew forth formulas that are not only poor in quality, pedestrian and trite, but deceiving, the myth can be exploded.

Poetry is made. For the poet like the child is a maker who does not have any privileged news from heaven. He has a potential and certain gifts, but he is subject to the same need for craft, for revising and for structure, as any other human. To believe any less is to do children a tremendous disservice. But it will take a giant upheaval in the present classroom to relinquish the myth; it will take a new sort of approach. It will take a combined effort on the part of educators, poet-teachers, classroom teachers, and parents. It is *not* easy – but it can be begun. There is a way to put our "shaken house" in "its new order."

CHAPTER XV

Rules of the Game

"That's not a regular rule: you invented it just now."
"It's the oldest rule in the book," said the King.
"Then it ought to be Number One," said Alice.

From *Through the Looking Glass, and What Alice Found There*
Lewis Carroll[1]

When are the formulas and prescriptives and gimmickry that have plagued the child too long going to be laid to rest?

Most of these are conceived as an easy way to instant poetry; like many word games they are not means to creativity, but ends in themselves that only prove a child can follow directions and be controlled. They do not enlarge the imagination nor contribute to a child's growth; indeed, they stifle both. Such gimmicks include a myriad of "mathematical" formula ideas such as Lusk's

	cat			car
+	tree	and	+	elephant
	pussy willow			fat miles per hour[2]

while others that supposedly integrate school subjects with poetry abound in profusion. Lusk's "trigger lines," or suggestion that children use social studies tests and then "select words or phrases or facts . . . and try to write a poem using these,"[3] links poetry to learning in a manner that is bound to turn children away from creativity. Jill P. Gann's idea that a limerick be written about a career for a "Creative Classroom Career Contest"[4] is far removed from the idea that writing a nonsensical verse, meant to exist in the realm of the ridiculous, can be a pleasure. Writing greeting cards, creating "your own poetry notebook cover," or putting in the words for a "Poem You

Can Finish"[5] is nothing but busy work – a substitute for what poetry is all about. Thomas G. Devine's suggestion that a "Completed Image Poem" may be created by writing a title and four subsequent lines which list a "sight, sound, smell and emotional response"[6] on respective lines is another manifestation of the belief that ease and instant writing is a substitute for poetry. Shuffling "vocabulary cards" to "string together a zany dream-narrative,"[7] to use the letters of the alphabet to ask "about how it would taste, if you eat the letter A,"[8] to suggest that poems are made by "using as many incorrect grammatical forms" as possible, to supply "outrageous last lines" for poems, and to use "line breaks"[9] as tricks are only a few of the gimmicks offered. Perhaps, as Ziegler suggests, the gimmicks give "sure-fire" results and "are good for beginnings, as confidence builders, and later on as occasional cures for writer's block. But beware of addiction. Gimmicky exercises can foster a stimulus/response approach to writing, with the students dependent on the teacher."[10]

A good writing formula, the editors of *Stone Soup* assert, serves to "revitalize both the children's and the teacher's interest in writing." Such writing affords children praise and success. But formulas, they also believe, "tend to emphasize form over content" and "discourage children from relying on their own resources for their ideas."

> This is the greatest fault we find with "creative writing" formulas. Kenneth Koch's formulas, for example, create instant "poetry." By playing on children's natural sense of the absurd, his formulas lead to the creation of clever sounding writing. But do these clever sounding poems mean something to the children who wrote them?[11]

Whether they have meaning to the children is hardly the point. Chances are that they do, for students have been *told* that they have *written a poem*, and their pride in having done so is justifiable. What other standards do children have than the approbation of adults and their peers?

This is all the more reason to view with suspicion the writings of teachers who proudly proclaim how they trick children into liking poetry. P. R. Brostowin in "Poetry by Seduction" published in *English Journal* writes:

> Fake them out. Make them think you're doing one thing while you're actually doing something else. A magic act: the teacher as illusionist. Not a noble attitude for an honest person. Not the right behavior for a professional. Seduction, trickery, fakery, deception. Yet if we analyze what novelists, playwrights and poets do, we see that they use the same technique. They stack the evidence in favor of their theme. We call their behavior artistic selection, but it's still trickery, or deception. The poet, especially, uses indirect language; she says something by saying something else. This is the essence of metaphoric language. In fact, all art is distortion. Lying, of a sort. Telling lies about little things in order to tell the truth about bigger things. It's true of literature, painting, sculpture and photography (when it's artistic.)[12]

Brostowin's apparent inability to understand the function of the metaphor, the pseudo-statement as opposed to actual falsehood, is no more surprising than Stephen Marcus's techniques for the "Compupoem," a poem written by a computer "which encourages concern for planning ahead, unity and coherence" and "includes specific advice on such things as nouns, adjectives, adverbs, and 'zen and the art of computer poetry'."

> Sheridan's Poem
>
> The words
>   masterful, serving
> for inspiration
>   gently, insistently
> solace

According to Marcus, "Compupoem helps people deal with aspects of language, including image-making and sentence structure, have fun, and at the same time develop their computer literacy."[13] But is this poetry? What of Donald Mainprize's "Rollercoaster Poems" where words are stacked "*down* the page," kept the same size, and must "*say something significant, to utter a meaningful truth about life on planet earth*"? One of Mainprize's examples:

Anger
is
when
your
fist
can't
stay
unclenched.
Penny Reich[14]

Another formula is suggested by Jesse Hise, an Arizona high school teacher, again in *English Journal*, where "C+C+WD+E = NP" or "A comparison plus a comparison plus a wild dream plus an emotion equals a nonsense poem." Hise makes the rules clear:

A. The poem should not make sense
B. Rhyming is not permitted.
C. Write the words in any form that looks like a poem to you.

An example reads:

I was standing with my elephant
In the sky backward
When the late angry students
Cried at the loss of sky.
The moon melted into a first base automobile
And hailstormed at my feet[15]

The surfeit of gimmickry published in leading educational journals reminds one of O'Gorman's note that "preschool classrooms are usually filled with junk: teachers' crutches that kids fall over."[16] Do those who read these journals, as well as those who edit and publish them, believe this is the stuff of poetry, the means by which poets write, and the way children may create and grow?

There are many teachers and poet-teachers who report success in using pictures and photographs to inspire children's writing. Ruth Whitman believes this "has been a successful stimulation to a poem, partly because it allows the student to write about things he might not want to talk about in his own person."[17] Gensler and Nyhart believe that empathy is engendered by photographs, that the "notion of liberating someone's voice from its black-and-white silence is particularly appealing to the students of junior high school age."[18] Others take children to the museums where they may respond to paintings, sculpture, and artifacts in many media.

Yet while a poet-teacher may choose works of art and is aware that it takes skill to elicit response to the work of an artist or photographer, commercial gimmicks offer cartoon characters, stick figures, and photographs with lines below for children to fill in their responses. What of a child who sees nothing in the pictures to which he can respond? The "Portrait of Mille Y. D." by Jacques Villon is seen by a sixth grade pupil as:

> A rock looked like a head's turkey.
> Forms of land were shaped like tents.
> Yellow forms looked like a lady sitting down.
> Some red shapes made a chair
> some blue forms looked like a tub but only half
>   of it
> some shapes formed a dolphin's fin.
>   Jose Trujillo[19]

Is this poetry or a series of similes that go no further than first associations that a child normally makes? While the perceptions are original, they are far from the process of being synthesized into a poem.

Is it time that the catalog poem as it is practiced in the classroom be laid to rest? Educator Glenna Sloan, author of *The Child as Critic: Teaching Literature in the Elementary School*, notes that "Catalogue verse is as old as Homer," and suggests that a theme be presented to children who "in a brainstorming session, call out their associations related to it, trying to express as many sensory reactions as possible."[20] This is little more than an attempt to find out what children know about a subject; a dull listing arranged to resemble the alignment of poetry; and has nothing to do with the catalog poem as it is crafted by the poet with careful selection and meaningful description. In sharp contrast to Elizabeth Barrett Browning's "How do I love thee? Let me count the ways" is a child writing:

Houses are big
Houses are small
Some are short
Some are tall
Some are warm
Some are cold
Some are new
Some are old
Whatever the case as you will see,
They are good to live in for you and me.[21]

Sloan believes that rhyming can be avoided, but even then the results are encyclopedic. A child whose work is published in an elementary school anthology in California begins:

Eyes can be sad
Eyes can be happy
Eyes can be scared
And eyes can be gentle
Blue, brown, hazel, green
and black.
Eyes can look up
Eyes can look down . . .[22]

All this, of course, suggests a sense of play and it is the opinion of many that poetry is indeed a perfect foundation for "useful play." The rationale for this may be found in the words of May Swenson:

> Notice how a poet's *games* are called his "works" – and how the "work" you do to solve a poem is really *play*. The impulse and motive for making a poem and for solving and enjoying a poem are quite alike: both include curiosity, alertness, joy in observation and invention.[23]

Teachers, knowing that games have rules, seize upon this idea for their own inventions, believing that the "atmosphere of a game" must be created in addition to formulation of "rules like a game."

Is it not time to abolish the "making new" of names for figures of speech and forms? If children are as curious, alert, and excited about poetry as poet-teachers and teachers would have us believe, if they enjoy playing with words, can they not learn the words *simile, metaphor, couplet, tercet?* Must they be taught about "talk-to-mes,"[24] when what is meant is *persona?* Must they be subjected to "triplets," "terquains," and "triangular triplets"[25] when what is meant is the three-stanza form, the tercet? Must children be told about septs, septets, lanternes, chain lanternes, which are not listed in any text on the subject of poetry? Do children need the haikon, a pictorial haiku, or "couplet cuties,"[26] or "alphabits"?[27] Is it not time for adults to protest misleading articles by those who tell them that "An easy poem to compose is the couplet. A couplet expresses a single unit of thought. It is usually written in iambic form (– /)."?[28] Inevitably following such misinformation is a series of poorly constructed opening lines with a "word bank" so that students can write a second line. It is no wonder that poet-teachers eschew the traditional when they see the products which both teacher and students think are poetry.

Yet, has the day not come when some honor be paid to tradition? Poets like Robert Frost, Richard Wilbur, Dylan Thomas and others who write in form, meter, and rhyme have been neglected too long in favor of those who believe that they will either rewrite the past or ignore a body of work representing some of the finest poetry written. Free verse, of course, should be equally honored by the tradition-bound. Poets will always be at war as to what constitutes structure and rhythm, whether or not content dictates form, and a myriad of other matters of the craft. But it is time to rescue the child from being pulled to and fro in a struggle over ideologies and methods. It is time to respect the child's right to know, for example, not only what a couplet really is, but something about the beauty and force of a piece of free verse. Both are part of a poetic inheritance.

Nowhere does this show itself more clearly than in the area of using music in the classroom in conjunction with writing poetry. There are teachers who view music, as Holbrook regards it, as a way in which "experience takes on a new structure and wholeness, as one could demonstrate by taking, say Mahler's *Ninth Symphony* or Beethoven's last piano sonata (Opus 111). Such a creative experience, when we possess it, can actually seem to bring us to the solution of a life-problem, even if we only say, 'It made my problem seem unimportant' (which is a way of noting the 'solving' effect of music, in soothing the nervous system by communicating a rich sense of content and structure)."[29] This is a traditional viewpoint, recognized as a legitimate use for listening to music.

Educators like Ruth Kearney Carlson, on the other hand, think of music as "a lesson on word imagery" where "music was played and pupils were asked to imagine a picture or story in each record." After playing music for which students were not given titles, "pupils commented on its meaning to them"[30] and then selected one of three records about which to write. The music was played during the time the children wrote and revised their work. First, however, the children were asked to jot down their ideas in an "Impressions Column." Carlson also relates how teachers may "accent the positive" by underlining the good parts of children's writing. One fifth grade child writes while listening to "Ride of the Valkyries":

> Bells – It made me feel like I heard doorbells. It felt *like it was the assembly line at a car plant.*

"In this case," Carlson comments, "the teacher underlined the simile which was more original."[31]

For young children Professors Anthony R. Angelo and Marie-Jeanne Laurent suggest listening to Debussy's "La Mer," or "Moon River" from "Breakfast at Tiffany's," or the theme music from "Star Wars" or "Close Encounters." A lengthy list of questions as to place, what is seen, questions about the melody, instrumentation, volume and rhythms are suggested. Discussion should center, they advise, on "How is the music full of sea? sky? moon? . . . Are you excited as you listen, or calmed? Why? . . . Can you identify colors with use of different instruments?"[32] and the final suggestion that pupils describe their reactions to the music.

Another article in the same journal by Claire Ashby-David and Denise Robinson notes that because "At the moment of birth poetry was wed to music and dance," the teaching of poetry "without reference to music or dance would be a pedagogical error."[33]

In the *Whole Word Catalogue 2* Zavatsky and Padgett suggest music by Stravinsky, Erik Satie, Charles Ives, Edgard Varèse's futuristic music "and for weirdness – music like you've never heard before – the electronic music of Karlheinz Stockhausen is highly recommended." An example of a poem by Hyam Kramer, a "gifted" seventh grader who "isn't afraid to 'write crazy' by jotting down whatever pops into his mind as he listens" begins:

Whirling, winding, ouch!
Wow! Hey shut-up!

No, not again!
Hey, stop it!
Good boy!

and later reads:

Quiet, slow, yes . . .
Now relaxation . . .
Slow, slow, slow . . .

Hark the herald angels . . .
Frankenstein?

Mother Goose lost her touch!
Stop drilling on my egg!

Pop, a chick was hatched!
Slow down, I hear something unusual!

"Hyam's dizzying, exclamation-punctuated poem reminds, stylistically, of Gertrude Stein, whom he has surely never read." Although most student writing "won't be of this sort," they write, "we include this example to suggest that a teacher must expect the unpredictable. No one knows exactly what kind of fantasies that music will whirl up inside young authors." In any case, "the name of the game is response."[34]

Students, Zavatsky and Padgett write, should be encouraged "(without saying so) to get in touch with the continual stream of imagery that the music is about to activate." First they will see a place, and as the "place becomes clear, things will begin to happen." If children have trouble, they should be asked, "What's happening now? What is changing?" or "What do you see now? What does that remind you of?"[35]

Gensler and Nyhart also believe that "Listening to records of instrumental music or to the sounds of animals, such as the recorded songs of whales, can help to free the flow of ideas."[36] In her report Ruth Whitman gives an example of this kind of writing.

Listening to the Song of
The Humpbacked Whale

I wish there were no prisoners.
It's what that song reminds me of.
Being captured, possible tortured,
unable to come home.
Helpless, not free, calling for help.
If only there were no prisoners
and everyone was free.[37]

Koch's belief that music "puts children in a dreamy, excited, creative mood" leads him to encourage children "to make some associations of the music with sounds, colors, places, times of year, feelings of happiness and sadness."[38] He also suggests recordings of birdcalls, railroad trains, ocean, and other sounds of civilization and nature. An example from a fifth grade boy, Charles Conroy, when Stravinsky was played, begins:

Blahhh

Tweet, twang, twoot
Tweet, tweet, blaah, tweet, tweet, blaah
Twinkle, twixt, twang, la, la, la, la
Swung sweurt, sleep, sleep, sleep
Blah, twang, sweurt, twoot, tweet, . . .[39]

Joseph Peck, listening to Mozart, writes

A Black Night

It was pure black outside
Out of nowhere came out a burglar
He shot me and I fell dead
He ran and ran
I had a funeral
Everyone was quiet[40]

Other uses for music or sound range from playing tapes, "jiggling, crumpling, tapping various objects,"[41] as suggested by Brendan Galvin, to crumpling wax paper as poet-teacher Imogene Bolls suggests.[42]

But is the best use of music to create a mood, to foster images? If student writing is any indication, those who say that children have a natural rhythm presume too much. Children do not naturally write in the poetic line: They must be taught to do so. If they indeed possessed such a gift, there would be no need for a teacher to explain how the writing of poetry differs from that of prose. What, then, is the point of playing music, of listening to its rhythms and sounds, and ignoring the fact that the very nature of music resides in order, in melody, in steady rhythm that might be used to indicate to children the importance of *sound and rhythm in poetry?*

Yet, it is a rare poet-teacher who senses that there is in music a unique opportunity for developing one of the most important pleasures that poetry offers – the sounds, the rhythms as they are crafted to reinforce the ideas within a poem. While most teachers ask children to "program" music, to find individual images or feelings or places, only a few teachers have written of the importance of the "disciplined and formal patterns" that spring from music, and how they may be felt. Langston Hughes's classes in jazz, which discussed music "from the folk music of the deep South and the jug and tramp bands with their improvised instruments to the best of the modern commercial arrangements such as Benny Goodman and Artie Shaw,"[43] were held so that children might learn of the "values of freedom and originality in folk expression and how it might be used in more disciplined and formal patterns."[43]

Martin Steingesser, in his article "Sharing the Blues," believes that writing blues lyrics reinforces the importance of expressing feelings and becomes an exploration into the basic elements of form – "a refreshing way to develop appreciation of the rhythmic elements in poetry." "The final shape and rhythm of each line," he writes, "should be found by testing it against an improvised melody on the blues scale." Children also learn the importance of revision. "If the line is too long or too short, it just won't *sing*. It is then an easy task to either condense or fill out a line and to change the word order where necessary until it sings smoothly and sounds right." Steingesser believes that the experience is more valuable than the poem, and suggests – that "Even if it takes a whole writing session to compose one three-line verse, the experience (know-how), satisfaction, and confidence gained from having themselves written well one such lyric will stay with the children."[44]

Another poet-teacher, Martin Robbins, uses music in his classes to establish the need for phrasing and accent in poetry. The value of sound in poetry is emphasized in lessons ranging from the use of rhyme, slant-rhyme and accentual-syllabic meters to an understanding of metrical feet. Music serves him as a joyous jumping-off place for examples of both "riming" and "timing," and offers more than a medium through which to elicit autonomous feelings. Children learn that their work can be strengthened by judicious use of rhythm, rhyme, assonance, alliteration and other tools of the craft.[45]

David Henderson, too, values the writing of songs, chanting, and listening to familiar song lyrics as a way to rhythm and teaches about tradition and styles "to establish the difference between traditions by using music, blues, and jazz. It's important to talk about tonal language and the oral tradition and about experiential things that are part of poetry. Many of the poems are not told straight-out. They are told tonally by rhythms and the juxtapositions in the images and language. Like blues and jazz and oral poetry, it sings."

> One thing I do not do, that I used to do, is discourage students from writing in couplets – sincere couplets that sound like a rhythm and blues song

Henderson also believes that "we learn to expand and change our perceptions" in the fields of poetry, music and even science, that children should not be "trapped by definitions derived from what has been done;"[46] yet his recognition of tonal language, rhythms, and juxtapositions is, like that of Langston Hughes and Steingesser, an acknowledgement that poetry is more than gimmickry and that children are capable of listening, learning, and striving for some structure. Music is too often called into service as a way to elicit imagery or feelings and neglected as a means of helping the child to see and value an order in which, like the poet, he may begin a process of selection leading to creativity. To respond to how a piece of music makes one feel or to what individual images, places, colors are present, is neither creativity nor poetry.

The need for teachers to find a quick way to write poetry with no worry about rhythm has afforded the haiku and cinquain untold popularity; the poor methods propounded for creating these would fill an entire book. One set of activity cards, "Fun Fantasies," informs teachers and children that they should "Write a Haiku (Japanese) poem. Haiku poems are usually about nature." With a first line of 5 syllables, a second of 7 syllables, and a third of 5, they offer an example

My beautiful tree
A bluebird is in my tree
I love my own tree[47]

To offer such a model, to equate this with the haiku of Basho:

Over the ruins
of a shrine, a chestnut tree
still lifts its candles[48]

or Issa's

Warbler, wipe your feet
neatly if you please, but not
on my plum petals![49]

is more than travesty. To believe that the strict rules that govern the writing of haiku – its use of season symbol, its association of idea, its invitation to the reader to enter into the picture – can be sloughed off with an instant seventeen syllable replacement by young children is not only fallacious but ridiculous. Haiku is an intensely difficult form, as poets know. The same irresponsibility is evidenced by an explanation of cinquain as an "American poem," with an example for students:

Football
I like football
Football is my best sport
My dad is a football
Player
Football[50]

Cinquain, as invented by Adelaide Crapsey, is a five line poem with twenty-two syllables arranged in a pattern of two, four, six, eight and two. One of her cinquains, "The Warning," reads:

Just now,
Out of the strange
Still dusk . . . as strange, as still . . .
A white moth flew: why am I grown
So cold?[51]

Countless misinterpretations of cinquain are widely practiced by teachers who use it as a basis for identifying parts of speech – nouns, verbs, participles, adjectives, and synonyms in an endless variety of combinations.

For those who can't stop at seventeen syllables, or twenty-two syllables the tanka with thirty-one syllables has been pressed into service and beyond that, other syllabic forms such as the sijo with forty-two to forty-eight syllables. If these syllable patterns do not please teachers, they invent their own, of which the haikon, terquain, and hexaduad are examples.

In an article, "Writing in First Grade" in the *Whole Word Catalogue 2*, Anne Martin suggests that all the " 'artificial devices' for getting around children's inhibitions about writing at higher grade levels" might be dispensed with if there were an "emphasis on reaching children and teachers at the primary level." This might, she feels, put an end to "the need for using tricks, props, or gimmicks to stimulate writing, because the children were so reluctant and afraid to write, due to their previous school experience."[52] Martin's suggestion is both insightful and important, but it will require devoted carefully prepared teachers willing to give extra time and to learn from workshops and classes which do not falsely assure them that teaching is easy.

It is doubtful that gimmicks, prescriptives, and formulas will ever disappear, for their use by a large majority of those connected with education ensures the continuation of standardized responses within safe, set patterns. For the educator they are, like the test, made to measure a child's ability to respond in acceptable ways. For the classroom teacher they are effortless shortcuts to build the children's confidence as well as remove the burden of individualized instruction. In addition, they provide a source of so-called creativity for teachers who devise their own gimmickry to share with others through publication in educational magazines. For the poet-teacher, who may use them only as beginnings, they make instant contact with students and assure them of immediate success. For the commercial publisher they are the magic pill offered to prove that writing poetry is easy. For the parent they are proof of the child's ability and creativity.

Is the state of excitement that the reader is told children often experience while writing poetry in the classroom also a gimmick, an artificially-induced euphoria? Richard Lewis asserts that

> this excitement of a child's involvement with language cannot take place, or even continue to grow, unless we, the adults, create an atmosphere where every child realizes that he, with his imagination and his senses, can use words to suit his way of seeing the world around him.[53]

The nature of this atmosphere varies widely as it is described by poet-teachers. Koch writes about the "lovely chaos" of his classroom, the "maelstrom of creation," the tremendous commotion, the "writing and talking and jumping about, the trash can going BOOM, the PA system going BOOP BOOP." The competitive atmosphere of his classroom, where he allows the children to "make a good deal of noise," not only precedes but is a part of the writing process. "All the time they were writing, there would be a few students, frantically excited, shouting at me."[54] Michelle Rae Moore, a poet-teacher in Stockton, California, speaks of the "supervised chaos" of her classroom where children "run about the room for a period of one minute like a kicked nest of hornets."[55]

Such an atmosphere suggests that children are indeed excited about their writing; often the very arrival and presence of the poet-teachers is occasion for the cheers and applause that start the juices going. Certainly this concept is tied up with the idea that poetry, if successful, involves not only the mind, but the body.

To Piaget, expression is made up of "gestures, movement and mimicry as much as of words" and this has been recognized as a necessary response both to the making of and listening to poetry. Richard Lewis, Claudia Lewis, and others note the value of dramatics and of dancing as legitimate outlets for these physiological feelings in children. This "thinking of the body" in Yeats's terms, the tension between the brain and body that Emily Dickinson noted in her response to poetry, is characterized by A. E. Housman as a "strong tremor of unreasonable excitement which words set up in some region deeper than the mind."[56] Such words "find their way to something in man which is obscure and latent, something older than the present organization of his nature."[57]

Poet-teacher Sandra Alcosser writes of how "I sometimes teach poetry by asking students to climb buttes or dismantle compost."[58] Sylvia Ashton-Warner describes in *Teacher* the pulse of physical energy that is released when a child spontaneously begins to dance, as though words touched something within her that needed a form of expression.

The importance of having children "express themselves with body and speech" is noted by Sewalk:

> There is a change in body language and perceptions when children learn how to read or write the words they are trying to tell me. When they don't know the word they are very spatial with their bodies. They stretch, extend and grasp their little bodies to circumscribe a universe that defines their "word," that defines their perception. In effect they become the word with their bodies; body = word; experience = that which they touch and see and hear.[59]

The idea that physiology is involved with the writing of poetry is anathema to teachers who demand a quiet classroom and a strictly cerebral response. Brownjohn believes firmly in the silent classroom; "working in silence produces better poems. There is no doubt about this. Everyone needs room to think and this means the least possible distraction."[60] McIntosh also believes that children "have to be led to their solitude if they are to write poetry for real."[61] Langston Hughes believes that "seldom is serious writing done in groups or in a room full of people." Poems, he felt, should "be put down quietly at home."[62]

But those who champion the use of the collaborative poem, popularized during the last decade, negate this attitude. Often called a communal, collective, or group poem, the collaborative can be written by a few students or by an entire class. Those who use the collaborative poem cite a number of reasons for its effectiveness. Koch believes that "two person collaborations have a particular charm for the chance they give to trick, tease, and outdo one's fellow poet, as well as to feel the immediate inspiration of his presence. . . . The finished product has a kind of magic; written by two, often at cross purposes, amid excitement and jokes, it turns out to be one poem – interesting, beautiful, funny, and sometimes even making sense."[63] The class collaborative poem, where a student contributes one line, is, in Koch's words, "easy to write, had rules like a game, and included the pleasures without the anxieties of competitiveness. No one had to worry about failing to write a good poem because everyone was only writing one line." To give the poem unity Koch suggested making up rules. "We ended up with the regulations that every line should contain a color, a comic strip character, and a city or country; also the line should begin with the words 'I wish'."[64] Lines were written down, shuffled about and read aloud to the great excitement of the children who were "talking, waving, blushing, laughing, and bouncing up and down."[65] Koch notes that the collaborative poem always made the children want to make up their own individual poems, and usually write them down.

Teachers who believe in putting a collaborative poem on a chalkboard, however, view the collaborative less as an exercise in game-playing and more as a way of giving some kind of help or instruction. Lopate maintains that children understand the difference between the collaborative as a "form of fun" and the poem written by the individual as "another activity entirely, more related to their daily schoolwork." He suggests that crazy ideas may be expressed in the collaborative where there is no sense of responsibility, ideas a student "would not want to put down in his or her own handwriting." A "visible genre" in its own right, the collaborative poem is more than "a tooling-up for individual work." It is a "visual model for the appearance of modern verse" as it shows students "the look of a poetic line, the uses of end-stops and enjambment."[66] It is also a way for Lopate to "introduce information about metaphors, images and similes painlessly as they come in the writing of the poem."[67] The teacher is also able to keep control of the poem, include all lines suggested uncritically, "or else select some ideas and ask the group to edit or improve lines."[68]

Lopate speaks of the wide gulf, however, between the "social euphoria of the collective poem" and the "lonely individual effort"[69] of the poem written by a single child. Individual writing involves waiting for the right moment – the "ripe" moment. To Lopate, ripeness and patience are important. "*Waiting*," he says, "*is half the discipline of writing*,"[70] and "unpopular as this fact may be, serious creative writing requires withdrawal."[71]

Thus, the collaborative poem is an example of writing viewed as a serious effort and a legitimate form by some, while to others it is a vehicle for teaching about the form and tools of poetry. It may also serve as an inducement to those not ready to commit themselves to paper to be part of a community effort. It is, in Lopate's words, a way to engage the child not ready to assume "author responsibility." To others, like Weinstein, "most group poems are more game than artistic creation."[72]

The collaborative poem is, indeed, a sort of surrealist game as it is practiced by most teachers, a form that offers little more than what Piaget calls the "collective monologue" where each child understands the speaker but is only interested in his own response to the subject, his own lines. There is little interest in cause or reason and almost no sense of true cooperation, for the lines follow a prescriptive pattern forever rooted in subjective imagery. Only occasionally do collaboratives offer anything beyond the most superficial of statements. They are merely another form of formula writing. The question arises, therefore, whether poetry is to be thought of as instant entertainment, tossed off quickly, or as the serious vehicle for expressing the voice and thought of a single individual. Is the poem an outcome of excitement, of a brainstorming session, or of quiet reflection? What atmosphere best serves a particular group of children and how does the teacher view his role at any given time – as a guide or as the dispenser of rules and gimmicks? Lopate's distinction is cogent for those who seek some answers to the values of excitement and physicality, the atmosphere for real creativity, and the teacher's role in all this.

Anne Martin's discussion on writing assignments is also pertinent:

> At first I used to worry about children who consistently said they could not think of anything to write. I would suggest things, or remind them of things they had told me and sometimes that worked for them. But I find now that often the best thing is just to ask them to sit quietly and think for a while. More often than not, something will emerge that is more real to the child than what I would have suggested. I think that a teacher's calm confidence that the child himself will come up with an idea is often more reassuring than tricky writing ideas invented by teachers.[73]

Arnstein, too, believes in the teacher as a "quiet reassuring presence" and shuns exhibitionism. It is, to Lopate, clear that "a good poetry teacher can exert a spell through the timbre of voice, the choice of words, the quality of concentration" that leads children into a "mood of inner stillness"[74] where creativity can function.

There are a number of implications in these viewpoints that bear examination; for while all poet-teachers recognize the involvement and interaction of mind and body not only in response to hearing poetry but in the actual process of writing, three viewpoints are expressed in regard to the atmosphere and the teacher's role in the classroom. One idea is that creativity is not functioning unless it is expressed in some bodily function – both talking and excitement *prior* to the writing experience and *during* the writing process. The energy, in other words, must be seen and heard as proof that creativity is taking place, and teachers must set the stage with their own physical displays of energy and entertainment. A second view is that teachers believe they can help the child by channeling this energy into warm-up exercises for the actual writing; making collaborative poems or listening to music is thus encouraged as a way to the unconscious. Moreover, those who take a third view and believe in the quiet classroom fall into two groups. To some teachers disorder is unthinkable because it is threatening to the role they must play as authorities and taskmasters; yet, to teachers like Lopate, Martin, and others, there is the recognition that the excitement and energy generated by mind and body are part of the creative process: that excitement displays itself not as an overt act, but transfers itself to the excitement felt in the work produced, and so can be given to the reader.

Psychology and theories about creativity may be enlightening in this regard, for Piaget points to the possibility that energy is diffused through too much talking and outward action when he writes that while speech "accelerates action it also runs the risk of supplanting it"[75]; and Arieti believes that creativity is fostered by solitude, inactivity, and daydreaming, conditions which the noisy classroom does not allow.

There can be no one way to involve children in poetry writing, no one method that will work in all classrooms, yet there would seem to be some value in establishing standards which recognize that the atmosphere be conducive to creativity, if poetry is to be written.

Poet-teachers often dwell on the success of a particular lesson, attempting to pinpoint what factors caused a certain positive response. Gensler cites a dream session which was successful because of the children's age, their knowledge of the teacher, and "the ways of poetry,"[76] the mood of the students and the weather. Arnstein writes of a relaxed atmosphere, good discussion, and weather as a prelude to good writing. Simon points to "an atmosphere of trust and confidence" where students do not need to run the risk of being thought foolish if they share feelings, or if they present work in "fragments rather than agonize over a finished product."[77] Richard Lewis believes in an "intimate and unhurried atmosphere"[78] where time and encouragement are present. As he views it

> Both children and teachers may all too frequently get locked into the dynamics that occur when learning buckles under to the demands of institutionalization – when what should be one of our most personalized, integrated human experiences becomes the victim of increasing fragmentation and expedience. We need not wonder then that the very activity enabling the *personal* and the *individual* to be expressed is usually at the lowest levels of priorities within many of our schools.[79]

To Mearns the creative atmosphere focuses not on lessons but a "skillfully set-up environment" where there is an abundance of "material for the creative impulses," and where teachers are "guides rather than instructors."[80] Larry Levinger, writing in *English Journal*, enjoins teachers to recognize the importance of creating a nourishing environment.

> We come into this world with the intention of speaking honestly, clearly, on behalf of ourselves and what is around us, and through myriad circumstances, we are distracted from our intention. To reconstruct intention, to dismantle distraction, something genuine must come from us. In this way something genuine will come from our students. The writing problem is at heart a problem in human relationships; its very existence indicates an unwillingness to be ourselves, inability to participate honestly in personal and interpersonal relationships. . . .
>
> As teachers we must place our allegiances where they belong –

> not in centralized and systematic cure-alls for the ills of education, but in instinct and intuition – the means by which we connect the emotional continuity of our lives with those of our students. In this we transform ourselves from the role of processors, makers of minds, educational technologists, to the realm of humanists, who like lovers, learn to trust and share, appreciate proximity, take joy, sorrow, growth, from the vitality of relationship.[81]

The best teachers are those who, given the potential of the child, discard what Harold Taylor calls "automatic responses to conventional stimuli."[82] "Knowledge," he writes, "is created freshly every time an individual human being takes hold of an idea and makes it part of his own understanding."[83] It is the aim of the teacher "to peel away layers of customary reality and to restore vitality and nourishment to the individual consciousness beneath."[84] This teacher embodies a love of wisdom, a sensitivity to people and ideas, a respect for fact, a generosity of outlook, the ultimate liberality of the honest mind, and the ability to instill in each student a desire to know and to learn.

CHAPTER XVI

Notes for a New Mythology

Who hath told you to renounce your authority? I do not know that, till this moment, you have had any over him. Hitherto you have been able to obtain nothing of him, except by cunning or force. Authority, the law of duty, has been unknown to him. But you have now many and various means of engaging his heart: Reason, friendship, gratitude, and a thousand other motives of affection, speak to him in a language he cannot misunderstand. Vice hath not as yet rendered him deaf to their voice. He is as yet susceptible only in natural passions.

From *Emile*
Jean Jacques Rousseau[1]

Old mythologies do not vanish easily, nor are foundations for new mythologies built without struggle. John Dewey's beliefs in the child's growth as the focus of the educational process, in the classroom as a field for the child's interests, thoughts, and actions, and in the teacher as a guide and co-worker who will aid in that growth are not unlike those of Rousseau. But Emile lived in a different society. His classroom was nature; he had no peers against which to test his experience and ideas; he had but a single tutor. The absolutes of eighteenth-century France have collapsed, even as the classroom of Dick and Jane in the early part of this century in America has disappeared. In its place is a schoolroom with a spectrum of students from broader, more diverse backgrounds, students who challenge educators and teachers, and the states and governments that support them. This is a difficult situation; it is a house – and even home – shaken and out of order. Parents, as well as school administrators, must reexamine values in an effort to answer questions about education that have plagued them for so long. Is the tradition of the child at the center and the teacher as guide, as co-worker, to be valued? Or does this new classroom demand that old orders be restored with the teacher reinstated as authority and taskmaster over the child? Of more particular concern here, is the contribution of the poet-teachers with their emphasis on divergent thinking to be encouraged? The ultimate consideration is whether under these conditions creativity can flourish as a process, or whether the need for standardization and product will supersede the expression of the individual child.

New problems call for new solutions, and none seem more exciting than the fact that this new classroom offers a richness that can have greater potential for creativity than ever before. The wealth of new ideas that come with divergent cultures and languages, the exposure to contrasting backgrounds and ideas, the openness to different forms of expression and opinion by students, teachers, and poet-teachers brings a new dimension that can foster creativity. If the change can be accepted as a positive force, if respect for growth through interaction with fresh viewpoints can seize hold, ways can always be discovered to combine the strengths of tradition with the American propensity to make new.

People must, as Steiner and Richards assert, have their mythologies; some semblance of belief and order by which to explain their very existence and resolve the chaos of their lives. If one mythology disappears, it must be replaced by another, and this new mythology must *not* be rooted in fancy, but in the reality that children have the potential for growth, for creativity, and for the writing of poetry — and that given this, with guidance by caring parents, educators, teachers, and poet-teachers, they can be led to learn the value of craft and the work that it requires to make a poem.

For children like poets are honest; like poets, they speak a truth that does not pander to the conventions or formulas of society but that, in Rousseau's words, is a "faithful expression" of their ideas. If children speak of "the glories" they know, it is not to give adults "news of heaven" but to make them aware of their rich invention, their imaginations, their curiosity for what they find on this earth. Unlike the mythological concept of the child-poet who needs no more than some instant replay from the unconscious, children need guidance as they grow to help them value their own dreams, wishes, experiences, imagination, memories, and their own voices, but they will not be content with incoherent fragments. They will learn to deal in rhythms and words which may be understood because they have known the joy of a discipline that will, of their images, make symbols that speak to others. These will not be playbacks of the reproductive imagination or productive imagination alone – but products of the creative imagination. Such poems need *making*; they need the educator, the parent, the teacher, and the poet-teacher to nourish and allow them to grow. Such poems need a David Holbrook, a Richard Lewis, a Phillip Lopate, a Herbert Kohl, a Claudia Lewis, a Hughes Mearns, a Langston Hughes, a June Jordan. It is to be hoped that they will also have a wide range of literature. But they can only be made when the impediments are discarded.

"The story of the leaders of the race," Mearns wrote in 1926, "is the story of those who cultivated the creative spirit in spite of the schools. Why is it, I wonder, that we have never taken that lesson to heart?" Those who have been the "masters of men" have not worked within the traditional educational pattern but "have fought their way to the right to be free. The mass has not been strong of will: a little fluttering of the wings, and then an acceptance – that is their story."[2]

Mearns's words are prophetic. Those who have emerged over the past half-century as creative teachers and educators have taken strong stands against the prevailing inertia of the classroom. Their innovative methods, if at times flamboyant, have drawn attention to the arts as a viable and important part of the curriculum. "In fact," Ronald Gross writes, "the theory and practice of radical school reforms are strikingly congruent with the concerns, impulses, and aspirations of those who see the arts as a central element of a humane education."[3] Some practitioners, it must be noted, have been responsible for continuing the myth of the child as poet, but others adopt a more reasonable course that poses an alternate view of the child as potential poet.

Kohl's suggestion that those who worked with the Teachers & Writers Collaborative keep diaries of their activities has been of value for insights into the methods of poet-teachers and their varying philosophies about their work. Some have been expanded into books while others appear as essays and statements in a variety of publications.

None is more relevant to the making of a new mythology than June Jordan's February 12, 1968 entry in "The Voice of the Children" Saturday Workshop Diaries, when she not only writes of Deborah Burkett's creative mimicry and the need for a child to internalize feelings, but makes clear her beliefs that the writing of a poem should be more than a playback of the world the child knows. The idea, espoused by Wirthschafter, that a black child living in the ghetto should reflect in her writing only street language, the things experienced and heard as a "black and poor child," is countered by Jordan when she answers that there are some children who are exceptional, who not only learn from their environment but in school and in the library. Would you have this child, Jordan asks, know "only what she fears and what threatens her existence?" Should a child parrot in her writing the language she hears everyday?

> Contrary to your remarks, a poet does not write poetry according to the way he talks. Poetry is a distinctively precise and exacting use of words whether the poet is Langston Hughes or Robert Burns.

Jordan's point is crucial to the understanding that a poem is not merely a reproduction of language, an experience, something observed or felt, but a crafted work. She goes on:

> One should take care to discover racist ideas that are perhaps less obvious than others. For example, one might ask: "Will I accept that a black child can write "creatively" and "honestly" and yet *not* write about incest, filth, violence and degradation of every sort? Back of the assumption, and there is an assumption, that an honest and creative piece of writing by a black child will be ungrammatical, mis-spelled, and lurid titillation for this white teacher, is another idea. That black people are only the products of racist, white America and that, therefore, we can be and we can express only what racist white America has forced us to experience, namely, mutilation, despisal, ignorance and horror.
>
> Fortunately, however, we have somehow survived. We have somehow and sometimes survived the systematic degradation of America. And therefore there really are black children who dream, and who love, and who undertake to master such white things as poetry. There really are black children who are *children* as well as victims. And one had better be pretty damned careful about what one will "accept" from these children as their own –

> their own honest expression of their dreams, their love, and their always human reality that not even America can conquer.
>
> According to your letter, one might as well exclude 19th, 18th, 17th and 16th century literature from the libraries frequented by ghetto students. For inasmuch as they are young, inasmuch as they are children, *they will learn*, and they will assimilate and happily, they will master.
>
> Do you suppose that ghetto schools should merely extend the environment that has murdered millions of black children? The inculcation of self-respect and healthy race identity does not follow from the mere ventilation and reinforcement of desperation in every one of its hideous forms.
>
> No great poet has emerged without knowledge and mimicry of precedent. Even William Blake is no exception to this generality. And yes there *are* black children who will insist on becoming not merely "great black writers," but great writers who are black the way Shakespeare was an Englishman.
>
> I think Deborah may be one of these children. I hope so. And I will continue to try and serve the kids who come on Saturdays, one at a time, as this child and that child – rather than as black children wholly predictable and comprehensible in the light of statistical commonplace.[4]

Jordan's voice must be heard in the new mythology, for her letter makes clear that poetry has to do more than bemoan the desperation or record the environment of the writer. Good poetry is a synthesis that through a careful process of *making* destroys neither the environment and its reality, nor the fantasies of the unconscious, but keeps them intact even as it creates something new. It is the vehicle through which the child learns, assimilates, and masters.

Jordan, unlike many others, understands that the child must not only be conscious of self, but can learn from models and traditions of the past. Stevenson's poem "Travel" has awakened in the child the knowledge that she can go beyond her immediate environment; that she can select and make clear the images, the pictures she wishes to see, choosing some, discarding others. Her dream, like her environment, is not that of Stevenson's but his poem has touched in her a responsive chord. She is both dreamer and realist, knowing that she can go, but can also return home. Her work, like the model, is understood by Jordan and the reader because it is rooted in universal symbolism. She is communicating beyond the single, wishful image that characterizes what many think is poetry, because she enlarges the meaning for herself and for others.

Jordan is a creative teacher because she will stand up for the fine models that the new mythology needs. She does not confine her students to the poets of one age and one environment but offers them a choice as to subject matter and form; she does not disdain meter, rhyme, the poets of childhood, nor the poets of any century. She resists directives to limit the child, to wall in the imagination, to reduce the child to gimmicks and formula, to keep students within the strictured bounds of their own narrow environment. She will "continue to try and serve" the children she teaches, "one at a time," recognizing that each is entitled to learn, assimilate, and master in unpredictable and incomprehensible ways.

The new mythology must have such teachers aware of a child's potential. From Jordan's workshops come real poetry, such as that of Vanessa Howard who wrote at age thirteen:

> i am frightened that
> the flame of hate
> will burn me
> will scorch my pride
> scar my heart
> it will burn and i
> cannot put it out.
> i cannot call the fire department
> and they cannot put out the fire within my soul
> i am frightened that the flame
> of hate will burn me
> if it does
> i will die[5]

The new mythology must have those who encourage the voices of children, who recognize, like Jordan, that

> It would be something fine if we could learn how to bless the

> lives of children. They are the people of a new life. Children are the only people nobody can blame. They are the only ones always willing to make a start; they have no choice. Children are the ways the world begins again and again.
>
> But in general, our children have no voice – that we will listen to. We force, we blank them into the bugle/bell regulated lineup of the Army/school, and we insist on silence.
>
> But even if we cannot learn to bless their lives (our future times), at least we can try to find out how we already curse and burden their experience: how we limit the wheeling of their inner eyes, how we terrify their trust, and how we condemn the raucous laughter of their natural love. What's more, if we will hear them, they will teach us what they need; they will bluntly formulate the tenderness of their deserving.[6]

Here are echoes of Rousseau, formulated for a new century, a new time. They are spoken, too, by others such as Mearns who writes that the real poetry of children will "be natural and youthlike, with no conscious attempt either to imitate an adult form or even to please adults."[7] The new mythology recognizes that the teacher, while not authoritarian, must be there to guide.

Yet where, in the new mythology, does praise – or encouragement – fit in? "Flattery they hate," writes Mearns, "these children; and praise they are apt to suspect; but their own ability thus put to them is something that they themselves can appraise as worthy."[8] Arnstein's observation that children walk away from their work with disinterest may give a clear picture of her school and the children within it. So does Mearns's assessment of his students' disdain of flattery. But the situation has changed: today's youth glories in early fame and believes that its self-expression is art, beyond reproach. It is fashionable to accept anything children write and praise it. Fortunately there are those who point to a need for standards. Kantor writes:

> Arguing that we cannot evaluate creative writing is a "cop out" which signals to students that anything goes, that no piece of creative work is better, or worse, than any other. This kind of relativism can lead only to a profusion of mediocrity . . .[9]

Bernd believes that when teachers accept less than the best from children

> we are, unquestionably, being unfair to poetry. We are failing in a miserable way to do justice to the arts and artists in general. In a larger sense, we are failing the children themselves. How do we dare accept the mediocre and praise it? How can we, in conscience, give children the impression that a work of art, or any work of worth, is *easy*? On the one hand, we decry the lack of quality in our daily lives, from commercial television to automobiles to mousetraps, and at the same time discourage the pursuit of excellence. We are not true to ourselves, and even more shattering to contemplate, we are betraying our future.

"Use praise," Bernd adds, "but set the standards high. A well-turned phrase or an original metaphor is one thing. Being a poet is another."[10] Bernd would agree with Chambers that leading children to believe that "all art is simply narcissistic, that is easy to do; that it is about taking a lovely ego trip" leads in the end to the belief that "most children grow up rejecting art as something for self-indulgent bums, or at best, a sort of hobby for people with too much time on their hands." Too often, he asserts, the writing of poetry is a means for children to view art as "a way of getting attention for themselves."[11]

The teacher who is part of the new mythology will, in Kantor's words,

> need to allow students some breathing room, some space in which to test out ideas, no matter how fanciful or far-out. We don't have to praise that which is mediocre, but we may want to accept, at least for a while, genuine expression of feeling. Eventually, of course, we must be able to sense that point at which a student feels confident enough about his own writing that he can non-defensively receive constructive criticism and use it to advantage.[12]

Jacobs would make a distinction between constructive criticism and fault-finding. "Fault-finding as I use the term is negative. It tears down. Criticism, on the other hand, is constructive."

> In criticism, one recognizes that the composing act is a serious use of one's craftsmanship, one's creative energies. So, starting with respect for the composing act, one is on the side of the writer. That one points up wherein one thinks the writing has been better done, or less well done is not to tear down the work, but rather to help the writer think again, and perhaps improve the writing which has been done. Of course the writer reserves the right to accept, reject, or modify the criticism.

"Teachers," Jacobs believes, "should be somewhat like editors in this respect, aids to helping the children do the best they can."[13] Teachers, as Summerfield declares, should be there to guide, "to foster a set of standards."[14] But these standards cannot be acquired overnight; they cannot be learned in a few hours at a language arts convention or by reading a few easy how-to articles. It takes time to learn that poetry is not a message where the reader is told how to feel and behave; not a greeting card or a commercial, badly rhymed doggerel, a series of quick disconnected images, nor a recorded experience. "What is important to understand," writes Herbert Read, "if you would appreciate the pure essence of poetry, is that it does not preach or argue; it deals with ideas by means of images."

> Poetry is not made up of words like pride and pity, or love and beauty. These are cotton wool words – they can be squeezed into poultices or spread over wounds; they can be used to gag people's mouths or to pull over their eyes. The poet distrusts such words and always tries to use words that have a suggestion of outline and shape, and represent things seen, as clear and precise as a crystal. This does not mean that ideas should not be present in a poem . . . it means that ideas are poetically expressed in images – that the poet thinks or feels in images. That is why some poems cannot be explained – that is to say, translated into cotton-wool words. They shimmer in the mind suggestively, like tantalizing puzzles.[15]

But images by themselves, as poets know, are not the only essentials of poetry. The new mythology will question the idea that *any one can teach poetry*. While it is true that any one can instruct children to write by formula, it will make clear that such writing is not poetry. It will encourage those who believe poetry has something to offer to learn more about poetry, as Ruth Whitman indicates in recommending workshops for teachers. It will place value on learning about literature written for adults and also on a body of literature that has served children for centuries. It will question the idea that children's work as models can provide the broad symbolism, the enlargement of spirit that literature offers. The new mythology will also explore the wisdom of allowing those who understand nothing of the psychology of children to teach. It will question the remark of a poet-teacher who does not understand why the imagination of a first grade child is so much more active than that of an eighth grader; or the comment of the teacher who wonders why children "enumerate"[16] in lists. It will urge that classroom teachers, who have a knowledge of children and their emotional needs, must work in combination with poet-teachers, who bring knowledge of another sort. Ruth Whitman writes:

> If the poet's view of the world and his way of dealing with the world is to be handed on in education, there has to be a real living poet at the beginning of each chain of inheritance. What was surprising and instructive to me was to see that the other conductors in this chain do not have to be poets themselves, so long as they have had a true working contact with one. That is why poetry boxes, apparatus, how-to books, prescriptions and essays are essentially useless for teaching the sources of poetry.[17]

If, according to Whitman, "The only effective way to hand on techniques of access to the sources of poetry is through a working poet,"[18] then surely the new mythology must continue to support the work of the state Poets-in-the-Schools program and such groups as Teachers & Writers Collaborative.

Yet there are two further considerations which must be explored. First, what if the poet-teacher asks children to imitate his own work? Poet-teacher James Humphrey writes that "the poet-teacher has no right to expect the student to share his/her attitudes, opinions or experiences. I don't want the student to become a shadow of me; rather I want to help all the students to see their own possibilities for themselves."[19] There are those, however, who encourage the sort of imitation that completely stifles the child's natural voice.

The following poem, purportedly written by two fifth grade girls – and dozens of similar poems – suggest that there are poet-teachers whose consideration for the voice of the child is lacking; who foist on students images, words, and ideas that are not only derivative of their own minds and work, but false to the emotions, thoughts, and understanding of middle-graders.

> Slaves of desire wriggle
>   into me, my being
> Unaware of the force
>   which holds me back –
> but me and Dean Martin
> free them from
>   the magical taste
> of silly metaphors.
>   We repell
> against the evil poet god,
> with white roses.
>   We capture
> him and he becomes our
> friend. Never again do we think
> of poems as
>   dragonfireless words.[20]

This lack of respect for the child's voice is not only irresponsible but unjust: It is a disregard of the value of process and, as Mearns notes, a use of product which many have "turned to their own uses."[21]

Second, what happens in the classroom when a poet-teacher cannot be found – or afforded – but the teacher genuinely wishes to give children the experience of creating poetry? Ruth Whitman's call for a working poet is admirable but not always possible. Mearns, Arnstein, Claudia Lewis, Lopate, Jordan, Whitman, Kohl, and others have given clues. The sources of writing are first to be found in the reading of poetry which involves literature of all times and leads to discussion. The beginnings, as Jordan states, are in creative mimicry of those who have gone before. Inadequate models will produce inadequate products; this is self-evident. But if the teacher introduces good poetry and is more concerned with process than product, the beginnings of poetry may evolve in unforeseen ways.

While self-expression, the attention to the unique experiences, memories, and ideas of each child must always be elicited, the new mythology does not ask for instant poems. It takes from the work of Sexton, Martin, and others the belief that the habit of writing in a journal or "personal writing book" or diary is of great importance. To Sexton this is a "way of keeping things alive."[22] The value of the students keeping a journal has never been stressed enough by poet-teachers who need, because of time, money, and school pressures, to have them produce instant poems. Yet there are hopeful signs – among them the recognition of long-term writing and of letting work ripen and of revising.

In addition to keeping things alive the journal serves as training in observation and the use of the senses; it relates the individual to the world about him and lifts him from a preoccupation with the narcissistic. While the syncretism in children's writing creates a lovely fantasy at times, growth demands that they also be aware of reality. Mearns speaks of how "a considerable portion of our own energy . . . was spent with individuals in making them believe that the everyday happenings of their own lives were alive, dramatic even, interesting to others and worthy of serious portrayal."[23] Poets and teachers know the difficulty of alerting children to the possibilities within their lives, but this has become even more of a task as children today glue themselves to television screens.

Ruth Whitman wrote in 1970 that "children's senses are becoming atrophied," yet the situation has since deteriorated dramatically. It becomes harder to encourage children, or even to expect them to make their own images as the screens produce pictures for them! The journal may also serve as a memory bank and as a spur to the regaining of sensitivity.

In addition to the journal, the role of the teacher is important in keeping the sensibilities of children alive. The enjoinder to go into memories, to recall, to "Close your eyes . . . and try to get pictures in your mind" is practiced by some teachers. Willis asks children to "pretend your mind or your eyes are watching a movie screen," to look for pictures and sounds, to list "everything within a five foot radius" and then she sends them to some "unusual place" where, with "a period of enforced quiet" they note what they see and smell. Eavesdropping, listening, and watching beyond school with a "quieting of self in order to pick up all the fascinating information your senses are bringing in" is also advised. Looking at things through a camera lens, she notes, will also enable children to see "fresh things," such as "cracks in the sidewalks" and note how "leaves become interesting."[24]

While movie screen and camera lens may be ways of making things more vivid and exciting to some, the knowledge that observation and image-making need nothing more than the physiological equipment of a healthy child is recognized by most. Poet-teacher Robert King suggests that children "look closely at things they do (swinging, jumping rope, playing football, rollerskating, throwing a paper wad) to write more concisely and vividly of common personal actions."[25] Steinbergh and McKim write:

> I ask the children to take their time with the objects, to stay with them for a while. This watchfulness, I say, is part of being a poet. I ask them to choose something they can identify with, something that shares some of their own characteristics.[26]

Most teachers will recognize that careful observation is preferable to perfunctory looking. Observation is *not* a game but a way of training children to look outside of themselves, to be aware of the world surrounding them. It is through observation that children begin to relate themselves to others, to lay the foundation for their unique response to life. Children – and adults – who live only within themselves lose perspective; they do not grow. Leah Wilcox notes how a quiet walk with a teacher who asks children to look for things "not noticed before or things that could be described in a new way"[27] is a way to metaphoric observation.

The new mythology will rejoice with O'Gorman, Kohl, and Jordan as they describe the trips they plan and take with their children to become aware of "the CITY, its zoos, museums, streets, subways, stores, parks and people."[28] Observations and sensory responses remembered from these excursions are not poetry but lead to poetry. Bly writes:

> The Japanese say, Go to the pine if you want to learn about the pine. If an American poet wants to write of a chill and foggy field, he has to stay out there, and get cold and wet himself. Two hours of solitude seems about right for every line of poetry.[29]

Certainly children are too young to spend hours of observation but they can learn to value it whether or not they become poets. The knowledge that they can make their own observations, that their reactions and opinions do not need to be handed to them is preparation for life itself. Claudia Lewis asserts that

> those who lose touch with the sharp sensory equipment they are born with – who forget how to observe and how to feel the impact of their own impressions – have lost one of the basic tools that the writer of any age must use in his efforts to perceive and clarify reality.[30]

Too few teachers and poet-teachers value observation beyond the immediate classroom. The new mythology notes that it has been one of the most neglected areas in the creative writing program, not only because it develops sensory powers, but because it provides a means to the "making" of a true poem. Although it is an unpopular idea with poets who believe poetry comes from the exploration of the unconscious, evocation of personal images does *not* provide symbolism to others. This must be done through some area, some object, some field to which all who read and listen can relate. The Romantic tradition, like its predecessors, chooses nature and its neglect by the poet-teachers in urban schools today has severely limited the ability of these poets or their students to communicate adequately. Mickey Mouse, Superman, King Kong, recordings of sounds, and the trappings of surrealism can in no way substitute for the relationship to nature that Rousseau recognized as one of the foundations of education:

> No artist can execute any thing beautiful but by imitation. All the models of true taste are to be found in nature. The farther we depart from this master the more preposterous are our designs; as, in that case, we deduce our models from such objects as happen to delight us; and the beauty of imagination, subject to prejudice and caprice, is nothing more than that which pleases those who direct us.[31]

It is nature, Rousseau writes, that has showed man the way to live; in nature is a model for all life, and his writings seem amazingly apt today.

> I would always remain as near to nature as possible, in order to gratify the senses she hath bestowed on me; being well assured that the more natural were my enjoyments, the more I should find them real. In the choice of objects for imitation, I should take those of nature always for models; in the gratification of appetites nature should have always the preference; in matters of taste I should consult her ever.[32]

Rousseau believed that by understanding nature man begins to understand himself; this can be clearly seen in the poetry that has stood the test of centuries.

The statement in the *Whole Word Catalog* that "City kids are notoriously oblivious to natural phenomena"[33] suggests that little effort is made to introduce urban children to observation of nature beyond slides, pictures, tapes, and recordings. In this way children are turned back upon themselves, to dwell in their own world of memories or images or – in most cases – escape from reality and fantasy in the realm of the unconscious. Human nature is mistaken for nature itself. It is heartening, therefore, to read the account of one New York poet-teacher, Julie Alvarez, who writes:

> We spent the next half hour sitting in a circle on the floor talking about what we missed about our native countries. Then – these incredible teaching aids! – it started to snow and the kids raced to the window to watch. It struck me that we had been concentrating on the awful replacements and losses, but had not mentioned the startling new things we had never encountered before: snow for one![34]

Alvarez's "teaching aids" will be welcome in the classroom of the new mythology.

Yet care must always be taken lest children, absorbed in observation, write poems incorporating *only* facts. This is the province of journalism, the mere reproductive reportage of the world as found in much writing by children. Facts, as Langston Hughes used them, are the basis for "fiction and poetry if used creatively." To Steiner, "The radical flaw in the naturalist tradition is to describe accurately – like taking a photograph," whereas "enduring realism is achieved through magic and the supreme liberties of art."

CHAPTER XVII

Further Notes for a New Mythology

He requires an experience, he hath not yet attained, and sentiments to which he is as yet a stranger, to be susceptible of that complex impression which is the general result of all these sensations.

From *Emile*
Jean Jacques Rousseau[1]

The new mythology believes that children are capable of being led to make their own magic – their own poems. The liberties which they take in their syncretic schemes often lend themselves to the making of poetry. Those who guide them, however, should, as Mearns hopes, retain "a memory of their own childhood" if they are to be "compatriots of the young." If teachers are to identify and encourage the magic, they ought to keep "in some part of their being, an egotistic celebration of the unusual and unique self of their earlier days."[2] They should, as Simon notes, find themselves involved in the conflicts which children experience and remember how it was to go through the difficulties "inarticulate & mute, or struggling amid clichés to find language to fit our feelings."[3] They must guide the children by recalling earlier days and how they worked to find a voice with which to speak of the problems that beset them.

The new mythology will also have teachers who have enough respect for children to recognize that even in the early grades, children can distinguish the difference between lyric, narrative, and dramatic poetry, that they can use persona or speak through a mask with freshness. When Piaget speaks of the "well known phenomenon of animism among very young children,"[4] or their use of anthropomorphism when "phenomena are animated with real life or with a dynamic character drawn from life,"[5] he is describing a use of the imagination common to both children and poets – an ability to creep into the skin of someone or something else; to adopt a different voice and point of view. "Often children and adults can be freer and more expressive," Steinbergh and McKim write, "if they can return to a less rational logic and imagine themselves to be something or someone else."

> The use of a persona allows us to say what we might not ordinarily reveal. Masks provide us with ways of internalizing metaphor, extending imagination and becoming more truly ourselves. There is an endless number of such persona; some of these include objects (natural and man-made), vegetables and animals (real and imaginary), and the lives of other people.[6]

The Mineral, Animal and Vegetable Poems written by children working with Steinbergh and McKim are rich in originality and feeling. Catherine Miller's "Radish Poem"

> Once quite pale
> As Someone sampled me
> Now quite red . . .
> Tinged by embarrassment[7]

is a striking example of how the mask can be used without prescriptive beginnings.

The teacher of the new mythology will recognize that fill-in phrases such as "I wish I were a . . ." or "If I were . . ." or "I don't want to be . . ." are not the stuff of poetry, but merely directives which may be part of the *preparation* for writing, but have no place in the poem itself. The teacher who guides the child toward developing creativity will not only encourage use of the dramatic voice but will demonstrate respect for children's intelligence by refusing to call this voice "Talking Jismoes" or "My Friend America,"[8] "Being Hysterical"[9] or "Myth Poems."[10] This teacher will not ask children to pretend they are insane or that they stutter by writing in "Weird Voices."[11]

This does not imply that children should speak only of the happy things. As Richard Lewis notes

> We cannot allow children to think that writing is that which must be "pretty." I think too often we give children the impres-

> sion that we are looking for "beauty" in their writing. We don't give them the impression that we are looking for something that is genuinely their own voice.[12]

It is understandable that in an attempt to release children from the burden of writing about the beautiful or the pretty, many poet-teachers have asked that they explore the strange and often bizarre. But while the real voice of children need not be smothered under high-flown words or concepts, neither should it strain to be crazy and incoherent. As teacher John Bennett states, "One of the myths that has arisen in teaching poetry is that we teach our charges to lie in order to be poetic. This is unfortunate."

> If we do not teach our students to tell their personal truth as they write, then we continue to propogate a deadly falsehood of poetic license in the name of creative expression.[13]

Between the personal truth which Bennett champions, and the fragmented and often weird images advocated by other teachers, there is a middle ground. The teacher who does not blindly follow prescriptives and formulas will recognize the charm of the lyrical voice and its personal truth; the need for the narrative voice and its objective stance; and the possibilities for releasing the imagination through the dramatic voice. Children should be encouraged to experiment so that what might be first written as a dull lyrical piece can become more exciting as a mask. The same work that is written in a pedestrian narrative may come alive when the persona, often combined with apostrophe, is explained. Children's uninspired poetic asides, didactic verses, or the injunction for the reader to behave in a certain way can be avoided when the voice is changed. A cursory look at any anthology of children's work will show that the use of the narrative voice, the impersonal telling of a story or event, or description is used more frequently than the lyrical and the possibilities for the dramatic voice have hardly been touched. Yet children who love to play and pretend, who still cling to anthropomorphism and animism, who enjoy dramatic play, have seldom been introduced to the power which the mask or apostrophe or dialogue can confer upon their work.

"There is no limit," writes Kohl, "to the forms of writing that children will experiment with" if, as he explains, "they are convinced that the teacher does not want a correct answer to an unambiguous question, but rather to hear what they have to say."[14] This is as true for the writing of poetry as prose, and ultimately must involve a discussion of the need for form and what Bedoya recognizes as the control children not only need, but actively seek. Control does not imply a rigid approach, a tight adherence to classical metrics and rhyme, an unyielding insistence on excellence in grammar and handwriting, but it does imply that a "formal structure"[15] is often needed as children themselves discover when their work does not satisfy. It is as if they themselves know that poor form can only produce poor work, and the more they write, the more they recognize that some rhythm must accompany their writing just as it controls their rope jumping or basketball dribbling or even breathing and eating. Perhaps this is what adults refer to as the "natural rhythm" of the child. Perhaps it is what poet Charles Olson means by the line which comes "from the breath, from the breathing of the man who writes, at the moment when he writes."[16]

The teacher who has respect for children, who wishes them to grow, recognizes like Brownjohn that "Until the children are used to writing poems it will be necessary for you to go through much of their work and help them put it into lines . . . taking out odd words or rearranging sentences can make all the difference. . . ."[17]

The new mythology will have teachers who care enough to help; to admit that if they do not know, they will search for the answers in partnership with students. They will recognize, as Kohl suggests, that "It is a mistake to assume that all children have the energy and devotion necessary to write novels or poems"[18] but they will not give up easily. They will be teachers who tailor what is meaningful for their students in the age and area in which they are growing up. They will, like high school teacher Heidi Bowton, consider that if they are teaching a group of remedial students who "have missed large blocks of the school year through detainment at juvenile hall or work camps," who are "unfamiliar and hostile to conventional forms of poetry," they must plan writing that touches what these students know and what they may dream. They will spend time and energy listening to their students, noting that bragging as one aspect of their personality is found in Nikki Giovanni's *Ego-Tripping*, and they will build lessons that eventually end in poems that have the creative mimicry of which Jordan spoke

. . . raised like somebody
I am going to be somebody some day

I'll grow up and finish school to be somebody
I'm not a quitter I will go on to be somebody . . .[19]

The new mythology will have innovative teachers like Rolly Kent, the Tucson Arizona Public Library's poet-in-residence, who carries on the tradition of the first bards – who listened and recorded what they heard – as he weaves into poems the "connection between the day-to-day world of survival and the world of feelings" of children. Like Grace Conkling, he knows that the urgency of what a child may have to tell is hindered by the writing process. "I am not a teacher," he writes. "I'm a poet. I have no method that is readily teachable to someone else."

> The whole viability of what I do with kids depends on being with them and being with myself. So every session with kids is different. I am suspicious of methods: methods make it tempting to avoid interacting with others. Besides, methods also make it easy to think one knows something "important."[20]

In *Talk about the World*, a collection of poems by children between four and eight years old, Kent relates how he learned that although children can write, "their imaginative energy gets diverted into the effort needed to spell and assemble sentences. Tape-recording seemed a possibility, but ultimately was too distracting and awkward. Finally I just took dictation. The kids could talk; I handled the pencil. I then found that the success of this method depended on asking questions or posing situations which could continually involve the kids so they'd want to talk. When I understood that kids simply enjoyed the fun of talking, the poems became by-products of the play and interplay of children with each other and me."[21]

The poems in this collection are an interplay of fantasy and reality, each beginning almost as if Kent had started in the midst of the thought inside the child's head. "I want to talk about how the world is/the big wide ball with all the cities in it," a six year old begins. A second grade child's poem starts "It feels like I'm in another country." The natural rhythm of children's speech is heard as a kindergarten child, towards the end of a long sequence on hiding, says

OK, I'm hiding . . .

You can't see me!

Come look for me.

You can't find me,
You can't find me![22]

Here the children's voices come through, telling of observations, ideas, dreams and wishes, without prescriptives or gimmicks. It is as though one could hear the expectancy of the teacher listening, the child talking. Here are echoes of Rousseau and Emile, Kohl in his classroom, Lopate patiently waiting for the "ripe" time for a child to write, Mearns evoking with wise humor what secrets children are willing to give.

The reader can almost hear hidden associations at work as a first grader says "When I'm the giant/I like to eat corn . . . ;" of a group of eight second graders in a fresh sort of collaborative effort:

And everyone had to
get into a ship, the pilgrims
came to America.
In America, everyone had enough
and snacks . . .[23]

The natural use of sound and repetition comes through in another work by six third graders with a refrain that reads:

Mary Lou, Mary Lou,
I believe in you![24]

The image true to childhood is evoked naturally in

It's sad when someone dies, all
you can do is cry or yell
or fix your dolly . . .[25]

There will be poet-teachers, too, like Richard Brown who believe that poetry can be begun by students if they are given a "beginning working-vocabulary of prosody, mechanics and an ability to write one or two of the basic verse-forms." This is "not poetry" but a knowledge that in the haiku there is "the demand for terseness," a brush with metaphor, and the "beginnings of free verse" that lead the student to understand something about the "illusion of freedom." Through the limerick Brown feels students will learn that meter and rhyme can be effective tools, that grow familiar and comfortable with practice and repetition.

> I am old-fashioned by today's standards. I love my students and they know it! I do not use paper bags, records, seashells and pictures as stimulus; these items are not in us, these are tangibles made tangible by a power, higher than us. We have however a power latent in most of us, that can transform the intangible into the tangible; that is poetry![26]

One of the most urgent and important things that the new mythology must do is to take a critical look at the overuse – and often misuse – of a number of the tools of poetry that are meant to enhance and add significance to the intent of the poem. When John Ciardi asks, "How does a poem mean?"[27] he speaks of all the various elements that contribute to the meaning; the use of rhythm, sound, imagery, choice of language, tone, metaphor, simile – and lesser devices such as alliteration, consonance, assonance, and synesthesia. In an effort to coax out the poet in the child, many poet-teachers and teachers seize on one of these devices, enjoin children to elaborate upon it, and substitute for poetry itself what is merely an exercise in the use of one poetic tool.

It is time to recognize that metaphor and simile have been pressed into poor service when they no longer serve as vehicles for the fresh, original observation, but as trite statements that only prove a child can make comparisons in color, shape, size, or other analogous features. "The big clouds look like pillows,"[28] one child writes, or "The sun looks like gold."[29] Often written in catalog fashion, they become spin-offs of pop culture; "Love is . . ." and "Happiness is . . . having nice friends."[30] Often they make factual and banal statements – "The sky is as blue as the sea."[31] Because simile and metaphor are natural operations of the mind, a way to understand concretely, young children use them naturally and with originality. But when they become license to make "wild and crazy comparisons" that are a product of the child's autonomous imagination – "The blue in the flag is a boy with chickenpox"[32] – they are no longer metaphor but subjective imagery. They have lost any symbolic meaning.

Closely allied to this is the enjoinder to use synesthesia, a type of analogy that perceives and interprets the data of one sense in terms of another. Thus, a color may be elicited to represent a certain chord or note in music. Synesthesia is not a device which children use spontaneously. They use color for identification and description; they do not deal in abstract thought; they do not normally associate color or sound with feelings. Prodded by teachers to emulate Mary O'Neill's *Hailstones and Halibut Bones*, children produce either the most obvious and pedestrian comparisons – "gold is the sun"[33] or "blue is a lake"[34] – or asked by teachers to make "weird" comparisons, they may write "A tree is as green as a roaring lion."[35] In either case, a catalog of such listings is not poetry but forced synesthesia masquerading as poetry.

The new mythology recognizes that rhyme is a difficult tool for children to use well; yet in censuring its use, many adults working in the classroom search for a substitute that will change a dull prose line into poetry. Some teachers wisely choose repetition to give structure and form. Others choose syllabication. But too often children are urged to *describe* sounds or noises – "A clink sounds like a drink of pink water"[36] – or employ onomatopoeia which, in the English language, is limited. Arguments against the use of anything but a child's natural rhythm seem to rely more on the fact that many poet-teachers and teachers are unwilling – or unable – to teach metrics. The new mythology will welcome the few teachers, like Martin Robbins, whose essay in *Poemmaking*, "Riming is Timing," proves that children can learn that alliteration "can reinforce meaning,"[37] that phrasing and alignment can be studied, that assonance can aid in the use of rhyme, and that rhyme can be used well. Indeed, Robbins's children not only used rhyme but learned about phrasing, metrical feet, and other ways of "making a poem work."[38]

The new mythology does not argue with the fact that children like to play with words, but it will examine the beliefs of those who ascribe to words a magic that can unlock the secrets of the unconscious through word-association. It will not quibble with the assertion that, for some, words may kindle images and that word games are certainly a good bit of fun. But it will regard words as raw materials – tools. The tendency to paste together "found" words or arrange the letters of words in patterns, or write acrostics, has blinded many to the viewpoint of Ted Hughes and Mearns: Words, they assert, are secondary to the feeling, the absorption in the thing about which the child – or poet – is writing. Words do not lead, but follow an idea. The new mythology believes, as does Mearns, that there is danger in becoming a "wordist,"[39] because children let the words substitute for the voice behind them.

The new mythology recognizes that good poetry must spring from the child's own life-experience as well as his imaginative life, but it questions whether poet-teachers and classroom teachers do not overemphasize methods to reveal a child's inner feelings. In an effort to bring to light the child's true feelings, they probe the memories, experiences, dreams, and thoughts, inventing "honesty-promoters"[40] to urge students to tell of their angers, joys, fears; they ask children to search their memories for imagery, and often interpret what the child is saying. Poets spend lifetimes probing their unconscious, spinning out hidden dreams. The new mythology seriously doubts that children can – should – or will disclose their private feelings and thoughts in the classroom. They may offer a memory, an experience, an image – what they think adults want to hear – but these are not poetry. They must be reinforced, altered, and rediscovered before the poem is born.

The new mythology deplores the substitution of the poetic device for the poem itself. To sanction this would be to believe that a child who uses rhyme is, ipso facto, writing a poem. It regards all of this emphasis on devices and tools as helpful, *if* children understand that poetry is made up of many elements. It strongly urges that adults learn to distinguish the difference between a tool of poetry and the crafted poem itself.

Parents who are interested in a new mythology from which to develop children's potential in writing and the arts may wish to provide a home environment that encourages children to work and play in creative ways. Parents will make sure that children are not pushed from activity to activity but are allowed time for thinking and day-dreaming. E. Paul Torrance believes the home can provide alternatives, materials and books which enrich imagery and awareness of nature as "models of creation;"[41] in addition children should be encouraged to write, to express themselves in words and drawings and be accorded praise. Word play and games are also advised, as are alternates to the dittoed fill-ins, the standardized art drawing that still plagues many classrooms. While he advocates publication of children's work, it is unclear whether he sanctions the publishing of formula work. His strong stance against dittoed kindergarten art indicates that he might be opposed to the gimmicks and fill-ins that glut so many publications today.

It is strange, however, that many in the field of education and psychology take a strong stand against parents' attempt to develop creativity in their children. Although full of good intentions, parents often, according to Arieti, "show inhibiting anxieties, such as worrying whether their children appear unusually introverted, peculiar. They are more concerned with external success and popularity than with inner growth and creativity; between practicality and creativity, many parents choose practicality."[42] Love and security are often discussed as prerequisites to creativity, although this is not borne out in fact. Arieti suggests that contrary to the belief that early experience and conflict may drive some children toward creativity, his own experience indicates that "the love of a good mother, accompanied by the faith that the child will be a worthwhile and creative individual" can play a vital role in the creative development of the child.

> The child introjects; he learns to share mother's feeling; he accepts her prophecy. Now he must prove that his mother is right. The image of the trusting mother will sustain him throughout his life – in moments of doubts, tribulations, and impulses to withdraw from the pains of the innovating search.[43]

Yet as Mearns and Arieti both state, such a love "is hardly a sufficient causative factor. Too many are the mothers who nourish similar feelings for their children; too few are the children who respond to such wishes by becoming creative."[44] The plans and hopes can indeed backfire. The promotion of creativity is seen by most educators as the province of the educational system.

This last point is moot; for on a practical level, it would seem that the home, as the first environment of the child, provides the first encounters with books, music, nature, language, play, and the creative spirit – that is, the ability to think in fresh combinations, as when a child is exposed to blocks that, arranged in different ways, can become a bridge or a house, a road or a castle. Educators know that children who have heard good books write in a different rhythm; that those who have not sat in front of the television screen hours upon end are far more capable of making their own images. The research of Torrance and others shows that children's ability to create drops off at about five years of age, nine years of age, and at the beginning of junior high school: it cites as reasons, hindrances in creative thinking blamed on education; "premature attempts to eliminate fantasy; restrictions on manipulativeness and curiosity; overemphasis or misplaced emphasis on sex roles; overemphasis on prevention, fear and timidity; misplaced emphasis on certain verbal skills; emphasis on destructive criticism; and coercive pressures from peers."[45] If this is true, it would seem the home might serve as a balance by offering books of fantasy, by permitting games and materials to spur curiosity, by refusal to categorize stereotyped sex role models, and by allowing time for the child to build up self-confidence within the family situation. While these are matters for psychologists and educators, the creative parent will not turn over the education of a child to the schools alone, or creativity may, indeed, die.

Torrance asserts that teachers can help by treating unusual questions and unusual ideas with respect; by believing in the value of children's ideas; by providing time and materials for self-initiated learning and giving credit for this; and by providing periods of time for doing work which is not evaluated. But perhaps one of Torrance's most valuable suggestions is that there must be a recognition that there is no "one supreme educational method to which all children will respond. Perhaps the most that we can realistically hope for is to determine what methods are most effective with what types of categories of learners. Many convergent lines on research are beginning to make it clear, that when we change our methods of teaching, or the nature of our instructional materials, that children with different kinds of mental abilities become the star learners and non-learners."[46]

This viewpoint bodes well for the new mythology because it suggests that teachers will learn to value their own creativity and be willing to try new ways when the old do not work. They will also know there is still a place in the child's world for order and the knowledge that rules must be learned before they can be broken. Ginsberg's "ghostly Academics in Limbo screeching about form" will still have the support of a few who recognize that to throw out all tradition is to cheat themselves and the children of growth. There will be teachers, too, who value the importance of humor; who do not take themselves or their children so seriously that they cannot laugh. With this knowledge and with respect for the power of levity they will come to know that poetry is more than a receptacle for high-flown declarations of Beauty, Wisdom, and Truth. It is not the celestial abode nor the heaven that is found in children, but their laughter and play here on earth that matters.

> I'm sitting in New Orleans
> eating my gumbo.
> My gumbo has shrimp, crab
> sausage and chicken, honey child
> My gumbo go down my
> throat and hit my spot.
> Me be asking for lst, 2nd, 3rd,
> and 4th. My grandma say
> I gonna turn into a big
> pot of gumbo.
> My gumbo be screaming!
>
> Naeemah Sabree[47]

Those who are part of the new mythology – educators, teachers, and poet-teachers, parents and children – will look at poetry not as something apart from life, but as a vital and sustaining part of it, expressing every observation, feeling, experience, wish and dream, emotion and idea that is part of being alive. And as adult poets make their work a record of their own human experience, seeking to engage an audience through their pseudo-statement and metaphor, so should children be led to do the same. But the new mythology listens to those who recognize that not every word put down is a poem, that it is order and craft that lead to creativity and the making of a poem. "Writing," asserts Kohl, "must be taught qualitatively – how can one best express oneself, in what way?"[48] And Mearns answers:

> We must all learn control. The sign of the best artist is just that. The creative force must not be permitted to waste itself; it must

> be directed: slowed up, stopped when necessary, let go to the limit, thinned out, spread wide; but unless the direction comes from the creative artist himself he is nothing more than a machine or an enslaved person. Control is one of the greatest subjects of study.[49]

Control is order, the same order that I. A. Richards pits in opposition to the "natural." Poet Ishmael Reed would also define it as craft, for

> Even if you write bizarre stuff, fantasy or new fiction or discontinuous literature, you still have to have craft. I think craft and hard work are crucial beyond inspiration. It took me a long time to learn my craft . . .[50]

Can the child be a creative artist who, like the adult, learns control and craft? Can these be taught to the young? Is it possible to understand the nature of creativity clearly enough to learn something about its workings that will offer any clues? The knowledge that creativity is wasted every moment in every classroom must be of deep concern to the new mythology. And it is to this problem as well as to that of control that it must, ultimately and underlying all other considerations, address itself.

CHAPTER XVIII

Creativity and Reality

The poet who is not a realist is dead. And the poet who is only a realist is also dead. The poet who is only irrational will only be understood by himself and his beloved, and this is very sad. The poet who is all reason will even be understood by jackasses, and this is also terribly sad. There are no hard and fast rules, there are no ingredients prescribed by God or the Devil, but these two very important gentlemen wage a steady battle in the realm of poetry, and in this battle first one wins and then the other, but poetry itself cannot be defeated.

From *Memoirs*
Pablo Neruda[1]

In his paper "Towards a Theory of Creativity" published in 1954, C. R. Rogers maintains that there is a "desperate social need for the creative behavior of creative individuals."[2] To fight stereotypes, to face the "fantastic atomic age" which he foresees, "creative adaption seems to represent the only possibility that man can keep abreast of the kaleidoscopic change in his world."[3]

> Unless individuals, groups and nations can imagine, construct and creatively revise new ways of relating to these complex changes, the lights will go out. Unless man can make new and original adaptions to his environment as rapidly as his science can change the environment, our culture will perish.

Rogers, as a scientist, believes that a product of creation must be "symbolized in words or written in a poem, or translated into a work of art or fashioned into an invention."[4] Mere subjective fantasies may be novel but cannot be defined as creative. "Creativity always has the stamp of the individual, upon its product, but the product is not the individual, nor his materials, but partakes of the relationship between the two." Rogers's definition of the creative process is

> *the emergence in action of a novel relational product, growing out of the uniqueness of the individual on one hand, and the materials, events, people, or circumstances of his life on the other.*[5]

Rogers asserts that creativity "exists in every individual and awaits only the proper conditions to be released and expressed"[6] and although this individual may not be always conventional or conforming his product will be "socialized." Creativity is not then some isolated fantasy that relates only to the "I" but one that includes the uniqueness of the individual as a "new aspect of himself-in-relation-to-his-environment with others."[7] Teachers, parents, and all those who would foster creativity will value the individual worth and potential of each person; will provide a *"climate in which external evaluation is absent"*[8] and with empathy, will give the individual freedom to think.

Rogers's strong plea for the creative individual is based upon his belief that there must be "creative behavior in adapting ourselves to our new world if we are to survive," and the urgency of what he wrote thirty years ago grows ever more pressing. But can we view the making of a poem in the same light as Rogers views creativity in the sciences?

Many agree that we can, for poetry alters the way that adults – and children – see the world. To Steiner, poetry is the "best evidence of how life is for ourselves." Poets, above all, are honest men – they do not prostrate themselves before false gods. It is poetry that helps men and women know who they are, and what their relationship is to the world, as well as what they can become and make of their environment. Even if children are not capable of becoming poets – and there are few who will be – children nevertheless become exposed to the knowledge that their voices can make a difference; that they can make themselves heard. Rogers's points are cogent for creative living as well as for actual creation.

Children find out who they are through creative work, for such work enlarges their capacities for understanding and learning. Many who work with children describe creativity as a means to fresh insights, a way to self-confidence and communication. Poetry is an expression of creativity for everyone – teacher, poet-teacher, parent, educator, and child, either as writer or reader. Certainly poetry – through its assertions and metaphors, its imaginative view of the world, its different way of looking at reality, its ways of reshaping reality – mirrors human vision.

The creative process itself, the stages through which we must go to effect a synthesis, is a source of fascination. There have been numerous educated guesses made and psychological studies conducted, theories proposed and countered, both by those who create and those who either admire the creative mind or wish to discover its sources. Of interest is H. Poincaré's genesis of mathematical creation, written over fifty years ago. Mathematical creation, he writes

> does not consist in making new combinations with mathematical entities already known. Any one could do that, but the combinations so made would be indefinite in number and most of them absolutely without interest. To create consists precisely in not making useless combinations and in making those which are useful and which are only a small minority. Invention is discernment, choice.[9]

Poincaré speaks of the necessity of preparation for the creative act; the background that is essential before "the appearance of sudden illumination, a manifest sign of long, unconscious prior work" which first appears and must be followed after "some days of voluntary effort."[10] He speaks of the rest required over a period of time, the working of the unconscious, and the return to "discipline, attention, will and therefore, consciousness."[11] The interplay of the conscious and unconscious and the relationship between the contingencies of the external world are all germane to the act of creation. A great deal of scientific and psychological data have been amassed over the past fifty years, with many new hypotheses about the creative process; but none stress so clearly as does Poincaré the need for the interaction of individuals with their environment as well as with the modes of the mind. Nor does any theory, translated into a framework which considers the child as potential poet, show more emphatically the realization that it is *not only* background, but spontaneity, inspiration, conscious and difficult work, and unconscious prompting that can lead to the making of a poem. It is not any *one* of these, but all taken together, each in its proper time, that leads to creation.

A revealing study of the creative process is the subject of Arieti's *Creativity: the Magic Synthesis.* It examines the creative mind from the psychological, scientific, and artistic point of view. A number of Arieti's beliefs, already discussed, are fruitful for understanding both the similarities and the differences between the adult as poet and the potential of the child. In addition, to Arieti:

> Creativity is one of the major means by which the human being liberates himself from the fetters not only of his conditioned responses, but also of his usual choices. However, creativity is not simply originality and unlimited freedom . . . Creativity also imposes restrictions. While it uses methods other than that of ordinary thinking, it must not be in disagreement with ordinary thinking – or rather it must be something that, sooner, or later, ordinary thinking will understand, accept, and appreciate. Otherwise it would be bizarre, not creative.
>
> A creative work cannot be considered in itself only; it must also be considered in reference to man. It establishes an additional bond between the world and human existence . . . Creative work thus may be seen to have a dual role: at the same time as it enlarges the universe by adding or uncovering new dimensions, it also enriches and expands man, who will be able to experience these new dimensions inwardly. It is committed not just to the visible but, in many cases, to the invisible as well. Indeed, it is the perennial (and almost always unverbalized) premise of creativity, to show that the tangible, visible, and audible universe is infinitesimal in comparison to the one that awaits discovery through exploration of the external world and of the human psyche. A new painting, poem, scientific achievement, or philosophical understanding increases the numbers of islands of the visible in the ocean of the unknown. These new islands eventually form those thick archipelagos that are man's various cultures. Thus any creative product has to be considered from two points of view: that is, as a unity in itself; and as part of a culture, either a specific culture or the general cultural patrimony of mankind.[12]

Creativity demands, as Rogers, Poincaré, and Arieti all assert, that the product, the thesis, the invention, the poem are not the "isolated fantasy," the "useless combination," or the outgrowth of "unlimited freedom," but *the result of control and discipline.* Thus any discussion of poetry written by children must take into account what is meant by the "raw" or the "cooked" poem; whether or not children are capable of the same kind of poetry as adults. "Art at its truest," Kostelanetz writes, "disciplines the ego, rather than exploiting it or indulging it."[13] Holbrook notes the need for inner order and Mearns speaks of the necessity for "language design," for "fashioning" into words "the turbulent undercurrent of my life, of whose meaning and significance I am not fully aware until I have so fashioned it."[14]

Some concept of what a poem is – for poetry cannot be defined – may serve well to explore the differences between a child's poetry and art poetry. "Today," writes poet Robert Francis, "many poets eschew magic. Instead of a mysterious rabbit, they give us the hat itself, the empty hat, the old hat with the sweaty headband. After all (they seem to be reminding us) no hat we really wear has a rabbit in it."[15] In contrast is the poetry of those who embrace the rabbit. Steiner writes that

> in every mature and completed work of art a totality of vision is implicit. Even a short lyric poem makes defining statements about two spheres of reality – the poem itself and that which lies outside of it (in the sense that a vase defines two areas of space.) But in the majority of instances we cannot wholly document the continuities between a mythology and its aesthetic embodiment. We conjecture, we read "between the lines" (as if the poem were a screen and not, as it must be, a lens) or we extrapolate about what we know of the author . . .[16]

"Entrenched in our poets," Steiner continues, "is the belief that art reveals to us, through allegory and metaphor, the 'real' world of which our own is but a corrupt or fragmentary image." The Western mind, he notes, "seeks an ascent from the transitory to the real through philosophy or science or the sudden illumination of poetry and grace."[17]

How we view poetry, then, what we wish it to do for us, has a great deal of bearing on our praise or condemnation of the kind of thing children write. But to excuse mediocrity in the work of children who do not possess the fully developed faculties of the adult poet may also be to excuse the environment or the educational system, or the teacher who has not developed the potential inherent in the child. "The sadness, if not tragedy, of this devaluing of a child's ability to imagine and to create," Richard Lewis writes, "is not only the limiting of an individual's potential but the degree to which the individual will have been made to forfeit his or her right of access, both as a participant and creator, to the vast heritage of human expression."[18]

The qualities which the poet and child have in common are: a rich inner life; a sense of an inner reality that can be communicated to others, that speaks with honesty and a sense of its own truth and that rises above the limits of reality to state, in Williams's terms, its dream. Both children and poets have strong emotions, sharp sensory responses. They both need to verbalize, to play with language. Their paleological minds seek and find analogies that offer unlimited possibilities for expression. They have energy, dreams of glory, wishes that cannot be stilled, and, in the beginning, a spontaneity which, if kept alive, serves them well. Underlying all this they have the ability to think in concrete imagery, to make pictures, and to glory in the use of the imagination.

These qualities and modes of the mind are sustained by poets; they are a part of whatever is created. They are given to the normal child, but unless they are kept alive, nourished and encouraged, they are apt to lose their strength and even vanish. If guided, they are qualities which may grow in intensity and carry over into adult life.

Paleological thinking, the thought process which establishes links between objects and words, is strong in young children who, as a part of their growth, are trying to relate things to each other, to classify, to understand themselves in relationship to the world. They see similarities everywhere, and these similarities become the means for making total identifications. Children are trying to give meaning to what they see so they associate by means of the link, the predicate that identifies these things in their minds. The child, as Piaget notes, *perceives* comparisons but does not *compare* perceptions, as in the example of the moon as *full* as a suitcase. The paleological mind does not, in fact, use logic but seizes on some predicate as a basis for identification. Thus, even a word can open up hundreds of possibilities for identification, and there is no way of knowing what predicate will be seized. This is why children's writing is often unclear; often the predicate has been hidden, as in the example of the "affectionate" sugar. Great originality can result from the use of this mode of thinking because the potential is endless, and the child goes off on what Arieti calls an "orgy of identification."

Poets also use this mode of thinking, but there is a marked difference. For in the making of their poems, their metaphors, they also use logic and reason to *reject* the links which do not suit what they are saying. As an example, Shakespeare perceived many similarities between the world and the stage. In thinking of the world, Shakespeare noted its properties, searched for links between the two images, and with imagination and logic selected only those links which applied to both the world and the stage. (While the world has oceans, for example, the rational mind cannot accept the idea of a stage with oceans.) What Shakespeare seizes for his metaphor are those links which can be easily understood by the ordinary mind, that will not, as Arieti states, appear bizarre and impossible. In creating his new metaphor, Shakespeare destroys neither the world nor the stage. They remain images in their own right. Yet the reader, the listener, will gain a fresh insight on both world and stage in the new unity.

Children, on the other hand, are seldom capable of this kind of metaphor, because they often bypass reason and tend to *accept* rather than *reject* links which do not fit into their schemes. There is, according to Arieti, great variation from child to child in the use of paleologic thinking; further, it is a mode of thinking that is often discarded by both child and adult.

Children are, however, able to make similes, which they do easily on the basis of color, shape, or by classification. While teachers and educators attempt to elicit the fresh and unusual, children are more apt to mimic and write in clichés which may satisfy the assignment. Once their work is accepted as poetry, no further attempt is made to lead the children on to fulfill the potential that they actually possess.

Such work is easy to obtain but falls short of being poetry for several reasons. In the first place, children stay within the framework of their own subjective thinking; their work *appears* to be original, but it is doubtful that they are actually giving what Lopate asks for in the way of "emotional truth." Asked to write quickly or asked to produce something – even trained to express their feelings and urged to use their sensory equipment – they may succeed in writing something that tells how they view or think about things. But they are still too bound up in self: Their images *remain* images and do not rise to the level of symbolism and create a new unity. Their response to a picture or a piece of music remains in some cases that of unbridled imagination, purely subjective and meaningful only to the individual child.

Therefore, while children can effect a simile or even a metaphor, while they can relate subjective images, the process of creativity stops precisely at this point. Their work is called imaginative because they have used their own imagery. It is called spontaneous because they have written it quickly and it is called original because it is in their own handwriting. But it is *not* poetry. It is not poetry because there has been no attempt made to lead them beyond the subjective response, to discipline imagination, or to translate their personal images into universal symbols and, thereby, to communicate.

The recent injunction by educators and teachers to provide an audience for children's writing; the belief that work be published and read by others, the insistence that children enjoy hearing and reading "books" by their peers, may foster self-confidence in children who enjoy being praised and "published." But there is sad confusion here. Rather than developing the potential for communication through the poem itself, helping children to find a way beyond the subjective image, and encouraging the symbol, educators and teachers replace the absent symbol with audience. Thus, the child's potential is not reached. There is no reason why communication cannot exist on both levels, but it will not happen until adults recognize this curious misunderstanding which roots itself in misapprehensions about the role of the poet and poetry itself.

There are few teachers who recognize that the child has potential to incorporate this communication. Some poet-teachers are aware of these possibilities and make conscientious attempts to develop them in students. But finding the time for individual attention and guiding the process demands a commitment that can rarely be afforded. Thus, formulas and gimmickry become replacements for what should be attention to the best in models, to the slow process of creativity, and to the discipline and craft required for the making of poetry. It is time to stop equating the lie of the child with the pseudo-statement of the poet. The child's lie is a purely subjective image; poets' pseudo-statements are symbolic of their dreams, their wish for communication with the world and with their listeners.

Another quality of creativity which is often praised in both poet and child is that of spontaneity. Spontaneous action is unrestrained: It does not rely on premeditation. Springing from impulse, it admits no effort. As Arieti states:

> spontaneity means a certain range of possibilities immediately available to a person's psyche because of that person's intrinsic qualities and past and present experiences. These possibilities, however, do not tend to remain spontaneous. Learning, as well as the formulations of aims and goals, tends to eliminate what proves to be useless from the repertory of the mental flow.[19]

"Man's spontaneity and originality," according to Arieti, "manifest themselves in a flow of images, feelings and ideas." The quality of spontaneity in the poets, then, is tempered by a conditioned rejection of what is meaningless to their work, of what experience and craft has taught them is of no value. Children, because they are less experienced and even less aware of the origin and nature of their feelings, try, without stopping to think, "to put them into action with no or very few modifications." But this is not creativity. It is merely an outpouring of images and ideas and feelings which masquerade as creativity and the poem.

Still another creative quality is that of sensitivity. In the young child the need to touch, smell, see, and hear everything is part of a natural curiosity to understand. But as the child grows, as certain objects or sounds become familiar they are no longer explored or thought about. The atrophying of the sensitivities as well as that of the imagination are observed by many teachers and poet-teachers who work hard to keep these faculties alive. This loss is another tragedy of an age where children sit before a screen instead of going to explore, to smell, to taste even a raindrop on the tip of the tongue. The plea for observation, for being alert to detail, for perception through all of the senses is made by those who recognize that unless sharp sensory equipment is kept alive, it loses its vigor.

The love of language and words is another basis for comparison between poet and child. Children are discovering the joy of understanding and using words and may indulge in a great deal of word play. Sound must be a consideration here. Those who work with young children note that the use of end rhyme is a form of order which gives pleasure, most probably because it limits the number of words which can be absorbed. (Later, when children learn that rhyme is merely a tool or ornament, they will accept the fact that it is not necessary.) Yet the traditional nursery rhyme has always elicited a satisfactory response from the young. This may have something to do with the physiological pleasure derived from a repetition of pattern that can be brought to a happy conclusion or, indeed, a way of regulating language. Or it may simply be that the ear delights in pleasant sounds that in themselves form a sort of order.

Iona and Peter Opie write that "Rhyme seems to appeal to a child as something funny and remarkable in itself, there need be neither wit nor reason to support it."[20] Dr. Isaac Watts's belief that children would remember best what is said in verse and rhyme still holds weight, for even adults will use the old verse, "Thirty days hath September" to remember the number of days in each month.

The pattern of words is also crucial to poetry. Those who assert that children have natural rhythm believe, it would seem, in what is simply a natural way of speaking. A look at any anthology of children's free verse writing will show that, with rare exception, few children write in what may be called poetic cadence, a music or sound traditionally associated with poetry. This is an art which must be learned either through listening to models or through some prescribed pattern, whether it is the natural breath line, syllabic count, or what is now contrary to fashion, the study of metrics. It is possible to teach children this art, although few teachers will attempt it, and most poet-teachers view traditional meters as irrelevant and dead. A teacher who is willing to introduce alliteration, assonance, and consonance may have some results, but too often attention to such figures of speech becomes an end in itelf rather than taking its place in the total poem. They are merely totems and touchstones. To *talk* about a noise or sound does not *make* the sound; nor does what many call children's natural ability to make onomatopoeia hold much ground. There are not that many words in the English language which elicit the sense of what they are and those that exist become clichés. The hundredth time a bee *buzzes* or a wind *whispers* or a ghost *moans* becomes boring. The sound in a poem is effected by a careful making process which a majority of children are neither equipped or able to do. It must be noted, however, that children who have heard good literature read in their early years produce poetry with far greater sensitivity to cadence than those who have not, which suggests that imitation and mimicry lie at the heart of both sound and rhythm.

Poets, of course, are far better equipped to handle words and rhythms. They have learned to eliminate superfluous words and phrases and have evolved their individual styles. In addition, they have escaped from the fetters of the language arts classroom where adjectives are equated with poetic expression. If they use figures of speech, they place them judiciously and select them carefully for their effect in relation to the total poem. Poets, in short, have gone beyond the teacher's injunction to indulge in "orgies" of alliterative sentences, or fill in sentences that prescribe the use of certain kinds of words. They do not set out systematically to put a color in every line or two modifying clauses or to write a poem which begins with a word and ends with a synonym. The word games they play are self-engendered.

The rich inner life and the poem as wish or dream are common to both child and poet, for they are a way of looking at the world which places self in the center – a self that is not only honest, but trusts itself to see things that others do not. Children, who are ego-centered, believe that their view of the world is the right view, and it is only with growth that they begin to relate to the externals. In their syncretism then, they bypass reality. Their sense of animism and anthropomorphism allows them to believe, for example, that the moon is following them; everything is endowed with life as *they* know it. This is, of course, the belief of primitives who do not use logic, but who build a myth of how, for example, the moles eat the moon. Everything is satisfactorily explained in terms of their own myths, and logic has no place. This was noted in various views of the moon expressed through poetry. Furthermore, children use everything that they know, weave everything into their writing whether there is justification or not. There is no difference in their minds between cause and effect. Poets, too, may do this. Blake, for example, builds a myth on just such a basis: Everything he sees and knows goes into his vision. He loses himself in his myth, bypasses reality just as the child. Poets more bound to reality, however, select from all the images those which suit their vision – theirs is a different sort of communication which recognizes reality but transcends it – and bring back to their readers symbols of that world which they can relate to and understand. "Incredible as it may seem," Arieti writes, "the creative person tries to find the phantasmic universal and transfers it into a platonic universal."[21]

To effect such a universal, however, requires that poets impose upon the disorder of everything that is presented to them in imagery, in their perception, in their conscious and unconscious, some order. The poets' order is directed by a desire to make what they do not know clear either for themselves or for others: They are making a synthesis, not like the child, hindered by syncretism. While children want to put everything they know into their work, poets discipline themselves and their imagination, selecting only such material as suits their poems. The poet is concerned with metaphor in its broadest sense; the child uses simile or metaphor only as a figure of speech. Poets strive to direct themselves and their readers, to unveil the hidden meaning; the child's hidden meaning is usually locked inside, incapable of verbalization. Poets express their feeling and emotion by means of symbol; children do so by direct subjective response insofar as they can formulate it.

The poet's order is an important part of the made poem. To find the form that will carry the force is one of the most difficult labors of the poet and involves rejection of work, revision, and experimentation. It requires a discipline that is not demanded of the child, either in form, in use of the imagination, in rhythm, or even in idea.

To make clear the difference between the poet's order and the child's lack of it, let us assume that a teacher or poet-teacher, asking children to write a poem, calls for a response to the word "green" in the hope that this word, this color may elicit some response, some image, some sensory data, some memory, some idea. A child may respond, as did one working in Larrick's classroom:

> Green is like a meadow of grass
> Banana peels that are not ripe
> And broccoli.
>
> Beth Smith[22]

This is an eight-year-old speaking, identifying and classifying all things that might be green. Similarly, a fourth grade student of Koch's writes:

Green is the color of chalk.
Green is grass.
Green is the color of a shirt.
Green is peas.
Green is the color of a Christmas tree.
One night I was walking down a street. Then suddenly I
turned green. Then the street turned green.
When I walked down the next block that turned green too.
Virginia Dix[23]

A fifth grade pupil in Koch's class also responds to green:

Green is the color of the universe
A steeple of stars all green
Towers over the world
The stars look like emeralds
Scattered through the greenish hue
Of the universe so green.
On a dark green planet
Eight trillion green years away
A frog sits in the green night
All you can see is a shimmer of green
On the skin of green algae
In that green planet
Eight trillion green years away
Through endless miles of green void.
Galorp, galorp, burble, gurble
The frog disappears in the dark green night.
In that green world an animal lives on green oranges.
It wanders through the green endlessness of the universe.
Through the emerald green spire
To that small green planet
Eight trillion green years away.
Jeff Morley[24]

The word green conjures up in the mind of the first child a few things of the earth that are green. No one could quibble with her ability to classify things that are green or to arrange them in lines. But is this poetry? Such facts could be found in an encyclopedia. There is nothing fresh about her observation.

The second example begins with the same sort of classification and recognition, but in the last three lines it becomes more personal as it shows that the child begins to explore her inner self, to weave a fantasy about a green street. But the elaboration is quickly aborted.

The child who wrote the third example begins with a pseudo-statement that may be accepted readily by the reader who cherishes "suspension of disbelief." The boy goes on to tell about his universe, selecting things that are green and turning those that are not into green. He is fantasizing about a green world and his work may interest us because he is indeed creating a certain scheme that we believe to be childlike. We commend him for his imagination: Some may even wish to say that he has written a poem. He has gone further than the second child, not telling but showing his world so we may see it. But what does it communicate to us? Simply that a child has a vivid imagination and although we may wish to enter this world for a time and marvel at its invention, the poem, once read, is slightly more than a fantasy. A majority of children are capable of such writing.

But poetry does more. In "Fern Hill" Dylan Thomas writes of his boyhood days:

> Now as I was young and easy under the apple boughs,
> About the lilting house and happy as the grass was green[25]

Here green is used to describe the color of something we know – grass – and it is this image of grass which establishes the reality of Fern Hill. But green also becomes a symbol as Thomas associates it not only with the spirit of the place but as he links it, through simile, with his own youthful spirit. The next time green appears

> And as I was green and carefree, famous
> among the barns

it is color that not only reinforces his concept of a happy spirit but of carefree spirit. In the same stanza he tells us that "green and golden

I was huntsman and herdsman . . ." As the sun is young only once and sheds on him a golden light, the use of green with golden establishes that youth is a unique time, never to return.

In the next stanza we are told that there is "fire green as grass" which is a pseudo-statement that establishes the fact that he sees everything through his youth as happy and carefree. The next stanza tells of

> the spellbound horses walking warm
> Out of the whinnying green stable

which followed his first encounter with love and a sun "that grew round that very day." In the next stanza he states that the "children green and golden" will soon follow time "out of grace." In the last stanza we learn that

> Time held me green and dying
> Though I sang in my chains like the sea.

Green is thus invoked not only as image by the poet for his reality, fantasy, spirit, memory, dreams, and experience, but is transformed into symbols that communicate to us our own youth. We are transported beyond the Fern Hill of Thomas to our own Fern Hill. There we may not only relive the poet's childhood but our own as well. There we better understand and see with new eyes. Like the poet, we are transported from the "phantasmic universal" into the "platonic universal."

This is the poet's order. His imagination, unleashed but controlled by his logic, allows the reader to understand what youth is about. His sprung rhythm is perfectly suited to the exuberance of his youth, to the music and sounds as well as the expanse of Fern Hill. He has allowed his fantasies to be unleashed, yet he controls them so that we are not cast adrift by the bizarre nor clusters of incoherent images.

It is doubtful that children could write such poems. Their knowledge of rhythm, of language does not permit such nuances; their memories and experience are not broad enough; their feelings cannot be so easily recalled; their images are not yet ready to be transported into symbols or such an elaborate concept. They cannot fully control either fantasy or reality. Such a metaphor is the poet's domain.

Yet the potential is there, waiting, and if we do not stifle children with formulas and fill-ins, if we offer them other means to order which are within their grasp, they will come to know that structure is basic to art, that control and discipline are basic to poetry as to life. In properly writing the haiku and cinquain the potential is there for children to learn that their natural verbosity can be controlled with surprising results while their voices need not be silenced by complicated form or necessity for rhyme. Children can learn to use the couplet, the tercet, the quatrain, even if unrhymed; they can learn in the limerick something of metrics, and yes, even rhyme, on occasion. Children thus exposed, it has been ascertained, show a marked improvement in their prose writing.

It is important to recognize that not every child will be a poet. Poetry is a making and involves a craft that is not easy. But this does not mean that children should be less exposed to poetry and the poet-teacher; indeed, there should be a cry for an army of poet-teachers who are trained not only in what real poetry is but in the ways of the child. And these must be people who have respect for children and know what they can do as well as what they cannot do – not because they are rural children or urban children or advantaged or disadvantaged children, but because they are young and full of potential.

Poetry dies in the schools too often because in this society it is not respected. It is tacked onto language arts, it is mutilated by gimmickry, it is castigated as a frill. It is thought of as some esoteric region of the mind, as a luxury. It is in such an atmosphere that a false mythology can exist. And not only exist and grow but flourish – because those who nourish it do not really understand that poetry is a way of growing, of coming to grips with the self and its relationship to the external world, of communicating with all the other selves who are also striving to grow and communicate the meaning of their lives through universal symbols. They believe instead that poetry is a sort of therapy for children, an inner revelation of individual experience and dreams that will reveal the problems of the child and they, the adults, will either learn his secrets of how to cope – because the child is giving them a priceless secret and message from another world – or they feed upon the child's product and create for themselves a utopia on earth where they are the impressarios of the child prodigy.

It is time to recognize the difference between myth and reality, between syncretism and unbridled spillage of emotion, between uncontrolled imagination and the potential children have for a synthesis that is honest and true to childhood. We must also face the fact that the syncretic world topples; the child moves from precausality to logic; and the child, like the educator, teacher, poet-teacher, and parent, must face reality. The child's inner world suffers a change but this does not portend disaster. Rather it suggests that when the paleologic mode begins to diminish, it should be strengthened; that the imagination should be honored but not allowed to run rampant. It suggests that when a child's work becomes imitative and trite, it should be guided to a new spontaneity; that when the sensitivities begin to atrophy, they should be rekindled; that if the individual voice grows faint, it should be allowed to listen to literature that will eventually entice it to add its own song.

What can educators, teachers, and parents do to keep creativity alive? It must depend on what we believe creativity to be. Those who have examined the creative process come up with limited answers because the process varies, and because there is limited scientific knowledge as to how the mind actually works.

Those who believe creativity is the ability to be spontaneous and original and accept the image as the poem, those who believe that speaking of a past experience or telling about a dream or wishing for something or finding a concrete image to describe a color – those in short who accept whatever is written as poetry – will be content with whatever children write and they will praise these children and call them poets.

But those of us who believe that poetry is more – that it can not only draw into itself all the variety of man's experience and feeling, but give this back with fresh understanding of the possibilities of man – must be counted. We will listen to the spirit of the Romantics who place the individual and his emotions at the center of things, even as we place the growth of the child and his potential at the center of education. But we will also recognize that the individual, and the child, is in danger when the self places itself above nature, and when self-discipline vanishes. We will oppose those who would constrain children's spirits by speaking out for an environment in which the self is free, but we will not tolerate that freedom to be translated as license to abandon all guidance and order. We will respect children and provide what is needed not only for their growth but for the creative spirit which makes life the more meaningful. And, as Rousseau, we will know why we do so.

> You must endeavor to be happy, my dear Emilius; this is the end which every sensible Being proposes; it is the first desire imprinted in us by nature, and which never abandons us. But where is happiness? Who enjoys it? Every one is in pursuit of it, yet no one finds it. We spend our whole lives in search of it, and yet never attain it. My young friend, when I took you in my arms as soon as you were born, and calling heaven to witness the engagement I made, devoted my days to the happiness of yours, was I aware of the charge I undertook? No: I only knew that by ensuring your felicity, I should secure my own. By making this useful search on your account, I rendered the benefit common to both of us.[26]

REFERENCES

I – THE CHILD AS NATURAL POET

1. Williams, *The Collected Earlier Poems of William Carlos Williams*, p. 126.
2. Whitman, *Leaves of Grass: Poems of Walt Whitman*, p. 27.
3. Duncan, "Pages from a Notebook," *The New American Poetry*, ed. Allen, pp. 404-405.
4. James, *The Turn of the Screw*, p. 71.
5. Ibid., p. 12.
6. Dostoevsky, *The Brothers Karamazov*, p. 151.
7. Duncan, "Pages from a Notebook," pp. 404-405.
8. O'Gorman, *The Storefront*, p. 42.
9. Wordsworth, "Preface to the Lyrical Ballads," *The Complete Poetical Works of Wordsworth*, p. 791.
10. Wordsworth, "Preface to Ode: Intimations of Immortality," p. 353.
11. Wordsworth, "Ode: Intimations of Immortality from Recollections of Early Childhood," p. 354.
12. Wordsworth, "Preface to Ode," p. 353.
13. Rilke, *Letters to a Young Poet*, p. 19.
14. Ibid., p. 18.
15. Meek, "The Signal Poetry Award," *Signal 35*, May, 1981, p. 67.
16. Arbuthnot, *Time for Poetry*, p. xv.
17. Fosburgh, "Child Poets Reveal Candid Visions of the World They See," *New York Times*, Sept. 4, 1969.
18. Richard Lewis, "The Child as Creator," UPI, Feb. 1982.
19. Kohl, "Poets on Poetry," *Teacher*, April 1977, p. 50.
20. Mearns, *Creative Youth*, pp. 3-4.
21. Mearns, *Creative Power*, p. 112.
22. Mearns, *Creative Youth*, p. 28.
23. Richard Lewis, "The Child as Creator," UPI, Feb. 1982.
24. Cheifetz, "A Love Letter to My Church," *Journal of a Living Experiment*, pp. 305-308.
25. Richard Lewis, "A Place for Poetry," *Publishers' Weekly*, July 10, 1967, p. 120.
26. Gensler and Nyhart, *The Poetry Connection*, p. 17.
27. Claudia Lewis, *A Big Bite of the World*, p. 33.
28. Rousseau, *Emilius and Sophia: of a New System of Education*, Book II, p. 301.
29. Ibid., p. 128.
30. Holbrook, "Creativity in the English Programme," *Creativity in English*, ed. Summerfield, p. 1.
31. Ibid., p. 4.
32. Steiner, *Tolstoy or Dostoevsky*, p. 233.
33. Rousseau, *Emilius*, Book II, p. 307.
34. Olson, "Letter to Elaine Feinstein," *The New American Poetry*, ed. Allen, p. 397.

II – THE CHILD AND IMAGINATION

1. Williams, *The Collected Earlier Poems of William Carlos Williams*, p. 423.
2. Lopate, *Being with Children*, p. 304.
3. Murphy, *Imaginary Worlds*, p. 24.
4. Ibid., p. 22.
5. Brown et al., *The Whole Word Catalog*, p. 30.

6. Koch, *Wishes, Lies, and Dreams*, p. 270.
7. Ibid., p. 8.
8. Ibid., p. 33.
9. Ibid., p. 49.
10. Ibid., p. 198.
11. Ibid., p. 193.
12. Ibid., p. 137.
13. Ibid., p. 129.
14. Southern Nevada Teachers of English, *An Invitation to Poetry*, unpaged.
15. Kimzey, *To Defend a Form*, p. 98.
16. Gensler and Nyhart, *The Poetry Connection*, p. 26.
17. MacAdams, "A Talk about Teaching Poems to Kids," *The Whole Word Catalogue 2*, p. 20.
18. Ibid., p. 19-20.
19. Murphy, *Imaginary Worlds*, p. 8.
20. *Scholastic Voice*, Jan. 13, 1976, p. 8.
21. Tiedt, *Individualizing Writing in the Elementary Classroom*, p. 9.
22. *Imagine and Write*, pp. 4-19.
23. Wiener, *Any Child Can Write*, p. 147.
24. Larrick, *Green Is Like a Meadow of Grass*, p. 62.
25. Ibid., p. 63.
26. Ibid., p. 19.
27. Ibid., p. 20.
28. Ibid., p. 42.
29. Hoffman, "Magic—Black and Otherwise," *The Whole Word Catalog*, p. 20.
30. Ibid., p. 25.
31. Veitch, "The Trapdoor Method," *The Whole Word Catalogue 2*, pp. 63-66.
32. Percy, *The Power of Creative Writing*, pp. 18-19.
33. Coleridge, *Biographia Literaria*, p. 347.
34. Kant, *Critique of Pure Reason*, p. 41.
35. Tennyson, *The Poetical Works of Alfred, Lord Tennyson*, p. 130.
36. Lindsay, *Collected Poems*, p. 67.

III – SYMBOLISM AND INNER REALITY

1. Whitman, *Leaves of Grass*, p. 372.
2. U.S. Bureau of American Ethnology, *Forty-Sixth Annual Report of the Bureau of American Ethnology to the Secretary of the Smithsonian Institution, 1928-1929*, p. 397.
3. Ibid., pp. 484-485.
4. *Stone Soup*, Sept. 1977, pp. 28-29.
5. Rubel and Mandel, *The Editors Notebook*, p. 8.
6. Ibid., p. 9.
7. Ibid., p. 7.
8. *Spicy Meatball Number Five*, p. 7.
9. *Cricket*, Jan. 1978, p. 93.
10. Arnstein, *Children Write Poetry*, p. 132.
11. *Reflections*, Vol. I, Issue 2, 1983, p. 19.
12. *Cricket*, Oct. 1974, p. 91.
13. Richard Lewis, "The Child as Creator," UPI, Feb. 1982.
14. Steiner, *Tolstoy or Dostoevsky*, p. 253.
15. Holbrook, "Creativity in the English Programme," *Creativity in English*, ed. Summerfield, p. 9.
16. Ibid., p. 1.
17. Ibid., p. 7.
18. Ibid., p. 9.

19. Piaget, *The Language and Thought of the Child*, p. 238.
20. Robbins, "Riming is Timing," *Poemmaking*, eds. Whitman and Feinberg, p. 87.
21. Piaget, *The Language and Thought of the Child*, p. 109.
22. Ibid., p. 140.
23. Richard Lewis, "The Magic Fish and the Yellow Print," *Childhood Education*, March 1976, p. 254.
24. Piaget, *The Language and Thought of the Child*, p. 183.
25. Ibid., p. 272.
26. Alwan and Alwan, *The Moon is as Full as a Suitcase*, p. 13.
27. Piaget, *The Language and Thought of the Child*, p. 186.
28. Ibid., p. 150.
29. Ibid., pp. 151-152.
30. Claudia Lewis, *A Big Bite of the World*, p. 85.
31. Ziegler, "Poetry is Like," *The Whole Word Catalogue 2*, p. 165.
32. Ibid.
33. Piaget, *The Language and Thought of the Child*, pp. 13-14.
34. Ibid., p. 22.
35. Ibid., p. 43.
36. Ibid., p. 211.
37. Koch, *Rose, Where Did You Get That Red?*, p. 105-106.

IV – THE OUTER CLIMATE

1. Pound, *Personae*, p. 96.
2. Ginsberg, "Notes from Howl and Other Poems," *The New American Poetry*, ed. Allen, pp. 414-418.
3. Kris, "On Inspiration: Preliminary Notes on Emotional Conditions in Creative States," *The International Journal of Psychoanalysis*, Vol. 20, 1939, p. 379.
4. Ibid., p. 380.
5. Ibid., p. 381.
6. Ibid., p. 377.
7. Ibid., p. 378.
8. Kostelanetz, *The Old Poetries and the New*, p. 41.
9. Ciardi, "Manner of Speaking," *Saturday Review*, May 20, 1972, pp. 14-19.
10. Lusk, *Homemade Poems*, p. 38.
11. Greenberg, *Teaching Poetry to Children*, p. 33.
12. Magers, "Make-A-Poem," *English Journal*, Oct. 1975, p. 50.
13. Southland Council of Teachers of English, *Sunspots I*, Spring 1975, p. 10.
14. Cheyney, *The Writing Corner*, p. 91.
15. Spencer, *Flair, Vol. 1, Creative Writing*, p. 4.
16. Marmor, *Psychiatry in Transition*, p. 3.
17. Ibid., p. 10.
18. Ibid., p. 11.
19. Ibid., p. 12.
20. Ibid.
21. Ibid., p. 14.
22. Koch, *Wishes, Lies, and Dreams*, p. 43.
23. Ibid., p. 25.
24. Manning, "The Freshness of the Morning: The Poetry Children Write," *The Times Literary Supplement*, Oct. 30, 1970.
25. Rousseau, *Emilius and Sophia: of a New System of Education*, Book III, pp. 84-85.
26. Whitman, *Report to the Council on the Arts and Humanities of the Commonwealth of Massachusetts*, p. 3.
27. Whitman and Feinberg, *Poemmaking*, p. viii.

28. Fosburgh, "Child Poets Reveal Candid Visions of the World They See," *New York Times*, Sept. 4, 1969.
29. Claudia Lewis, *A Big Bite of the World*, p. 7
30. Ibid., p. 27.
31. Ibid., pp. 7-8.
32. Ibid., p. 16.
33. Ibid., p. 15.
34. Ciardi, "Manner of Speaking," p. 14.
35. Sisson, "Alternative Offered to a 'cornucopia of perspectiveless drek'," *Minneapolis Tribune*, Feb. 3, 1974.
36. Leland Jacobs, letter to author.
37. Chambers, "Letter from England," *The Horn Book Magazine*, June, 1981, pp. 347-350.
38. Lopate, *Journal of a Living Experiment*, p. 332.
39. Kohl, "Poets on Poetry," *Teacher*, April 1977, p. 49.
40. Kohl, *Teaching the Unteachable*, p. 25.

V – HILDA CONKLING: CHILD-POET

1. Lindsay, *Collected Poems*, p. 254.
2. Hilda Conkling, letter to author.
3. Griffin, "I Have a Dream for You, Mother," *Yankee*, Feb. 1982, p. 90.
4. Hilda Conkling, letter to author.
5. Grace Conkling, *Imagination and Children's Reading*, p. 6.
6. Ibid., p. 7.
7. Ibid., p. 11.
8. Ibid., p. 14.
9. Ibid., p. 15.
10. Ibid., p. 16.
11. Ibid., p. 20.
12. Ibid., p. 21.
13. Ibid., p. 25.
14. Hilda Conkling, letter to author.
15. Ibid.
16. Ibid.
17. Ibid.
18. Hilda Conkling, conversation with author.
19. Ibid.
20. Griffin, "I Have a Dream for You, Mother," p. 91.
21. Ibid., p. 90.
22. Ibid., p. 91.
23. Hilda Conkling, conversation with author.
24. Hilda Conkling, letter to author.
25. Hilda Conkling, conversation with author.
26. Ibid.
27. Griffin, "I Have a Dream for You, Mother," p. 90.
28. Piaget, *The Language and Thought of the Child*, p. 258.
29. Hilda Conkling, *Poems by a Little Girl*, p. v.
30. Piaget, *The Language and Thought of the Child*, p. 257.
31. Ibid., p. 244.
32. Ibid., p. 243.
33. Mearns, *Creative Power*, p. 74.
34. Ibid., p. 72.
35. Ibid., p. 86.
36. Ibid., pp. 86-87.

37. Ibid., p. 86.
38. Grace Conkling, *Wilderness Songs*, p. 8.
39. Ibid., p. 19.
40. Hilda Conkling, *Poems by a Little Girl*, p. 15.
41. Ibid., p. 3.
42. Ibid., p. 68.
43. Hilda Conkling, letter to author.
44. Ibid.
45. Griffin, "I Have a Dream for You, Mother," p. 91.
46. Hilda Conkling, *Poems by a Little Girl*, p. vii.
47. Ibid., pp. vii-viii.
48. Griffin, "I Have a Dream for You, Mother," p. 90.
49. Ibid., p. 87.
50. Untermeyer, "Hilda and the Unconscious," *Dial*, Aug. 1920, p. 187.
51. Ibid.
52. Ibid., p. 188.
53. Ibid., pp. 188-189.
54. Hilda Conkling, *Poems by a Little Girl*, p. v.
55. Ibid., p. xiv.
56. Ibid., p. xv.
57. Ibid., p. xix.
58. Hilda Conkling, conversation with author.
59. Untermeyer, "Hilda and the Unconscious," p. 188.

VI – HILDA CONKLING: HER WORK

1. Grace Conkling, *Wilderness Songs*, p. 58.
2. Hilda Conkling, letter to author.
3. Ibid.
4. Williams, *Harriet Monroe and the Poetry Renaissance*, p. 276.
5. Grace Conkling, *Wilderness Songs*, p. 36.
6. Ibid., p. 46.
7. Ibid., p. 49.
8. Ibid., p. 14.
9. Hilda Conkling, *Poems by a Little Girl*, p. 6.
10. Ibid., p. 20.
11. Ibid., p. 40.
12. Ibid., p. 41.
13. Ibid., p. 42.
14. Ibid., p. 63.
15. Ibid., p. 83.
16. Ibid., p. 58.
17. Ibid., p. 64.
18. Hilda Conkling, *Silverhorn*, p. 96.
19. Hilda Conkling, *Poems by a Little Girl*, p. 27.
20. Ibid., p. 32.
21. Ibid., p. 34.
22. Ibid., p. 118.
23. Ibid., p. 119.
24. Hilda Conkling, *Silverhorn*, p. 88.
25. Ibid., p. 134.
26. Hilda Conkling, *Poems by a Little Girl*, p. 23.
27. Ibid., p. 69.
28. Hilda Conkling, *Silverhorn*, p. 155.

29. Hilda Conkling, *Poems by a Little Girl*, p. 4.
30. Hilda Conkling, *Silverhorn*, p. 109.
31. Ibid., p. 125.
32. Ibid., p. 127
33. Ibid., p. 135.
34. Ibid., p. 112.
35. Ibid., p. 136-137.
36. Ibid., p. 152.
37. Ibid., p. 151.
38. Ibid., p. 156-157.
39. Ibid., p. 67.
40. Ibid., p. 81.
41. Ibid., p. 91.
42. Ibid., p. 98.
43. Ibid., p. 111.
44. Ibid., p. 159.
45. Hilda Conkling, *Poems by a Little Girl*, p. 120.
46. Hilda Conkling, *Silverhorn*, p. 158.
47. Griffin, "I Have a Dream for You, Mother," *Yankee*, Feb. 1982, p. 90.
48. Ibid., p. 91.
49. MacBean, *Marjorie Fleming's Book*, p. xviii.
50. Ibid., p. xviii-xix.

VII – OTHER CHILD-POETS

1. MacBean, *Marjorie Fleming's Book*, p. 110.
2. Ibid., p. 1.
3. Ibid., p. 87.
4. Ibid., p. 128.
5. Ibid., p. 106.
6. Ibid., pp. 41-42.
7. Ibid., p. 78.
8. Ibid., p. 79.
9. Ibid., p. 49.
10. Ibid., p. 51.
11. Ibid., p. 29.
12. Ibid., p. 132.
13. Ibid.
14. Ibid., p. 140.
15. Ibid., pp. 204-205.
16. Carasso, *The Candle Burns*, p. 5.
17. Ibid., p. 6.
18. Ibid., p. 5.
19. Ibid., p. 85.
20. Ibid., p. 83.
21. Ibid., p. 82.
22. Ibid., p. 84.
23. Ibid., p. 44.
24. MacBean, *Marjorie Fleming's Book*, p. 150.
25. Hilda Conkling, *Poems by a Little Girl*, p. v.
26. Crane, *The Janitor's Boy*, p. 40.
27. Ibid., p. xv.
28. Ibid., p. 38.

29. Ibid., p. 37.
30. Ibid., p. xiv.
31. Ibid., p. xv.
32. Ibid., p. xiv.
33. Ibid., p. 33.
34. Ibid., p. xiv.
35. Ibid., p. 78.
36. Ibid., p. 75.
37. Ibid., p. 54.
38. Ibid., p. 68.
39. Ibid., p. 32.
40. Ibid., p. xvi.
41. Ibid., p. xviii.
42. Barnstone, *The Real Tin Flower*, p. v.
43. Ibid., p. vi.
44. Ibid., p. 1.
45. Ibid., p. 2.
46. Ibid., p. 4.
47. Ibid., p. 22.
48. Ibid., p. 10.
49. Ibid., p. 30.
50. Ibid., p. 6.
51. Ibid., p. 19.
52. Ibid., p. 24.
53. Ibid., p. 33.
54. Ibid., p. 53.
55. Ibid., p. 27.
56. Ibid., p. 3.
57. Ibid., pp. 50-51.
58. Farrell, *The Horn Book*, Feb. 1969, p. 61.
59. Sutherland, *Bulletin of the Center for Children's Books*, March, 1969, p. 107.
60. *Booklist*, Jan. 1, 1969, p. 493.
61. Thomas, *School Library Journal*, Jan. 1, 1969, p. 64.
62. Grosvenor, *Poems by Kali*, p. 37.
63. Drouet, *Arbre, mon ami*, unpublished translation by Lloyd Alexander.
64. de Boisdeffre, "Pour Conclure," *Une Histoire Vivante de la Littérature d'Aujourd'hui*, pp. 622-625, unpublished translation by Lloyd Alexander.
65. Ibid.
66. Jean Cocteau, Lettre à Robert Goffin, *Foudre natale*, Dutilleul, 1955, unpublished translation by Lloyd Alexander.
67. Barthes, "La Littérature selon Minou Drouet," *Mythologies*, pp. 153-160, unpublished translation by Lloyd Alexander.

VIII – LANGSTON HUGHES: POET-IN-RESIDENCE, 1949

1. Hughes, *The Dreamkeeper and Other Poems*, p. 12.
2. Warren Seyfert, letter to author.
3. Eunice H. McGuire, letter to author.
4. Hughes, (report) *Three Months at the Laboratory School*, p. 1.
5. Warren Seyfert, letter to author.
6. Hughes, report, p. 12.
7. Irene Breckler, letter to author.
8. Hughes, report, pp. 2-3.
9. Alice Wirth Gray, letter to author.

10. Dartha Cloudman Reid, letter to author.
11. Judith Hayes Weir, conversation with author.
12. Anonymous, letter to author.
13. Phoebe Liebig, conversation with author.
14. David Zimmerman, letter to author.
15. Hughes, report, p. 3.
16. David Zimmerman, letter to author.
17. Lois Grass Kuhr, letter to author.
18. Catherine DeCosta Wilder, letter to author.
19. Anonymous, letter to author.
20. Lois Grass Kuhr, letter to author.
21. Phoebe Liebig, conversation with author.
22. Anonymous, letter to author.
23. Hughes, report, pp. 6-7.
24. Ibid., p. 9.
25. Ibid., p. 11.
26. Ibid., p. 10.
27. Ibid.
28. Phoebe Liebig, conversation with author.
29. Dartha Cloudman Reid, letter to author.
30. Hughes, report, p. 5.
31. Ibid., pp. 5-6.
32. Ibid., pp. 3-4.
33. Ibid.
34. Ibid.
35. Ibid.
36. Ibid.
37. Ibid., p. 5.
38. Warren Seyfert, letter to author.
39. Helen Rand Mills, letter to Charlemae Robbins.
40. Alice Wirth Gray, letter to author.

IX – THE POET AS TEACHER

1. Rousseau, *Emilius and Sophia*, Book III, p. 7.
2. Howard, *Mabel Mapes Dodge of "St. Nicholas,"* p. 207.
3. *St. Nicholas*, 1922, p. 214.
4. Ibid., p. 326.
5. *St. Nicholas*, 1923, p. 662.
6. *St. Nicholas*, 1924, p. 326.
7. Ibid.
8. Kantor, "Creative Expression in the English Curriculum: an Historical Perspective," *Research in the Teaching of English*, Vol. 9, no. 1, pp. 5-30.
9. Mearns, *Creative Power*, pp. 75-76.
10. Ibid., p. 257.
11. Ibid., p. 270.
12. Ibid., p. 271.
13. Ibid., pp. 256-257.
14. Ibid., p. 188.
15. Ibid., p. 11.
16. Ibid., p. 48.
17. Ibid.
18. Ibid., p. 28.
19. Ibid., p. 41.

20. Arnstein, *Children Write Poetry*, p. iv.
21. Ibid., p. 184.
22. Ibid., p. 67.
23. Ibid., p. 69.
24. Ibid., p. 3.
25. Ibid., p. 51.
26. Ibid., p. 61.
27. Ibid., p. 62.
28. Ibid., p. 83.
29. Ibid., pp. 82-83.
30. Ibid., p. 32.
31. Ibid.
32. Lopate, *Journal of a Living Experiment*, p. 327.
33. Ibid., p. 14.
34. Rousseau, *Emilius*, Book IV, p. 203.
35. Ibid., p. 206.
36. Ibid., p. 213.
37. Kohl, *36 Children*, p. 107.
38. Ibid., p. 42.
39. Herbert Kohl, conversation with author.
40. Lopate, *Journal of a Living Experiment*, pp. 193-194.
41. Ibid., p. 192.
42. Hoffman, "Creating Worlds," *The Whole Word Catalog*, p. 42.
43. Metcalf, "Sitting on the Chimney: Poetry Workshops with Adolescents," *Poemmaking*, eds. Whitman and Feinberg, p. 98.
44. Berger, "A Grave for My Eyes," *Journal of a Living Experiment*, ed. Lopate, p. 186.
45. Morley, "Wishes, Lies and Dreams Revisited," *Teachers & Writers Magazine*, Vol. 15, No. 2, November-December, 1983, p. 1.
46. Lopate, *Journal of a Living Experiment*, p. 191.
47. Ibid., p. 193.
48. MacAdams, "A Talk about Teaching Poems to Kids," *The Whole Word Catalogue 2*, p. 18.
49. McGovern, *A Poetry Ritual for Grammar Schools*, p. 10.
50. Alvarez, "Bilingual Poetry-in-the-Schools," *Teachers & Writers Magazine*, Vol. 10, No. 2, Winter, 1979, p. 6.
51. "Celebrating our 15th year – 1967-1982," *Teachers & Writers Collaborative*, p. 1.
52. Schiff, *Artists in Schools*, p. 28.
53. Lopate, *Journal of a Living Experiment*, pp. 328-329.
54. Ibid.
55. Kiesel, "A Poet's Elementary School Journal," *American Poetry Review*, May/June 1974, p. 63.
56. Folkins, "The School Board Sucks," *American Poetry Review*, May/June 1975, p. 35.
57. Karen Swenson, letter to author.

X – A BASIS FOR MODELS

1. Sandburg, *The Complete Poems of Carl Sandburg*, p. 476.
2. White, *Time of the Indian*, preface.
3. Ibid., p. 14.
4. Lopate, "Getting at the Feelings," N.Y. *Times Sunday Magazine*, Aug. 31, 1975.
5. Holman, *At the Top of My Voice*, p. 17.
6. *Spicy Meatball Number Five*, p. 7.
7. Holman, *At the Top of My Voice*, p. 9.
8. *Stone Soup*, May/June 1980, p. 9.
9. *Reflections*, Vol. I, Issue 2, 1982, p. 12.

10. *Language Arts*, Feb. 1983, p. 183.
11. Moore, *See My Lovely Poison Ivy*, p. 3.
12. *Wombat*, September/October 1979, p. 25.
13. *A Magic Place Is*, p. 71.
14. Anonymous.
15. *A Magic Place Is*, p. 29.
16. McCord, *One at a Time*, p. 41.
17. Hunt, "Plagiarism and Appreciation," *Easy Thing for You to Say*, ed. Simon & Harer, pp. 40-42.
18. Elizabeth Hall, letter to author.
19. Jordan, " 'The Voice of the Children': Saturday Workshop Diaries," *Journal of a Living Experiment*, ed. Lopate, p. 144.
20. Ibid., p. 145.
21. Stevenson, *A Child's Garden of Verses*, p. 13.
22. Jordan, *The Voice of the Children*, pp. 145-146.
23. *Wombat*, March/April/May 1980, p. 28.
24. Ibid., p. 23.
25. Baker, *Blue Smoke*, p. 13.
26. Ziegler, *The Writing Workshop*, pp. 19-20.
27. Richard Lewis, "A Place for Poetry," *Publishers' Weekly*, July 10, 1967, p. 119.
28. Claudia Lewis, *A Big Bite of the World*, p. 34.
29. Ibid., p. 166.
30. Ibid., p. 36.
31. Ibid., p. 290.
32. Ibid., p. 196.
33. Ibid., pp. 259-260.
34. Ibid., p. 34.
35. Hill, "How to Tell a Sheep from a Goat – and Why It Matters," *The Horn Book Magazine*, Feb. 1979, p. 101.
36. Meek, "The Signal Poetry Award," *Signal No. 35*, May, 1981, p. 67.
37. Mearns, *Creative Power*, p. 211.
38. Stewig, *Read to Write*, p. 11.
39. Koch, *Wishes, Lies, and Dreams*, p. 30.
40. Ibid., p. 32.
41. Ibid.
42. Gensler and Nyhart, *The Poetry Connection*, p. 10.
43. Nold, "Reality Next to Imaginary: Poetry Writing with Children," *Teachers & Writers Magazine*, Vol. 7, Issue 2, Winter, 1976, p. 27.
44. Zavatsky, "Using *There Are Two Lives*," *The Whole Word Catalogue 2*, p. 155.
45. Ibid., p. 154.
46. Ziegler, "The First Poems of Gerry Pearlberg," *Teachers & Writers Magazine*, Vol. 9, No. 3, Spring, 1978, p. 44.
47. Ibid., pp. 42-43.
48. Ibid.
49. Mernit, "Writing, Not Fighting," *Teachers & Writers Magazine*, Vol. 12, No. 3, Spring, 1981, p. 21.
50. Greenberg, *Teaching Poetry to Children*, p. 13.
51. Brown et al., *The Whole Word Catalog*, p. 19.
52. Ibid., p. 113.
53. Rubel and Mandel, *The Editors Notebook*, p. 12.
54. Koch, *Rose, Where Did You Get That Red?*, p. 6.
55. Ibid., p. 6.
56. Ibid., p. 7.
57. Ibid., p. 13.
58. Ibid., p. 94.
59. Ibid., p. 39.
60. Natalie Robins, broadside.

XI – FURTHER MODELS AND RELATED MATTERS

1. Carroll, *The Work of Lewis Carroll*, p. 752.
2. Holbrook, "Creativity in the English Programme," *Creativity in English*, ed. Summerfield, p. 8.
3. Ibid., p. 2.
4. Ibid., p. 11.
5. Ibid., p. 18.
6. Ibid., p. 19.
7. Ibid., p. 10.
8. Ibid., p. 13.
9. Ibid., p. 14.
10. Ibid., p. 9.
11. Kohl, *Stuff*, p. xi.
12. Padgett and Gallup, "Teaching Poetry Writing to Rural Kids," *The Whole Word Catalogue 2*, p. 41.
13. Roethke, *On the Poet and His Craft*, p. 130.
14. Whitman, *Report to the Council on the Arts and Humanities of the Commonwealth of Massachusetts*, p. 5.
15. McGovern, *A Poetry Ritual for Grammar Schools*, p. 13.
16. Kimzey, *To Defend a Form*, p. 133.
17. Ibid., p. 88.
18. Ibid., p. 89.
19. Gensler and Nyhart, *The Poetry Connection*, p. 27.
20. Ibid., p. 9.
21. Ibid., p. 10.
22. Ibid.
23. Willis, "Linguistics and Creative Writing," *Teachers & Writers Magazine*, Vol. 7, No. 3, Spring, 1976, p. 38.
24. Brownjohn, *Does It Have To Rhyme?*, p. 89.
25. Kohl, "Poets on Poetry," *Teacher*, April 1977, p. 50.
26. Koch, *Wishes, Lies and Dreams*, p. 256.

XII – POETRY AND LANGUAGE ARTS

1. de Giovanni, *Borges on Writing*, p. 72.
2. Mountsier, *Singing Youth*, p. vii-viii.
3. Smith, "Poetry in the Schools – at the Mercy of Genius," *American Poetry Review*, Sept/Oct. 1976, p. 17.
4. Ibid., p. 18.
5. McIntosh, "Poetry is Like Nothing Without the Poet," *Teachers & Writers Magazine*, Vol. 12, No. 2, Winter, 1981, p. 11.
6. Kohl, *Stuff*, p. x.
7. Kohl, *Teaching the Unteachable*, p. 7.
8. Arrington, "Writing Rights," *Educating Children*, Vol. 20, No. 3, 1975, pp. 24-25.
9. Hopkins, *Let Them Be Themselves*, p. 87.
10. Arnstein, *Children Write Poetry*, p. 56.
11. Ibid., p. 77.
12. Holbrook, "Creativity in the English Programme," *Creativity in English*, ed. Summerfield, p. 19.
13. Chambers, "Me or It," *The Horn Book Magazine*, June, 1981, pp. 348-349.
14. Ibid., p. 348.

15. Summerfield, "A Short Dialogue on Some Aspects of that which We Call Creative English," *Creativity in English*, ed. Summerfield, pp. 37-38.
16. Ibid., p. 39.
17. Ibid., p. 40.
18. Ibid., p. 41.
19. Ibid., p. 43.
20. Ibid., p. 44.
21. Koch, *Wishes, Lies and Dreams*, p. 43.
22. Ibid., p. 196.
23. Ibid., p. 47.
24. Mearns, *Creative Power*, p. 47.
25. MacAdams, "A Talk about Teaching Poems to Kids," *The Whole Word Catalogue 2*, p. 21.
26. Summerfield, "A Short Dialogue," p. 22.
27. Ibid., p. 24.
28. Ibid., p. 23.
29. Lopate, *Journal of a Living Experiment*, p. 100.
30. Ibid., p. 101.
31. Ibid., p. 104.
32. Ibid., p. 105.
33. McGovern, *A Poetry Ritual for Grammar Schools*, p. 17.
34. Brownjohn, *Does It Have To Rhyme?*, p. 7.
35. Rubel and Mandel, *The Editors Notebook*, pp. 8-10.
36. Donna Northouse, letter to author.
37. Kohl, *Teaching the Unteachable*, p. 21.
38. Ibid., p. 50.
39. Ibid., p. 51.
40. Mearns, *Creative Power*, p. 154.
41. O'Gorman, *The Storefront*, p. 7.
42. Richard Lewis, "The Magic Fish and the Yellow Print," *Childhood Education*, March 1976, p. 254.
43. Burrows, "The Young Child's Writing," *Explorations in Children's Writing*, ed. Evertts, p. 87.
44. Staudacher, *Creative Writing in the Classroom*, p. 55.
45. Albert, "Process Approach to Compositions Receiving Too Much Attention," *New York Times*, Jan. 1, 1980.
46. Jackson, *Turn Not Pale, Beloved Snail*, p. 190.
47. Ibid., p. 191.
48. Hughes, (report) *Three Months at the Laboratory School*, p. 4.
49. Cherner, "The Power of Imagery," *Teachers & Writers Magazine*, Vol. 13, No. 3, Jan/Feb 1982, p. 5.
50. Ziegler, "A Few Notes on Revision," *The Whole Word Catalogue 2*, p. 61.
51. Brownjohn, *Does It Have To Rhyme?*, p. 88.
52. Ibid., p. 87.
53. Schacter, "Videotaped Authors Advise Student Writers," *English Journal*, March, 1980, p. 86.
54. Mearns, *Creative Power*, p. 10.
55. Bower, "An Outline for a Crafted Writing Course, *Connecticut English Journal*, Spring 1979, p. 110.
56. Schiff, *Artists in the Schools*, p. 90.
57. Dunlap, "Flights of Fancy," *Teacher*, Nov. 1975, pp. 82-85.
58. Nold, "Reality Next to Imaginary: Poetry Writing with Children," *Teachers & Writers Magazine*, Vol. 7, No. 2, Winter, 1976, p. 27.
59. Claudia Lewis, *A Big Bite of the World*, p. 285.
60. Bond, "Playing with Form in Poetry," *Poemmaking*, eds. Whitman and Feinberg, p. 7.
61. Arnstein, *Children Write Poetry*, p. 113.
62. Lopate, "Getting at the Feelings," *Teachers & Writers Magazine*, Vol. 5, No. 2, Winter, 1974, p. 11.

63. Brown et al., *The Whole Word Catalog*, p. 33.
64. Source withheld.
65. Simon, *Easy Thing For You to Say*, ed. Simon & Harer, pp. 18-19.
66. Bedoya, *Easy Thing For You to Say*, ed. Simon & Harer, p. 18.
67. Grapes, *Easy Thing For You to Say*, ed. Simon & Harer, p. 19.
68. Arnstein, *Children Write Poetry*, pp. 104-105.
69. Whitman, "Poetry in the Classroom," *American Poetry Review*, Mar/Apr. 1982, p. 50.
70. Mearns, *Creative Power*, p. 248.
71. Richards, *Science and Poetry*, p. 44.
72. Ibid.
73. Richards, *Principles of Literary Criticism*, p. 61.

XIII – PROCESS AND PRODUCT: CHILDREN AS YOUNG AUTHORS

1. Shakespeare, *Hamlet*, Act II, Scene 2.
2. Rousseau, *Emilius and Sophia*, Book I, p. 272.
3. Ibid., p. 275.
4. Chukovsky, *From Two to Five*, p. 86.
5. Ibid.
6. Rousseau, *Emilius*, Book II, p. 275.
7. Whitman and Feinberg, *Poemmaking*, p. viii.
8. Claudia Lewis, *A Big Bite of the World*, pp. 7-8.
9. Lusk, *Homemade Poems*, p. 19.
10. Wirtschafter, "Frantic Letters and Memos," *Journal of a Living Experiment*, ed. Lopate, pp. 127-128.
11. Brownjohn, *Does It Have to Rhyme?*, p. 16.
12. Tiedt, *Individualizing Writing in the Elementary Classroom*, p. 1.
13. Ibid., p. 24.
14. Kamler, "Research Update: One Child, One Teacher, One Classroom: The Story of One Piece of Writing," *Language Arts*, September, 1980, pp. 692-693.
15. Pakula, "A Fifth Grade Publishing Company," *Teacher*, Jan. 1976, p. 80.
16. Ibid., p. 82.
17. Ibid., p. 83.
18. Ibid., p. 84.
19. Jackson, *Turn Not Pale, Beloved Snail*, p. 152.
20. Gonzales, *An Author Center for Children*, p. 2.
21. Ibid., p. 1.
22. Olsen, "Teacher Encourages Creative Writing by Children," *La Verne Leader* (Ontario, Calif.), Oct. 14, 1979.
23. Lopate, *Journal of a Living Experiment*, p. 108.
24. Copeland, "Share Your Students: Where and How to Publish Children's Work," *Language Arts*, September, 1980, pp. 635-638.
25. McKim and Steinbergh, *Beyond Words*, p. 25.
26. Mearns, *Creative Power*, p. 266.
27. Lusk, *Homemade Poems*, p. 26.
28. Zimmerman, "The Creative Writing Class: Writers in Search of an Audience," *English Journal*, October, 1979, p. 52.
29. Brown, "Teachers & Writers & Me," *Journal of a Living Experiment*, ed. Lopate, p. 224.
30. Koch, *Wishes, Lies and Dreams*, p. 6.
31. Advertising brochure for *Stone Soup*, 1982.
32. Ibid.
33. Nold, "Reality Next to Imaginary: Poetry Writing with Children," *Teachers & Writers Magazine*, Vol. 7, No. 2, Winter, 1976, p. 25.

34. Kralik, "Poetry: Take a Chance," *English Journal*, Oct. 1975, p. 53.
35. Advertising brochure, Southwest Regional English Teachers Conference, Oct., 1982.
36. Maitland, "Underneath That Sneaker Canvas, a Poetic Soul," *New York Times*, Sept. 4, 1975.
37. *The Reading Teacher*, Winter, 1982-83, p. 8.
38. Advertising brochure, National Council of Teachers of English, Kansas City Convention, 1978.
39. Department of Education, San Diego (Calif.) County, letter to author, Oct. 10, 1980.
40. North Area Publications Committee, Minneapolis Public Schools, *Guidelines for Preparing Material for Publication in "Right On,"* Feb. 21, 1974.
41. "Write On! Young Author's Awards," *Los Angeles Times*, May 2, 1978.
42. *If You Feel Like It*, p. 64.
43. *Highlights for Children*, May 1981, p. 37.
44. *Wombat*, April/May/June, 1982, p. 25.
45. Kantor and Perron, "Thinking and Writing: Creativity in the Modes of Discourse," *Language Arts*, Vol. 54, No. 7, Oct. 1977, p. 743.
46. Lee Bernd, letter to author.
47. *An Invitation to Poetry*, unpaged.
48. Ibid.
49. Lopate, "Time as an Ally: Homage to Aunt Forgie," *Teachers & Writers Magazine*, Vol. 8, No. 2, Winter, 1977, p. 4.
50. Bly, *Talking All Morning*, p. 290.
51. Burrows, "The Young Child's Writing," *Explorations in Children's Writing*, ed. Evertts, p. 89.
52. Herman, "Is the Display of Creative Writing Wrong?", *Elementary English*, January, 1970, p. 36.
53. Ibid., p. 37.

XIV: EXPLODING THE DREAM

1. Steiner, *Tolstoy or Dostoevsky*, p. 219.
2. Ibid., p. 232.
3. Ibid., p. 3.
4. Ibid., p. 256.
5. Ibid., p. 257.
6. Ibid., p. 258.
7. Ibid., pp. 233-234.
8. Piaget, *The Language and Thought of the Child*, pp. 158-159.
9. Ibid., p. 159.
10. Zavatsky, "Dream Workshop," *The Whole Word Catalogue 2*, p. 84.
11. Gensler and Nyhart, *The Poetry Connection*, p. 26.
12. Richard Lewis, "Acting Out Daydreams," *Parabola*, Spring, 1982, p. 47.
13. Holbrook, "Creativity in the English Programme," *Creativity in English*, ed. Summerfield, p. 4.
14. Williams, *The Selected Essays of William Carlos Williams*, pp. 281-282.
15. Ibid., p. 281.
16. Ibid., p. 283.
17. Ibid., p. 282.
18. Koch, *Wishes, Lies and Dreams*, p. 8.
19. Ibid., p. 86.
20. Richard Lewis, "Acting Out Daydreams," *Parabola*, Spring, 1982, p. 50.
21. Holbrook, "Creativity in the English Programme," p. 4.
22. Koch, *Wishes, Lies and Dreams*, p. 137.

23. Ibid., p. 11.
24. Arieti, *Creativity: The Magic Synthesis*, p. 145.
25. Ibid., p. 142.
26. Ibid., p. 9.
27. Ibid., pp. 9-10.
28. Ibid., p. 142.
29. Whitman, "Poetry in the Classroom," *American Poetry Review*, March/April 1973, p. 51.
30. Zavatsky, "Dream Workshop," p. 79.
31. Ibid., p. 80.
32. Ibid., p. 84.
33. Ibid., p. 81.
34. Ibid., p. 82.
35. Kohl, "Poets on Poetry," *Teacher*, April 1977, p. 48.
36. Martin, "Personal Writing," *The Whole Word Catalogue 2*, p. 30.
37. Ibid.
38. Ibid., p. 31.
39. McIntosh, "Poetry is Like Nothing Without the Poet," *Teachers & Writers Magazine*, Vol. 12, No. 2, Winter, 1981, p. 10.
40. Lourie, "Kenneth Koch's *Wishes, Lies and Dreams:* The Scriptural Fallacy," *Teachers & Writers Magazine*, Vol. 5, No. 2, Winter, 1974, p. 24.
41. Ibid., p. 23.
42. Weinstein, "West Virginia Poetry in the Schools: a Daybook," *Teachers & Writers Magazine*, Vol. 6, No. 1, 1974, p. 52.
43. Sewalk, "Bilingual Poetry Workshops: a Journal," *Poemmaking*, eds. Whitman and Feinberg, p. 68.
44. Kimzey, *To Defend a Form*, p. 16.
45. Conkling, *Silverhorn*, p. 151.
46. Arnstein, *Children Write Poetry*, p. 180.
47. Mountsier, *Singing Youth*, p. 53.
48. Ibid., p. 59.
49. Commager, *The St. Nicholas Anthology*, p. 529.
50. Arieti, *Creativity*, p. 8.
51. Ignatow, *Open Between Us*, p. 66.
52. Lepson, "Fingerpainting with Words," *Poemmaking*, eds. Whitman and Feinberg, p. 103.
53. Ibid., p. 102.
54. Ibid., p. 101.
55. Ibid., p. 103.
56. Calas, "The Challenge of Surrealism," *Art Forum*, Vol. XVII, No. 5, Jan. 1979, pp. 24-29.
57. Ibid.
58. Preminger, *Princeton Encyclopedia of Poetry and Poetics*, p. 821.
59. Ignatow, *Open Between Us*, p. 82.
60. Simpson, *A Company of Poets*, p. 218.
61. Ibid., p. 219.
62. Ibid., p. 221.
63. Zavatsky, "Dream Workshop," p. 84.
64. Shapiro, "The New Poetry: a Literary Breakdown," *Los Angeles Times*, April 19, 1970.
65. O'Gorman, *The Storefront*, p. 53.
66. Lee Bernd, letter to author.
67. Bronowski, *The Identity of Man*, pp. 63-64.

XV – RULES OF THE GAME

1. Carroll, *The Works of Lewis Carroll*, p. 105.
2. Lusk, *Homemade Poems*, p. 33.
3. Ibid., p. 32.

4. Gann, "Creative Classroom Career Contest," *Instructor*, March 1981, p. 120.
5. *Scholastic*, March, 1976.
6. Devine, "Poetry in the English Class," *Connecticut English Journal*, Spring, 1979, p. 7.
7. Zavatsky, "Dream Workshop," *The Whole Word Catalogue 2*, p. 84.
8. Bedoya, *Easy Thing For You to Say*, ed. Simon & Harer, p. 18.
9. *Scholastic Voice*, Jan. 13, 1976, p. 9.
10. Ziegler, "The Seasons of a Writing Workshop," *Teachers & Writers Magazine*, Vol. 10, No. 1, Fall, 1978, p. 36.
11. Rubel and Mandel, *The Editors Notebook*, pp. 14-15.
12. Brostowin, "Poetry by Seduction," *English Journal*, Sept. 1980, p. 59.
13. *SCWriP Newsletter*, 1980, unpaged.
14. Mainprize, "Rollercoaster Poems," *English Journal*, Oct. 1979, pp. 45-46.
15. Hise, "Writing Poetry: More than a Frill," *English Journal*, Nov. 1980, pp. 19-20.
16. O'Gorman, *The Storefront*, p. 56.
17. Whitman, "Poetry in the Classroom," *American Poetry Review*, March/April, 1973, p. 51.
18. Gensler and Nyhart, *The Poetry Connection*, p. 31.
19. Alwan and Alwan, *The Moon is as Full as a Suitcase*, p. 20.
20. Sloan, *The Child as Critic*, p. 101.
21. Source withheld.
22. *The Human Puzzle*, Kenter Canyon Elementary School, p. 19.
23. Swenson, *Poems to Solve*, Introduction.
24. Wiener, *Any Child Can Write*, p. 188.
25. Encyclopedia Britannica Educational Corporation, *Ditto Resource Book*, 1975.
26. Spencer, *Flair, Vol. I: Creative Writing*, p. 28.
27. Jory, *Discovery: Discover the Magic of Poetry*, p. 5.
28. Kahl et al., *Potpourri 76*, unpaged.
29. Holbrook, "Creativity in the English Programme," *Creativity in English*, ed. Summerfield, p. 10.
30. Carlson, *Sparkling Words*, pp. 65-66.
31. Ibid., p. 202.
32. Angelo and Laurent, "Sharing Poetry with Young Children," *Connecticut English Journal*, Spring 1979, p. 45.
33. Ashby-Davis and Robinson, "Teaching Poetry through Music and Dance," *Connecticut English Journal*, Spring 1979, p. 47.
34. Zavatsky and Padgett, "Writing to Music," *The Whole Word Catalogue 2*, pp. 210-212.
35. Ibid.
36. Gensler and Nyhart, *The Poetry Connection*, p. 27.
37. Whitman, *Report to the Council on the Arts and Humanities of the Commonwealth of Massachusetts*, p. 8.
38. Koch, *Wishes, Lies, and Dreams*, p. 245.
39. Ibid., p. 230.
40. Ibid., p. 239.
41. Galvin, "Writing More Cemently: Some Strategies for Teaching Poetry-Writing," *Connecticut English Journal*, Spring 1979, p. 89.
42. Bolls, "Wax Paper Poems, *Apollo's Diary*, Nov. 1976.
43. Hughes, *Three Months at the Laboratory School*, p. 10.
44. Steingesser, "Sharing the Blues," *Teachers & Writers Magazine*, Vol. 9, No. 2, Winter, 1978, pp. 24-25.
45. Robbins, "Riming is Timing," *Poemmaking*, eds. Whitman and Feinberg, p. 84.
46. Kohl, "Poets on Poetry," *Teacher*, April 1977, p. 49.
47. *Fun Fantasies: Activity Cards for Creative Writing.*
48. *Haiku Harvest*, unpaged.
49. Behn, *More Cricket Songs*, unpaged.
50. *Fun Fantasies.*
51. Crapsey, *Verse.*
52. Martin, "Writing in First Grade," *The Whole Word Catalogue 2*, p. 304.
53. Richard Lewis, "A Place for Poetry," *Publisher's Weekly*, July 10, 1967, pp. 119-120.

54. Koch, *Wishes, Lies, and Dreams*, p. 50.
55. Moore, *Easy Thing For You to Say*, ed. Simon & Harer, p. 53.
56. Housman, *The Name and Nature of Poetry*, p. 43.
57. Ibid., p. 45.
58. Sandra Alcosser, letter to author.
59. Sewalk, "Bilingual Poetry Workshops: a Journal," *Poemmaking*, eds. Whitman and Feinberg, p. 69.
60. Brownjohn, *Does It Have to Rhyme?*, p. 89.
61. McIntosh, "Poetry is Like Nothing Without the Poet," *Teachers & Writers Magazine*, Vol. 12, No. 2, Winter, 1981, p. 11.
62. Hughes, *Three Months at the Laboratory School*, p. 4.
63. Koch, *Wishes, Lies, and Dreams*, p. 280.
64. Ibid., p. 5.
65. Ibid., p. 6.
66. Lopate, "Helping Young Children Start to Write," *Research on Composing: Points of Departure*, eds. Cooper and Odell, p. 138.
67. Kohl, "Poets on Poetry," p. 55.
68. Lopate, "Helping Young Children Start to Write," p. 137.
69. Ibid.
70. Lopate, "The Moment to Write," *The Whole Word Catalogue 2*, p. 75.
71. Lopate, "Helping Young Children Start to Write," p. 142.
72. Weinstein, "West Virginia Poetry in the Schools: a Daybook," *Teachers & Writers Magazine*, Vol. 6, No. 1, 1974, p. 52.
73. Martin, "Personal Writing," *The Whole Word Catalogue 2*, p. 35.
74. Lopate, "Helping Young Children Start to Write," p. 147.
75. Piaget, *The Language and Thought of the Child*, p. 16.
76. Gensler, "Dream Poems in Broad Daylight," *Poemmaking*, eds. Whitman and Feinberg, p. 6.
77. Kohl, "Poets on Poetry," p. 50.
78. Richard Lewis, "The Magic Fish and the Yellow Print," *Childhood Education*, March 1976, p. 254.
79. Ibid.
80. Mearns, *Creative Power*, p. 259.
81. Levinger, "The Human Side of Illiteracy," *English Journal*, Nov. 1978, pp. 26-29.
82. Taylor, *Essays in Teaching*, p. 8.
83. Ibid., p. 9.
84. Ibid., p. 8.

XVI – NOTES FOR A NEW MYTHOLOGY

1. Rousseau, *Emilius and Sophia*, Book IV, p. 161.
2. Mearns, *Creative Power*, p. 258.
3. Gross, "The New Radical Alliance," *Cultural Affairs*, Summer 1970, pp. 17-18.
4. Jordan, " 'The Voice of the Children,' Saturday Workshop Diaries," *Journal of a Living Experiment*, ed. Lopate, pp. 146-147.
5. Jordan, *The Voice of the Children*, p. 86.
6. Ibid., pp. 93-94.
7. Mearns, *Creative Power*, p. 265.
8. Ibid., p. 21.
9. Kantor, "Evaluating Creative Writing: a Different Ball Game," *English Journal*, April 1975, p. 72.
10. Lee Bernd, letter to author.
11. Ibid.
12. Kantor, "Evaluating Creative Writing," p. 74.

13. Leland Jacobs, letter to author.
14. Summerfield, "A Short Dialogue on Some Aspects of that Which We Call Creative English," *Creativity in English*, ed. Summerfield, p. 42.
15. Read, *This Way Delight*, p. 140.
16. Arnstein, *Children Write Poetry*, p. 166.
17. Whitman, "Poetry in the Classroom, *American Poetry Review*, March/April, 1971, p. 51.
18. Ibid.
19. Humphrey, "A Practical Guide for Making Audiotape Collages for Poetry Workshops," *Poemmaking*, eds. Whitman and Feinberg, p. 63.
20. Holograph.
21. Mearns, *Creative Power*, p. 258.
22. Sexton, "Journal of a Living Experiment," *Journal of a Living Experiment*, ed. Lopate, p. 49.
23. Mearns, *Creative Power*, 267.
24. Willis, "Observation Writing," *The Whole Word Catalogue 2*, p. 140.
25. Robert King, letter to author.
26. McKim and Steinburgh, *Beyond Words*, p. 73.
27. Wilcox, "Literature: the Child's Guide to Creative Writing," *Language Arts*, May 1977, p. 550.
28. O'Gorman, *The Storefront*, p. 56.
29. Bly, *Talking All Morning*, p. 165.
30. Claudia Lewis, *A Big Bite of the World*, p. 36.
31. Rousseau, *Emilius*, Book IV, p. 230.
32. Ibid., p. 243.
33. Brown et al., *The Whole Word Catalog*, p. 24.
34. Alvarez, "Bilingual Poetry-in-the-Schools," *Teachers & Writers Magazine*, Vol. 10, No. 2, Winter, 1979, p. 7.
35. Steiner, *Tolstoy or Dostoevsky*, p. 50.

XVII – FURTHER NOTES FOR A NEW MYTHOLOGY

1. Rousseau, *Emilius and Sophia*, Book III, p. 13.
2. Mearns, *Creative Power*, p. 62.
3. Simon, "Afterword," *Skins of Change*, eds. Kennedy and Simon, p. 83.
4. Piaget, *The Language and Thought of the Child*, p. 205.
5. Ibid., p. 204.
6. McKim and Steinbergh, *Beyond Words*, p. 72.
7. Ibid., p. 79.
8. Brown et al., *The Whole Word Catalog*, p. 8.
9. Lusk, *Homemade Poems*, p. 40.
10. Greenberg, *Teaching Poetry to Children*, p 61.
11. Brown et al., *The Whole Word Catalog*, p. 10.
12. Richard Lewis, "A Vital Experience," *Explorations in Children's Writing*, ed. Evertts, p. 95.
13. Bennett, "Poetry, Too, Is a Moveable Feast," *English Journal*, October 1975, p. 47.
14. Kohl, *Teaching the Unteachable*, p. 25.
15. Bedoya, *Easy Thing For You to Say*, ed. Simon & Harer, p. 18.
16. Simpson, *A Company of Poets*, p. 157.
17. Brownjohn, *Does It Have to Rhyme?*, p. 87.
18. Kohl, *Teaching the Unteachable*, p. 25.
19. Heidi Bowton, letter to author.
20. Rolly Kent, letter to author.
21. Kent, *Talk about the World*, foreword.
22. Ibid., unpaged.
23. Ibid.

24. Ibid.
25. Ibid.
26. Richard Brown, letter to author.
27. Ciardi, *How Does a Poem Mean?*
28. *The Horn Book*, June 1957, p. 234.
29. Shaefer and Miller, *Young Voices*, p. 87.
30. Holograph, Braille Institute of America contest.
31. Koch, *Wishes, Lies, and Dreams*, p. 92.
32. Ibid., p. 145.
33. Carlson, *Sparkling Words*, p. 178.
34. *Wombat*, April/May 1983, p. 23.
35. Koch, *Wishes, Lies, and Dreams*, p. 93.
36. Ibid., p. 120.
37. Robbins, "Riming is Timing," *Poemmaking*, eds. Whitman and Feinberg, p. 85.
38. Ibid., p. 87.
39. Mearns, *Creative Power*, p. 52.
40. Lusk, *Homemade Poems*, p. 24.
41. Torrance, "Ten Ways of Helping Young Children Gifted in Creative Writing and Speech," *Creativity: Its Educational Implications*, ed. Vernon, p. 212.
42. Arieti, *Creativity: The Magic Synthesis*, p. 362.
43. Ibid., p. 29.
44. Ibid., p. 30.
45. Torrance, "Ten Ways of Helping Young Children," p. 242.
46. Torrance, "Toward the More Humane Education of Gifted Children," *Creativity: Its Educational Implications*, p. 60.
47. *Bay Leaf and Fool's Gold*, p. 88.
48. Kohl, *Teaching the Unteachable*, p. 25.
49. Mearns, *Creative Power*, p. 157.
50. Kohl, "Poets on Poetry," *Teacher*, April 1977, p. 50.

XVIII – CREATIVITY AND REALITY

1. Neruda, *Memoirs*, p. 265.
2. Rogers, "Towards a Theory of Creativity," *Creativity*, ed. Vernon, p. 137.
3. Ibid., p. 138.
4. Ibid.
5. Ibid., p. 139.
6. Ibid., p. 140.
7. Ibid., p. 146.
8. Ibid., p. 147.
9. Poincaré, "Mathematical Creation," *Creativity*, ed. Gowan, p. 80.
10. Ibid., p. 83.
11. Ibid., p. 88.
12. Arieti, *Creativity: The Magic Synthesis*, pp. 4-5.
13. Kostelanetz, *The Old Poetries and the New*, p. 81.
14. Mearns, *Creative Power*, p. 9.
15. Francis, *Pot Shots at Poetry*, p. 205.
16. Steiner, *Tolstoy or Dostoevsky*, p. 249.
17. Ibid., p. 253.
18. Richard Lewis, "The Child as Creator," UPI, Feb. 1982.
19. Arieti, *Creativity: The Magic Synthesis*, pp. 6-7.
20. Opie, *Lore and Language of Schoolchildren*, p. 17.
21. Arieti, *Creativity: The Magic Synthesis*, p. 74.

22. Larrick, *Green is Like a Meadow of Grass*, p. 27.
23. Koch, *Wishes, Lies and Dreams*, p. 202.
24. Ibid., p. 211.
25. Thomas, "Fern Hill," *The Collected Poems of Dylan Thomas*, pp. 178-180.
26. Rousseau, *Emilius and Sophia*, Book V, pp. 202-203.

SELECTED BIBLIOGRAPHY

Adoff, Arnold, ed. *It is the Poem Singing in Your Eyes: Anthology of New Young Poets.* New York: Harper & Row, 1971.

Allen, Donald M., ed. *The New American Poetry.* New York: Grove Press, 1960.

Allen, Terry, ed. *The Whispering Wind: Poetry by Young American Indians.* New York: Doubleday & Company, 1972.

Alwan, Ameen, and Alwan, Georgia, eds. *The Moon is as Full as a Suitcase: Poems and Prose by Children.* Los Angeles: Los Angeles County Museum of Art, 1979.

Arieti, Silvano. *Creativity: the Magic Synthesis.* New York: Basic Books, 1976.

Arnstein, Flora J. *Children Write Poetry: a Creative Approach.* New York: Dover Publications, 1967.

———. *Poetry and the Child.* New York: Dover Publications, 1970.

———. *Poetry in the Elementary Classroom.* New York: Appleton-Century-Crofts, 1962.

Ashton-Warner, Sylvia. *Teacher.* New York: Simon and Schuster, 1963.

Barbe, Walter B., comp. *Creative Writing Activities.* Columbus, Ohio: Highlights for Children, 1965.

Barnstone, Aliki. *The Real Tin Flower: Poems about the World at Nine.* New York: Crowell-Collier Press, 1968.

Baron, Virginia Olsen, ed. *Here I Am! An Anthology of Poems Written by Young People in some of America's Minority Groups.* New York: E. P. Dutton & Co., 1969.

Barras, Jonetta; Hubbard, Grigsby; and Crider, Sheila. *Poems by People Six to Thirteen.* D.C. Commission on the Arts, 1979.

Barthes, Roland. "La Littérature selon Minou Drouet," *Mythologies.* Unpublished translation by Lloyd Alexander.

Behn, Harry. *Chrysalis: Concerning Children and Poetry.* New York: Harcourt Brace Jovanovich, Inc., 1971.

Behn, Harry, trans. *More Cricket Songs: Japanese Haiku.* New York: Harcourt Brace Jovanovich, Inc., 1971.

Bennett, John, ed. *The Inkwell #15.* East Lansing, Michigan: 1976.

Bly, Robert. *Talking All Morning.* Ann Arbor: University of Michigan Press, 1980.

Book About Rainbows, A: Poems by Bernard Shepherd. A Seventy-Five Press Book. New York: Teachers & Writers Collaborative, 1974.

Bronowski, Jacob. *The Identity of Man.* Garden City: Natural History Press, 1965.

Brown, Hannah; Lopate, Phillip; Sklarew, Debra; and Vorsanger, Jessie, eds. *The Memories of Kindergartners.* New York: Teachers & Writers Collaborative, 1978.

Brown, Rosellen; Hoffman, Marvin; Kushner, Martin; Lopate, Phillip; and Murphy, Sheila, eds. *The Whole Word Catalog.* New York: Teachers & Writers Collaborative, 1972.

Brownjohn, Sandy. *Does It Have to Rhyme? Teaching Children to Write Poetry.* London: Hodder and Stoughton, 1980.

Carasso, Katharine. *The Candle Burns.* New York: Henry Harrison, 1936.

Carlson, Ruth Kearney. *Sparkling Words.* Geneva, Illinois: Paladin House Publishers, 1973.

Cattonar, Joanna, and Farragher, Shaun, eds. *Let's Ride the Air Today: Poems from the Dillon County Total Arts Program Poetry and Creative Writing Component.* Columbia, South Carolina: South Carolina Arts Commission, 1977.

Chambers, Aidan. "Letter from England: Me or It." *The Horn Book* (June 1981) 347-350.

Cheyney, Arnold. *The Poetry Corner.* Glenview, Illinois: Scott, Foresman and Company, 1982.

———. *The Writing Corner.* Glenview, Illinois: Scott, Foresman and Company, 1979.

Chukovsky, Kornei. *From Two to Five.* Translated by Miriam Morton. Berkeley: University of California Press, 1963.

Ciardi, John. *How Does A Poem Mean?* Boston: Houghton Mifflin Company, 1959.

———. "Manner of Speaking." *Saturday Review* (May 20, 1972) 14-19.

Cocteau, Jean. Letter to Robert Goffin, reproduced in *Foudre Natale.* Dutilleul, 1955. Unpublished translation by Lloyd Alexander.

Coleridge, Samuel Taylor. *The Complete Works of Samuel Taylor Coleridge. Vol. III; Bibliographia Literaria.* New York: Harper & Bros., 1954.
Commager, Henry Steele, ed. *The St. Nicholas Anthology.* New York: Random House, 1948.
Conkling, Grace Hazard. *Imagination and Children's Reading.* Northampton, Massachusetts: The Hampshire Bookshop, 1928.
______. *Wilderness Songs.* New York: Henry Holt and Company, 1920.
Conkling, Hilda. *Poems by a Little Girl.* New York: Frederick A. Stokes Company, 1920.
______. *Shoes of the Wind.* New York: Frederick A. Stokes Company, 1922.
______. *Silverhorn: the Hilda Conkling Book for Other Children.* New York: Frederick A. Stokes Company, 1924.
Cornish, Sam, and Dixon, Lucian W., eds. *Chicory: Young Voices from the Black Ghetto.* New York: Association Press, 1969.
Crane, Nathalia. *The Janitor's Boy and Other Poems.* New York: Thomas Seltzer, 1924.
______. *Lava Lane and Other Poems.* New York: Thomas Seltzer, 1925.
______. *Venus Invisible and Other Poems.* New York: Coward-McCann, 1928.
Cullinan, Bernice; Karrer, Mary K.; and Pillar, Arlene M., eds. *Literature and the Child.* New York: Harcourt, Brace, Jovanovich, Inc., 1981.
Danish, Barbara. *Writing as a Second Language: a Workbook for Writing and Teaching Writing.* New York: Teachers & Writers Collaborative, 1981.
Day, Robert, and Weaver, Gail Cohen, eds. *Creative Writing in the Classroom: an Annotated Bibliography of Selected Resources (K-12).* Urbana, Illinois: National Council of Teachers of English, 1978.
de Boisdeffre, Pierre. "Pour Conclure," *Une Histoire Vivante de la Littérature D'Aujourd'hui.* n.d., 622-625. Unpublished translation by Lloyd Alexander.
di Giovanni, Norman Thomas; Halpern, Daniel; and MacShane, Frank, eds. *Borges on Writing.* New York: E. P. Dutton & Co., Inc., 1973.
Ditto Resource Book. Encyclopedia Britannica Educational Corp., 1975.
Drouet, Minou. *Arbre, Mon Ami.* Paris: René Juillard, 1956. Unpublished translation by Lloyd Alexander.
Dunning, Stephen; Eaton, M. Joe; and Glass, Malcolm, eds. *For Poets. Poetry 2: a Scholastic Literature Unit, Series 4100.* Scholastic Book Services, 1975.
Eckel, Jim, and McGrath, Jim, eds. *Sun Five, 5th Journal of Self-Expression by the Students and Staff of the Department of Defense Overseas Schools in the Pacific, Japan, Okinawa, Korea, the Philippines.* Okinawa, Japan: D.O.D. Dependent Schools, Pacific Region, Education Division, Curriculum Branch, 1979.
Evertts, Eldonna L., ed. *Explorations in Children's Writing.* Urbana, Illinois: National Council of Teachers of English, 1970.
Francis, Robert. *Pot Shots at Poetry.* Ann Arbor, Michigan: University of Michigan Press, 1980.
Gensler, Kinereth, and Nyhart, Nina. *The Poetry Connection: an Anthology of Contemporary Poems with Ideas to Stimulate Children's Writing.* New York: Teachers & Writers Collaborative, 1978.
Ghiselin, Brewster, ed. *The Creative Process: a Symposium.* New York: New American Library, 1952.
Ginsberg, Allen. "Notes from *Howl and Other Poems,*" *The New American Poetry,* edited by Donald M. Allen. New York: Grove Press, 1960, 414-418.
Gonzales, Dolores G. *An Author Center for Children.* Privately printed, 1979.
Gowan, John Curtis, ed. *Creativity: Its Educational Implications.* New York: John Wiley & Sons, Inc., 1967.
Greenberg, David. *Teaching Poetry to Children.* Portland, Oregon: Continuing Education Publications, 1978.
Gregory, Horace. *The Shield of Achilles: Essays on Beliefs in Poetry.* New York: Harcourt, Brace and Company, 1944.
______. *Spirit of Time and Place: Collected Essays of Horace Gregory.* New York: W. W. Norton, 1973.
Griffin, Kathryn. "I Have a Dream for You, Mother." *Yankee* (February 1982) 85-92.
Gross, Ronald. "The New Radical Alliance." *Cultural Affairs* (Summer 1970) 17-18.
Grosvenor, Kali. *Poems by Kali.* New York: Doubleday & Company, 1970.

Haines, John. *Living off the Country: Essays of Poetry and Place.* Ann Arbor, Michigan: University of Michigan Press, 1981.

Hall, Donald. *Goatfoot Milktongue Twinbird: Interviews, Essays, and Notes on Poetry, 1970-76.* Ann Arbor, Michigan: University of Michigan Press, 1978.

Hausman, Gerald, comp. *The Shivurrus Plant of Mopant and Other Children's Poems.* Santa Fe: The Giligia Press, 1968.

Hill, Helen M. "How to Tell a Sheep from a Goat – and Why it Matters." *The Horn Book Magazine* (February 1979) 100-110.

Holman, Felice. *At the Top of My Voice and Other Poems.* New York: Charles Scribner's Sons, 1970.

Hopkins, Lee Bennett, ed. *City Talk.* New York: Alfred A. Knopf, Inc., 1970.

______. *Let Them Be Themselves: Language Arts Enrichment for Disadvantaged Children in Elementary Schools.* New York: Citation Press, 1969.

______. *Pass the Poetry, Please! Using Poetry in Pre-Kindergarten-Six Classrooms.* New York: Citation Press, 1972.

Housman, A. E. *The Name and Nature of Poetry.* New York: Macmillan, 1936.

Howard, Alice B. *Mary Mapes Dodge of St. Nicholas.* New York: Julian Messner, 1943.

Howard, Vanessa. *A Screaming Whisper.* New York: Holt, Rinehart and Winston, 1972.

Huck, Charlotte S. *Children's Literature in the Elementary School.* 3d ed. updated. New York: Holt, Rinehart and Winston, 1979.

Hughes, Langston. *The First Book of Rhythms.* New York: Franklin Watts, Inc., 1954.

Hughes, Ted. *Poetry in the Making.* London: Faber and Faber, 1967.

______. *Poetry Is.* New York: Doubleday & Company, Inc., 1967.

I Never Saw Another Butterfly . . . Children's Drawings and Poems from Terezin Concentration Camp 1942-1944. New York: McGraw Hill Book Company, 1964.

If You Feel Like It . . . an Anthology of Poetry by the Children of Santa Barbara County. Santa Barbara, California: Santa Barbara County Schools, 1975.

Ignatow, David. *Open Between Us.* Ann Arbor, Michigan: University of Michigan Press, 1980.

Imagine and Write: My Weekly Reader Creative Expression Series, Book 3. Columbus, Ohio: My Weekly Reader, Education Center, 1967.

Invitation to Poetry, An. Nevada: Southern Nevada Teachers of English, n.d.

It Just Takes Time . . . a Collection of Student Writing, Kindergarten-Grade 12. Los Angeles: Los Angeles City Schools, 1977.

Jackson, Jacqueline. *Turn Not Pale, Beloved Snail: a Book about Writing among Other Things.* Boston: Little, Brown and Company, 1974.

Jordan, June, and Bush, Terri, comps. *The Voice of the Children.* New York: Holt, Rinehart and Winston, 1970.

Jory, Dennis, ed. *Discovery: Discover the Magic of Poetry.* Lompoc, California: Lompoc Junior High School, 1978.

Joseph, Stephen M., ed. *The Me Nobody Knows: Children's Voices from the Ghetto.* New York: Avon Books, 1969.

Judy, Susan, and Judy, Stephen. *Gifts of Writing: Creative Projects with Words and Art.* New York: Charles Scribner's Sons, 1980.

Kahl, Marilyn; Plank, Lois; and Sprague, Dee, eds. *Potpourri 76: a Collection of Teaching Ideas for Elementary and Secondary Schools.* Los Angeles: Southland Council of Teachers of English, 1976.

Kant, Immanuel. *The Critique of Judgement.* Translated by James Creed Meredith. Oxford, England: Clarendon Press, 1952.

______. *Critique of Pure Reason.* Translated by Norman Kemp Smith. New York: St. Martin's Press, 1965.

Kennedy, Sarah, and Simon, John Oliver, eds. *The Skins of Change.* Berkeley, California: Aldebaran Review, 1975.

Kennedy, X. J. *An Introduction to Poetry.* 4th ed. Boston: Little, Brown & Company, 1978.

Kent, Rolly, ed. *South Side: 21 Poems by Children from Tucson's Southside.* Tucson, Arizona: Friends of the Tucson Public Library, 1982.

______. *Talk about the World: Spoken Poems by Children.* Privately printed, 1979.

Kimmins, C. W. *Children's Dreams.* London: Longmans, Green and Company, 1920.

Kimzey, Ardis. *To Defend a Form: the Romance of Administration and Teaching in a Poetry-in-the-Schools Program.* New York: Teachers & Writers Collaborative, 1977.
Koch, Kenneth. *Rose, Where Did You Get That Red? Teaching Great Poetry to Children.* New York: Random House, 1973.
______. *Wishes, Lies, and Dreams: Teaching Children to Write Poetry.* New York: Chelsea House Publishers, 1970.
Kohl, Herbert R. "Poets on Poetry." *Teacher* (April 1977) 48-52.
______. *Teaching the "Unteachable": the Story of an Experiment in Children's Writing.* New York: The New York Review, 1967.
______. *36 Children.* New York: New American Library, 1967.
Kohl, Herbert, and Cruz, Victor Hernandez, eds. *Stuff: a Collection of Poems, Visions & Imaginative Happenings from Young Writers in Schools – Opened & Closed.* New York: The World Publishing Company, 1970.
Kostelanetz, Richard. *The Old Poetries and the New.* Ann Arbor, Michigan: University of Michigan Press, 1981.
Kris, Ernst. "On Inspiration: Preliminary Notes on Emotional Conditions in Creative States." *International Journal of Psychoanalysis* Vol. 20 (1939) 377-389.
Larrick, Nancy, ed. *Green is like a Meadow of Grass: an Anthology of Children's Pleasure in Poetry.* Champaign, Illinois: Garrard Publishing, 1968.
______. *I Heard a Scream in the Street: Poems by Young People in the City.* New York: M. Evans, 1970.
Larrick, Nancy, and Merriam, Eve, eds. *Male & Female under 18: Frank Comments from Young People about their Sex Roles Today.* New York: Avon Books, 1973.
Lewis, Claudia. *A Big Bite of the World: Children's Creative Writing.* Englewood Cliffs, New Jersey: Prentice-Hall, Inc., 1979.
______. "The Pleasant Land of Counterpane." *The Horn Book* (October 1966) 542-547.
Lewis, Richard. "Acting Out Daydreams." *Parabola* (Spring 1982) 48.
______. "The Child as Creator." UPI (February, 1982).
______. "The Forest of the Mind: Nurturing Imagination in Children and Teachers." *Today's Education* (April-May 1980) 47E-49E.
______. "The Magic Fish and the Yellow Print." *Childhood Education* (March 1976) 252-256.
______. "A Place for Poetry." *Publishers' Weekly* (July 10, 1967) 119-120.
______. "A Vital Experience." *Explorations in Children's Writing,* edited by Eldonna L. Everrts. Urbana, Illinois: National Council of Teachers of English, 1970, 93-95.
______ed. *Miracles: Poems by Children of the English-Speaking World.* New York: Simon and Schuster, 1966.
Lopate, Phillip. *Being with Children.* New York: Doubleday & Company, Inc., 1975.
______. "Getting at the Feelings." *New York Times Sunday Magazine* (August 31, 1975).
______. "The Moment to Write." *The Whole Word Catalogue 2,* edited by Bill Zavatsky and Ron Padgett. New York: Teachers & Writers Collaborative, 1977, 74-78.
______. "Time as an Ally: Homage to Aunt Forgie." *Teachers & Writers Magazine* (Winter 1977) 2-14.
______, ed. *Journal of a Living Experiment: a Documentary History of the First Ten Years of Teachers & Writers Collaborative.* New York: Teachers & Writers Collaborative, 1979.
______. *Memories of Oatmeal by Zaphasdemdaj.* New York: Teachers & Writers Collaborative, 1980.
______. *Ways of Looking.* New York: Teachers & Writers Collaborative, n.d.
Lusk, Daniel. *Homemade Poems: a Handbook.* Hermosa, South Dakota: Lame Johnny Press, 1974.
McAllister, Constance, comp. *Creative Writing Activities.* Columbus, Ohio: Highlights for Children, 1980.
MacBean, L. *Marjorie Fleming's Book: the Story of Pet Marjorie*; and Brown, John, M.D., *Marjorie Fleming: a Story of Childlife Fifty Years Ago.* New York: Boni and Liveright, 1920.
McCord, David. *Pen, Paper and Poem.* New York: Holt, Rinehart and Winston, 1973.
McGovern, Robert. *A Poetry Ritual for Grammar Schools.* Ashland, Ohio: Ashland Poetry Press, 1974.

McGovern, Robert, and Snyder, Richard, eds. *The Young Voice II: Poems by Ohio High School Students.* Ashland, Ohio: Ashland Poetry Press, 1973.
McKim, Elizabeth, and Steinbergh, Judith W. *Beyond Words: Writing Poems with Children.* Green Harbor, Massachusetts: Wampeter Press, 1983.
MacLeish, Archibald. *Poetry and Experience.* Boston: Houghton Mifflin, 1961.
Macrorie, Ken. *Uptaught.* Rochelle Park, New Jersey: Hayden Book Company, 1970.
Magic Place Is, A . . . an Anthology of Poetry by Children of Santa Barbara County. Santa Barbara, California: Santa Barbara County Schools, 1977.
Making It Strange: a New Design for Creative Thinking and Writing. Series by Synectics Inc. New York: Harper and Row, 1968.
Manning, Rosemary. "The Freshness of the Morning: the Poetry Children Write." *The Times Literary Supplement* (October 30, 1970) 1249-1250.
Marmor, Judd, *Psychiatry in Transition*, Selected Papers of Judd Marmor, M.D., New York: Brunner/Mazel, 1974.
Mearns, Hughes. *Creative Power.* New York: Doubleday, Doran & Company, 1929.
———. *Creative Youth: How a School Environment Set Free the Creative Spirit.* New York: Doubleday, Page & Company, 1925.
Meek, Margaret, and Hunt, Peter. "The *Signal* Poetry Award." *Signal* (May 1981) 67-75.
Miner, Marilyn E., and Kahl, Marilyn D., eds. *Sunspots I, Spring 1975.* Los Angeles: Southern California Council of Teachers of English, 1975.
Morse, David, ed. *Grandfather Rock: the New Poetry and the Old.* New York: Delacorte Press, 1972.
Morton, Miriam, ed. and trans. *The Moon is like a Silver Sickle: a Celebration of Poetry by Russian Children.* New York: Simon and Schuster, 1972.
Mountsier, Mabel, ed. *Singing Youth, an Anthology of Poems by Children.* New York: Harper & Brothers, 1927.
Mueller, Lavonne, and Reynolds, Jerry D. *Creative Writing.* River Forest, Illinois: Laidlaw Brothers, 1977.
Murphy, Richard. *Imaginary Worlds: Notes on a New Curriculum.* New York: Teachers & Writers Collaborative, 1974.
My Mind is an Ocean: Poems Koans and Prophecies from Kids Seven to Twelve Years, collected by Dancing Dick. San Rafael, California: Spiritual Community Publications, 1973.
My Own Book. Scholastic Magazine (March 1976).
Neruda, Pablo. *Memoirs.* Translated by Hardie St. Martin. New York: Farrar, Straus, & Giroux, 1977.
Nims, John Frederick. *Western Wind: an Introduction to Poetry.* New York: Random House, 1974.
O'Gorman, Ned. *The Storefront: a Community of Children on 129th Street & Madison Avenue.* New York: Harper & Row, 1970.
Opie, Iona, and Opie, Peter. *Lore and Language of Schoolchildren.* Oxford: Clarendon Press, 1960.
Options in Education, Program #64, February 7, 1977. The National Public Radio & The Institute for Public Leadership.
Padgett, Ron, ed. *My Intelligent Brain: an Anthology of Student Writing from JHS 52.* New York: Teachers & Writers Collaborative, 1978.
Percy, Bernard. *The Power of Creative Writing: a Handbook of Insights, Activities, and Information to get Your Students Involved.* Englewood Cliffs, New Jersey: Prentice-Hall, Inc., 1981.
Piaget, Jean. *The Child's Conception of the World.* London: Routledge and Kegan Paul, 1929.
———. *The Language and Thought of the Child.* 3d ed. London: Routledge and Kegan Paul, 1959.
Poemball: *Poems and Calligraphy by Students at Fillmore Arts Center.* Washington, D.C.: Fillmore Arts Center, 1979.
Poetic Forms for Authorship. Encyclopedia Britannica Educational Corporation, n.d.
Preminger, Alex, ed. *Princeton Encyclopedia of Poetry and Poetics.* Princeton, New Jersey: Princeton University Press, 1974.
Randall, John Herman, Jr. *The Making of the Modern Mind: a Survey of the Intellectual Background of the Present Age.* Boston: Houghton Mifflin Company, 1940.

Read, Herbert, sel. *This Way, Delight: a Book of Poetry for the Young*. New York: Pantheon Books, Inc., 1956.
Richards, I. A. *Coleridge on Imagination*. Bloomington, Indiana: Indiana University Press, 1960.
______. *Principles of Literary Criticism*. New York: Harcourt, Brace and World, Inc., 1928.
______. *Science and Poetry*. 2d ed. London: Kegan Paul, Trench, Trubner & Co., Ltd., 1935.
Rilke, Rainer Maria. *Letters to a Young Poet*. Translated by M. D. Herter Norton. New York: W. W. Norton & Company, Inc., 1934.
Roethke, Theodore. On the Poet and His Craft: Selected Prose of Theodore Roethke, edited by Ralph J. Mills, Jr. Seattle: University of Washington Press, 1965.
Rousseau, Jean Jacques. *Emilius and Sophia: of a New System of Education*. 2d ed. in 4 vol. London: T. Becket and P. A. deHondt, 1763.
Rubel, William, and Mandel, Gerry. *The Editors' Notebook*. Santa Cruz, California: Stone Soup, 1976.
Schaefer, Charles E., and Mellor, Kathleen C., eds. *Young Voices*. New York: The Bruce Publishing Company, 1971.
Schiff, Bennett. *Artists in Schools*. Washington, D.C.: National Endowment for the Arts, U.S. Office of Education, 1973.
Shallcross, Doris J. *Teaching Creative Behavior: How to Teach Creativity to Children of All Ages*. Englewood Cliffs, New Jersey: Prentice-Hall, Inc., 1981.
Shapiro, Karl. "The New Poetry: a Literary Breakdown." *Los Angeles Times* (April 19, 1970).
Simon, John Oliver, ed. *Bay Leaf and Fool's Gold: the California Heritage Poetry Curriculum*. Oakland, California: Oakland Unified School District, 1982-3.
______. *The Night I Jumped Off the World*. Berkeley, California: Hillside School, 1975.
______. *Surrounded by the Quiet World*. Oakland, California: Hawthorne School, 1983.
______. *Where the Hawks Hide*. Oakland, California: Oakland Unified School District, 1983.
Simon, John Oliver, and Harer, Katharine, eds. *Easy Thing for You to Say*. Oakland, California: California Poets in the Schools, 1980.
Simon, John Oliver, and Kennedy, Sarah. *A Raindrop has to do her Work: Poetry from California Poets in the Schools*. Berkeley, California: Aldebaran Review, 1979.
Simpson, Louis. *A Company of Poets*. Ann Arbor, Michigan: University of Michigan Press, 1981.
______. *An Introduction to Poetry*. 2d ed. New York: St. Martin's Press, 1972.
Sloan, Glenna Davis. *The Child as Critic: Teaching Literature in the Elementary School*. New York: Teachers College Press, Columbia University, 1975.
Spencer, Zane A. *Flair: Vol. I: Creative Writing*. Stevensville, Michigan: Educational Service, 1975.
Spicy Meatball, No. 1 through 5, written and collated by the students of P.S. 75, Manhattan. New York: Teachers & Writers Collaborative, c. 1973-74.
Staudacher, Carol. *Creative Writing in the Classroom*. Belmont, California: Pitman Learning, 1968.
Steiner, George. *Extraterritorial: Papers on Literature and the Language Revolution*. New York: Atheneum Publishers, 1971.
______. *Tolstoy or Dostoevsky: an Essay in the Old Criticism*. New York: Alfred A. Knopf, Inc., 1959.
Stewig, John Warren. *Read to Write: Using Children's Literature as a Springboard for Teaching Writing*. 2d ed. New York: Holt, Rinehart and Winston, 1980.
Summerfield, Geoffrey, ed. *Creativity in English: Papers Relating to the Anglo-American Seminar on the Teaching of English at Dartmouth College, New Hampshire, 1966*. Champaign, Illinois: National Council of Teachers of English, 1968.
Taylor, Harold, ed. *Essays in Teaching*. New York: Harper & Brothers Publishers, 1950.
This Book's Got Taste: an Anthology of Stories and Poems written by Mr. Breindel's class 1974-75 P.S. 75 Manhattan. New York: The Print Center, 1975.
Tiedt, Iris M. *Individualizing Writing in the Elementary Classroom*. Urbana, Illinois: National Council of Teachers of English, 1975.
Tolstoy, Leo. *What is Art?* and *Essays of Art*. Translated by Aylmer Maude. London: Oxford University Press, 1930.
True, Michael, ed. *Poets in the Schools: a Handbook*. Urbana, Illinois: National Council of Teachers of English, 1976.

U.S. Bureau of American Ethnology. *Forty-Sixth Annual Report of the Bureau of American Ethnology to the Secretary of the Smithsonian Institution, 1928-1929.* Washington, D.C.: Govt. Printing Office.

Untermeyer, Louis. "Hilda and the Unconscious." *Dial* (August 1920) 186-190.

Vernon, P. E., ed. *Creativity: Selected Readings.* New York: Penguin Books, 1970.

Voice and the Word VII, The. Ashland, Ohio: The Ohio Poets' Association, n.d.

White, James L., ed. *Angwamas Minosewag Anishinabeg: Time of the Indian.* St. Paul, Minnesota: Community Programs in the Arts and Sciences, 1976.

Whitman, Ruth. "Poetry in the Classroom." *American Poetry Review* (March/April 1982) 25-26.

———. *Report to the Council on the Arts and Humanities of the Commonwealth of Massachusetts, 1972.*

Whitman, Ruth, and Cornish, Sam, comps. A Small Teaching Anthology. Commonwealth of Massachusetts Council on the Arts and Humanities, n.d.

Whitman, Ruth, and Feinberg, Harriet, eds. *Poemmaking: Poets in Classrooms.* Lawrence, Massachusetts: Massachusetts Council of Teachers of English, 1975.

Wiener, Harvey S. *Any Child Can Write: How to Improve Your Child's Writing Skills from Preschool through High School.* New York: McGraw-Hill, 1978.

Williams, Ellen. *Harriet Monroe and the Poetry Renaissance: the First Ten Years of "Poetry."* Urbana, Illinois: University of Illinois Press, 1977.

Williams, William Carlos. *The Selected Essays of William Carlos Williams.* New York: Random House, 1954.

Wilson, Jane B., ed. *Children's Writings: a Bibliography of Works in English.* Jefferson, North Carolina: McFarland & Company, 1982.

Witucke, Virginia. *Poetry in the Elementary School.* Dubuque, Iowa: Wm. C. Brown Co. Publishers, 1970.

Wordsworth, William. *The Complete Poetical Works of Wordsworth.* Boston: Houghton Mifflin Company, 1932.

Wuertenberg, Jacque. *Helping Children Become Writers.* 2d. ed. Tulsa, Oklahoma: Educational Progress Corp., 1980.

Zavatsky, Bill, and Padgett, Ron, eds. *The Whole Word Catalogue 2.* New York: Teachers & Writers Collaborative, 1977.

Ziegler, Alan. *The Writing Workshop, Vol. 1.* New York: Teachers & Writers Collaborative, 1981.

Selected Publications: *American Poetry Review, Apollo's Diary: A Poetry Newsletter, Art Forum, Booklist, Bulletin of the Children's Book Center, Childhood Education, Connecticut English Journal, Cricket, Ebony Jr., Educating Children: Early and Middle Years, Elementary English, English Journal, Highlights for Children, The Horn Book Magazine, Instructor, Language Arts, Literary Cavalcade, Poetry Shell: A Magazine of Verse, The Reading Teacher, Reflections: A National Student Poetry Magazine, Research in the Teaching of English, St. Nicholas: An Illustrated Magazine for Boys and Girls, Saturday Review, School Library Journal, Signal: Approaches to Children's Books, Stone Soup: The Magazine by Children, Teacher, Teachers & Writers Bi-Monthly, Teachers & Writers Collaborative Newsletter, Teachers & Writers Magazine, Three R's: Reading, Writing and Radio, Times Literary Supplement, Today's Education, Wombat: A Journal of Young Peoples' Writing and Art.*

INDEX

Permission Acknowledgments

Pages 349 to 354 constitute an extension of the copyright page. Permission to reprint copyrighted materials in this book is gratefully acknowledged to the following publishers and copyrights holders:

ASSOCIATION FOR CHILDHOOD EDUCATION INTERNATIONAL
Excerpts from "The Magic Fish and the Yellow Print" by Richard Lewis in *Childhood Education*, Vol. 52, No. 5 (1976). Reprinted by permission of Richard Lewis and the Association for Childhood Education International, 11141 Georgia Avenue, Suite 200, Wheaton, Maryland 20902. Copyright © 1976 by the Association.

ATHENEUM PUBLISHERS, INC.
Lilian Moore, "Bedtime Stories" from *See My Lovely Poison Ivy*. Text copyright © 1975 by Lilian Moore. Reprinted with the permission of Atheneum Publishers.

JULIAN BACH LITERARY AGENCY
Excerpt from *Being With Children* by Phillip Lopate © 1975 by Phillip Lopate. First published by Doubleday & Company, Inc., 1975 and reprinted by courtesy of Julian Bach Literary Agency, Inc.

BASIC BOOKS, INC.
Excerpts from *Creativity: The Magic Synthesis* by Silvano Arieti. © 1976 by Silvano Arieti. Reprinted by permission of Basic Books Inc., Publishers.

GEORGES BORCHARDT, INC.
Excerpts from *Tolstoy or Dostoevsky: An Essay in the Old Criticism* by George Steiner, © 1959. Reprinted by permission.

PETRA CABOT
Excerpts from *Creative Power* by Hughes Mearns, Doubleday & Company, Inc., 1929. Copyright 1929 by Hughes Mearns. Reprinted by permission of Petra Cabot.

CALIFORNIA POETS IN THE SCHOOLS
Excerpts from *Bay Leaf and Fool's Gold*, The California Heritage Poetry Curriculum, Oakland, California 1982-3, © 1983 by the Oakland School District, and *Easy Thing For You to Say*, edited by John Oliver Simon and Katherine Harer, 1980, © by California Poets in the Schools. Reprinted by permission of John Oliver Simon.

CHELSEA HOUSE
Excerpts from *Wishes, Lies, and Dreams: Teaching Children to Write Poetry* by Kenneth Koch, Chelsea House Publishers, 1970. Copyright © 1970 by Kenneth Koch. Reprinted by permission of Chelsea House Publishers.

CHILDREN'S ART FOUNDATION
Excerpts from *The Editors' Notebook* by William Rubel and Gerry Mandel, 1976; "Why the Moon Changes Shape" by James Lindbloom from Vol. 6, No. 1 (September 1977) of *Stone Soup*; "White Season" from Vol. 8, No. 5 (May/June 1980) of *Stone Soup*. All reprinted with the permission of the Children's Art Foundation, Santa Cruz, California.

COMPAS
Excerpt and selection from *Angwamas Minosewag Anishinabeg: Time of the Indian*. St. Paul, Minnesota: Community Programs in the Arts and Sciences, 1976. Reprinted by permission of COMPAS.

HILDA CONKLING
Selections from *Poems by a Little Girl*, Frederick A. Stokes, 1920 and *Shoes of the Wind*, Frederick A. Stokes, 1922. Copyright 1920, 1921 and 1949 by Hilda Conkling. Reprinted by permission of Hilda Conkling.

CRICKET MAGAZINE
"The Night Sky" by Anne Elizabeth Murdy and "The Moon" by Joya Moller. Reprinted by permission of *CRICKET Magazine*, © 1974 and 1978 by Open Court Publishing Company.

DOUBLEDAY & COMPANY, INC.

Excerpt from *The Identity of Man* by Jacob Bronowski. Copyright © 1965 by Jacob Bronowski. Excerpt from *Poems of Kali* by Kali Grosvenor. Copyright © 1970 by Kali Grosvenor. Excerpts from *Creative Youth: How a School Environment Set Free the Creative Spirit* by Hughes Mearns. Copyright 1925 by Doubleday & Company, Inc. All published and reprinted by permission of Doubleday & Company, Inc.

DOVER PUBLICATIONS, INC.

Excerpts from *Children Write Poetry: A Creative Approach* by Flora J. Arnstein, Dover Publications, Inc., 1967. Copyright © 1967 by Dover Publications, Inc. Copyright © 1951 by Mrs. Flora J. Arnstein. Reprinted by permission of Dover Publications, Inc.

ROBERT DUNCAN

Excerpts from "Pages From a Notebook, from *The Artist's View*, No. 5, © 1953 by Robert Duncan. Reprinted by permission of the author.

FARRAR, STRAUS AND GIROUX, INC.

Excerpt from *Memoirs* by Pablo Neruda. Copyright © 1974 by the Estate of Pablo Neruda. Translation copyright © 1976, 1977 by Farrar, Straus and Giroux, Inc. Reprinted by permission of Farrar, Straus and Giroux, Inc.

ALLEN GINSBERG

Quotations from "Notes for *Howl* and Other Poems," from *Fantasy 7006*, © 1959 by Allen Ginsberg. Reprinted by permission of the Andrew Wylie Agency.

DR. JOHN CURTIS GOWAN

Excerpts from *Creativity: Its Educational Implications*, John Curtis Gowan, Ed., John Wiley & Sons, Inc. 1967. Reprinted by permission of Dr. John Curtis Gowan.

HARCOURT BRACE JOVANOVICH, INC.

Seven lines from *The People, Yes* by Carl Sandburg, copyright 1936 by Harcourt Brace Jovanovich, Inc.: renewed 1964 by Carl Sandburg. Three lines from *More Cricket Songs: Japanese Haiku*, translated and © 1971 by Harry Behn. Reprinted by permission of Harcourt Brace Jovanovich, Inc.

HARPER & ROW, PUBLISHERS, INC.

Excerpts from *Singing Youth, An Anthology of Poems by Children*, Mabel Mountsier, editor, Harper & Brothers, 1927, and *The Storefront: a Community of Children on 129th Street & Madison Avenue* by Ned O'Gorman, Harper & Row, 1970. Copyright © 1970 by Ned O'Gorman. Reprinted by permission of Harper & Row, Publishers, Inc.

DAVID HIGHAM ASSOCIATES LIMITED

Excerpts from "Fern Hill" in *The Collected Poems of Dylan Thomas*, published by J. M. Dent. Reprinted by permission of David Higham Associates Limited.

HIGHLIGHTS FOR CHILDREN

Eight line poem from *Highlights for Children*, May, 1981. Reprinted by permission of Highlights for Children.

HODDER & STOUGHTON

Excerpts from *Does It Have To Rhyme?* by Sandy Brownjohn. Hodder & Stoughton, 1980. Reprinted by permission of Hodder & Stoughton Educational.

HOLT, RINEHART AND WINSTON, PUBLISHERS

Excerpt and poem from *The Voice of the Children* collected by June Jordan and Terri Bush. Copyright © 1968, 1969, 1970 by The Voice of the Children, Inc. Copyright © 1970 by June Meyer Jordan. Reprinted by permission of Holt, Rinehart and Winston, Publishers.

THE HORN BOOK, INC.

Excerpt from "The Clouds of Spring" by Brenda Lynch, from *The Horn Book Magazine*, Vol. XXXIII, No. 3. Copyright © 1957 by The Horn Book, Inc., Boston. Excerpt from a review by Diane Farrell of *The Real Tin Flower: Poems About the World at Nine* by Aliki Barnstone, from *The Horn Book Magazine*, Vol. XLV, No. 1. Copyright © 1969, The Horn Book, Inc., Boston. Excerpts from "How to Tell a Sheep from a Goat" by Helen M. Hill, from *The Horn Book Magazine*, Vol. LV, No. 1. Copyright © 1979, The Horn Book, Inc., Boston. Excerpts and poem from "Letter from England: Me or It" by Aidan Chambers, from *The Horn Book Magazine*, Vol. LVII, No. 3. Copyright © 1981 by Aidan Chambers. Reprinted by permission of The Horn Book, Inc.

HOUGHTON MIFFLIN COMPANY

For permission to quote "White Season" from *Pool in the Meadow* by Frances M. Frost, published by Houghton Mifflin, 1933.

HUMANITIES PRESS INC.

For passages from *The Language and Thought of the Child* by Jean Piaget. London: Routledge & Kegan Paul Ltd., 1959. Reprinted by permission of Routledge & Kegan Paul Ltd.

INSTRUCTOR PUBLICATIONS, INC.

Excerpts from "A Fifth Grade Publishing Company" by Arnold J. Pakula. Reprinted from *Teacher* January 1976. Copyright © 1976 by Macmillan Professional Magazines. Passages from "Poets on Poetry" by Herb Kohl. Reprinted from *Teacher* April 1977. Copyright © 1977 by Macmillan Professional Magazines. Excerpt from "Flights of Fancy" by Virginia M. Dunlap. Reprinted from *Teacher*, November 1975. Copyright © 1975 by Macmillan Professional Magazines. Used by permission of The Instructor Publications, Inc.

INTERNATIONAL SOCIETY FOR GENERAL SEMANTICS

Excerpts from "Toward a Theory of Creativity" by C. R. Rogers. Reprinted from *ETC.* Vol. 11, No. 4 by permission of the International Society for General Semantics.

ROLLY KENT

Excerpt and lines from *Talk About the World: Spoken Poems by Children*, 1979. Reprinted by permission of Rolly Kent.

ALFRED A. KNOPF, INC.

"Dreams" from *The Dream Keeper and Other Poems* by Langston Hughes. Copyright 1932 by Alfred A. Knopf, Inc., and renewed 1960 by Langston Hughes. Reprinted by permission of Alfred A. Knopf, Inc.

RICHARD KOSTELANETZ

Excerpts from *The Old Poetries and the New*, by Richard Kostelanetz, published by the University of Michigan Press in 1981, and reprinted by permission of the author.

NANCY LARRICK

Excerpts and student writing from *Green Is Like a Meadow of Grass: An Anthology of Children's Pleasure in Poetry*, selected by Nancy Larrick. Garrard Publishing Company. Copyright © 1968 by Nancy Larrick. Reprinted by permission of Nancy Larrick.

RICHARD LEWIS

Excerpts from "Acting Out Daydreams," originally published in *Parabola* Magazine, Spring, 1982 issue. Copyright © 1982 by Richard Lewis. Passages from "The Child as Creator," originally commissioned by United Press International and published in February, 1982. Copyright © 1982 by Richard Lewis. Excerpts from "The Magic Fish and the Yellow Print," published in *Childhood Education*, Vol. 52, No. 5, March, 1976. Copyright © 1976 by the Association for Childhood Education International and reprinted by permission of Richard Lewis and the Association. Excerpts from "A Place for Poetry," originally published in *Publishers Weekly*, July 10, 1967. Copyright © 1967 by Richard Lewis and reprinted by permission of Richard Lewis.

LITTLE, BROWN AND COMPANY

Excerpts from *Turn Not Pale, Beloved Snail: A Book About Writing Among Other Things*, by Jacqueline Jackson. Copyright © 1974 by Jacqueline Jackson. Little, Brown and Company 1974. "This is My Rock" from *One At a Time* by David McCord. Copyright 1929 by David McCord. First appeared in *The Saturday Review*. By permission of Little, Brown and Company.

LOS ANGELES COUNTY MUSEUM OF ART

Three lines by David Lorenzo and six lines by Jose Trujillo from *The Moon is as Full as a Suitcase: Poems and Prose by Children*, edited by Ameen and Georgia Alwan, published by Los Angeles County Museum of Art, 1979. Reprinted courtesy of the Los Angeles County Museum of Art.

MACMILLAN PUBLISHING COMPANY, INC.

Excerpts and verse reprinted with permission of Macmillan Publishing Company from *The Real Tin Flower* by Aliki Barnstone. Copyright © 1968 by Aliki Barnstone. Copyright © 1968 by Macmillan Publishing Co., Inc. "The Moon's the North Wind's Cooky" from *Collected Poems* by Vachel Lindsay. Copyright 1914 by Macmillan Publishing Co., Inc., renewed 1942 by Elizabeth C. Lindsay. Ten lines from "Being the Dedication of a Morning to Hilda

Conkling, Poet." Reprinted with permission of Macmillan Publishing Company from *Collected Poems* by Vachel Lindsay. Copyright 1923 by Macmillan Publishing Co., Inc., renewed 1951 by Elizabeth C. Lindsay.

JUDD MARMOR, M.D.

Passages from *Psychiatry in Transition: Selected Papers of Judd Marmor, M.D.*, published by Brunner/Mazel, New York, 1974. Copyright © 1974 by Judd Marmor. Reprinted by permission of Judd Marmor.

MASSACHUSETTS COUNCIL OF TEACHERS OF ENGLISH

Passages and student writing from *Poemmaking: Poets in Classrooms* edited by Ruth Whitman and Harriet Feinberg. Copyright © 1955, Massachusetts Council of Teachers of English. Reprinted by permission of Harriet Feinberg.

ROBERT McGOVERN

Passages from *A Poetry Ritual for Grammar Schools* by Robert McGovern, Ashland Poetry Press, Ashland, Ohio, 1974. Copyright by Robert McGovern, 1974. Reprinted by permission of Robert McGovern.

ELIZABETH McKIM and JUDITH W. STEINBERGH

Excerpts from *Beyond Words: Writing Poems with Children* by Elizabeth McKim and Judith W. Steinbergh, Wampat Press, 1983. Copyright © 1983 by Elizabeth McKim and Judith W. Steinbergh. Reprinted by permission of the authors.

NATIONAL COUNCIL OF TEACHERS OF ENGLISH

Excerpts from *Creativity in English*, Geoffrey Summerfield, editor, 1968; from *Explorations in Children's Writing*, Eldonna L. Evertts, editor, 1976; from *Research on Composing: Points of Departure*, Charles R. Cooper and Lee Odell, editors, 1978. Passages from articles in *Elementary English*, *Language Arts* and *English Journal*. Published by the National Council of Teachers of English, and reprinted by permission of the National Council of Teachers of English.

NEW DIRECTIONS PUBLISHING CORPORATION

Four lines from "Gulls" and sixteen lines from "The Unknown" by William Carlos Williams from *Collected Poems of William Carlos Williams*. Copyright 1938 by New Directions Publishing Company. "Dum Capitolium Scandet" by Ezra Pound from *Personae*. Copyright 1926 by Ezra Pound. Lines from "Fern Hill" by Dylan Thomas from *Poems of Dylan Thomas*. Copyright 1945 by the Trustees for the Copyrights of Dylan Thomas. Reprinted by permission of New Directions Publishing Corporation.

THE NEW YORK REVIEW OF BOOKS

Excerpts from *Teaching the Unteachable* by Herbert Kohl. Reprinted with permission from *The New York Review of Books*. Copyright © 1962 by Herbert Kohl.

THE NEW YORK TIMES

Excerpts from articles by Albert Burton, Jr., of January 1, 1980, Lacey Fosburgh of September 5, 1969, and Leslie Maitland of September 4, 1975. Copyright © 1969/75/80 by The New York Times Company. Reprinted by permission. Excerpt from article "Poetry in the Sixties – Long Live Blake! Down with Donne!" by Louis Simpson, December 28, 1969. Copyright © 1969 by The New York Times Company. Reprinted by permission.

PANTHEON

Excerpt from *This Way Delight: A Book of Poetry for the Young*, selected by Herbert Read. Copyright 1956 by Pantheon Books, Inc. Reprinted by permission of Pantheon Books, Inc.

PETER PAUPER PRESS, INC.

For "Over the ruins" from *Haiku Harvest: Japanese Haiku, Series IV*, translated by Peter Beilenson and Harry Behn, copyright © 1963 by the Peter Pauper Press. Reprinted by permission of Peter Pauper Press.

PRENTICE-HALL, INC.

Excerpts from *A Big Bite of the World: Children's Creative Writing* by Claudia Lewis, © 1979 by Prentice-Hall, Inc. Excerpts from *The Power of Creative Writing* by Bernard Percy © 1981 by Bernard Percy. Published by Prentice-Hall, Inc., Englewood Cliffs, New Jersey 07632. Reprinted by permission of Prentice-Hall, Inc.

RANDOM HOUSE, INC.

Excerpts from *Rose, Where Did You Get That Red? Teaching Great Poetry to Children* by Kenneth Koch. Copyright © by Kenneth Koch, 1973. Random House, 1983. Reprinted by permission of Random House, Inc.

REFLECTIONS

Two student poems, "First Snow" and "A Moon Child's Goodnight" in *Reflections*, Vol. 1, Issue 2. Reprinted by permission of Reflections, Duncan Falls, Ohio.

SATURDAY REVIEW

Excerpts from "Manner of Speaking" by John Ciardi © 1972 Saturday Review Magazine Co. Reprinted by permission.

CHARLES SCRIBNER'S SONS

Felice Holman, "At the Top of My Voice," and "They're Calling" from *At the Top of My Voice and Other Poems*. Text copyright © 1970, Charles Scribner's Sons. Reprinted with the permission of Charles Scribner's Sons.

KARL SHAPIRO

Excerpts from "The New Poetry; a Literary Breakdown" by Karl Shapiro, *Los Angeles Times*, April 19, 1970. Reprinted with the permission of Karl Shapiro.

JOHN OLIVER SIMON

Excerpt from *The Skins of Change, Fourteen Young Poets*, edited by Sarah Kennedy and John Oliver Simon, Aldebaran Review no. 17. Reprinted by permission of John Oliver Simon.

WILLIAM JAY SMITH

Excerpts from "Poetry in the Schools – at the Mercy of Genius" by William Jay Smith, *American Poetry Review*, September/October 1976. Reprinted by permission of William Jay Smith.

SMITHSONIAN INSTITUTION PRESS

By permission of the Smithsonian Institution Press from *Forty-Sixth Annual Report of the Bureau of American Ethnology to the Secretary of the Smithsonian Institution, 1928-1929*, "Indian Tribes of the Upper Missouri," Edwin Thompson Denig, pp. 375-626, Smithsonian Institution, Washington, D.C. 1930.

KATHRYN GRIFFIN SWEGART

For quotes from "I Have a Dream for You, Mother" by Kathryn Griffin, published in *Yankee*, February, 1982. Copyright by Kathryn Griffin Swegart and reprinted with permission of the author.

TEACHERS & WRITERS COLLABORATIVE

Excerpts and student writing from *Imaginary Worlds: Notes on a New Curriculum* by Richard Murphy, 1974; *Journal of a Living Experiment: A Documentary History of the First Ten Years of Teachers and Writers Collaborative* by Phillip Lopate, 1979; *The Poetry Connection: An Anthology of Contemporary Poems with Ideas to Stimulate Children's Writing* by Kinereth Gensler and Nina Nyhart, 1978; *Spicy Meatball Number Five* written and collated by the students of P.S. 75, Manhattan (Luis Mercado, principal) with the help of the Teachers & Writers Collaborative team, Teri Mack, Karen Hubert, Sue Willis, and Phillip Lopate project director, 1973-1974; *To Defend a Form: the Romance of Administration and Teaching in a Poetry-in-the-Schools Program* by Ardis Kimzey, 1977; *The Teachers & Writers Bi-Monthly*, *Teachers & Writers Collaborative Newsletter*, and *Teachers & Writers Magazine*, 1970-1983; *The Whole Word Catalog*, Rosellen Brown, Marvin Kushner, Phillip Lopate and Sheila Murphy, editors, 1972; *The Whole Word Catalogue 2*, edited by Bill Zavatsky and Ron Padgett, 1977; *The Writing Workshop, Vol. 1*, by Alan Ziegler, 1981. All published by Teachers & Writers Collaborative, New York, and reprinted by permission of Teachers & Writers Collaborative.

SUSAN CAMBIQUE TRACEY

Poem from *The Power of Creative Writing* by Bernard Percy, © 1981 by Bernard Percy and published by Prentice-Hall, Inc., 1981. Poem copyright by Susan Cambique and reprinted by permission of the author.

UNIVERSITY OF CALIFORNIA PRESS

Excerpts from *From Two to Five* by Kornei Chukovsky, Translated and Edited by Miriam Morton, Foreword by Frances Clarke Sayers. University of California Press, 1983. This translation © 1963 by Miriam Morton. Reprinted by permission of the University of California Press.

WOMBAT

Student writing from *Wombat, A Journal of Young People's Writing and Art*, Sept/Oct. 1979; March/April/May, 1980; April/May/June, 1982 issues. Reprinted by permission of Jacquelin F. Howe, publisher.

YALE UNIVERSITY PRESS
For "Days" from *Blue Smoke* by Karle Wilson Baker, Yale University Press, 1919. Copyright 1919 by Yale University Press, and reprinted with permission of Yale University Press.